Crime and Punishment in the Ancient World

Crime and Punishment in the Ancient World

Israel Drapkin, M.D.

Foreword by
Thorsten Sellin

Lexington Books
D.C. Heath and Company/Lexington, Massachusetts/Toronto

Library of Congress Cataloging-in-Publication Data

Drapkin, Israel, 1906–
  Crime and punishment in the ancient world / Israel Drapkin :
foreword by Thorsten Sellin.
    p. cm.
    Bibliography: p.
    Includes index.
    ISBN (invalid) 0–669–01279–3 (alk. paper)
    1. Criminal law—History. 2. Punishment—History. 3. Crime and
criminals—History.   I. Title.
K5015.4.D73 1989
345'.009—dc19
[342.5009]   76–54458   *18191888*

Published simultaneously in Canada
Printed in the United States of America
International Standard Book Number: 0–669–01279–3
Library of Congress Catalog Card Number: 76–54458

11–19–90

The paper used in this publication meets the minimum requirements of
American National Standard for Information Sciences—Permanence of
Paper for Printed Library Materials, ANSI Z39.48–1984. ∞™

89 90 91 92 8 7 6 5 4 3 2 1

To our great-grandchildren, Dorina, Harel, and Shai,
who have enlivened my later years

Contents

Foreword

Nearly forty-five years ago, a young Chilean psychiatrist, on a professional visit to the United States, came to talk with me about matters of interest to criminologists. His name was Israel Drapkin, and our meeting was the beginning of a lasting friendship. Since then, we have had many opportunities to work together on committees of the United Nations and on boards of directors of international organizations dealing with questions of "the prevention of crime and the treatment of offenders." I have followed, with admiration, the progress of his professional career and his publications. When he asked me to write a foreword to this, his latest book, I gladly accepted, even though my knowledge of the specific subject matter of the work is deficient.

One who studies the law of crimes and the rules and practices of punishment usually finds enough contemporary problems to occupy his attention without extending his inquiries beyond the borders of his country or delving into the history of basic concepts and institutions. When he does, he usually does not roam far afield. My own interest in the history of punishment was kindled more than sixty years ago; but in the numerous articles and books it has prompted me to write, I have rarely ventured beyond the limits of the United States and Europe, nor into centuries prior to the Middle Ages. Therefore, the ancient history of the penal systems of much of the world is for me, as I suspect it is for most American criminilogists, mostly unknown territory. Professor Drapkin has explored it, however, and has recorded his findings in this book, the reading of which has permitted me to fill some wide gaps in my knowledge—a pleasurable experience that I hope many other readers will want to share.

Thorsten Sellin

Preface

Life must be lived forward, but can only be understood backward.
—Kierkegaard

This book sets out to record the history of criminal law, including the definitions of the various types of crimes and their respective punishments. It attempts to reveal some of the many facets of crime and punishment in the shadowy period that preceded civilization through the development of oral and written law as reflected in a variety of ancient and early societies. The history of behavioral limitations begins not with the written law but with the concepts of taboo and revenge. Primitive man was unable to write, but he had an overriding urge to communicate with his fellowmen and to record his crucial experiences for future generations. In fact, cave paintings discovered from Norway to Spain, on the continents of Africa and Australia, and in such remote places as Easter Island give us a glimpse into primitive man's way of life. Criminological theory cannot ignore such primordial origins, where we find some institutions that still exist in certain areas of the world and are an undeniable link to man's primitive ancestors. The history of later crime and punishment is somewhat easier to write, because there are many more recorded documents dealing with the negative aspects of human behavior than otherwise.

The Sources of Aggression

According to an ancient Hindu saying, there are seven basic human emotions: joy, anger, anxiety, adoration, grief, fear, and hate. Hate is the most common and the least acknowledged of these emotions. When uncontrolled, it is self-defeating and even self-destructive; when harnessed, it is the inspiration of much wit and wisdom.

Human society began with the tribe, which had a strong sense of "we" as opposed to "they." These poles are not necessary antagonistic, but hostility is inherent in them, as expressed in the struggle for food, territory, or power. Human history is irrevocably marred by man's self-inflicted wounds. From primitive cannibalism to the atrocities of our last two world wars, man's saga is one of brutality to his own kind—due, perhaps, to the lust for power inherent in every human being. And if we accept Lord Acton's aphorism that power corrupts, we should also admit that it is a strong aphrodisiac.

Richard E. Leakey and Roger Lewin have theorized that man's perverse drive toward self-destruction shows that the human species is somehow "deranged," and Konrad Lorenz regards man as the outcome of a terrible biological blunder whose only hope is to ritualize his aggressive tendencies through socially acceptable forms of behavior.

What is the source of man's aggressive tendencies? A number of contemporary scientists have proposed a variety of solutions to this riddle. One such group, the *endogenists,* is convinced that man is inherently aggressive and that these tendencies are part of his genetic structure. Like all large apes, man was once a vegetarian, and his evolution into hunter-killer, and perhaps cannibal, involved more than a mere change in diet. Conflicts with his fellowman, particularly those involving the fundamental territorial instinct, were settled through killing, as was the case in so many other species. The endogenist approach has a certain appeal, in that it relieves man of the responsibility for his behavior and attributes it to genetics and instincts.

The *exogenists* regard the endogenist approach as nothing more than an extremely dangerous fiction. They do not deny man's basic relationship with the animal world, nor his evolution from vegetarian to carnivore, but they do deny that these traits have become part of man's genetic structure. They are convinced that man's development and achievements are, to a large extent, due to his ability to cooperate with his fellowman and that, in the same way, his aggressiveness is due to the natural conflicts arising from his social life.

The debate between endogenists and exogenists is not a new one. The roots of man's aggressive tendencies are the subject of a long and bitter debate between the Scholastics and the theoreticians of the "social contract"— followers of Jean Jacques Rousseau. The Scholastics—who based their philosophy on the writings of the Church fathers, especially St. Augustine— were convinced that man was conceived in sin and, therefore, was born evil. Rousseau credited man with being "good" at birth but subject to the influences of the society in which he lives. This controversy was stoked much later when Cesare Lombroso developed his theory of the "born criminal," which is undoubtedly endogenist.

Students of prehistory do not use the term *crime* in relation to primitive man. The only exception may be Raymond Arthur Dart, who devoted a chapter of his *Adventures with the Missing Link* to the "antiquity of assassination." He describes his studies of the Australopithecinae, who bludgeoned his victim to death with extremely accurate blows. Only man, claims Dart, could have wielded such a weapon with such precision; therefore, this was a clear case of "murder." In his studies of the Peking Man, the Chinese prehistorian Wu Rukang describes similar findings in a different manner. "Some skulls have been destroyed by external blows," he says, indicating that "the people living between two and six hundred thousand years ago used to kill each other." He does not, however, use the term *murder*.

Yet primitive man had no notion of law or crime. For him, the acceptability of human behavior depended on whether or not it served his personal interest or that of his group. "Desire" and "need" were one and the same, and it was this relationship that governed individual behavior. Inacceptable behavior became "crime" only after it was defined that way in writing, and written law did not exist until historical times.

Man's ancestors lived in a world in which killing was simply an expression of the struggle for survival, a part of the natural process of selection. The notion of crime did not exist. Crime is a rather complex legal and sociological concept that is linked to man's development in society and to the values he has placed on human life, property, territory, power, and so on; but the notion of crime cannot be properly applied to any type of human behavior during prehistoric times. Only later, when men started to live in larger communities, did there possibly appear the first limitations or prohibitions on individual conduct, determined by the group's authorities in order to cope with the social needs of the group. These prohibitions could have been similar to what the Polynesian people understood as "taboo"—something forbidden by social customs or demands or because of some magical or religious meaning.

Organization of the Book

Part I of this book deals with the evolution of crime and punishment from the chronological or longitudinal point of view, starting from prehistoric times and continuing to the fall of the Roman Empire. The contrasts among primitive people and cultures are fairly astonishing. It is one thing to realize that ancient China—far removed from the West, practically without religion, and organized on a secular basis—had its own legislation, very different from that of all other contemporary societies. It is even more difficult to grasp that other people—neighbors in time and in geographic location—had sharply differing basic concepts in their legislation; for instance, whereas the Sumerians preferred a system of pecuniary retribution, Hammurabi originated the concept of "an eye for an eye."

Part II deals with countries and peoples that, though extending beyond the fall of the Roman Empire, are included in the book because their criminal law was still primitive in nature or was historically close to that of the ancient period.

I am neither a historian nor a lawyer but a self-made criminologist (there were no courses in this field in Latin America when I was young enough to study for a second degree)—a discipline to which I have devoted the past fifty years of my life. I have also had a keen and abiding interest in human history. Therefore, after my retirement from active academic life, my criminological knowledge and experience, matched with my historical "hobby," produced this blended work. The merit of this book, if any, is that it puts together, in a handy way, a large amount of information that otherwise would require a great deal of bibliographic search and labor.

This book makes no claim to original research. Nevertheless, thanks to the way in which the data have been collated, summarized, and organized, both the professional and the layman may find in it the answers to many of their questions about its subject matter. It has been written in a simple language, avoiding technical or professional jargon; nor has it been gratuitously embellished with graphs, charts, and quantitative data. In a volume such as this, footnotes are not needed to cover every statement, and quotations are frequently given without attribution to avoid pedantry. On the other hand, I am personally responsible for every single statement I make here, and the respective written sources appear in the bibliography. Finally, this is not, of course, a text of comparative penal law because that was not its purpose.

Until the appearance of a better book on this subject, I hope that this one will achieve its modest objectives. Although it does not cover the subject inclusively and does not promote a thesis, it will not have been written in vain if it facilitates inquiry and sheds light on the crucial field of the evolution of crime and punishment.

Acknowledgments

I t would be almost impossible to mention all those whose published works served me as an inexhaustible fountain of constructive thinking and information and those whose advice and criticism contributed to the format and content of this book. Nevertheless, I must single out the following people for my special indebtedness: Professor Emeritus Thorsten Sellin, not only for willingly writing the foreword to this book but also for his many and most valuable observations regarding the original manuscript; Professors Reuven Yaron, Mordehai Ravello, and Zeev Falk of the Faculty of Law of the Hebrew University of Jerusalem, as well as Professor Cheryl Exum of Boston College, for reading the first few chapters of the manuscript and making a number of productive remarks; Rabbis Josef Green of Jerusalem and J. Newman of Netanya, Israel, for their assistance in the preparation of the chapters on the Persians and the ancient Hebrew law, respectively; Sri Paripurnanand Varma, president of the All India Crime Prevention Society, for his critical evaluation of the chapter on India; Professor Taro Ogawa of the Law Department of Asia University, Tokyo, for doing the same with the chapter on feudal Japan; and Yamada Asameon and Akio Yamaguchi for translating for me some Japanese texts dealing with punishments in various stages of the historical evolution of Japan; Professor Antonio Beristain of the Faculty of Law of San Sebastian, Spain, for commenting on the chapter dealing with the Basques.

I am very much indebted and would like to express my sincere gratitude to the Faculty of Law of the Hebrew University of Jerusalem for supporting much of the technical work in preparing this volume; the last two deans of that faculty, Professors Joshua Weisman and Itzhak England, for their most valuable suggestions; the members of its Research Committee, for the generous grant they accorded me; and the academic and clerical staff of the Institute of Criminology of the same faculty for their friendly cooperation and economic assistance.

I must also mention a number of my personal friends for their generous contributions, which greatly facilitated the completion of this work. Special among them are Dr. Luis Lamas of New York; Richard and Ruth Hirschfeld of Houston; Olga Heinemann and Jacobo and Sara Glushankof of Buenos Aires; and Aron Eisen, Israel Pollak and Sam Sebba of Israel. To all of them I express here my most sincere gratitude.

Evelyn Grossberg, Aliza Yahav, and David Hornik helped prepare the first English version of my original manuscript. Their editing was indispensible, and I appreciate it very much.

Special acknowledgment and thanks are due to Michael McCarroll, former vice-president and general manager of Lexington Books, for his abiding interest in my work; and to Margaret N. Zusky, editor at Lexington Books for transforming the original version of my manuscript into its final form.

Last but not least, I must mention Rebecca, my life's companion for more than half a century, without whose mere presence at my side I would never have accomplished the few modest things I have achieved during my long academic career, especially this book.

Part I
The Ancient World

1
The Legacy of Primitive Man

> Aujourd'hui comme hier, on n'obtien rien que par la violence; c'est
> l'instrument efficace; il faut seulement savoir s'en servir.
> —Anatole France, *L'Ile des Pingouins*

Prehistoric Violence, Art, and Taboo

Prehistory is the study of man's evolution, from both the biological and
cultural points of view, prior to the existence of written documents. Here
almost everything is assumed, since no historical records are available, besides
some archaeological remains and a few dating techniques. Prehistory is not
simply the evolutional stage through which man passed a long time ago. It is
a period that, properly understood, might contribute to a better evaluation of
our present-day situation, with a more valid perspective than the one based
on a narrow study of our history. The dating processes—such as the
bristlecone pine rings, radiocarbon 14, and others—have contributed enor-
mously to such an understanding.

Traditionally, paleontologists have held that the first humans appeared
from 15 to 20 million years ago. In recent years, however, molecular anthropologists, who study chemicals instead of fossils (one of the most promising
tools for deciphering the mysteries of human evolution since Darwin), have
reached a radically different conclusion—namely, that our ancestors may
have emerged as recently as 4.5 million years ago. Today it is believed that
the first true man, *Homo erectus,* emerged in the East Indies and Africa only
about 1.5 million years ago. Be that as it may, the specifics of human
evolution—the details of how and when our ancestors changed into apes and
at what point the human line became distinct—are still subjects of exploration
and controversy.

Archaeology's basic aim, which has contributed so much to the
understanding of our remote past, is to establish the chronology of a site by
studying where each layer of structures that represent a historical period
begins and ends. After a given level is defined, its age may be determined by
evaluation of the existing evidence: a dated inscription, a seal or tablet with

a king's name, and similar items. When a given object has been dated, it can be assumed that the other objects on the same level belong to the same epoch. Therefore, archaeology, with the cooperation of other sciences, is trying to recreate the environment of early man—what he created for himself at any particular time—and thence to deduce how he lived.

From the archaeological point of view, it was during the Lower Paleolithic, the oldest period of the Old Stone Age, that man fashioned the oldest known tool in Africa, learned to use and control fire, roamed in small bands of five to twenty individuals, lived in caves, had the most rudimentary social structure, and organized large-scale elephant hunts in Europe. This was the situation some 2.5 million years ago. During the Middle Paleolithic, which lasted from about 100,000 to 40,000 years ago, the Neanderthal man appears in Europe; ritual burials existed in the Middle East, suggesting the belief in an afterlife; woolly mammoths were hunted in Europe, where the cave bear became a cult focus. The Upper Paleolithic (from about 40,000 to 10,000 years ago) was when Asian hunters crossed the Bering Land Bridge and started to populate America; the oldest known written records—lunar notations—were made on bone, in Europe; man reached Australia; the first artists decorated the walls and ceilings of caves in Southern France and Northern Spain; figurines were sculpted for nature worship; and the invention of the needle made sewing possible. During the Mesolithic Age, from about 10,000 to 9,000 years ago, the bow and arrow appeared in Europe, and the first pottery was made in Japan. The Neolithic Age (from about 9,000 to 5,000 years ago) saw the domestication of sheep in the Middle East, the dog in North America, and the goat in Persia; Jericho, the oldest known city, was settled; the first crops—wheat and barley—were cultivated in the Middle East, where the pattern of village life grew; Catal Hüyük, in present-day Turkey, became the largest Neolithic city; the loom was invented and cattle were also domesticated in the Middle East; and agriculture began to replace hunting in Europe. During the Copper Age (from about 5000 to 3100 B.C.), copper was traded in the Mediterranean area; corn was cultivated in Mexico; the oldest known massive stone monuments were built in Brittany; sail-propelled boats started to be used in Egypt; the first city-states appeared in Sumer; cylinder seals begin to be used as marks of identification in the Middle East; the first potatoes were cultivated in South America; the wheel appeared in Sumer; rice started to be cultivated in the Far East; silk moths were domesticated in China and the horse in southern Russia; Egyptian merchant trading ships started to ply the Mediterranean; and the first pictographic writing was invented in the Middle East, marking the end of prehistoric times.

There is no doubt that man's unique endowments allowed him to go beyond the narrow limits of the biological evolutionary processes, to carve out a cultural evolution that embraced the arts, the sciences, and everything else that distinguishes man's behavior from that of the animal. There were certainly great moments of human invention, from flint tools to the arch and the wheel, to geometry, to the theory of relativity and modern technology. All of them show the progression of man in his search to understand and control the natural world in which he lives. Nature, his biological evolution, has fitted man to all kinds of environments, not to specific ones. His imagination, his reason, his emotional subtlety and thoroughness permitted him to not accept a given environment but to change it for what he considered a better one. The series of inventions by which man has been able to remake his environment constitute not a biological but a cultural evolution. Man's imaginative gifts allow him to make plans, inventions, and new discoveries in different ages and cultures that represent a richer progression and more intricate conjunction of human gifts. Thanks to them, the first human cultures—the Hassuna culture and the Halaf farmers—appeared in Northern Mesopotamia during the Neolithic era. Soon afterward, the Ubaidian culture of Southern Mesopotamia developed, and finally came the Sumerians, with their first great civilization. All this has been possible because man felt conscious of something about himself—body and spirit—that was outside his day-to-day struggle for existence and his night-to-night struggle with fear. He felt the need to develop his qualities of thought and feeling and to reach, as nearly as possible, an ideal of perfection. During the ages, he has managed to satisfy his needs in various ways—through myths, dance and song, systems of philosophy, and the order he has been able to impose on our visible world.

Parallel to this evolution is the first evidence of man's conscious artistic motions that might be considered *prehistoric art,* belonging to the Upper Paleolithic era and consisting of the first cuttings on stone and bones. It is not known whether they had a practical, magical, or simply decorative meaning, but they were indeed purposely made. They were not only the expression of art—the conscious use of skill and creative imagination—but might have been used as a means for transmitting certain ideas and experiences. That is, they were, in a way, a system of nonportable writing, since they were usually done on the walls of the caves where people lived. (The Sumerian cuneiform tablets are considered the first human writing because, since they were small, they were portable.) The same is true with the first rock-wall paintings, whereby the hand of a man, dirtied with sweat, was pressed on a rock within a cave; these date about 25,000 years ago. Such cuttings and paintings have been discovered in many places around the world, from Norway to South Africa (Bushman rock paintings were discovered in 1986 in a number of caves in the Drakensberg mountains in Natal), from East to West, and even in such isolated places as Easter Island. The first intentional use of color (ochre) appeared only some 15,000 years ago, but it is still not known whether it was done for amusement or for experimental purposes, with some kind of ritual intention.

Related to the subject matter of this book, it is worthwhile to mention that in the Paleolithic cave of Addaura, in Sicily, there is an engraved scene of many human figures moving around a central one, which is in a severely contracted position, presumably because he was tied in such a manner that if he straightened out he would strangle himself—a form of torture or ritual not unknown in ancient times. The scene shows, in the most vivid colors that *homo sapiens* has ever had, together with the gift of creation, the potential for self-destruction.

There is no doubt that Paleolithic art possesses a coherent and continuous tradition, revealing a certain type of social organization as well as some sort of beliefs as expressions of basic elements of a primitive culture. Paleolithic people undoubtedly had admirable human qualities, as Ashley Montagu wrote in a letter published in the *New York Times* of 14 July 1985:

> The Neanderthal man walked perfectly erect, wasn't knock-kneed, had a much larger brain than we have, and was characterized by a highly developed spiritual life. He buried his dead with care and compassion—frequently on a bed of flowers—and tenderly cared for the child, the injured and the crippled. Furthermore, there is every reason to believe that among them there were no sociopaths or psychopaths.

Art is a part of the culture of the people who created it and must be studied along with bones and stones, pottery, houses, and graves. Its chief interest to archaeologists lies in the details of dress and ornaments, hunting weapons, weighted digging sticks, fishing methods, dances and ceremonies, and sometimes even penal practices. Many such details may be seen in the painted primitive shelters. The basic controversy is over the dating of many such findings, since no one date can be applied to all of them. Whatever the case, we must guard against segregating prehistoric art and technique because they lack a material life as well developed as ours, when in fact they participated, by their form as by their function, in the process of human evolution.

It is difficult to imagine that the Australopithecus or the Pithecanthropus had even the faintest idea of behavioral prohibitions. Killing a fellowman in case of need or in self-defense was the accepted way of life. Homo hominis lupus was the norm of yesterday as well as today. Such concepts could not have developed until man began to settle in groups of hundreds or thousands. Only then could there have been the social motives to instigate such prohibitions or limitations and the establishment of an authority that could enforce them. Before then, perhaps the witch doctor, peering at the entrails of sacrificial goats, was the one who could decide. These early limitations may have been similar to what the Polynesians—much later—coined with the expression *tabu,* or *taboo:* something forbidden because of its magical, religious, or social implications. Religious taboos, for example, prohibited profane contact—be it by touch, word, or deed—with a person or object of sacred or damned nature. Violation of these taboos was believed to arouse the wrath of supernatural forces against the entire community. Primitive fertility symbols were "untouchable," as were the totem poles that marked the entrance of the early American Indian communities, as they still do in some areas of Africa and Asia.

Early Social Forms

Among primitive people, society was largely structured and based on *kinship,* an indispensable basis for such a purpose. The discovery of kinship apparently had a profound effect in human development. For instance, all human societies hold to an incest taboo rule, which involves kinship; kin recognition and incest taboo are always coexistent, even though we do not know the meaning or reason. The fact is that man has consistently adhered to this taboo ever since, no matter how complex his civilization has become. It is true that he has added many different factors and has elaborated and altered it in endless minor variety, but he has always stuck to it.

Many unlettered peoples have dealt with kinship with the intention of elaborating a wider meaning to it. This has been done in two main directions. The first consists in the extension of kinship to all human beings with whom one has personal relations—that is, over the whole society in the largest sense. This type brings with it the need of marrying kin, creating two rigorously divided groups: one whom one may or must marry and the other who is taboo. This type of society is found mostly among Australian aborigines and in some regions of Melanesia; elsewhere it is rather rare. The second type applies kinship over a segregated group of persons, resulting in *sibs* (kindred, relatives, blood relations, or kinsmen), *clans* (groups comprising a number of people who have common ancestors), *households* (people who dwell under the same roof and form a family), and the like. Carrying this process even further, it may perhaps result in a *phratry* (a kinship subdivision within the same clan, usually an exogamus group typically comprising several totemic clans) and a *moiety* (one of two approximately equal parts constituting a tribe). This biological kinship usually ramifies, through marriage—endlessly overlapping and crisscrossing—to include large segments of highly diluted kinness, as is the case with all relatives except siblings.

Extended families, sometimes difficult to distinguish by definition, have been designated *clans.* These clans may include persons of doubtful kinship but reckoned as such by virtue of their clan membership. The clan contains, actually or potentially, an artificial extension of the true blood kinship. This is why clans have usually a name, whether totemic (symbolic) or not. In fact they need a name, whereas the lineage family, consisting of genuine kinship, is an indisputable unit even without a name. This preoccupation with kinship groups has a direct influence on cross-cousin marriage and on the need for property conservation through generations. There are an almost infinite number of systems—some of them very simple structures, others showing the most unexpected combinations of possible social forms.

Taking all this into consideration, it is impossible to deny inventiveness among primitive people, even in their sociological settings and systems, which show an unbelievable degree of ingenuity and imaginativeness. On the other hand, *political organization* is something that primitive people, in general, have not achieved to any notable degree. And when some of them have done so—as in some areas of Africa and in Peru and Mexico—they are excluded from the concept of primitivism. Throughout history, however, the high civilizations have always had a considerable degree of political organization. It seems that primitive societies were more interested in organizing different forms of social structures and some institutions concerned with interpersonal relations. Nevertheless, some traits of kinship can be detected even in higher civilizations, because kinship is biologically and psychologically inescapable.

Primitive Ethics and Law

There is no universal morality; there are only local and temporal ones. Morality is not a man's inborn gift; it took many centuries of heredity and experiences before it was more or less established. Places in which elderly people were killed or expelled from the community—as among the Eskimo—to eliminate nonproductive mouths are found practically nowhere today. This was never considered a crime, just an established custom.

In early times, morality and religion were not synonymous. When someone killed an ox, a slave, or the wife of his neighbor, he owed a compensation, but he did not have to implore the pardon of the gods. For a very long time, religion (man's duties toward his gods) had nothing to do with morals (man's duties to his fellowmen), and often enough they were in aggressive opposition. A religion's request to exterminate prisoners of war only retarded the evolution of ethics. The children sacrificed to Moloch, Krishna's demand that Indian virgins should engage in sexual orgies with priests, the Holy Office of the Inquisition, organized by the most religious nations of Europe; and so many other similar historical examples are the best confirmation that morality and religion are not the same thing. More than religion, the basic need to assure the general welfare of the community moved the people to defend it against all kinds of dangers. From this natural need of mutual defense derived, also, the first reciprocal duties from one to another and to the community as a whole. No society can survive in chaos, and those torn by schisms soon disappeared. Slowly, man's life—especially his adult life, for his usefulness to the community—began to be respected. The same happened with private property and avoiding dangerous conflicts with other members of the group. And in such a way the first rudiments of law, which is nothing else than the collective morality codified, started to appear.

Law and morality are not natural gifts. The real natural law is a law of the strongest; it dominates the entire history of mankind. Man's earliest societies knew no law. They relied on the forces of custom, magic, religion, and social pressures to achieve their desired ends. The community's reaction to antisocial behavior was governed and dictated by a simple basic drive: *revenge.* In its earliest stages, the group determined that the account to be settled between victim and wrongdoer was a private affair. It was up to the victim to extract vengeance; neither the clan, the tribe, nor the community as a whole would interfere. And to rule out the possibility of future attacks, the victim often found it best to wreak his vengeance to the utmost; killing the wrongdoer ensured that the victim would never suffer at his hands again. The injured party was, therefore, victim, judge, and executioner; the burden of protecting his person and property was his and his alone. Private revenge was the initial form of vengeance.

Revenge is an inherent, if unconscious, element of man's psychological structure; Steinmetz stresses that. Nor was it originally conceived of as a legal institution or as a vehicle of justice. It was for the victim to determine the extent of the damage, and it is little wonder that the measure of vengeance was generally out of all proportion to the injury sustained. This, in turn, created a new imbalance: the wrongdoer became victim and could exercise *his* right to vengeance. The conflict thus established could continue indefinitely, despite the fact that these early communities could ill afford the resulting loss of life and destruction of property. The dire consequences of such an unbroken cycle of revenge forced these primitive societies to develop certain restrictive measures, some of which appear in the first laws and codes of historical times. The first restriction took the form of what is known as *blood revenge.* "Blood" refers to the question of family relationship rather than to the mode of vengeance—the blood tie or bond uniting a group of individuals in varying degrees of kinship. Blood revenge placed the responsibility of punishing the wrongdoer in the hands of the group rather than the individual victim. An injury suffered by a member of a family, clan, or tribe was considered a blow to the victim's entire community, and revenge was exacted from the wrongdoer's family or community. Revenge was now the domain of the community rather than the individual. Perhaps this is the remote origin of what became known as *collective punishment,* in which an entire community pays for a single member's crime.

As religion became an institutionalized force and the fear of divine wrath as well as the belief in an afterlife took root, the concept of *divine revenge* was a natural development. Injurious behavior was defined as an affront to the gods, who might express their wrath in the form of earthquakes, fires, plagues, and the like. The punishment that would assuage divine wrath was to be determined and executed by the priests within their temples. It was within this framework that the concepts of *asylum* (refuge for the wrongdoer), *tregua dei* (a period of peace "in the name of god"), and *talio* (a limitation of the consequences of revenge) first developed. They may be found in various codes that span different chronological periods, and they are aimed at limiting the excesses of revenge. Later, it was realized that the *talio* was weakening the welfare of the community, and the system of *compensation* was established. Every crime was redeemable, and once the problem settled in such a way, the group was satisfied and did not consider it its duty to apply severe punishments as a means of preventing future misbehaviors. This situation lasted for a long time. Even the Roman Twelve Tables considered compensation for theft; and in the early German law, the life of an individual had a tariff according to his status in the community—expensive was the life of a nobleman or a priest but cheap the life of a peasant, woman, or slave.

The power of the religious institutions was gradually joined, and eventually eclipsed, by the power of the state. *State revenge,* which was essentially the origin of *public justice,* gradually displaced all other forms of meting out punishment. Rather than answering to the victim, his clan, or the priests, the wrongdoer was now judged and punished by the state alone.

The development of the concept of revenge and its limitation was not a linear process; the various forms of vengeance often existed side by side during the same chronological period. What evolved was not so much a code that suited punishment to misdeed but a framework that limited the destructive powers of revenge, which so often wreaked havoc on these early societies, deciminating whole clans. The culmination of this evolution of limitations— state revenge and public justice—belongs to the historical era, with its first written codes and laws. These earliest codes were not formed in a void; they express concepts and beliefs that previous generations could not express in writing but transmitted orally from one generation to the next.

Individual and social needs slowly created the public opinion of the group and its customs, from which derived morality and law whose evolution was related to the basic characteristics of each nation. In the beginning, when men lived from hunting and fishing, the entire catch belonged to the community and was distributed equally among its members; this primitive communism had no rich and poor people. But with the development of agriculture appears the concept of *family property:* those who worked a piece of land, usually the members of the same family, were entitled to benefit from the fruits of their work. Much later appeared the notion of *private* or *individual property.* Parallel to such a development there was also a kind of *industrial development,* which has so influenced civilization by creating rivalries and stimulating wars, slavery, and so on. Humble were its beginnings, based on the carving of silex by percussion, the first but not the last implement for war. Later came the club, the dart (short or long), the arch and arrow, and so on—used both for hunting and for defense—as well as the shields made from the bark of trees and the cuirasses from animals' skins. The art of killing was the first to develop, and it has not yet stopped. The tremendous use of fire—not only for the preparation of food but also for the elaboration of pottery and, much later, for working with metals—caused it to be considered a divinity.

Then came the *division of work;* each member of the community specialized in a given work (hunting, fishing, etc.), which contributed to industrial development and, as a direct consequence, slavery, which persists, in different forms, to the present.

The Protohistoric Period

The heritage of the first nonwritten codes lies within the rather vague boundaries of what we term *protohistory*—the period that was the very border between prehistory and history. Protohistory concerns itself mainly with the legends and myths that have been passed down through oral tradition—material that reflects early man's beliefs, concepts, and fears. This evidence, though of doubtful empirical value, nevertheless reflects an important step in man's development, an era marked by man's gradual departure from nomadism, a step that had far-reaching consequences for all aspects of human evolution.

The nomadic way of life, which still exists among the Bedouins of the Arabian, Palestinian, Syrian, and North African deserts, is structured around seasonal migration, according to the needs of the herd. Migration is never arbitrary; the tribe moves over a well-established route during fixed seasons, from one field to another, from one water source to the next. These nomads have their own system of trade and barter in order to obtain the necessities that are not provided by their herds.

It is difficult to pinpoint exactly when man began the transformation from nomad to settler and even more difficult to accurately define his motives for doing so. A scarcity of game may have forced him to make his first awkward attempts to wrest his living from the soil; or he may have begun to cultivate purely by accident. What is certain is that he could not have become a settler without the existence of certain factors, including the certainty of a crop surplus that could be stored for a period of time and the domestication of various animals, which he could then utilize for his own purposes. Both these factors, as already mentioned, imply a consequence: man, within society, began to accumulate property.

Man's settled life began some 10,000 years ago in an area known as the Fertile Crescent—a misnomer at best, since the area is neither remarkably fertile nor crescent-shaped. Favorable climatological conditions and better terrain encouraged the growth of agriculture, and man began to settle in concentrations that could be considered hamlets or villages. Until recently, the oldest known permanent farming community was at Jarmo, in what is modern Kurdistan, at a site that dates from approximately 7000 B.C. An even earlier settlement at nearby Karim Shahir provides clues to the most rudimentary stages of farming, when man still lived as a semi-nomad, migrating when his crops had exhausted the land. The ruins of Jericho provide striking evidence of an even older settlement and of man in transition from food collector and hoarder to food producer, from wanderer to settler. Archaeological finds at this site, at the northern end of the Dead Sea, include tools that point to an early agricultural system that probably supported as many as 2,000 people.

Man's development from hunter to farmer, from nomad to settler, altered his relationship not only with his environment but with his fellowman as well. Man became a farmer and a settler, and he grew more and more dependent on the society of others. As a nomad, he had been subject to nature's dictates, but as a settler he was forced to become better attuned to the needs of society. Conflicts were no longer limited to the primitive territoral instinct; instead, they were the result of a more sophisticated sense of private property. New social structures necessitated the inception of a new social order, an order that could come into being only as man's systems of communication became more reliable.

Another consequence of all these developments is the appearance of the first governments; some of them were tyrannical, while others authorized a greater individual liberty. Nomads have a very weak central authority but a very strong paternal one, whereas hunting and fishing communities usually had a rather strong central authority but a very weak paternal one. The early forms of government were related to the need of common defense against enemies. Usually, they were constituted by a small group of people under the leadership of one chief, who was considered the most sage and strong. In the same way as the fear of natural phenomena created the gods, the fear of enemies created autocratic governments. People living in little mountainous territories, like those of classical Greece, preferred free republican systems; and the nomads, without territory to defend, never knew despotism. Wars and industrial developments determined the form of government of each people. Religion also affected the forms of government; sovereigns always tried to give to their orders a divine sanction and were always united with the clergy. Many ancient governments were no more than omnipotent theocracies. In short, the evolution of the different peoples was the direct outcome of a number of factors: the ethnic origin and the local environment; the development of agriculture and industry; the fight for survival; the legends, myths, and religious beliefs; the nature of leaders; and so forth.

Diseases abounded in the Palaeozoic era (some 500 million years ago) as well as in the Golden Age of early man (some 10,000 years ago), as demonstrated by the archaeological investigations of human and animal remains of those times. Tuberculosis existed in the Stone Age. The attitude toward disease was rather an emotional reaction to pain and to fear. The frightened man was driven into the realm of fantasies about God and evil spirits, the outcome of his own anxiety. It is possible that the sick and old people were simply killed as annoying encumbrances. The mentally ill were probably no exception, although the Chinese tradition of being kind to them would suggest that killing was not the only "treatment" employed. As primitive man developed, he soon discovered that one might influence the sick by means of what we now call hypnosis. The shamans of certain Siberian tribes definitely practiced it, and in some parts of the East (Cochin China, the Malay Archipelago), priests indulged in a form of hypnotic treatment, using an assistant as medium. Our knowledge of primitive psychiatry is less than fragmentary, but it seems that the psychological energies of early man were dedicated more to the problem of getting rid of the uncertainties and fears generated by illness than to realistic efforts to eliminate the sickness itself.

2
Ancient Civilizations of Mesopotamia

History begins at Sumer.
—Samuel N. Kramer

From the Origin of the Written Word to Mass Communication

The events and achievements of people living at a given time, which are contemporary by calendar, are not necessary contemporary in experience unless other people know of them. The creation of the written word heralded an era in which communication between people could be preserved for future reference. Nevertheless, communications, during most of history, have been limited, slow, and desultory. One of the more tantalizing questions for the historian is how, when, and where knowledge of an event occurring in one place reached other parts of the earth. Very frequently, this has been a crucial fact, shaping the course of history. We must count not only on what happened in a given place at a given time but on the accessibility of these events to people living elsewhere. Contemporaneity is a relative and variable term, depending not only on what happened when and where but also on who knew what, when, and where. Among the most important changes in human experience, few have been more drastic than our suddenly enlarged sense of contemporaneity, thanks to the modern means of mass communications; events that occur at a given time and place enter the experience of larger and larger numbers of people, not only on the day of their occurrence but almost at the very moment. These apparently unimportant notions are in fact fundamental and have been pondered and discussed by human beings since the unknown date when our early ancestors first awoke to consciousness.

Whatever the case, the discovery of writing was a prerequisite to the establishment of centralized rule, since records could be kept, history recorded, and decrees issued. Thanks to archaeology—which has so enriched our understanding of the historical evolution of the law—we know that the written word was born at approximately the same time in Egypt and in Mesopotamia, toward the end of the fourth millenium B.C. With the "decoding" of Egyptian hieroglyphics and Mesopotamian cuneiform writing, nearly 2,000 years of history were added to Western man's knowledge of the ancient world.

Egyptian hieroglyphics may have developed from prehistoric rock painting or "picture writing," like that found in the Stone Age caves. The Egyptians never developed an alphabet as we know it, but their rebus-style system of writing was nevertheless an efficient means of communications for those days; it served both rulers and poets. Excavations at Nippur, the Sumerian religious and cultural center in Southern Mesopotamia, have unearthed the oldest known evidence of writing in the form of tablets with pictographic script, which date from approximately 3100 to 2800 B.C. This script was the forerunner of cuneiform "wedge-shaped" writing, which came into being around 2500 B.C.

The first signs of recorded history were found also on votive statues, stelae, vases, plaques, sacred stones, and markers that were inscribed with the donor's name, rank, and achievements. Contracts of land sales and other transactions, the first known legal documents, appeared around 2400 B.C. And when writing became more versatile, its uses went beyond the simple and concrete; man began to believe that the written word had magical powers. Engraved amulets were worn to ward off evil spirits; death came when a divine scribe recorded a man's name in the Book of Fate.

Written tablets are the most informative archaeological artifacts in Mesopotamia. Because they were prepared on unbaked clay, great care had to be taken in handling. Today there are a number of elaborated techniques for such purposes. Besides these tablets, water jugs, storage vases, drinking vessels, and dishes are among the numerous finds in almost any archaeological site. For this reason, pottery has sometimes been called the alphabet of archaeology. Before archaeologists started their work in Mesopotamia—a bit more than a century ago—very little was known of the empires that flourished there 4,500 years ago, such as the Babylonian and the Assyrian. The scanty information from the Bible and the works of Greek and Roman historians was vague and even contradictory. And from older people—such as the Sumerians, for example—nothing at all was known. After a few years of excavation, some remarkable facts were revealed. Mesopotamia had the first people on earth to live in cities, study the stars, use the arch and wheeled vehicles, write epic poetry, and compile a legal code. This archaeological work has never stopped, and the pursuit of the past continues in a number of different sites. Therefore, it is unpardonable that, according to Boyce Rensberger, writing in the *New York Times* of 16 April 1979, the Syrian authorities are suppressing recent discoveries in the ruins of the 4,500-year-old kingdom of Ebla, in which is now Syria, because they may confirm certain biblical accounts and suggest that Ebla was linked to the Hebrews of Biblical times. Not one of the approximately 15,000 tablets has been made available, even in a readable photograph, to the Italian archaeological team conducting the Ebla archaeological research. In such a way, present-day antagonisms affect our knowledge of the past.

It was during the 1,500 years of Sumerian rule, all of them within the Bronze Age, that the written word became an institution, a fact of life. Society became dependent on documentation; and the complexities of man's social behavior were recorded and defined. The written law—beginning with the earliest known code of the Sumerian king Ur-Nammu—became indispensable to the rulers of the early city-states of Sumer and Akkad.

Sumerian History and Social Structure

The early Sumerian codes of written law cannot be fully understood without some knowledge of the structure and history of the Sumerian-Akkadian city-states. It was not until modern archaeologists began to uncover evidence of the city-states that rose to power some 5,000 years ago that the complexity of this ancient society came to light. These early inhabitants of Mesopotamia were the first men to establish cities and to face the challenges of a multi-leveled "urban" society; they had sailboats made of reeds on which they navigated further east. (Thor Heyerdahl, the Norwegian explorer, was able to duplicate such early navigation when—by the end of 1977 and the beginning of 1978—he went from Iraq to Karachi on his boat made of reeds, the Tigris, on a ten-week voyage.) Their philosophers dealt with the questions of liberty and tyranny; their politicians with those of war and peace; their rulers with power struggles and territorial conflicts that differed only in magnitude from modern-day warfare; and they deliberated issues that plague modern man to this day.

The little we know of Sumerian history is based primarily on the *List of Sumerian Kings,* which was compiled thousands of years after the rise of the first city-states. Although the list's authors may have often mistaken legend for fact, they have provided us with a chronicle of Sumerian history from the earliest city-states, which gained control over the surrounding area, to the end of their supremacy around 1950 B.C.

The Earliest Written Legal Documents

The very forces that eventually divided and destroyed the Sumerian empire were also responsible for the development of juridical institutions, for the need to define the rights and obligations of individual members of the community. Perhaps the most powerful of these forces was that brought about by the shift from communal to private ownership. During prehistoric times, land belonged to the community as a whole; as man settled and began to work the land, he developed the concept of private property. Fields, livestock, and crops were no longer communal property; one man labored, and the fruits of his labors were his alone. Gradually, more and more stress was placed on ownership, on the concept of "mine"—"my work," "my fields," "my livestock," "my home." Inevitably, the concept of private property was accompanied by that of "infractor"—one who takes something belonging to another. Society could no longer function without imposing certain norms, without a ruling power that determined limits of acceptable social behavior. This was the beginning of a system of legal institutions.

From the juridical perspective, *institutions* are those situations, relationships, or basic ordinances that are indispensable for the peaceful and harmonious social coexistence of a human community. Ideally, institutions serve the needs of the community and adapt to the fluctuating needs of society, achieving the delicate balance between protecting the individual and preserving a certain peaceful social framework. Legal institutions derived from sociological needs: when one of society's members behaved in a manner contrary to prescribed norms, he was punished. Ancient legal codes were actually no more than a collection of precedents—lists of actual cases, including the verdict given in each specific case. These specific cases became the basis of a general rule, as opposed to modern-day general rulings, which are applied to specific cases.

ntral role of written law in Sumerian society was a direct conse- the Sumerians' high regard for private property. As early as 2500 B.C., man began to inscribe private transactions on clay tablets. The popularly held conception that the oldest code of law is that of Hammurabi has been refuted by archaeological evidence. Today, as mentioned earlier, the oldest code in our possession is that of Ur-Nammu, who founded the Third Dynasty of Ur in approximately 2050 B.C.; his reign preceded that of Hammurabi by some 300 to 400 years. However, the first references to written law are found even earlier, in about 2400 B.C., when Ur-Engur, king of Ur, stated that he had administered justice "following the laws of the gods." Urukagina, king of Lagash in approximately 2350 B.C., claimed to have compiled all existing ordinances into one code, although only records of administrative reforms have been discovered till now. The Urukagina reform document is in itself of great significance for the history of legal development. This document determines that the entire population has the right to know the justification behind each conviction and punishment. Both the thief and the woman convicted of adultery were to be stoned to death with stones inscribed with their infractions. The seriousness with which female adultery was considered was due to the introduction of strange elements within the family, and the cult of the ancestors could be tainted with sacrilege. In the Hammurabi

Code, the old Hebrew law, and even classical Greece, the adulterous wife received the death penalty. The Urukagina tablet also refers to the people's struggle against tyranny and oppression and points to reforms that were introduced to prevent abuses by the nobles. There is also a mention of a bitter struggle between temple and state, in which the populace supported the church.

Although the code of Urukagina has not come to light, it is reasonable to assume that such a code did exist. Indeed, the degree of similarity that exists between all early Mesopotamian codes leads us to the conclusion that they were based on earlier texts. Each of the early Mesopotamian codes, from that of Ur-Nammu to that of Hammurabi, are based on similar legal principles. Each begins with a prologue proclaiming the king's appointment by the gods to rule over the city-state and to maintain security and preserve order. The prologue is followed by the body of legal principles; and each code ends with an admonition that those who do not follow the king's laws will be cursed. This similarity is impressive evidence of the degree of contact that existed between the city-states.

The tablet containing Ur-Nammu's Code, deciphered by Samuel N. Kramer, is not the original, or even a contemporary copy, but a poorly preserved clay tablet inscribed several hundred years later. The tablet's prologue proclaims Ur-Nammu's selection by the gods as the city's ruler and lists his achievements: the elimination of the abusers and exploiters of the people; the establishment of a uniform system of weights and measures; the institution of moral and social reforms; and the initiation of rules that ensured that the "orphan should not become the prey of the rich, the widow the prey of the powerful, and the man of the shekel the prey of the man of the mina" (a mina contained 60 shekel).

The tablet is so badly damaged that only five of the laws could be deciphered with any degree of certainty. One refers to a kind of trial by water ordeal and another to returning a slave to his rightful owner. The other three read as follows:

If [a man to a man with an instrument] . . . has cut his foot, he will have to pay ten silver shekel.

If a man to a man with a weapon the bones of . . . has broken, he will have to pay one silver mina.

If a man to a man with an instrument has cut the nose, he will have to pay two-thirds of a silver mina.

Although the code itself is in poor condition, hundreds of tablets unearthed in the ruins of Nippur, in the area where the temple scribes lived, paint a rather clear picture of the administration of justice during this period.

Court records were known as *ditilla,* meaning a completed lawsuit. Among these records are court notarizations of agreements; contracts referring to marriages, divorces, child support, gifts, sales, inheritance, slaves, and the hiring of boats; and pretrial investigations, subpoenas, thefts, damage to property, and so forth. Justice was administered by the *ensi,* the governors of the cities within the city-state, who represented the king. The temple served as courtroom, but its role was merely to provide a hall in which oaths and ordeals were administered. There were no professional judges; the thirty-six men listed as judges in each city were from all walks of life—merchants, scribes, temple administrators, and so on. They all received some training at the *adubba,* the school of the temple, and all had a basic judicial knowledge. The *mashkim* was a kind of court clerk and bailiff who prepared the case for the court and was responsible for ensuring that proper court procedures were followed.

A lawsuit was initiated by one of the parties to the case, or by the state if state interest was involved. Testimony consisted of statements made by witnesses, usually under oath; by one of the parties, also under oath; or in the form of written documents or statements of "experts" or high officials. The verdict was usually expressed in the imperative: "must," "ought to," and the like. If damage to the victim was of such a degree that the guilty party was incapable of paying the indemnification, the *ensi* could determine that the victim would be compensated by the palace or temple. One of the tablets mentions the "seven royal judges of Nippur," who seem to have constituted a kind of court of appeals.

A small clay tablet, no more than five to ten centimeters in length, reveals the story of "A Sumerian Trial of a Case of Murder." The case took place during the reign of Urninurta, king of Isin, in about 1850 B.C. Three men murdered a temple employee. The victim's wife knew of the murder but remained silent. Eventually, the crime was discovered, and the trial was held at the court of Nippur. Nine witnesses testified against the three accused and the woman, asking for the death penalty for all four. Two witnesses came to the wife's defense, stating that she had had nothing to do with the murder, that she had suffered during her husband's lifetime, and that her situation was even worse following his death. The three accused were convicted and sentenced to be executed before the victim's house, but the woman was acquitted.

The phenomenon of juvenile delinquency is often regarded as peculiar to modern society, but it has existed since ancient times. One of the oldest cases is perhaps that found on a tablet entitled "A Father and His Perverse Son." The tablet opens with a rather friendly conversation between the father, who was a scribe, and his son, during which the father exhorts his son to go to school, to work diligently, and not to loiter in the streets. His tone then changes, and he begins to reprimand his son for his deplorable behavior.

Despite the fact that the father has never demanded anything from him, nor required his son to support him, as do other fathers, his son refuses to follow in his footsteps as a scribe, the most difficult but most useful of all professions. The text has a happy ending, in which the father blesses his son. It is in this text that the Sumerian word for "humanity"—*namlulu*—first appears, not in the context of "mankind" but as a behavioral norm.

The Code of Lipit-Ishtar

About one century after Ur-Nammu, the Amorite Semitic king of Isin, Lipit-Ishtar, compiled a code in the Sumerian language. The discovery of this code, which is almost certainly rooted in the cultural and juridical heritage of Sumer, dates from approximately 1900 to 1800 B.C. The code—clearly related to that of Hammurabi, which it precedes by some two centuries—provides material for studying the developing of legal concept in Southern Mesopotamia. The original tablet contained some 1,200 lines of text, of which only 400 could be deciphered by F.R. Steele in 1948. This code also begins with a prologue of some hundred lines, describing the king's appointment by the gods to "establish justice and care for the well-being of the Sumerians and the Akkadians." Only three of the laws that could be deciphered have a particular penal and criminological significance. They could be translated as follows:

> If a man entered the orchard of [another] man and was seized there for stealing, he shall pay ten shekel of silver.
>
> If a man cut down a tree in the garden of [another] man, he shall pay one half a mina of silver.
>
> If a girl-slave or a slave of a man has fled into the heart of the city and it has been confirmed that she [or he] dwelt in the house of [another] man for one month, he shall give slave for slave. If he has no slave, he shall pay fifteen shekel of silver.

In all of these cases, the transgressor is required to pay pecuniary compensation, which has no relation to the talionic concept introduced later by Hammurabi. And although the Sumerian and Babylonian codes are separated by two or three centuries, they come from cities relatively close to one another and have similarities that suggest that they derive from a common but as yet unknown source. The code of Lipit-Ishtar is another link in the chain from Ur-Nammu to Hammurabi and from Hammurabi to the Assyrians, the Hebrews, and the civilizations that were to follow.

The Laws of Eshnunna

After the downfall of the Third Dynasty of Ur, a number of cities in the Sumerian world were established beyond the original boundaries. One of these was the city-state of Eshnunna, located some fifty kilometers north of modern Baghdad. Of the little we know of its history, we can only be certain that Eshnunna was conquered and destroyed by Hammurabi, king of Babylon, in about 1720 B.C.

Two clay tablets with the Laws of Eshnunna, known as "A" and "B," were discovered in 1945 and 1949. Despite the efforts to decipher the laws, much of the material remains a mystery. The author of the code is also unknown, and the laws cannot be attributed to one particular king. According to Reuven Yaron, it is possible that they are only slightly older than the Hammurabi code, but even this conclusion is indefinite.

The Eshnunnian society consisted of two social classes—*awilum* and *muskenum*—both constituted by free citizens. The *awilum* were the upper class, and the *muskenum* the lower one. There were also slaves—the *uardu*. It is interesting to note the similarity of the expression *muskenum* to *maskin*, "poor" in Arabic, undoubtedly a derivation from the Akkadian; to *misken*, "unfortunate" in Hebrew; and to *mesquin* in French, *meschino* in Italian, and *mezquino* in Spanish—all referring to stinginess and avarice and all derived from the Arabic *maskin*.

Both classes—*awilim* and *muskenum*—were equal before the law and certainly had more legal rights than the slaves did. But not all *awilum* had equal social status; some were governors, others rich merchants, landowners, and so on, while still others were poor countrymen or simple soldiers. The place of the *muskenum* on the social scale is not clearly determined. They made up the majority of the population, and among them were small proprietors, shepherds, liberated slaves, army privates, and so forth. Some of them worked under contract, and the law protected them from abuse at the hands of the *awilum*, particularly in relation to salary. The slaves' fate depended, to a great extent, on the goodwill of the two upper classes. However, they were also protected by law. If a freeman decided to put himself in bondage in order to pay his debt, the law limited the time he would work as a slave. Surprisingly, a slave could marry the daughter of an *awilum,* and their children were freemen from birth. Prisoners of war were slaves, at the very bottom of the social scale.

The Laws of Eshnunna are a loose compilation of legal rules, precedents, and ordinances from a variety of sources. The two known tablets are written in Akkadian, the lingua franca in the Near East. (The Akkadians were Semitic inhabitants of Central Mesopotamia before 2000 B.C., and their language was used from about the twenty-eighth to the first century B.C.). It seems that these tablets were "private," not "official" copies. They may have been used by those dealing with legal problems, such as functionaries of the courts, or for the instruction and education of apprentices to scribes.

Only two sections of the laws deal with problems of jurisdiction. All the others relate to laws of persons; questions of capacity, marriage, and divorce; laws of property, including hiring and unauthorized use of boats; problems of harvesting, loans, inheritance, breach of contract, conflicts concerning land or cattle, loss of property, and the like. There were also five types of offenses mentioned: theft, burglary, and related matters; kidnapping or forcible seizure of persons; homicide and bodily injuries; sexual offenses; and damages caused to animals.

The main aspects of the Laws of Eshnunna with penal implications are as follows.

Section 12. "A man seized in the crop field of a *muskenum* in broad daylight, shall weigh out ten shekel of silver. [He] seized at night in the crop—he shall die, he shall not live." (Unlawful entry is an offense that precedes theft; punishment depending on whether the offense was committed in daylight or at night—compensation in the first case and death in the second.)

Section 23/24. "If a man had nothing upon a man, yet distrained [seized forcibly] the man's slave woman, detained the distressee in his house and caused [her] to die, he shall replace two slaves women to the owner of the slave woman. If he had nothing upon him, yet distrained the wife of a *muskenum,* the son of a *muskenum* detained the distressee in his house and caused [her or him] to die—[it is] a case of life: the distrainor who distrained shall die."

Section 25. "If a man claimed consummation, but his father-in-law wronged him and gave his daughter to [another]—the father of the daughter shall two-fold return the bride money [dowry] he received."

Section 26. "If a man brought bride money [for?/to?] a man's daughter, but another [man] without asking her father [and?/or?] her mother, forcibly seized her and deflowered her—[it is] a case of life indeed: he shall die."

Section 27. "If a man took a man's daughter without asking her father [and?/or?] her mother, and also did not fix the marriage feast [and?/or?] contract for her father [and?/or?] her mother—should she [even] dwell in his house the days of one year [she is] not a 'wife.' "

Section 28. "If, however, he fixed contract [and?/or?] marriage feast for her father [and?/or?] her mother and took her, [she is] a 'wife.' The day she will be seized in the lap of a man, [he?/she?] shall die, [he?/she?]

shall not live." (The basic difference here is whether there was or was not a previous contract.)

Section 31. "If a man deflowered a man's slave woman, he shall weigh out one third of a mina silver, and the slave woman [remains] her owner's indeed."

Section 42. "If a man bit the nose of a man and severed [it]—he shall weigh out one mina silver. An eye—one mina; a tooth—half a mina; an ear—half a mina; a slap in the face—he shall weigh out ten shekel silver." (Here, there were talionic measures, only compensatory ones.)

Section 43. "If a man severed a man's finger, he shall weigh out two-thirds mina silver." (This provision is unique and without parallel in all the other Eastern sources.)

Section 44/45. "If a man threw a man to the floor in an altercation and broke his arm—he shall weigh out half a mina silver. If he broke his leg—he shall weigh out half a mina silver.

Section 46. "If a man hit a man and broke his . . . —he shall weigh out two thirds of a mina silver."

Section 47. "If a man injured a man in a . . . —he shall weigh out ten shekel silver."

Section 48. "And/for . . . one-third of a *mina* to a *mina,* they shall cause him to seize litigation, but a matter of life [belongs] to the king himself." (In the last six sections, the punishments are only of a compensatory nature. In the last one, it seems that if the parties cannot reach an agreement, the issue will be settled through litigation.)

Section 49. "If a man is seized in [possession of] a stolen slave, a stolen slave woman, slave shall drive slave, slave woman [shall drive] slave woman."

Section 53. "If an ox gored an ox and caused [it] to die, both ox owners shall divide the price of the live ox and the carcass of the dead ox." (This ingenious solution represents a kind of *kadi*—Muslim religious judge—justice.)

Section 54/55. "If an ox [was a] gorer and the ward [authorities] have made [it] known to its owner, but he did not guard his ox and it gored a man and caused [him] to die—the owner of the ox shall weigh out two third of a mina silver. If it gored a slave and caused [him] to die—he shall weigh out fiften shekel of silver." (Here again, there is a difference in the compensation, depending on whether the victim is a freeman or a slave.)

Section 56/57. This is the same as in the previous two sections, but instead of an ox it deals with the case of a "vicious dog."

Section 58. "If a wall was threatening to fall and the ward have had [it] made known to the owner of the wall, but he did not strengthen his wall, and the wall collapsed and caused a son of a man to die—[it is a case concerning] life: decree of the king."

In the cases of an ox or a dog, the law imposes a penalty of forty to fifteen shekel of silver, depending on whether the victim is a freeman or a slave, because the damage could be foreseen, and had the owner behaved with caution, the accident could have been avoided. But death caused by the collapse of a wall that was in disrepair is a capital case, because it was predictable and therefore always preventable. The responsibility for prevention rested with the owner of the wall. It is likely that the ruling concerning the collapse of a wall and similar rulings were laid down following actual occurrences, thus setting the precedent that was recorded for future use. Hammurabi's code also contains a case regarding a wall that was in ill repair, but the ruling is talionic rather than compensatory.

The Laws of Eshnunna, like all these codes, are generally phrased in the language of statutory legislation—conditional sentences in the third person, followed by a sanction. All rulings deal with the objective consequences of the crime, without considering subjective or other factors.

These laws contain only fragmentary information regarding the administration of justice and court procedures. The *lugal* (king) was the highest judicial authority (Sections 48 and 58), and his representatives in the towns of the realm played a leading role in adjudication. Claimants could obtain satisfaction directly from the other party without initiating a lawsuit, but once the case was brought before the court, both litigants had to proclaim their readiness to abide by the court's ruling. The parties were bound not to renew litigation on the same subject. There is also little reference to the way in which a litigant presented his case, and no reference at all to witnesses or to whether or not the accused was ever required to undergo an ordeal, either in specific cases or in cases where evidence was wanting. Affirmative oaths were taken; a party could testify regarding a past occurrence, as in the instance when there was no registration of an alleged sale or when the sale had not been recorded in writing. In cases of rape, the rapist's claim that the woman had been a willing partner did not mitigate the crime or punishment. There is no mention, however, of the way in which the case was terminated or judgment executed.

The Laws of Eshnunna deal only with injuries inflicted by freemen upon freemen; they do not deal with slaves. There are no references to mens rea (intention to cause harm) or to premeditation. There is also no concept of subjective guilt, in contrast to the direct responsibility for actual consequences. In some cases, a subjective motive emerges as a material factor but is not explicitly mentioned in any legal provision. Similarly, there is no distinction between *crime* (as part of public law) and *tort* (concerned only with the parties involved). *Delicts* necessarily resulted in penal measures. *Sanctions* were of a relatively simple nature: for bodily injuries, the majority were of a pecuniary nature (usually from ten to sixty shekel), but more serious offenses were punishable by death. Specific modes of execution are not mentioned. In some cases, the death penalty was mandatory; in others, it was applied when compensation was impossible because the guilty party could not meet the demands of his victim. Death was the only form of corporal punishment. No other forms of physical punishment were sanctioned.

In all three of these early codes, the concept of *talio* is noticeable by its absence. These codes fixed a system of pecuniary rather than talionic compensation. It was not until the Code of Hammurabi, and later in the Hebrew laws, that talionic compensations first appear. Modern man tends to recoil from the dictum "an eye for an eye, and a tooth for a tooth," regarding it as primitive and barbaric. It is therefore worthwhile to remember that this "barbaric" notion was preceded by a more humane one—one that established a monetary compensation for damages rather than putting vengeance in the hands of the state.

The Code of Hammurabi

From the beginning of the third millenium B.C., groups of Amurru, or Amorites—Semitic invaders from the Syrian and Arabian deserts—made sporadic but increasingly frequent attacks on the dwellers of Mesopotamia. The flourishing Sumerian city-states finally fell under the incessant attacks, and the Amorites established a dynasty that was to rule, from its center in Babylon, for some three hundred years. Babylonian history actually begins in 1980 B.C., when the Ur dynasty fell and the Sumerians ceased to exist as an ethnic, linguistic, and political entity. The Babylonian king Hammurabi, who came to power in about 1750 B.C., eventually came to rule over a united kingdom that stretched from the Persian Gulf to the Habor River. Under Hammurabi, Babylonian government became highly centralized, with a tight network of governors and officials who represented the king's interests in all aspects of public life. The king held a position of supreme authority; his total control was undisputed.

Babylon retained the basic sociopolitical structure and the two social classes that existed in the city-state of Eshnunna: the *awilum* and the *muskenum*. There were also slaves. Babylonian society was characterized by a strong family unit; although polygamy was permitted, marriage was largely monogamous, and only one woman had the legal right to the title of spouse.

At the time of Hammurabi's rise to power, Mesopotamia was divided into a number of rival city-states. During the first thirty years of his reign, Hammurabi cautiously avoided wars with his neighbors, but he finally assaulted and conquered the city-state of Larsa. Over the next decade, Hammurabi gradually achieved control over Assyria, until his domain included virtually all of Mesopotamia. In the fortieth year of his reign, about 1700 B.C., Hammurabi issued his famous code of law. Like the early Sumerian codes, it was not a systematic collection of laws on a given subject, nor was it a complete collection of existing laws. Hammurabi's greatness lies in his attempt to achieve legal uniformity through his realm. The term *Hammurabi's code* is somewhat misleading. Like all Sumerian codes, this one, too, was copied by scribes, and additions and amendments were incorporated without mention of whether the decision was that of the king, court, or the scribes themselves.

Like previous codes, the Code of Hammurabi is divided into three parts: the prologue, the legal clauses, and the epilogue. The prologue and epilogue are the Akkadian equivalents of those appearing in the codes of Ur-Nammu and Lipit-Ishtar. With the exception of these two parts, there is no evidence that Hammurabi borrowed directly from previous codes. In the prologue, Hammurabi claims to have been elected by the gods to reign over Babylon and to preserve justice among its people. It ends with blessings for those who respect its laws—and curses for those who do not. The epilogue states: "These are the prescriptions for justice established by Hammurabi, in accordance with the wishes of the gods, who guided the kingdom along the proper path." The epilogue emphasizes the code's strength as a tool of social reform, designed to prevent oppression and facilitate justice.

Although the 282 legal clauses of Hammurabi's code are similar to those of earlier codes, both in form and in content, a certain degree of change is clearly evident. The very number of legal provisions is greater, their arrangements more systematic. The fact that Hammurabi claims authorship of the code and the fact that its provisions are purely secular are further proof of the power of the state. Perhaps the most interesting development was the institution of the talionic principle. The state's reaction to deviant behavior was essentially one of vengeance: death for death. The code also introduced the principle of *expressive* or *sympathetic punishment,* a form of corporal punishment in which the part of the body that had committed the crime was either amputated or mutilated.

Hammurabi's code covers the following subjects: (1) offenses committed during trial (sections 1–5); (2) patrimonial rights (sections 6–126); (3) family and inheritance laws (sections 127–195); (4) bodily injuries (sections 196–214); (5) rights and obligations of certain people, such as physicians (sections 215–223), veterinarians (sections 224–225), barbers (sections 226–227), masons and builders (sections 228–233), and boatmen (sections 234–240); (6) prices and salaries (sections 241–277); and (7) slaves (sections 277–282).

Twenty-seven clauses apply capital punishment in a variety of cases; others sentence the offender to suffer talionic or sympathetic punishments. If a person took something belonging to another, his fingers or hand were amputated (the other hand could be cut off if the crime was repeated); he would lose his lower lip if he kissed a married woman (also mentioned later in the Middle Assyrian laws) and one or more fingers in cases of indecent assault; emasculation was the punishment in cases of rape, and the removal of the tongue for calumny. An ordeal by water was also inflicted in certain cases.

In cases where it was impossible to exact punishment from the offender himself, various punishments could be inflicted upon a member of his family in his stead (later prohibited by the ancient Hebrew law). Homicide was a capital offense, which could never be punished by compensation. The offender was to suffer the death penalty. However, he could obtain at least temporary asylum by fleeing to a temple, a shrine, or a site on the kingdom's borders, or by leaving the country. Punishment was also determined according to the social class of the victim. For example: "If a man puts out the eye of an *awilum,* they shall put out his eye. If he breaks his bone, they shall break his bone" (section 196). "If he puts out the eye of a *muskenum* or breaks his bone, he shall pay one mina of silver" (section 197).

Various professions were regarded as having specific responsibilities before the law and were legally bound to fulfill certain obligations. The following provisions dealt with the surgeon's obligations: "If a surgeon has . . . opened an eye infection or a cataract with a bronze instrument [surgical knife] and so saved the man's eye, he shall take ten shekel" (section 215). If it is the one of a muskenum or his son, "he shall take five shekel" (section 216). "If he killed the man, his hands should be cut" (section 217). "If a surgeon has . . . opened an eye infection or a cataract with a bronze instrument and thereby destroyed the man's eye, they shall cut off his hands" (section 218). "If he killed the slave of a muskenum, he will give an equivalent slave" (section 219). "If he destroyed his eye, he shall pay half of the price of the slave" (section 220). "If he cured a broken bone of an awilum or he has revived his sickness, he will receive five shekel of silver" (section 221). "If it is the son of a muskenum, he will receive three shekel of silver" (section 222). "If it is the slave of an awilum, he will receive two shekel of silver" (section 223). Whether the surgeon received a fee or suffered some form of punishment depended on his success or failure; the fee itself or the degree of punishment depended on the social status of the patient.

Similar sections relating to masons and builders contain the following two clauses: "If a builder has built a house for a man and has not made it strong enough, and the house he has built collapses and causes the death of the house holder, the builder should be put to death" (section 229). "If it causes the death of the son of the owner of the house, they shall put to death the builders' son" (section 230).

Ladislao Thot mentions the fact that jails did exist in Babylon; the most important was called the "lake of the lions." These "jails" were no more than deep cisterns in which people were imprisoned. On the other hand, there is no specific mention of the system of asylum, although the institution existed in fact.

Although we can say with relative certainty that the talionic concept originated with Hammurabi, it is much less simple to pinpoint the motives behind this development. Archaeology has yet to provide us with documentation explaining the shift from compensatory to talionic punishments. Thus, the riddle remains unsolved: Why did the Babylonian civilization exchange a more humane form of sanction for one grounded in the more primitive realm of vengeance?

Middle Eastern Laws after Hammurabi

Soon after Hammurabi's death, his empire began to disintegrate, and it reached a rather inglorious end when King Samsu-Ditana was killed in battle during the brief but destructive invasion of the Hittites in 1600 B.C.

The Hittites were ruled by a constitutional monarchy, in which the king answered to a council of noblemen, the Pankus. The Hittite Laws, discovered in a number of cuneiform clay tablets, date from approximately the fifteenth century B.C. They contain some 200 clauses relating to civil and penal matters. Offenses are clearly defined, with sanctions ranging from payment of fines to the death penalty, forced labor, and mutilation (to which only slaves were subject). There is no evidence of the talionic principle that appeared in Hammurabi's code. For example, sections 7 and 8 determine that "whoever blinds or throws out the teeth of a freeman will pay from his possession twenty silver shekel," but if the victim is a slave, only ten shekel. Sections 11 and 12 state: "Whoever breaks the arm or the leg of a freeman will pay from his possession twenty silver shekel," but if the victim is a slave, only ten shekel. Sections 13 and 14 state: "Whoever tears off the nose of a freeman will pay from his possession a silver mina," but if the victim is a slave, only three silver shekel. Sections 15 and 16 state: "Whoever mutilates the ear of a freeman will pay from his possession twelve silver shekel," but if the victim is a slave, only three shekel. It is interesting that the compensation for injuries that deform the face (nose, ear) are equal to or greater than those for injuries to other parts of the body, such as fractures of arms or legs.

The Hittites were only one of a long list of would-be conquerers who preyed on the weakened Amorite dynasty of Babylon. The Kassites ruled for some four centuries and were finally ousted by the Elamites, who, in turn, were conquered by the Assyrians.

The powerful Assyrian empire reached its peak in 671 B.C., when Esarhaddon invaded Egypt and subjected this mighty nation to his rule.

Before that, the Assyrians developed a rich literature, as expressed in the wonderful Assyrian Creation Tablets, found by the English archaeologist George Smith at Kuyunjik, on the site of the ancient city of Nineveh. They were found in the "library" of King Assur-bani-pal, who reigned about 700 B.C. and was such a great patron of letters and learning that he sent scribes to the ancient cities of Babylon to make copies of rare and ancient works. It is particularly interesting that many of the thousands of this kind of clay tablet, containing masterpieces of the past, include the warning: "Whosoever shall carry off this tablet, or shall inscribe his name upon it, side by side with my own, may Ashur and Belit overthrow him in wrath, and may they destroy his name and posterity in the land." Two tablets tell the Babylonian story of Creation and of the Flood. Their date is about 2000 B.C., and they state that "man was brought into existence so that the gods might have worshipers." The story of the Flood, also known as the Epic of Nimrod, contains a very lengthy and detailed account of it. Its style was indeed majestic, as shown in the following verses:

> During six days and nights
> Wind, flood, storm evermore fiercely overwhelmed the land;
> When the seventh day came, storm and flood ceased the battle,
> Wherein they had contended like a host;
> The sea lulled, the blast fell, the flood ceased.
> I looked for the people with a cry of lamentation,
> But all mankind had turned again to clay.

Assyrian art was also impressive, as may be admired at the Assyrian Sculpture Gallery in the British Museum, London. Colossal winged bulls with human heads—protected genies from the eighth century B.C. palace of King Sargon at Khorsabad—are indeed most forceful. And when King Sennacherib conquered Judea 2,700 years ago, an Assyrian artist who was in his army translated into stone reliefs sketches—perhaps the earliest example of combat "photography"—of his battles. These sketches were kept on the walls of the king's palace at Nineveh but were brought to the British Museum, in accordance with the best colonial tradition. These sketches also provide the only existing "portraits" of Jews from the Biblical period.

The Old Assyrian Laws, also known as the Cappadocian Tablets, date approximately from the fifteenth century B.C. and relate mainly to commercial disputes. The more important Middle Assyrian Laws, from about the twelfth century B.C., consist of fifty-nine sections that deal in detail with offenses against the wives of freemen. Two badly damaged tablets from the same period seem to refer to cases of theft, for which thieves could either be fined, flogged, or required to give a number of days of service to the king. No real code of laws remains from the neo-Assyrian period (from about the middle of the eighth century B.C. until the end of the Assyrian empire), although there are a large number of cuneiform tablets that deal mainly with private transactions. The courts evidently consisted of a single judge (Babylonian courts generally had several), and certain types of offenses were not brought before the court. Instead, punishment was meted out by the victim himself— which might be regarded as a return to the protohistoric system of vengeance.

In 612 B.C., the Assyrian giant toppled under the combined efforts of the Medes and the Chaldeans. For more than seventy-five years, the Chaldeans reigned over what is termed the neo-Babylonian Empire, which reached its heights under Nebuchadnezzar II. It is the neo-Babylonian culture, which extended from the seventh to the fifty century B.C., that has furnished us with a detailed account of the history of the ancient world. However, the innumerable tablets contain only an unfinished draft of a "code" or lawbook, similar to Hammurabi's code. Punishments for the inflictions of blows or injuries are severe: for hitting a married woman, the offender suffers the amputation of a finger. On the other hand, a married woman who hits her husband pays thirty lead mina and may also be given twenty cane strokes. The talio is applied only in cases of murder, but the murderer may escape capital punishment if he gives a slave and his family to the victim's son. If not, he is to be executed on the grave of the deceased.

Those who ruled Mesopotamia after Hammurabi produced a number of laws that were basically similar to Hammurabi's code, though none of the laws in our possession applied the talionic principle. The harsh talionic measures seem to have been rejected by even the most warlike peoples, who preferred a system of monetary compensation. The many peoples who ruled over Mesopotamia all had an impact on the evolution of the criminal law. The Egyptian civilization, which developed almost parallel to that of Mesopotamia, underwent a very different evolution, which was expressed in a rich and highly distinctive culture.

The Impact of Mesopotamia's Civilization

Mesopotamia's influence on its contemporaries in Egypt, Persia, and India, however inspiring, did not endure. Curiously, its seed took deepest root not among its neighbors but in the West. For instance, to a very large extent, it might be stated that the tremendous technological and scientific development of our present-day Western civilization is the outcome of an evolution started in the Near East some 10,000 years ago. Western man's positive, pragmatic, and rational outlook found a congenial spirit in the Mesopotamian view of the world. Transfigured by the monotheistic Hebrews and transmitted by the philosophical Greeks, Mesopotamian concepts penetrated the Western ethos and are responsible, in no small proportion, for our turbulent history of tensions between reason and faith, hope and despair, freedom and authoritarianism, progress and defeat.

One of Mesopotamia's most precious legacies was the written law, originating in an awareness of the rights of the individual as well as by a penchant for controversy and litigation. Mesopotamian law evolved into a lofty ideal, conceived to be divinely inspired, for the benefit of all society. Words derived from the Sumerian and Babylonian legal traditions occur throughout the vast and heterogeneous commentaries on Hebrew law, known as the Babylonian Talmud. To this day, the orthodox Jew uses a Sumerian term when he speaks of divorce. And when he participates in the reading of the Torah in the synagogue, he still touches the pertinent place in the scroll with the fringes of his *tallit* (prayer shawl), wholly unaware of the fact that he is thus reenacting the scene in which the ancient Mesopotamian impressed the hem of his garment on a clay tablet as proof of his commitment to the provisions of the legal record.

It is probably no exaggeration to say that Mesopotamian law shed its light over much of the civilized world. Greece and Rome were influenced by it through their contacts with the Near East, and Islam acquired a formal legal code only after it had conquered the region that is now Iraq, the homeland of ancient Mesopotamia. Just how much of modern law goes back to Mesopotamian origins has yet to be determined.

Moving westward through the channels of Judaism, Hellenism, and Christianity, Mesopotamia's legacy to mankind eventually reached the modern world. In *technology,* that legacy included such prosaic miracles as the wheeled vehicle and the seeder-plough. In *science,* it included the beginning of *astronomy* and a numerical system based on 60, still in use today in dividing the circle into degrees, the hour into minutes, and minutes into seconds. Mesopotamia's astronomical observations led to the eventual discovery of the seasonal equinoxes and the regularity of the phases of the moon. And astronomy's pseudoscientific adjunct, *astrology,* revealed, through its interpretations of the "writing in heaven," the fixed relationships of the stars. It was Mesopotamia that invented zodiacal names, such as the Bull, the Twins, the Lion, the Scorpion, and many others. In *architecture,* it created the ziggurat, a high pyramidal staged tower whose angles were oriented to the cardinal points.

Mesopotamia also gave Western civilization two of its most important *political institutions:* the city-state and the concept of a divinely sanctioned kingship. The city-state spread over much of the Mediterranean world, and kingship—the notion that a ruler's right to rule was bestowed by the gods and that he was accountable to them for his stewardship—passed into the very fiber of Western society. It is hardly a coincidence that British monarchs today go through coronation ceremonies so reminiscent of those of Mesopotamia. Nor can it be a coincidence that activities traditionally associated with monarchs appeared in the early archives of Mesopotamian kings. Through highly efficient government bureaucracies—which used sophisticated book-keeping and accounting systems—the Mesopotamian rulers administered the building and repair of roads, the construction of hostelries for travelers, the sailing of the seas for trade and barter, the arbitration of political disputes, and the writing of international treaties.

There are innumerable other contributions, but a few should be mentioned—for example, a rich and complex system of *rituals and myths,* such as the notion of the netherworld, the concept of water as the source of all creation, the account of the creation of the world, the notion that natural catastrophes are divine punishment for wrongdoing; rituals for new year ceremonies, and the like. In *literature*—besides the stories of creation, paradiser the Flood, the Cain and Abel rivalry, the tower of Babel, and so many others—the epic of Gilgamesh is really extraordinary; "The Good Life," translated by E.A. Speiser, reads as follows:

> Gilgamesh, whither rovest thou?
> The life thou pursuest thou shalt not find.
> When the gods created mankind,
> Death for mankind they set aside,
> Life in their own hands retaining.
> Thou, Gilgamesh, let full be thy belly,
> Make thou merry by day and by night.
> Of each day make thou a feast of rejoicing,
> Day and night dance, dance thou and play!
> Let thy garments be sparkling fresh,
> Thy head be washed; bathe thou in water.
> Pay heed to the little one that holds on to thy hand,
> Let thy spouse delight in thy bosom!
> For this is the task of [mankind]!

Several of Aesop's fables have Sumerian predecessors. *Music* (and *musical theory*) is another Mesopotamian contribution. Harps and lyres of Ur are mentioned, together with ten other unidentified musical instruments. The first musical record in history carries the origins of music and musical theory back to more than 1,000 years before the first known Greek musical notations and consists of the first musical scale and a coherent musical system.

All this is still only a small fraction of the total—the visible part of the iceberg. Future discoveries will undoubtedly add new facets to this picture and will surely bring many surprises. In any case, Mesopotamia, with its unique combination of geography and human genius, created a culture without precedent, and the land between the Tigris and the Euphrates rivers will always be considered the "cradle of civilization."

3
Pharaonic Egypt

In the dimness of prehistory, man began to settle in the long valley
ribboned by the Nile.

—Lionel Casson, *Ancient Egypt*

The Land and the People

Egypt occupies the northeastern extreme of Africa, bordering the Mediterranean and the Red seas. Geographically, it consists of two different regions: Lower Egypt, the northern part, containing the delta of the Nile; and Upper Egypt, the southern part, comprising the narrow strip of cultivatable land on both sides of the river, as far south as Aswan.

The Nile is the source of life for Egypt. Constituted by the Blue Nile, which rises in Ethiopia, and the White Nile, starting in Uganda, it flows for more than 4,000 miles to the Mediterranean. It creates, in the midst of a sterile land, an elongated oasis that has nurtured civilization for thousands of years. The river provided prosperity to those people who lived along it, and the desert, gave them security. These two natural characteristics not only facilitated their existence but also molded their mentality. Each year, the Nile, swollen by the torrential rains of Ethiopia, inundates the land and, when the waters recede, leaves a layer of fertile silt, which the Egyptians called the "black land" to distinguish it from the "red land" of the desert. Without the river, the land would have been barren; with it, the pharaohs ruled for 3,000 years and created an astonishing civilization.

The region was inhabited from the Middle Paleolithic Age; a number of human skeletons dating from 60,000 to 80,000 years ago were discovered a few years ago in the Kubbaniye area, northwest of Aswan. These people came, perhaps, from Asia, crossed the Isthmus of Suez, and pushed back to the desert the black population established throughout the delta and along the Nile. The called the land Kemi (black land), while the neighboring people called it by the Semitic word *Misr,* which is still the country's name in both Hebrew (Mitzrayim) and Arabic.

More than 5,000 years ago, the Egyptians learned how to harness the annual flood, and they started on the way to becoming a nation. Their first practical calendar was based on the seasons of the year, as determined by the behavior of the river: inundation, recession of the waters, and drought. The same factors that created different types of work—building the pharaoh's projects, planting in the mud, and harvesting—later produced the social organization. The people started to build dikes to control the annual floods, basins to trap the water when inundation receded, and canals to irrigate the fields; and they also sank wells. The land was divided in a number of properties whose values depended on receiving the benefit of flooding. This produced a number of incessant wrangles before the courts over rights to use the waters of the river.

All this created a rich economy; even the Bible mentions the "fleshpots of Egypt." Grain was the chief product, and it was frequently exported to other countries. Another commodity was the tall reed called papyrus, which grew along the banks of the river, especially in the swamps of the delta. The Egyptians taught themselves to prepare an excellent type of paper from the stalk of this reed. It was the most convenient writing material of the ancient world until the twelfth century A.D., when paper began to displace it. Because papyrus was lightweight and could be rolled up, it was more handy than the clay tablets of Mesopotamia, and it soon became the most popular means for writing letters or records and keeping accounts. The fibers of the papyrus also served to make ropes, baskets, mats, sandals, and stools. With the river mud, the people prepared dried bricks for building their huts and palaces. Instead of olive oil—rather scarce along the river—they had abundant castor, flax seed, and sesame oil, which they used for cooking, cleaning, and lighting. In the delta as well as along the river, there were abundant cattle, pigs, and goats, as well as all sorts of water birds.

The river was also a perfect artery of communication. The earliest record of a sail is a picture on an Egyptian pot of about 3200 B.C. There were rafts, barges, punts, and grain freighters, as well as "yachts" for the rich and powerful. Sailors and ferrymen were in constant demand; some of them appear in inscriptions on pharaohs' tombs.

The Egyptians' reverence for the river is a natural one, since it transformed Egypt into one of the most prosperous nations of the ancient world, whose civilization lasted through three millenia of history.

The Ancient Sociopolitical Structure

The story of the ancient civilizations that grew and prospered on the banks of the Nile forms one of the most fantastic chapters in human history. Egyptian architectural and artistic achievements have a grandeur and sophistication that still have the power to astound modern man. Although ancient Egyptian culture may have begun at almost the same time as that of the Sumerians, its course was to be a very different one. Whereas the Sumerians and other Mesopotamian peoples lived in a vast open plain that created the conditions for almost continuous warfare (the reason why they disappeared so soon), Egyptians lived in the relative security of endless stretches of desert—a natural boundary that discouraged potential invaders. Instead of fighting among themselves, the Egyptian tribes that settled along the Nile learned to cooperate in their battle against the river's annual floods. Such cooperation is perhaps the key to the extraordinary culture that flourished in ancient Egypt over a period of some twenty-seven centuries.

The first step toward unity in ancient Egypt took place in approximately 3100 B.C., when one monarch—the first pharaoh, whom legend has named Menes—united the upper and lower parts of the country and founded the first of Egypt's thirty dynasties, establishing his capital at Memphis, just south of the Nile Delta. The Early Dynastic Period (3100–2686 B.C.) includes the first two dynasties. Hieroglyphic writing appears from the very beginning, as revealed by the Rosetta Stone, so called for the place where it was found by one of Napoleon's officers in 1799. The stone was a fragment of a stele inscribed not only with hieroglyphics but also in demotic (an ancient Egyptian script dominant in the country from about 650 B.C. to 450 A.D., which succeeded the hieratic script, a cursive form of hieroglyphics) and in Greek. Thanks to its multiple text, Jean-François Champollion, a French philologist, was able to solve the enigma of the hieroglyphs in 1822.

The Old Kingdom (2686–2181 B.C.) covers the next four dynasties. During the reign of Djoser, the outstanding pharaoh of the third dynasty, the first stone buildings were erected, as the Step Pyramid at Sakkarah. During the fourth dynasty, the most important rulers were Khufu, Khafre, and Menkaure. They built the Great Pyramids and the Sphinx at Gizeh, but the pharaohs' absolute power started to weaken, and internal strike led to anarchy, which created the First Intermediate Period (2181–2040 B.C.), characterized by the dissolution of the royal power—many kings with short reigns—covering the next four dynasties. Then came the Middle Kingdom (2040–1786 B.C.), with the eleventh and twelfth dynasties, during which Pharaoh Mentuhote, once again achieved the reunification of Egypt, and established his capital at Thebes. Temples and sculptures on a colossal scale made their appearance. The Second Intermediate Period (1786–1567 B.C.), from the thirteenth to the seventeenth dynasties, shows another decline of central authority; the power was seized by the Hyksos kings, infiltrating from Asia. Under their impact, the traditional Egyptian culture suffered a steep decline. The so-called New Kingdom (1567–1085 B.C.) included the seventeenth, nineteenth, and twentieth dynasties and such famous pharaohs as Ahmose I, who expelled the Hyksos; Thutmose III, who expanded the empire to the Euphrates; Hatshepsut, who built the temple at Deir el Bahri; Amenhotep IV, also known as Akhenaton, who tried but failed to impose monotheism; Tutankhamen and Haremhab, who built elaborate temples and tombs in the Valley of the Kings; Seti I and Ramses II, who repelled the Hittite threat and carried on with an energetic building activity, at that time, the "Book of the Dead" was written on papyrus scrolls. During the rule of the other Ramesside pharaohs (Ramses III to IX) invasions of Libyans and Sea Peoples were repelled. During the entire period, temples and tombs were increasingly built. And during the Late Dynastic Period (1085–341 B.C.), the country was again divided, and there were pharaohs of Libyan origin as well as invasions of Nubians and Assyrians; during the twenty-sixth dynasty, the Persians conquered Egypt, and the thirtieth dynasty saw the last native pharaohs. During the Persian rule, Darius I commanded the codification of Egyptian law. There was also a kind of cultural renaissance, with the imitation of ancient Egyptian art and the last flowering of native art. Finally, the Ptolemaic Period (332 to 30 B.C.) started with the conquest of Egypt by Alexander the Great; after his death, one of his generals founded the Ptolemic dynasty, during which a number of temples were built.

From Menes to Cleopatra, whose demise spelled the end of the Egyptian empire, Egypt was ruled by an absolute monarch—the pharaoh, who stood at the peak of Egypt's social pyramid. Beneath him was the vizier—the prime minister, so to speak—and a relatively small class of nobles, who were followed by priests, officials and scribes, army officers and soldiers, artisans, unskilled laborers, and peasants. At the very bottom were the slaves.

Although the visier was the chief magistrate, the minister of war, the chief of police, and the superintendent of tax collection for the entire kingdom, he had no power of his own; he had to receive the backing of the pharaoh for every one of his main decisions. At first, the vizier was usually selected among the royal princes; later on, however, members of the nobility, frequently within a given family, were appointed. Afterward, any qualified person whom the king favored could become vizier.

Egyptian society was controlled by a relatively narrow segment of the population. Only the priesthood, the professional army, the scribes, and other members of the bureaucracy had any real influence. The professional army provided the ideal solution for those not blessed with the proper family ties. The scribes, who underwent a rigorous training program, also had the opportunity to rise to a relatively high social position, whether or not they belonged to a powerful family. The great majority of Egypt's people were menial laborers whose wages were paid in produce: bread, beans, onions, meat, salt, and so forth. What is probably the first recorded strike in history took place in 1170 B.C., during the twentieth dynasty, when the workers at the Necropolis of Thebes, who had not been paid for two months, sat down and refused to continue working.

Pharaonic Egypt was divided into more than forty provinces, known as *nomes*. Each of them was administered by a governor, or *nomarch*, under the pharaoh's authority. With the end of the Old Kingdom in 2181 B.C., the pharaonic image lost some of its godlike aura, and the governors of distant provinces often acted without either the permission or the knowledge of the king. Many of these governors developed a degree of independent authority and eventually established their own principalities. What had begun as a position of delegated authority was slowly transformed into one of hereditary power.

An additional threat to the pharaohs' power came from the priests, who grew in wealth and influence until, by the end of the eighteenth dynasty, the High Priest controlled one-third of Egypt's agricultural land and was almost as powerful as the king himself.

Egyptian Religion

Religion permeated the entire Egyptian life—socially, politically, and economically. Prehistoric Egyptians, like most early people, revered the wonders of nature and the fearsome traits of certain animals, such as the lion and the crocodile, or the tenderness of others, such as a cow's tenderness for her young. Therefore, the first divinities were frequently represented in animal form—such as Horus, the falcon-headed god; Anubis, the jackal-god of mummification; Hathor, the horned cow–goddess of love; Seth, the big-eared imaginary animal resembling a donkey; Thoth, depicted as an ibis or a baboon; Sobek, the crocodile-god; Khnum, portrayed as a ram; and so forth. Some of such live animals were kept in the temples, such as Apis, the sacred bull, which was maintained at Memphis. When they died, these animals were also mummified, like human beings. Besides animals, the Egyptians worshipped the sun, known by different names in the various cults. One of these names was Re, of nationwide recognition, with the center for its cult in Heliopolis, the "City of the Sun." Afterwards, even before the rise of the first dynasty, the usual transition from zoomorphic to anthropomorphic deities appeared, but they nevertheless kept the former ones. One of the earliest deities to undergo this fusion was Hathor, the goddess of love and childbirth, which had a head and body of a human being but retained the cow's horns. The same happened with Thoth and Anubis, among others. Later on, some gods—such as Ptah, the god of craftsmen, and Osiris, the ruler of the netherworld—had a complete human form, without any kind of animal adornment. According to a legend, Osiris had an evil brother, Seth, who was jealous of the devotion of his brother and slew Osiris. Thanks to the fidelity of his wife, Isis, who collected all the dismembered parts of his body, Osiris was resurrected. Their son, Horus, later avenged his father's murder by killing

Seth. The same myth claims that every pharaoh rules as Horus, and when he dies, he becomes Osiris and rules the underworld.

The religion of ancient Egypt was basically polytheistic, and the gods were close to man, each living its own daily life, with its own likes, dislikes, wants, and needs. The fortune of a god depended on the place of its origin, as was the case with Ammon of Thebes. Both the town and the god were almost unknown prior to the founding of the Middle Kingdom, precisely at Thebes. Ammon (hidden) was an invisible being and could be present everywhere. But as even spirits need a pictorial expression, he was shown in many different ways—as a ram, a goose, and a serpent, but most frequently as a crowned king; and when Ammon was merged with the sun-god Re, the crown showed the rays of the sun. The temple complex at Karnak, the most massive of all time, was erected in his honor. The worship of Ammon even became international, as he was the god of Nubia and, for a time, was also worshipped in Syria and Palestine. Most Egyptians, no matter which particular god they worshipped—national or local—envisaged the birth of the world as the rising of an earthen mound out of the chaos of primordial waters, but each main city claimed to be the site of this phenomenon.

Although Egyptians religions were fatalistic in nature, and every event was determined by the gods alone, their basic element was *maat*, which is almost impossible to translate precisely but involves a combination of such principles as order, truth, justice, and righteousness. *Maat* was the foundation of Egyptian theology, representing the gods' will; so for the peasant, *maat* meant working hard and honestly, and for the official, it meant dealing justly. However, a religion rooted in fatalism regarded such a concept as fixed and unchanging. Since it was created by the gods, there existed a permanent perfection of the world and human society, and there was no need for social reform. Such conservatism could not create the mythology of a Garden of Eden or of Armageddon.

The same attitude determined the Egyptians' conception of and emphasis on death and their beliefs concerning the afterlife. Tombs of the Neolithic Age reveal tools and food left with the dead for use by the departed. The preparation of tombs in which to spend eternity—particularly for the pharaoh, the nobles, and the wealthy—could take years and even decades. Besides the inscriptions on their walls, each tomb had a number of *ushebtis*—figurines expected to work the celestial fields. In the beginning, only the pharaoh and his family were considered divine and immortal. Later, the nobles were included, and finally, even ordinary mortals could share the blessings of the afterlife. To the Egyptians, the afterlife meant a corporeal existence; that is why they mummified their dead. There is no account that describes mummification, and the practice varied in detail at different times. Of course, only a few Egyptians could afford an elaborate burial. Paupers were buried in communal graves covered with sand, but the tombs of the pharaohs were a serious burden on the national economy.

This was the situation until the latter half of the eighteenth dynasty, when the Pharaoh Akhenaton launched a heretical revolt against the great god Ammon. But he did not succeed in establishing the worship of his god, Aton, or in eradicating the other gods. His monotheistic new creed never took root; and soon afterward, the worship of animals was not only revived but intensified.

Their religion served the Egyptians well. By uniting gods and pharaohs, and later uniting the people with them, their civilization could survive for nearly 3,000 years. And the Egyptian concept of the afterlife differed considerably from that of the people of Mesopotamia, who believed in a rather vague subterranean world that followed death. For the Egyptians, death was a bridge between two lives, the new life being essentially a continuation of life on earth, as stated in the so-called Book of the Dead, known to the ancient Egyptians as "The Book of Coming Forth by Day." In fact, the deceased was often accompanied to his new life by wives and slaves, who were slain in order to join their master.

Arts and Sciences

The Egyptians were not philosophers, but they excelled in the arts and sciences, and they showed remarkable inventiveness in the more practical aspects of life. They developed an architecture most suitable for kings and gods. From the early sun-baked bricks, they went to highly sophisticated buildings in stone. Within a brief span of two centuries, they finished the pyramids at Gizeh and started to build the mightiest royal sepulchres of all time. And art kept pace with architecture, thanks to the sense of beauty and symmetry of their craftsmen, which developed into a mature art distinctively Egyptian in concept and character. For three millenia, Egypt produced a graceful and spirited art, expressed in their monumental temples and tombs. Even today, thanks to modern equipment, archaeologists are discovering new monuments almost everywhere in the long valley of the Nile. The royal dead were buried in mammoth tombs—the pyramids. These remarkable structures illustrates ancient Egypt's achievements in both art and sciences. Archaeologists have also unearthed evidence of a sophisticated network of canals that carried water to the fields, as well as a system of dikes that held back the Nile. From the thirteenth century B.C. onward, they had anthropoid coffins for aristocratic burials. Within them were jewelry and pottery of the period. Unhappily, priceless Egyptian treasures have been looted since immemorial times. When Howard Carter discovered the tomb of Tutankhamon in the Valley of the Kings in 1922, it was a miracle that he found it intact, with all its incredible beauties.

Medical advancements made by the Egyptians far exceeded anything known in the ancient world. Their physicians diagnosed and treated illnesses;

performed surgery—including, perhaps, even trepanations of the skull (today there are some doubts about this); and prescribed herbal cures. The process of mummification remains something of a mystery. During the times of Imhotep, the "father of Egyptian medicine"—whom, centuries later, the Greeks identified with Aesclepius, their god of medicine—besides making a realistic effort to eliminate disease, all energies were dedicated to the problem of getting rid of the uncertainties, anxieties, and fears generated by illness, a medical principle valid even today.

The Egyptians were also among the first people to use simple arithmetic to measure their fields and estimate crop yields. Their observation of the heavens led to the development of a solar calendar of 365 days. They also divided each day into twelve units, which varied with the seasons. This method of measuring time remained the most efficient system until the invention of the mechanical clock in medieval Europe.

Crime and Punishment

Life in ancient Egypt was steeped in religion. All aspects of art, science, and literature were imbued with religiosity. These were not favorable conditions for the development of law, and although many ostraca include legal matters, complete with jargon, penalty clauses, and other miscellaneous items from different periods, archaeologists have yet to discover any code of law that could compare to that of the Sumerians.

From the limited information available, the vizier, as chief magistrate, and his deputies administered the pharaoh's justice. He presided over the Court of Six—the supreme judicial court of the state—which served as the court of appeals for provincial and district courts. It was the vizier's explicit duty not only to judge fairly but to observe the accused for signs of a violent character, to watch his movements, his facial expression, and so forth. This rather sophisticated notion is perhaps the earliest intimation of criminal psychology. The vizier was also bound never to avoid a petitioner and to punish only when convinced of guilt. During the Old Kingdom, all the decisions were made by magistrates acting on behalf of the vizier, whose power was delegated by the king.

Later, at the beginning of the New Kingdom, the high priest used to attend court trials held in the temple, at which the vizier presided. It is unclear whether the high priest influenced the court and, if so, to what degree. Other priests were often found among Egypt's judges, although there is no record of a specifically ecclesiastic court.

In theory, the same law was applied to all members of the community. One of the surviving papyri that illustrates the basic principle of social justice is known as the "Protest of the Eloquent Peasant." The document refers to a peasant who had been robbed by a thief with court connections. The peasant complained to the chief steward of the palace, who restored the stolen property to its rightful owner. Although the thief was higher born than the victim, he was required to make restitution.

There is written evidence of Egyptians' transactions regarding land, cattle, slaves, boats, and so forth. Transactions relating to family affairs often reached the courts. At first, the Egyptian family was basically monogamous, based on equal rights for husband and wife. Both could prepare independent wills, and each could dispose of family property, real estate, or movable goods as he or she saw fit. The total equality between the sexes in this area raised a number of legal problems, which gradually diminished as woman's status declined.

Since death was merely the beginning of another life, even the dead did not escape justice. Before burial, the deceased was brought before a priest and his peers, and his life was judged. If he was condemned, he was refused burial, and his name was erased from all records. Even kings were not exempt from his procedure. The bodies of those who died without having paid their debts or having received punishment for a given offense were punished posthumously. In fact, Plutarch is said to mention that Ptolemy IV Philopator ordered the crucifixion of the body of Kleomenes, king of Sparta, who led an unsuccessful uprising and was said to be a "wretched debauchee." Thus, Ptolemy applied the punishment for sedition to the body of the guilty man!

During the fourth and fifth dynasties of the Old Kingdom, there is evidence of important legal developments and reforms. There are mentions of lawbooks or codes and archives for recording judgments and punishments—such as forced labor, mutilations, and other corporal penalties; hanging for serious crimes, and so forth. The illegal practice of certain functions that were exclusive to the priesthood—including medical and surgical treatments—could be punished by hanging. There are some indications that torture was applied in ancient Egypt to obtain confessions. People sentenced to forced labor were held in fetters in specific areas of the cities or even in private homes. Their sentences were served in the building of temples, palaces, tombs, and pyramids, or in the gold and copper mines.

Places of refuge or asylum may have existed in such cities as Herakleopolis, some 120 kilometers south of Thebes, where slaves could escape their masters. The temple of Osiris in the delta of the Nile and even the statues of the pharaohs served a similar purpose. Documentation regarding criminal procedure is almost nonexistent. Archaeologists have discovered only a fragmentary, poorly preserved penal statute from the time of Haremhab, an army general who took the throne in approximately 1320 B.C., at the end of the eighteenth dynasty.

What could be the explanation for the relative paucity of material regarding the development of legal concepts in ancient Egypt? Papyrus sheets, ostraca, and limestone laminae have been discovered that include tax receipts and related records of Egypt's economy. However, almost nothing has been discovered that could give us a clear picture of Egypt's legal system. Perhaps the answer lies in the fact that the study of law did not have the importance it had in Mesopotamia, nor did it develop to the extent it did under the Hebrews. The pervasiveness of Egypt's fatalistic religion may have made earthly crimes and punishments seem rather insignificant and unworthy of a serious effort of judgment and reform. The quality of life on earth was determined by the gods; man could only attempt to make his stay more comfortable, not to imbue it with a magnitude that was reserved for the world to come.

4

The Ancient Hebrew Criminal Law

If I forget thee, O Jerusalem, let my right hand forget her cunning.
If I do not remember thee, let my tongue cleave to the roof of my
mouth; if I prefer not Jerusalem above my chief joy.

—Psalm 137:5–6

Prehistoric Palestine

According to Kathleen Kenyon, Palestine was one of the places where some
of the first steps were made in the long process by which man ceased to be
a savage, a hunter, and a collector of wild foods and became the inhabitant
of a civilized community. With the progress of archaeology, great advances
have been made in the study of the early Middle East. Here were discovered
the wild early wheats and their cultivated descendants, so it is reasonable to
deduce that this area played an important role in the genesis of agriculture.
On the other hand, the skeleton of what is believed to be of the world's oldest
domesticated dogs—dating back 12,000 years—was found in a human grave
in 1976, in the Huleh Basin site of Ein Mallaha. Similar finds in the Hayonim
Cave in western Galilee support the hypothesis that man had already
domesticated the dog at that time. If the domestication of the dog took place
12,000 years ago, it was some 2,000 to 3,000 years earlier than the
domestication of any other animal. This may be due to some ritual, since the
dog was buried with a man in the same grave, or perhaps to a more
pragmative motive—to become a better hunter. Only much later did man start
to exploit wild animals for domestic purposes, perhaps in the following order:
goats and sheep, cattle, wild boars (later, pigs), horses and asses.

The ecological background to the beginnings of human settlements thus
started to take shape. The earliest were found in Jericho, to the north of the
Dead Sea, in the Hindu Valley, and in Anatolia. Their Neolithic cultures were
not identical, but they had some similar features. It seems clear there is no one
center from which all progress spread, but a number of them in which the
same environmental peculiarities gave an impetus to further development
between the ninth and the six millenia B.C. One of these was Palestine.

Perhaps progress was uneven: gradual in some places, with a great spurt forward in others and then a slackening. Byblos, Ras Shamra, Mersin, and similar villages were more or less self-sufficient, providing their own food and making their own tools, weapons, utensils, and clothes from flint or other local stones, animal skins, or woven cloth. Some of them had handmade pottery, and there was some kind of trade among them—exchanging seashells, ornaments, or amulets. These Neolithic communities were small, spreading over an area of a few acres. An excess of population would have to form new villages, and since primitive agriculture tended to exhaust the land, the villages often had to move in order to get virgin fields to cultivate. Perhaps this was the way in which the Neolithic type of life was gradually diffused from its original centers, such as Jericho, to other places in the Fertile Crescent. It was here where the first great civilizations arose.

The discovery of the use of certain materials—chief among them copper—and their advantages over stone caused these early communities to develop beyond the Neolithic stage and to enter into some type of exchange in order to secure them. They had to produce extra foodstuffs or other natural products to pay the traders as well as the smiths who made the implements, who had no time to provide their own food. Thus the self-sufficiency of the small units began to break down, and the complex structure of civilized communities began to develop.

From approximately the beginning of the fourth millenium B.C., the two tips of the Crescent—Mesopotamia and Egypt—began to develop more rapidly than the rest of it. They established the first city-state and towns. When one of them took the lead, they united the rest and formed the first empires. By the end of that millenium, and for the next 3,000 years, the interplay of these two empires was the main theme of Near Eastern history. Since then, human history is mainly a record of man's beastliness to man. Massacre upon massacre, slaughter upon slaughter, even the high ideals were inevitably pressed into service to provide the needed justifications for self-destructiveness. This rivalry inevitably affected the fate of countries such as Palestine, which lay on the connecting routes.

Historical Background

The origin of the Jewish people is—like that of most ancient peoples—a blend of legend and truth, fact and fantasy. According to the biblical tradition, Abraham was supposedly the first Hebrew, who migrated from Ur to Haran, an Amorite settlement in northwestern Mesopotamia, and afterward to Canaan, in approximately 1800 B.C. By then, the city-states of Sumer, Akkad, and Babylon were already in decline or had disappeared altogether, and the Near East was dominated by the warring river empires of the Nile and Mesopotamia.

It is a rather complicated and very much debated issue to determine the origin of the word *Hebrew*. Some scholars thought to identify the Habiru—a social class of dependents living in different places of the Fertile Crescent during the greater part of the second millenium B.C.—with the Hebrews, but no basis for such an identification has been determined. Others consider that the name *eber* derives from *iuri*, rather than vice versa, and still others suggest that the term refers to the region known as *eber ha-nahar*, beyond the river Euphrates. The fact is that the exact origin is unknown. The Hebrews could have been a Semitic group of clans and tribes, with Hittite and Philistine elements. They came to be known as Israelites only after the patriarch Jacob was given the name of Israel. These two terms, *Hebrew* and *Israelite*, are mainly used in the Bible before the Babylon exile.

The word *Jew* can be traced to the Hebrew *yehudi*, originally applied to members of the tribe of Judah, the fourth son of Jacob. It is possible that this term passed into the English language from the Greek *ioudaios*, by way of the Latin *judaeus*, and is found in early English from about the tenth century A.D. onward. This expression is never used in the Bible. Finally, the term *Israeli* identifies the citizens of the modern-day state of Israel.

It is a well-known fact that the oral tradition is far from bearing the same proximity to factual truth as written history, but in the beginning, it was the only way to keep the records of important events. The Bible states that Ur, known today as Mugajjar in Iraq, was located some kilometers to the south of Nasirije, in the confluence of the Euphrates with the Shatt el-Hai. It was the native place of Terah, the father of Abraham. Aram, Abraham's brother, died in Ur. Terah took his family from Ur Kasdim to the land of Canaan, but when they came to Haran, they stopped (Gen. 2:31). And it was Abraham who, on behalf of Israel, established the covenant with God that made Israel the "chosen people" and Eretz Israel—the land of Israel—the "chosen land."

Whatever the case, it is quite probable that the Hebrews migrated from Mesopotamia, since Mesopotamian influences had a decisive impact on the early Jewish religious and philosophical tenets. The impact of Mesopotamia on the Hebrews was both direct and circuitous. If, as some scholars think, the Biblical saga of Abraham had a kernel of truth in it, and if the Hebrew patriarch lived in Ur in the days of Hammurabi, then he and his family may have assimilated Sumerian culture long before the Jews themselves were a nation. And the Hebrews' ancestors clearly seem to have lived in Mesopotamia from very early times. Cuneiform documents, ranging from as early as 1700 to about 1300 B.C., frequently mention a people called the Habiru, a name closely identified, as already mentioned, with the biblical word *Hebrew*. According to these texts, the Habiru were wanderers, nomads, even brigands and outlaws—men who sold their services as mercenaries to Babylonians and Assyrians, Hittites and Hurrians (ancient non-Semitic people prominent in northern Mesopotamia, Syria, and eastern Asia Minor at about 1500 B.C.) alike. As early as 1500 B.C., these archetypal ancestors of the "Wandering Jew" began the conquest of Palestine. There they came in contact with the Canaanites—Semitic people inhabiting ancient Palestine and Phoenicia from about 3000 B.C. The Canaanites had a cuneiform script, their "schools" followed the Mesopotamian curriculum, and their culture was deeply imbued with Mesopotamian beliefs and thoughts. There are, of course, a great and important number of doubts and an unending debate about all these facts.

But the Hebrews' most important contact with Mesopotamian culture began in 586 B.C., when the king Nebuchadnezzar destroyed Jerusalem and carried off its people into Babylonian captivity. The literacy and great learning of the Babylonians infiltrated the Hebrew mind and thought. When the exiles later returned to their homeland to create again the Judean state, they carried with them a number of Mesopotamian liturgical, educational, and legal practices. Some of these were carried over into Christianity and, through the Judeo-Christian tradition, reached Western civilization as a whole. From then on, the Jewish people were devoted to learning and research and, as Abba Eban wrote: "the constructive humility of scholarship, its respect for the supremacy of reason, its insistence on rationality, its skepticism toward unproven dogmas, its sense of social obligation, its intrinsic tolerance and its universal solidarities, have a refining and ennobling effect on the social order, irrespective of the practical results of its explorations" (*Jerusalem Post*, 10 December 1985).

Of the thousands and thousands of clay tablets found in Mesopotamia, and probably many more that are still to be uncovered, not too many have been found in Palestine. An extremely rare clay tablet covered with Akkadian cuneiform script was found in 1978 in Afek, near the source of the Yarkon river at Rosh Ha'ayin, among the debris of the Egyptian fortress built there by Ramses II, from which Egyptians ruled the country for about forty years. The nine-by-five-centimeters tablet, with a forty-one-line text written on both sides as well as on its rim, is a letter from Kukhlina of Ugarit—in northwestern Syria—to Hayya, the Egyptian ruler of Canaan; it was written some time between 1240 and 1230 B.C. The Ugarite asked the Egyptian ruler to make sure that justice was done and that the 250 measures of wheat that passed, presumably unlawfully, from one Aduya (a Semitic name) to one Tur Shimati should be restored to their former owner. In support of his request, couched in a ceremonious but humble style, the Ugarite sent a gift of a hundred shekels of blue wool and ten shekels of red wool.

Returning now to the biblical tradition, some time after the Hebrews settled in Canaan, they migrated to Egypt to escape a severe drought. It was not the first contact between the Hebrews and the Egyptians. This one probably took place 4,000 years ago in the Taurus mountain range, between Haran and Nineveh, where the migrating Semitic tribes were then living, and when the soldiers of Amenemhet II conquered all of Western Asia. The ties between these two peoples became closer as the Semitic tribes migrated southward, first to Canaan and then to Egypt itself. The trickle became a stream, and the power and numbers of these "hordes from the north"—the Hyksos—became so great that they took control of Egypt in 1730 B.C. The Hyksos, a loose federation of Semitic tribes including the Hebrews, ruled Egypt for 180 years before they were overthrown by a revolt against foreign rule. It was during the Hyksos period that Joseph became vizier.

It is strange that of all the periods in the joint history of Israel and Egypt, the one that has remained most strongly in the Jewish folk-memory is that of the bondage in Egypt. This period followed immediately after the liberation of Egypt from the rule of the Hyksos and lasted till the mass Exodus led by Moses, when Egypt was at the peak of its strength. The Exodus is perhaps one of the sources of Egyptian anti-Semitism, based on the description by the Egyptian priest Manetho at the beginning of the third century B.C. In recounting his country's history, he tells of a "people from the east," despised by the gods and consequently stricken with a loathsome disease. These people, he writes, "subdued Egypt by stratagem and force, only to be driven out subsequently in ignominy, before making their way to the land of Judea. Here they established their capital, Jerusalem, and adopted a law code based on the hatred of all human-kind except their own." Manetho's version of the Exodus became a wellspring and prototype of anti-Jewish propaganda, whose early exponents included the Romans Juvenal and Tacitus, to name just a few. Since then, the exodus from Egypt's bondage is celebrated every year at Passover, with its special character and meaning as the festival of liberation from slavery and the determination of the Jewish people to proclaim its heritage as a sovereign people, now in its own land—the state of Israel.

The biblical account of the Exodus does not answer a tantalizing question. Why did Moses turn right when he reached the Sinai, taking his flock on an arid, roundabout forty-year odyssey instead of heading directly along the Mediterranean coast to the Promised Land? The Old Testament hints that Moses headed inland to avoid a confrontation with the Philistines. Yet archaeological findings show that at the time of the Exodus—about the thirteenth century B.C.—the Philistines had not yet established themselves in the coastal region around Gaza. Was it because it was easier to take the people out of slavery than to remove the slave mentality from their minds? It took Moses decades in the desert to create a free Jewish nation that could enter the Promised Land. But archaeology tells us another story: the Israelites went into the desert to elude not the Philistines but the very people from whom they were escaping—the Egyptians. Trude Dothan, a Hebrew University of Jerusalem archaeologist—found the remains of a large Egyptian community at a site near the modern Arab town of Deir Al-Balah about 18 miles southwest of Gaza, which flourished during the reign of Ramses II.

During their desert wanderings, the Israelites are supposed to have received the Ten Commandments, the moral and legal foundations of Western civilization. Moses, who received them on Mount Sinai and was the undisputed leader of his people, died before the Israelites entered Palestine. They were lead by Joshua bin-Nun (son of Nun) in the conquest and apportionment of the land of Canaan. According to the Bible, he was Moses' attendant and commander; Moses appointed him as his successor because he, too, was a prophet-legislator. Besides the Canaanites, they found the Philistines on the coast. The Philistines were a subdivision of the ancient "sea peoples" of the Mediterranean, such as the Tjekker, the Denyen, the Sherden, and others. The Philistines were a naval power that first emerged in the eastern Mediterranean in the second half of the thirteenth century B.C. At that time, both the Egyptian and Hittite empires were in eclipse, so the Philistines, taking advantage of the situation, invaded Syria and Egypt. Ramses III, who reigned from about 1198 to 1166 B.C., defeated the invading forces after bitter fighting, but encouraged them to establish themselves on the southern coastal plain of Palestine, then under Egypt's control. This happened precisely when the Israelites, fleeing Egyptian bondage, were also infiltrating the land of Canaan. The two factions, both seeking a permanent place for living, had a number of clashes; the Bible mentions Samson's adventures in love and war, and the conflicts of David, especially the fateful duel with Goliath. The biblical image of the Philistines, not necessary a true one, is that of an overbearing, deceitful, and unscrupulous enemy; this image was obviously colored by their supremacy in war, due to their knowledge of and monopoly in metal working. Nevertheless, by the middle of the tenth century B.C., they merged into the local scene and vanished from history. They had five main towns, the Pentapolis: Ashkelon, Ashdod, Gaza, Gath, and Ekron. The first three were more important because they were established along the ancient Via Maris. Palestine, whose name derives from its association with the Philistines, has an impressive amount of their remains. Their pottery, beautifully designed and executed, had an amazing variety of shapes and ornamental motifs in red and black, on a white background, showing a clear Mycenaean influence, thus demonstrating their roots. Their burials in anthropoid clay coffins, of Egyptian origin, show their influence. As for the invasion of Canaan, the capture of Jericho is one of the most detailed reports in the Bible, but it did not happen in the thirteenth century B.C.; archaeologists have clearly shown that the city site was deserted at that time. It is possible that the biblical account of the conquest does not accurately represent a historical reality, because of the process of distortion of the oral tradition. Only afterward, from the establishment of the kingship to the destruction of the First Temple, did royal and temple scribes keep reliable sources. Furthermore, the Book of Joshua shows the conquest of Canaan as a displacement by strangers of an indigenous population, accompanied by mass slaughters and genocide. According to that account, it was God who ordered the extermination of the Canaanites—men and women, young and old—with the edge of the sword, but the weight of archaeological opinion, based on extensive excavations, is that there was no dramatic and bloody conquest, but a rather peaceful infiltration of Israelite tribes over many years into a land largely depleted of its Canaanite population.

Be that as it may, the Israelites finally settled in the southwestern corner of the Fertile Crescent sometime during the twelfth century B.C. The area, later known as Palestine, was characterized by its central location. It was the focal point of trade routes, and it lay directly in the path of nomadic tribes and warring armies. This lack of stability and the resulting exposure to a wealth of knowledge and a variety of beliefs, ideas, and philosophies, facilitated the development of a highly distinctive culture. The Israelites spoke Aramaic throughout much of the biblical period and even afterward. (It is interesting to note that as many as 30 percent of the Syrian families in Israel today still speak Aramaic dialect, known as Syriac. The same is true in a few villages in Syria, as wells as with Jews coming from certain parts of Kurdistan.)

According to the Bible, when the people of Israel entered the land of Canaan, they were distributed in twelve tribes and divided the land between them. But they were united in their unwavering monotheism, which eventually became the basis of Christianity and Islam. And the Bible is still the source of a rich literary, philosophical, and legal legacy.

From approximately 1300 to 1100 B.C., the Israelites had no organized central leadership. During times of crisis, they were led by a prophet or a judge, who was essentially a kind of dictator. These leaders combined both military and political powers and ruled by right of "divine inspiration." When a period of crisis ended, the leader stepped down, relinquishing his power. This period ended when external threats from the Philistine in the west and Trans-Jordanian tribes in the east threatened their mere existence. Then the people of Israel asked their leader, Judge Samuel, to appoint a more permanent leader. Accepting their petition, he appointed Saul as the first king of Israel, under whose reign the nation entered a period of wars against her neighbors, which continued during the kingship of David. It was under the monarchy that Israel acquired political unity and became a military power. The monarchy was instrumental in the transition from a loose confederation to a nation with a centralized governing power. King David established his capital, Jerusalem, on the site of a Jebusite (one of the former people of Canaan) city, on the hills of Judea, which already had its defending walls. From the walls built by David himself to the present Turkish wall, repaired and rebuilt by Suleiman the Magnificent between 1537 and 1542 A.D., the history of the Jerusalem walls is a story in itself.

During the reign of King Solomon (from 965 to 928 B.C.), there were no wars; he developed his kingdom with wisdom and magnificence, particularly the first Great Temple in Jerusalem. After his death, tribal loyalties divided the kingdom in two: Judah in the south and Israel in the north. Israel was destroyed by Sargon II, king of the Neo-Assyrian empire, in 721 B.C. Judah eventually succumbed to Nebuchadnezzar II of Babylon in 586 B.C.; he burned the Temple of Solomon and took the people to Babylon, so starting the first Jewish exile. It was a rather short one, because when Cyrus I of Persia conquered Babylon in 538 B.C., he authorized the Jews to return to their country and to rebuild their temple. The actual work started in the year 520 and was finished in 515 B.C. Not all the Jews returned from Babylon, but the state of Judah continued to function till the first century A.D., when Flavius Vespasianus Titus destroyed it in 70 A.D. With the distruction of the temple by the Romans, the organized Jewish resistance ceased, with the exception of a few local cases, and the long Jewish exile (*galut* in Hebrew) started, ending only in 1948 with the establishment of the state of Israel.

Social and Religious Structure

From the beginning of the monarchy until the destruction of the Second Temple, the basic social structure of the Jewish nation was rather simple. Because of the Sinaitic Covenant, every Israelite was considered freeborn. Their shared ancestry and common background ruled out social classes. The population was divided into Israelites proper, strangers (foreigners), and *slaves*. The foreigners enjoyed the same rights as the Israelites did, and the treatment of slaves was rather lenient. Slaves were either prisoners of war or those who sold themselves into bondage in order to pay off debts. Once the debt was paid, they regained their status as freemen, but whether or not the debt was paid, they were automatically liberated after six years of servitude.

The family was the nucleus of society, and although the father had complete authority, women were held in high regard, despite the fact that they had no legal status in the Bible. Polygamy was unusual, but concubines were tolerated, though they did not have the same rights as the legitimate spouse. The husband could repudiate his wife, but she could also, under certain circumstances and with the consent of the priesthood, divorce her husband. A husband could accuse his wife of adultery, but she could not accuse him. Not to have children was considered almost dishonest and a valid reason for divorce. The Mosaic legislation accepts the system of levirate. A "levirate marriage" (*yibbum* in Hebrew) is one between a widow whose husband died without offspring and the brother of the deceased, who is not willing to marry her, as prescribed in Deuteronomy 25:5–6. When the brother does not agree to marry the widow, the ceremony of *halizah* takes place, whereby the woman becomes released from the levirate tie and free to marry someone else. For such a purpose, she goes up to the gate unto the elders and says: "My husband's brother refuseth to raise up into his brother a name in Israel; he will not perform the duty of a husband's brother unto me." Then the elders shall call him and speak unto him, but if he stand and say: "I like not to take her," then the woman draw nigh unto him in the presence of the elders, loose his shoe from off his foot, and spit in his face, and she shall say: "So shall it be done unto the man that doth not build up his brother's house" (Deut. 25:7–10).

Landed property was inherited by the family, and children could not be disinherited. Daughters could inherit only when they had no brothers. Whereas in Mesopotamia and Egypt the priests gradually took over the most fertile land and thus became rich and powerful, the Jewish *kohanim* (priests) could not possess lands, as their closeness to God was regarded as a much more valuable possession.

If civilization is the culture of living in cities, it was built up by the Mesopotamians, the Sumerians, the Canaanites, and the Egyptians. The Mesopotamians developed irrigation, which facilitated the life in cities; the Sumerians provided the wheel and cuneiform writing; the Egyptians built great cities and mighty monuments; the Canaanites produced the alphabet, which enabled man to codify laws and to transmit ideas. So what was the contribution of the Jews? They did not build pyramids, statutes, idols, or representations of God in stone or wood. Instead, they gave the world the concept of one God, awesome and majestic, invisible and intangible—a God who is moral and compassionate, who deals with humanity on the basis of the law, not whim, as the gods of the pagans did, and the One who brings order in place of chaos. Their belief in a monotheistic God has spread from the Jews to the other great monotheistic religions. This concept of monotheism appears to transcend in importance for civilization the trifling contributions of other peoples.

Sources of Biblical and Talmudic Laws

The great Hebrew literature surviving in the Old Testament contains much that relates to Jewish law, especially in the Pentateuch, possibly compiled about the beginning of the fourth century B.C. out of documents of earlier centuries. The Hebrew code, though brief, is a little less advanced than that of Hammurabi and is perhaps nearer, in its degree of development, to the laws of Eshnunna than to any other of the earlier codes. That the Biblical laws and the long-known Code of Hammurabi show numerous similarities in content, terminology, and even basic arrangement is recognized by practically all students of the Bible. But the Hammurabi code itself, as has been shown in recent years, is an Akkadian compilation of laws based largely on Sumerian prototypes. There is a good reason to infer that the extraordinary growth and development of legal concepts, practices, precedents, and compilations in the ancient Near East goes largely back to the Sumerians.

In contrast to the lack of documentation regarding the ancient criminal codes of the Near East, there is an almost dizzying richness of sources regarding the ancient Hebrew law. Nevertheless, it should be understood that the general comments that follow are the usually accepted versions of the large body of legal and other sources. Moreover, this is not a chronological account of the development of the Hebrew-Israelite law, which is practically not feasible given the long and complicated process of compilation of the Bible and the codification of the Mishnah and the Talmud, all of which is still the subject for many arguments and debates. What follows, therefore, is meant only for legal students, criminologists, and laymen, not for biblical scholars.

The legal tenets within the Pentateuch were complemented by the interpretations of the Mishnah (the oral law) and the Talmud, which is not a sacred text but an encyclopedic, rambling, and sometimes even humorous collection of folk tales, proverbs, philosophical debates, legal arguments, historical comments, and much more. It provides a highly varied collection of mortal protagonists, strong-minded teachers, servants, merchants, soldiers, beggars, and even thieves and whores, as well as a rich assortment of incidents, confrontations, and dialogues. To understand the nature of the religious influence on the criminal law, and to grasp both the beneficial and the detrimental factors it has brought to bear—be it the Hebrew code or any other ancient code—it is indispensable to interpret, for today, the meaning of the religious language and symbols and to clarify when they speak eschatologically or literally or when they use a metaphor or an overstatement as a homiletic device.

Nothing is intrinsically sacred about "law" in general. History abounds with cases of injustice and atrocites, at both the individual and collective levels, that were neatly perpetrated in the framework of the law. The extermination of the Jews, along with other legally defined "subhumans," was carried out by the Nazis in the framework of the Nuremberg Laws. And legal abuses have not been confined to totalitarian nations. It is not so long ago that hungry men in England were legally hanged for stealing food (*furtus famelicus*), and women were burned at the stake if charged with witchcraft.

The Mishnah is divided into six parts or orders, in six categories: *Zeraim,* dealing with benedictions and vegetable offerings; *Mo'ed,* with festivals; *Nashim,* with women and marriage; *Nezikim,* with civil law and judicial organization; *Kodashim,* with animal offerings and sacrifices; and *Tohoroth,* with ritual purity and cleanness. These six *sedarim* (orders) were revised and edited by Rabbi Judah ha-Nasi, by the end of the second century B.C. The Talmudic and Mishnaic interpretations reflect the discussions of the Tannaism and Amoraim, scholars who elucidated and commented upon them. The Tannaic period refers to the time in which the Mishnah was nearly completed, until about 220 B.C. The Amoraim participated in completing the Mishnah and prepared the Talmud, from approximately 220 B.C. to 470 A.D. Later contributions illuminating Mishnaic and Talmudic text were made by Rashi (Rabbi Solomon ben Isaac, 1040–1105); Maimonides (born in Cordoba, Spain, in 1135 and died in Fostat, Egypt, in 1204), known in rabbinical literature as Rambam (acronym of Rabbi Moses ben Maimon) and considered to be the most illustrious figure of the post-Talmudic era; and Joseph ben Ephraim Caro, perhaps the last great codifier of the rabbinical law and an outstanding talmudic authority of the sixteenth century (1488–1575). He is the author of the famous *Shulhan Arukh*, published in Venice by the end of the sixteenth century. It contains the 613 commandments of Moses' Laws, of which 248 are *mandatory*, making compulsory the performance of certain acts, and the other 365 are *prohibitory*, forbidding the execution of other acts. The vast majority of the material that follows derives from these sources. The Talmud commentaries on the Mishah are an important part of the Jewish social and cultural structure.

Interest and Biases in the Study of the Ancient Jewish Law

Although the study of Biblical Law flourished during medieval times, the last comprehensive study of Mosaic law was in the middle of the last century. There appears to be a tendency to dismiss them as archaic, despite the fact that many of their humanitarian qualities are unparalleled in the ancient Mesopotamian codes. Any attempt to approach the study in the context of contemporary social norms is necessarily blurred by prejudice and distorted by modern biases. A study of biblical law must be grounded in an understanding of the cultural values and ethics that prevailed in the ancient Mideast and must be seen in the light of the early cuneiform codes.

The first major differences between the cuneiform and the biblical law is authorship. In the former, the king was called upon by the gods to establish justice within his realm and was inspired with absolute, cosmic truths, which the king incorporated into actual laws. Hammurabi claimed authorship of his code in sentences such as: "*My* words which *I* have inscribed on *my* monument," "The judgments that *I* have judged," "The decisions which *I* have decided," and the like. Moreover, he invoked curses upon whomever would erase his name or "who will damage *my* handiworks." Similar claims were made by other Mesopotamian kings regarding their codes of laws. The inspiration may have been divine in origin, but both the authorship and the execution of the laws were the king's. Jewish law was evolved through discussion among learned men; it was a group effort, not accredited to an individual.

According to the biblical concept, law is no more than a statement of God's will. The laws are referred to as the "words of God"—never of man. God is the only legislator; righteousness, the observance of his law, assures the well-being and prosperity of the individual and of the community as a whole. The divine authorship of the biblical laws transforms "crimes" into "sins"—violations of the will of God. Offenses are regarded as absolute wrongs transcending man's power to pardon. The laws regarding adultery provide the most striking example of the difference between the religious nature of the biblical laws and the secular nature of cuneiform laws.

In the cuneiform laws, the offended husband may decide whether or not to punish his adulterous wife and her paramour. Both will be treated equally: punished or pardoned. In biblical law, the situation is different; both the adulteress and her companion have sinned against God and *must* be put to death, as stated in Leviticus 20:10 and Deuteronomy 22:22–23. God, not the husband, is the offended party. No man can pardon or mitigate an injury to him. Cuneiform laws also grant the king, as the author of the law, the right to pardon.

There are also important differences regarding the principles surrounding homicide. It is in this area that the biblical laws have been considered primitive and archaic in their severity. In the earliest biblical law (Gen. 9:6), it is stated that murder is punishable by death, because man was made in the image of God. Indeed, a beast may not kill a man, because in doing so he destroys the image of God. If homicide has been committed by a goring ox, the beast *must* be stoned to death, yet its flesh may not be eaten. If the owner knew that his ox was viscious, but he was negligent in restraining it, both the owner and his ox are subject to death, although the owner can ransom himself by offering monetary compensation. This was the only case in which a monetary compensation was accepted, since the homicide was unintentional and not committed directly by the owner. A murderer was to be sentenced to death; there was no possibility of monetary compensation. Other Near Eastern laws contain no such ban; they all recognize the right of the victim's family to accept a settlement instead of the death of the guilty party. These two provisions, regarding the case of the goring ox and prohibiting compensation, sufficed to relegate biblical laws to the past as based on archaic and primitive values.

It was erroneously assumed that biblical and nonbiblical laws were part of a single line of historical development, in which composition (Sumerian laws) precedes the talionic principle (Hammurabi's code). In fact, the biblical laws follow totally different principles regarding homicide, as illustrated by the case of the goring ox. The Mesopotamian laws are concerned with safeguarding private property and remuneration of losses. Since the goring ox could not pay for damages it caused, the responsibility lay with its owner. From this point of view, biblical law might be considered unjust: Why should the owner destroy his ox—a penalty that provides no remuneration? Why should the owner suffer for an accident he could not prevent and for which he cannot be responsible? Precisely because biblical law considers human life invaluable, the penalty for taking a life is death. It is this sense of the value of human life that constitutes the fundamental difference between the biblical view of homicide and that of other ancient legal systems. The others affix a material value to human life; in the Assyrian laws, for example, the kinsmen of the victim may decide whether they prefer material compensation or the surrender of another human being—a slave, a son, a wife, a brother—or whether they prefer to take revenge. This view of life is also found in Hittite laws, which established that the killer must make amends by surrendering a member of his family according to the status of the victim and the degree or type of the homicide. This method of compensation probably grew out of the community's desire to recover its working or fighting strength after losing one of its members. Life had a price tag, in direct contrast to the biblical view, which forbids even eating the flesh of the ox that has killed a man.

This basic difference in values can also be seen in the treatment of offenses against property. Assyrian and Babylonian laws indicate the death penalty for certain types of these offenses, such as breaking and entering, trespassing at night, and theft. The Middle Assyrian laws even condemn to death the wife who has stolen from her husband. In contrast, biblical law is relatively lenient in such matters; indeed, no property offense is punishable by death. In some cases, the law may require a payment of double the damages or may excuse the householder who slays a thief who breaks in at night and is caught *in flagrante delicto* (Exod. 22:1ff).

Each of the various legal systems shows a certain degree of evolution as archaic concepts develop into more modern ones. For instance, the Hittite edict of Telepinus—about 1620 to 1600 B.C.—still permits the kinsmen of a slain man to choose between retaliation and compensation, whereas later laws permit only replacement or compensation. The earlier capital punishment for theft was later replaced by a pecuniary one. In the same vein, biblical laws may be considered archaic in comparison with talmudic laws: whereas the former insisted on the death penalty for homicide, the latter reached its virtual abolition, although it was never replaced by any kind of pecuniary compensation. The conditions required to carry out an execution were so numerous and complicated that it was practically impossible to inflict the death sentence.

Vicarious punishment—applying the penalty to a person other than the culprit—was adopted by many of the cuneiform laws but was repudiated by biblical lawmakers. The principle of talio in the cuneiform laws is carried out to such a degree that it recalls vicarious punishment. For example, the creditor who has mistreated the son of his debtor to such an extent that he dies, must lose his own son (Hammurabi code, 116); the man who strikes a pregnant daughter of another man, so that she has a miscarriage and dies, will lose his own daughter (Hammurabi code, 209–210, and Middle Assyrian laws, 50); a seducer must deliver his own wife to the seduced girl's father for prostitution (Middle Assyrian Laws, 55). There are also cases in which a dependent of the offender may serve as his substitute. For instance, Hittite law compels the slayer to deliver a number of persons to the kinsmen of the victim, whereas Assyrian law allows for the substitution of a son, brother, wife, or slave (depending on the specific situation), instead of vengeance. The members of a family and its dependents have no separate identity; they belong to the *pater familias*, and he may dispose of them at his discretion. On the other hand, biblical law (Deut. 24:16) specifically prohibits collective punishments in purely judicial, rather than theological terms: "Parents shall not be put to death for children, nor children for parents; each one shall be put to death for his own sin."

Vicarious punishment is replaced in biblical law by the principle of individual responsibility. Secular offenses such as murder, negligent homicide, seduction, and the like, are never collectively or vicariously punished; only the culprit himself is subject to punishment. The only two cases in which vicarious punishments are recorded in the Bible are those of Achan, who plundered holy objects from the booty of Jericho (Josh. 7), and the case of Saul's sons, who were put to death for their father's massacre of the Gideonites in violation of an oath to God (2 Sam. 21). Both offenses were in open defiance of God's will. Thus, an affront to the divine power is on a different scale from that which touches man alone.

As mentioned before, women have no legal status in the Bible. Nevertheless the Torah and the Talmud mention a number of episodes showing their courage, such as the heroism of the Jewish midwives in defying the pharaoh's command to kill all Jewish male infants (Exod. 1). The Talmud (Sota 12a) describes the key role of Jewish women in the redemption of the Jews from Egypt, mentioning two different episodes. When the pharaoh decreed the death of all Jewish male infants, Amram, the father of Moses and the leader of his generation, declared: "We labour in vain" and separated from his wife. His daughter Miriam reprimanded him by saying: "Your edict is crueller than Pharaoh's, because you have sealed the fate of both boys and girls." Persuaded by her appeal, he rejoined his wife, leading to the birth of Moses. The same section tells us that when the Jewish men were weary and discouraged and had all but given up the struggle to regain their freedom, the women would go out to the fields to their exhausted husbands, bring them hot soup and food, wash them, massage their aching bodies, and then have conjugal relations with them, leading to the birth of children. These women were not cowed by adversity, not destroyed by slavery, but kept the spark of freedom alive, even within Egypt.

The great impact of the ancient Hebrew laws on contemporary Western legislation is undeniable. For instance, when former U.S. Supreme Court Justice Earl Warren wrote the famed *Miranda* opinion, he prominently quoted the Rambam and noted the Talmud's strict rejection of self-incrimination. The philosophy of the Jewish law is also reflected in the problem of a man who, in his efforts to save the life of another person, damages private property but is not liable for damages. Under English law, the rescuer may indeed be liable. The Israeli legislation determines, on the other hand, that whenever possible the courts should look into the Jewish tradition for guidance in their decision making.

Terminological and Other Differences between Biblical and Talmudic Laws

What follows is a set of general comments on a body of legal material that is particularly complex and has been exposed to a number of discussions from several different points of view.

There is no one single legal term for *crime* and *criminal law* or *punishment* in the Scripture. Regarding punishment, there are several Hebrew root words for it: *chasah* means "to keep back, restrain"; *yasar*, "to chasten, instruct, teach,; *amash*, to fine; *paqad*, "to inspect, look after"; and *naqam*, "to be punished, to be avenged." Punishment was also associated with *chet* (sin), *challath* (erring), *avon* (perversity), and *tokechah* (the need for reproof or rebuke, criticism for a fault).

One of the several terms relating to criminal law is *halakhah*, derived from the Hebrew root *halakh*, meaning "to go." Originally, the term *halakhah* meant a particular law or decision in a given case, but it later came to embrace personal, social, national, and international relationships, as well as other practices and observances of Judaism. *Halakhot*, plural of *halakhah*, is also sometimes used as a generic term for the entire legal Hebrew system. There are five elements within the *halakhah* that merit clear differentiation: the *written law, statements handed down by tradition,* the *oral law, sayings of elders and scribes,* and *customs.*

The talmudic literature contains another term for *law: din* (plural, *dinim*), which is used to designate matters relating to the fourth order of the Mishnah—*Nezikin.* These include two general kinds of law: *dinei mamonot,* similar but not identical to civil law, which deals with matters of money, property, and the like; and *dinei nefashot,* referring to those criminal offenses that may call for capital or corporal punishments. The Talmud, on the other hand, terms every offense, no matter which is its nature, *averah* (transgression).

The reason for the absence of a single Hebrew expression for *law* is, perhaps, a reflection of the fundamental principle that the revealed will of

God is the only source of all Jewish legislation. Consequently, every punishable act constitutes a violation of God's will and is considered a deliberate rejection of his authority. The Mosaic law, therefore, makes no distinction between mandatory and prohibitory laws, since all transgressions are offenses against God. The only distinction is made with respect to punishment: The failure to follow a mandatory law will be punished by God, since only he can punish a transgression of a religious duty; but the transgression of a prohibitory law is considered a criminal act and, therefore, may be punished by man.

The Mosaic legislation delineated three general categories of crimes. *Crimes against natural or God-given rights* to life and limb are the most serious; they include unitentional homicide. Willful murder is punishable by death, unintentional homicide by banishment. Even the simplest injury or mutilation of the body is regarded with gravity and may be punished by retaliation. *Crimes against secondary or property rights* are considered private wrongs, committed against an individual and not against the state. The injured party may claim monetary damages when he brings the case to court. *Crimes against Mosaic commandments* include social, religious, and political offenses, such as sacrilege, false testimony, idolatry, public desecration of ceremonial laws, adultery, immorality, incest, and the like. These are offenses that affect the entire community, as they are thought to invoke God's wrath upon the nation, which can be appeased only when the offender is put to death by a human tribunal. Therefore, it is the duty of all the people of Israel to bring the culprit to justice.

The biblical laws determine seven categories of crimes, each with a corresponding punishment. The punishments were death, *karet* ("extirpation" or "excision"), banishment, flagellation, *lex talionis,* fines, and penal slavery. Each method of punishment is described in detail, with the exception of flagellation, which is mentioned only once (Deut. 25:1–3) and then rather vaguely: "If the wicked man deserves to be beaten, the judge shall cause him to lie down and to be beaten before his face according to the degree of his wickedness." The offenses for which flogging is administered are not specified. Mercy is emphasized; the punishment is to be carried out only according to the seriousness of the offense and must not exceed forty lashes. Another vague reference to corporal punishment is found in Deuteronomy 22:18, dealing with the husband accusing his bride of not having been a virgin. If he is unable to prove his charge, "the elders of that city shall take hold of the man and chastise him"; there is no mention of the nature of the punishment. The Amoraim interpreted the punishment as flagellation, because this was considered the most ignominious of all the punishments for a freeman.

When the Persian ruler of Babylon, Artaxerxes, authorized the scribe Ezra to return to Judea, he provided him with an official document that indicated only four types of punishments: death, banishment, confiscation of property, and imprisonment. The last two were unknown in biblical law and were most probably the types of punishment practiced in Babylon. Talmudic jurisprudence adds three punishments to the seven mentioned, which undoubtedly are of postbiblical origin: imprisonment, death at the hand of Heaven, and death at the hand of the people.

Victimizing people with words is worse than victimizing them in money matters (Talmud, Tractate Bava Metzia 58b). Some examples of "victimizing with words" are reminding a penitent of his errant past; reminding a proselyte of his origins; telling a person who has fallen on hard times that he deserves it because of his sins; knowingly giving people wrong directions; bargaining over the price of something you do not really intend to buy; and humiliating someone publicly, which is equal to murder. If a person commits adultery, he is executed by strangulation, but does not loose his share in the World-to-Come, whereas one who publicly humiliates his fellow has no such share. Rabbis said: "Rather throw yourself into a crematorium than publicly humiliate your fellow." If you victimize someone in money matters, you can always pay him back the amount of which you cheated him, but victimizing words, once spoken, cannot be taken back. In Pirkei Avot (the Words of our Sages) it is written that the boor and the wise person have seven characteristics: The wise person does not speak in the presence of one wiser than he; he does not interrupt his associate's words; he does not hasten to reply; he asks and replies to the point; he speaks of first things first and last things last; he admits he doesn't know when he doesn't; and he acknowledges the truth. The boor is just the opposite.

Any discussion of Jewish law must take into consideration the fact that Jewish sovereignty existed only until the destruction of the Second Temple. During the talmudic period, from 70 A.D. until the end of the fifth century, the Israelites were ruled by the Roman law; the Jewish law was suppressed, and discussions regarding crime and punishment were largely theoretical. Only informers were killed. The only corporal punishment carried out by the Jewish community was flogging. However, the theoretical nature of talmudic law in no way detracts from its worth. Talmudic penology might be considered an attempt to formulate the best laws for an ideal society.

Administration of Justice and Legal Procedure

The ancient Hebrews developed a highly structured system of courts, which were divided into three kinds of tribunals. The first was composed of three judges and was held at the gates of cities with more than 120 families. Each litigant could choose one judge, and the two judges decided on the third, thus ensuring an unbiased verdict. Witnesses could be disqualified if one of the parties involved presented evidence to prove that they were gamblers, usurers, bettors in pigeon races, and the like. Kinsmen, friends, and enemies were also excluded. If a witness was not disqualified on legal grounds, the other side could not reject him. These tribunals dealt mainly with civil cases and private conflicts and with a number of delicts, such as theft, bodily injury, payment of indemnities or restitution, and some cases of rape, seduction, slander, and so forth. Offenses punishable by flagellation could be tried either by these tribunals or by a higher court, but offenses punishable by death were tried by a higher court, composed of twenty-three judges selected from among the elders of cities with populations of more than 120 families. In Jerusalem, this tribunal was located in the temple court, not at the gates of the city. Such courts examined only capital cases, in which the life of the accused was in danger, and cases that involved "unnatural crimes" between man and beast (i.e. acts of bestiality).

The supreme court whose decisions could not be appealed with the Great Sanhedrin. This tribunal, which was held in the Chamber of Hewn Stone within the Temple of Jerusalem, was composed of seventy-one judges presided over by the high priest. Its main function was to interpret the law, but it also dealt with civil, criminal, and religious matters, including cases of idolatrous tribes or false prophets. Under certain circumstances, the Great Sanhedrin could also function as a political assembly that could meet, for instance, on the decision to start an offensive war. It could also serve as a municipal council in order to authorize additions to the city of Jerusalem or to the temple courts. After the destruction of the Second Temple, Rabban Johanan ben Zakkai established the Great Sandedrin at Yavneh, outside Jerusalem, where it functioned until 118 A.D.

Jurisdiction, Organization, and Functioning of the Great Sanhedrin

The jurisdiction of the Great Sanhedrin included not only the entire Holy Land but also those Jews who lived in neighboring countries. Foreign cases could be tried only under the following conditions: (1) the court had to convene within the Temple; (2) its members had to be ordained in Israel; and (3) in addition to the seventy-one members of the Sanhedrin, other judges were required to carry on with the regular work within the temple.

Despite the fact that the high priest presided over the Great Sanhedrin, he could still be put on trial. He could also appear as a witness, and others could testify against him. The king had no judicial functions, however; he could not be put on trial or act as a witness, nor could others testify against him. Thus, the Israelites were among the first peoples to clearly separate the executive from the judicial power.

The Sanhedrin was arranged in a semicircle so that its members might see each other and be able to look directly at the witnesses in order to observe their faces closely. This might certainly be considered an early stage of judicial psychology.

In front of the seventy-one judges were three rows of unordained students, who would eventually serve as junior members of the court. When a vacancy occurred in the Sanhedrin, following the death or resignation of a senior member, it was filled by a junior member who moved forward. There were also two or three clerks standing—one on the right, another in the center, and the third on the left. Their task was to record the opinions of the judges who argued for acquittal or conviction, so that they could compare notes in case of any discrepancy.

The Sanhedrin could also function as smaller courts—known as the Smaller Sanhedrin—each consisting of twenty-three judges. All the judges were qualified to hear and determine civil cases, but only priests and Levites could hear capital cases. The latter had to be clear of all suspicion as to their character and integrity, to be of pure Jewish ancestry, and to have no bodily defects. Therefore, very old persons (who might have forgotten the troubles of raising children and might perhaps be unmerciful), eunuchs, and the childless (because they might also have no feeling of mercy) were not obliged to serve as judges in the Sanhedrin.

In very few cases does biblical law place the responsibility of prosecuting offenders on a public body. Broadly speaking, and different from the Roman legal procedure of confrontation between prosecution and defense, the only polarity was between Hillel's (Hillel the Elder, who lived from approximately the end of the first century B.C. and the beginning of the first century A.D.) lenient interpretations of the law, versus Shammai's (Shammai the Elder, who lived at the same time as Hillel) sterner precepts. The court at all times must lean toward the accused. The concept *in dubio pro reo* is a stright crib from the Mishnah, like so much else in Roman law. Moreover, there was no subpoena; witnesses came forward prompted by religious or social motivations. As in other Near Eastern laws, it was the injured party who generally initiated the legal action, and there was a recognition—particularly in cases of capital crimes—that the private prosecution acted both in his interest and in that of the public at large. This same principle is also expressed in the execution of sentences, in which the entire community could participate in the punishment of the offender.

Justice, Judges, Witnesses, and Verdicts

Modern justice, in spite of its claims, is not very clear in its proclaimed aims. Is it for deterrence, for the punishment or rehabilitation of the offender, for the defense of society, for the simple but never admitted aim of vengeance, or for a loose combination of all of these? In Jewish law, the objective is clearly not punishment but the rehabilitation of the offender. He must be given an opportunity to atone for his sin, and the punishment serves as a tangible proof of his atonement. Its objective of justice is not to be the society's avenging angel but to keep the ship of state on an even keel.

The Torah provides two penal systems for the deterrence of criminals: punishments enacted by the Sanhedrin, according to halakhic procedures and constraints, and crown penalties enacted according to the king's trials. Although, according to *halakhah,* the court should not put a man to death or flog him on his own admission of guilt—it should be done only on the evidence of at least two witnesses—and without following all the other principles of procedure, the state is empowered to punish offenders by crown law, without needing to resort to the rules of evidence and penalties laid down in the Torah. The former system is according to true justice (based on the Torah); the latter is according to the justice of the realm and the exigencies of the times. Each system had its own penal code and its own judicial hierarchy. It was a recognition that human society requires a state apparatus to represent and execute *relative justice*—that is, state justice—which imposes order and security, whereas the penal code of the Torah, which represents *absolute justice*—untainted by exigencies of time, place, and social standards—is definitely not enough.

The two judicial systems had different objectives. For the Sandedrin, the penalty was enacted as a punishment and as a means of expiation of sins committed in the past, whereas crown or state justice was used as a deterrent and preventive measure against repetition of the offense in the future. On the other hand, penalties imposed by the Sanhedrin were absolutely binding, and there was no possibility of clemency because, being commandments of the Torah, no one has the capacity to commute them. This is not the case with state penalties, which are neither obligatory nor binding but are a prerogative of the monarch.

Human society cannot maintain itself without the means of deterrence provided by the state penalties; otherwise, people would be swallowing each other alive. Nevertheless, although most of the penalties in the Torah were intended for chastisement and expiation, there were four instances in which the religious courts could apply punishment for the specific purpose of admonishing and deterring others: a person inciting to idol worship; a stubborn and rebellious son; a man who presumptuously behaves against the majority ruling; and false witnesses. The Torah sentences all these to death by stoning and requires that it should be publicized in advance, so that the people will understand why the offenders were put to death. Crown penalties, however, are all intended for deterrent purposes, to ensure the stability of the social order.

Basically, both courts had two basic functions: to sit in judgment settling disputes about money or property and to rid society of evil. And judges should be well-to-do, so that they are not beholden to any section of the community, in spite of the fact that they are not necessarily the wisest of the people.

Section 32B of Sanhedrin deals with the rights and duties of witnesses before the courts, evidence procedure, and punishment for perjury. Jews were not supposed to know the law, but they were encouraged to study it, because only when the law had been knowingly transgressed could punishment be meted. Ignorance of the law was a valid excuse.

Witnesses—who had to be males—were examined by the judges, individually and separately, after being admonished to tell the truth regarding what they had seen or heard and not to base their statements on mere supposithat or hearsay. Only those who personally witnessed the crime gave testimony; all others were disqualified. Even the strongest circumstantial evidence was insufficient for conviction. In the realm of probability, for instance, things may be unlikely but not impossible. If a witness to a stabbing said that he saw the knife enter the body, the judge could ask if there had not been a hole there already. On the other hand, how could the judge know that the witness was speaking the truth? In being hard on him, did he not discourage him from coming forward? But if a witness could not bear interrogation, his testimony would be suspect and he should not be heard.

Witnesses were warned against giving false testimony in capital cases, lest the blood of the unjustly executed stain their hands forever. Perjury had to be proved to have been willful, since human error was considered a perfect plea. False testimony was punished according to the talionic principle. If the offender was convicted, the witness suffered the same penalty that his testimony would have brought upon the accused (Deut. 19:16–19). If the *lex talionis* could not be applied, as in cases in which the punishment was banishment, then he would be punished with thirty-nine lashes. Witnesses falsely testifying that the accused owed 200 *zuz* (silver coins) to his neighbor either paid the 200 silver coins or suffered the punishment of lashes, but not both. If several witnesses gave false testimony regarding the 200 zuz, they could divide the sum between them—but not the lashes. Each would receive thirty-nine lashes, because each was considered to have applied these lashes on the falsely accused.

Judges investigated the witnesses through a most detailed process of examination and cross-examination. A number of precise inquiries were made regarding the exact time of the alleged crime (date of the month, day of the week, hour of the day, etc.); the place where it was committed; the kind of weapon used; and whether or not the witness recognized the victim as an Israelite. Once the answers regarding time and place met with the judges' satisfaction, they continued their questioning regarding issues bearing directly upon the crime: the identification of the victim and of the accused, and so on.

After questioning, the witness was subjected to cross-examination, which had no direct bearing on the issue involved but was meant only to test his veracity. For example, he was asked whether the accused or the victim had worn light or dark clothes, whether the color of the surrounding area was white or black, and so forth. This was also done with the purpose of confusing and disturbing the witness. Witnesses could be moved from place to place, and there was no limit to the number of questions, nor was there any requirement that they be relevant to the case. From the earliest periods of Jewish jurisprudence, judges revealed a strong desire to abolish capital punishment, and one means to do so was by declaring the witnesses' testimony invalid. If their testimony stood up despite this willful harassment, it was an indication that they spoke the truth. Indeed, if only one of the witnesses was unable to provide definite answers to any of the judges' questions, or if one witness seriously contradicted another during the cross-examination, the testimony of all the witnesses was invalidated and the accused was acquitted. Under Mosaic law, the testimony of any set of witnesses, no matter how many, is considered one inseparable entity. Only the testimony of at least two competent eyewitnesses could establish a *prima facie* case, and no case could be tried without the testimony of at least two competent eyewitnesses. Witnesses could not offer additional evidence after all testimony had been heard. The number of judges who heard each case depended on whether the offense was civil or capital.

The students who sat in the three rows before the judges were entitled to express an opinion, with the agreement of the judges. Those who wished to argue in favor of conviction were usually quickly silenced, but an argument in favor of acquittal was heard out. If the student's argument was found to have substance, he was invited to sit among the judges until the end of the trial. A court of three judges could sit on a civil case, but in capital cases, the court could not contain fewer than twenty-three judges. In civil cases, the opening argument could be either for or against the defendant, but in capital cases, it could only be for acquittal, not for conviction. Although in civil cases, judges were permitted to argue either in favor of or against the defendant and to change their opinions, in capital cases, if a judge argued for conviction, he could later plead for acquittal, but he could not reverse his pleading for acquittal. In civil cases, the verdict could be reached even after sunset, but in capital cases, the verdict had to be reached during the day. In civil cases, the verdict might be reached the same day, but in capital cases, this could happen only if the verdict were acquittal. In cases in which the accused was to be convicted, the judges adjourned the court until the following day. More time for deliberation was needed before condemning a man to death; in pondering the matter overnight, the judges might find arguments in favor of acquittal. The judges were to leave the court in pairs, eat little, without wine, for the rest of the day, and discuss the case throughout the night. Early the next morning, they would return to the court, where they could either reiterate their previously held opinion or declare that they had decided in favor of acquittal. However, the judges could *not* change their argument from one that favored acquittal to one that favored conviction. If a consensus for acquittal was reached, the accused would be freed. If not, a new vote was taken: If the outcome was twelve for acquittal and eleven for conviction, the accused was declared innocent, but if there were twelve for conviction and eleven for acquittal or if there were eleven on each side and one judge who declared "I do not know," or if there were twenty-two for acquittal and one judge said "I do not know," the court had to add another judge, because the judge who could not decide was eliminated *ab initio*.

Unless a capital case was tried by a court of at least twenty-three members, the proceedings were considered null and void, so a retrial had to be granted. If a case was retried by a full Sanhedrin of seventy-one judges, and there were thirty-six votes for acquittal and thirty-five for conviction, the accused was acquitted and went free. But if there were thirty-six for conviction and thirty-five for acquittal, the court had to continue its discussions until one of the judges who favored conviction changed his mind. If no such change occurred, the accused was acquitted; the court followed the dictum *in dubio pro reo*.

In civil cases, if two judges voted in favor of the defendant and one against him, the verdict was in favor of the defendant. If two voted against the defendant and one in his favor, the verdict was against the defendant. If one of the three judges said "I don't know"—no matter what the decisions of the other two—the court was required to add more judges. In capital cases, if only a majority of one voted for conviction, then it was necessary to enlarge the tribunal with two temporary judges selected from among the students. If again there was only a majority of one vote for conviction, two more temporary judges were added, and so on until the total number of the members of the court reached the legal maximum of seventy-one.

The order of voting in civil and capital cases was also different. In civil cases, the vote was taken first from the senior judges, but in capital cases, the junior judges voted first so that they would not be influenced by the senior judges. Reversal of verdicts could be obtained in civil cases no matter what the original verdict, but in capital cases, verdicts could be changed only from conviction to acquittal, not from acquittal to conviction. Once a verdict was reached, it was carried out immediately. For a man to be found guilty, two conditions had to be met: that he be warned that what he was about to do was a crime; and that he be informed what the punishment was likely to be—not an easy matter to convey to someone pursuing his victim with a dagger!

Crimes and Punishments

The Philosophical Motivations and Character of Ancient Jewish Punishments

In the Jewish system of jurisprudence, punishment is of three distinctive characters: (1) retributive—punishing the criminal for his wrongdoing; (2) deterrent—a punishment so severe as to intimidate others from committing similar crimes; and (3) expiatory—an attempt to obtain the forgiveness of the deity, whose wrath had been incurred by the commission of the crime.

From the philosophical point of view, one of the most decisive elements in penology is the distinction of an act of punishment from an act of vengeance. The first and most important measure to be introduced was likeness: "an eye for an eye, and tooth for tooth" (Exod. 21: 23–25, Deut. 19: 21). At first, such a principle—demanding that the punishment be commensurate to the crime—makes it look like the codification of vengeance. In reality, it seeks to restrain humans' insatiable thirst for retaliation: Take a tooth and be done with it! This principle is not of Jewish origin; it is a derivation of the Babylonian culture that shaped much of early Hebrew life. The Babylonian usage was honored by all the neighbors of the ancient Hebrews. The basic difference was that whereas the Babylonian code applied its punishments according to the social class of the offender and the victim, the Jewish version, because there were no social classes among the Hebrews, viewed offenders and victims without favoritism.

In the biblical text, talionic punishments were characteristic of retributive justice, which was swift and effective. The capital punishment for willful murder did not require due process but was carried out by the blood-avenger family upon the first meeting with the murderer. Measure for measure was deemed to be God's justice, but the blood-avenger was to be restrained from administering a punishment that was more severe than the crime itself.

Talionic punishments were perhaps carried out in both biblical and postbiblical times, although during the talmudic period, due process was required in order to administer a retributive punishment. The majority of the Amoraim replaced talio with monetary compensation, because they considered the justice of the talio more apparent than real. In fact, they argued, not all eyes of men were equal in size and quality, therefore an eye for an eye was equal in name but not in value. Moreover, what eye can be taken from a blind man who has taken another's eye? What talio can be applied to a crippled fellow without legs who has injured another man's leg? Is it possible to take an eye from a healthy person without producing an injury that might endanger his life? The mere risk of exceeding the prescribed measure is enough to render talio indefensible. Except for those crimes deserving capital punishment or exile, most of the other crimes could be punished by compensation. In these cases, the dictum "an eye for an eye," so often misunderstood, could also be applied. Damages in such cases were assessed by the following elements: material damage, pain inflicted, cost of medical treatment, and humiliation suffered. Later, the victim would not be permitted to refuse compensation if it were found adequate by the court. Compensation had the added advantage of restoring something to the victim, at least from the monetary point of view.

Talionic punishments could be divided into "identical" and "equivalent" ones. The former was the true talio: death for homicide, wounding for wounding, and so on. The later met some characteristics of the offense rather than its measure: "The hand that sinned shall be cut off" (Deut. 25: 12), not "a hand for a hand." Talmudic penologists abolished "identical" punishment, but the "equivalent" type of talio continued to exist throughout the Middle Ages and can even be found in modern penal law of certain modern Arab states. The interesting fact is that although talmudic scholars affirmed the talionic principle, they abolished its practice.

The deterrent character of punishment is emphasized in the Mosaic law in Deuteronomy 13: 12: "And all Israel shall hear and fear, and shall do no more any such wickedness in the midst of Thee." The talio was considered the best possible deterrent, particularly since its application did not differentiate between rich and poor.

Its expiatory character is illustrated in cases of willful murder and idolatry. Murder was considered a crime against God, and only the blood of the murderer could expiate such a sin. For the protection of the unintentional manslayer—not of the willful murderer—from the fury of the *goel ha-dam,* the "blood-avenger," and to prevent the shedding of innocent blood, the state had to set aside *miklatim,* "cities of refuge." The Talmud prescribes that when a man was slain by an unknown hand, and elders of the city nearest to the site of the murder had to atone for the sin in a special ceremony: They washed their hands in the blood of an unworked heifer and declare their innocence of the crime. The murderer also had to atone for his crime in order not to be deprived of a share in "the world to come." In cases of idol worship or serving other gods, the responsibility for expiation rested with the entire community; if the community did not discharge its responsibility, the nation as a whole would incur God's wrath.

Capital Crimes and Their Punishment

The Mosaic law defines *thirty-six capital crimes,* dividing them into six categories:

1. *Eighteen moral abuses:* These refer to illegal or perverted sexual relations, including three types of adultery (a priest's daughter, when she is married; a man with a married woman; and a man with a betrothed virgin, whether by criminal assualt [rape] or by consent [seduction]); two types of unnatural sexual relations (a man with an animal and a woman with an animal); twelve types of incest (with one's own mother; with one's own stepmother; with one's daughter-in-law; with one's daughter; with one's daughter's daughter; with one's son's daughter; with one's stepdaughter; with one's stepdaughter's daughter; with one's stepson's daughter; with one's mother-in-law; with one's mother-in-law's mother; and with one's father-in-law's mother); and one case of unnatural relations between one man and another (homosexuality).

2. *Twelve violations of religious laws:* These include one type of blasphemy; seven types of idolatry (sacrificing children to foreign gods, since the sacrifice of children, per se, was forbidden; inciting others to worship idols; communal conversion from Judaism to idolatry; false prophecy; prophesying in the name of heathen deities; and inciting an entire community to embrace idolatry); one type of profanation of the Sabbath; and three types of witchcraft (phytonism, or claiming to speak for a spirit; necromancy; and magic or sorcery).

3. *Three types of crimes against parents:* These include cursing or bruising a parent; the case of the stubborn and rebellious son; and conviction of a child by the elders—the father alone could not condemn him—of being a stubborn or rebellious son.

4. *One crime of assault and murder.*

5. *One type of forcible abduction (kidnapping) and selling into slavery.*

6. *One type of treason—that of a rebellious elder.*

The Amoraim were convinced that only God had the right to punish man; thus, they were really opposed to capital punishment. However, no matter how strongly they opposed the principle, they could not completely ignore the biblical injunction and substitute another form of punishment. Throughout the Talmud, there are a number of expressions of opposition to capital punishment. They created so many legal restrictions that it was almost impossible to carry out the death sentence. A Sanhedrin that put one man to death in seven years was called "destructive." For the Amoraim, the same applied if one man was executed every seventy years, while still others were convinced that had they been members of the Sanhedrin, no one would have ever been executed. In fact, Jewish penologists always regarded capital punishment disfavorably and made every effort to avoid it.

Three types of capital punishment are specified in the Mosaic law, listed in a decreasing order of severity: stoning, burning, and decapitation. Strangulation is mentioned only in the Talmud and is therefore considered to be even less severe. An offender convicted of two crimes, both punishable by death but by different methods of execution, was executed by the more severe method. On the other hand, if there was any confusion regarding the methods to which two convicted men had been sentenced to be executed, then both were executed by the milder method.

Stoning is the most frequently mentioned capital punishment in the Bible. Of the thirty-six capital crimes, eighteen were punishable by stoning. Nine other crimes were also regarded as punishable by stoning: sexual relations with one's own mother or with one's father's wife (i.e., stepmother), between two males, or with one's daughter-in-law; a man's unnatural relations with an animal; a female's relations with an animal; cursing one's father or mother; inciting other people or an entire community to embrace idolatry; and magic or sorcery. In all these cases, partners in a given crime suffered the same punishment. Both men and woman were subject to the same punishment. Stoning by the people was then a procedure often prescribed for crimes felt to threaten the well-being of the nation as a whole, among which were the sexual crimes.

Stoning doubtlessly existed before it was adopted as a method of execution. The Bible mentions several instances of mob-stoning (Exod. 8: 22, 17: 4; 1 Sam. 30: 6; and 1 Kings 12: 18). These cases were not the outcome of legal procedure but the reaction of an enfuriated mob. The Talmud does not mention mob-stoning. The Amoraim were looking for a more humane mode of execution.

A thief found breaking into a home is condemned to be stoned, because of the murder he might have committed. If he is killed by the owner, the owner is not considered guilty—but only if this occurs before sunrise. It is assumed that the burglar would kill anyone who opposed him, and therefore he may be killed, in self defense, with impunity.

In biblical times, the site of execution by stoning was originally outside the encampment or town, and later at the seat of justice: the gate of the city. In one instance (Deut. XXII:21) it is mentioned that the offender should be stoned at the site where the crime was presumably committed. The Bible does not mention an executioner; therefore, it can be assumed that the community as a whole acted as executioner (Deut. XVII:5; XXI:21 and XXII:21; and Lev. XXIV:14). However, the prosecuring witnesses were to cast the first stones, as the responsibility for the conviction rested with them. The physical act of execution was the severest possible test of the witnesses; knowing that they were to personally execute the man they convicted would most likely deter them from falsifying evidence. In cases where the intentional murderer flees to a city of refuge, the elders of the city in which the murder was committed must fetch him and deliver him into the hands of the blood-avenger so that he die (Deut. XIX:11–12).

Certain rules were applied in all cases of execution, whatever method was used. Once sentence was passed, the convicted person was removed from the court for execution. The site of execution was far from the court, so that the judges should not appear too anxious to carry out the sentence, and to allow as much time as possible to find some reason for vindicating the condemned man. A court officer stood at the door of the court with a cloth in his hand. Another one, mounted on a horse, was located at some distance, but near enough to see the first officer. The judges who had convicted the accused were not permitted to participate in the procession to the place of execution. They were to remain in the courthouse, and if one of them were to decide that he knew of a valid argument which could vindicate the condemned man, the first officer was to give a signal with the cloth he held in his hand to the mounted officer, who would then return the procession. If during the procession the condemned man or one of the public declared that he had an argument in favor of acquittal, the procession was halted and the convict returned to court. There was no limit to the number of times the convict could be returned to court. On the first two occasions, the accused is returned to court, whether or not his argument seems worthy of consideration, because the stress may have confused him and made him unable to express himself intelligently. After the second incident, the court appointed two of its members to accompany the condemned man and to listen to any new argument. He would be returned to court for a rehearing only if they decided that the new argument was worthy of consideration. If the judges were to find him innocent, the condemned man was acquitted. Otherwise, he was sent back to be executed. In each case, a herald went before the procession, proclaiming the name of the man to be executed and his crime. He also announced the names of the prosecuting witnesses, in case there were witnesses in the crowd who could provide alibis against them. The herald also declared that anyone with information that might save the convicted man should come forward.

When the condemned man was about ten cubits from the place of execution, he was asked to confess in order to grant himself a share in the world to come. At a distance of about four cubits from the scaffold, the officers stripped the condemned person, except for a loincloth in the case of a man and a single garment in the case of a woman. Only then did the actual execution take place.

As stoning was considered the most severe of the four methods of capital punishment, the Amoraim tried to modify it by introducing the "stoning house," which was to be twice the height of a man, from which the condemned man was thrown so that he should die with as little agony as possible. It was not made higher in order to avoid mutilation by the fall and thus cause him unnecessary posthumous shame. The Amoraim, in their attempt to provide the condemned man with a swift and relatively painless death, determined that there was really no difference if the condemned was killed by stones thrown at him or if he was thrown down into the stones. To comply with the Scripture that the first witness "lay hands on" the condemned man, he was required to push him from the roof of the stoning house, and the second witness was to put him to death if he had not died from the fall. Thus, there was no need for the general public to participate, eliminating all traces of *vindicta publica*.

The execution was carried out as follows: The first witness knocked the condemned man down so that he lay face down at the edge of the roof of the stoning house. The witness then pushed him to the ground, where the second witness was to make sure that he lay on his side rather than face down, so as to preserve his dignity. If the man did not die from the fall, the second witness was to take a stone so heavy that two men were needed to lift it, and to drop it on his chest. If the man still did not die, he was stoned by all the people (cf. Deut. 17: 7) until death.

Although hanging is not specifically mentioned as a method of capital punishment, convicted offenders were hanged after death as a posthumous punishment (Deut. 21: 22), perhaps with a deterrent purpose. In these cases, a beam was raised and the body was hanged with both hands tied together.

Following execution, the body had to be buried on the same day in one of two special graveyards: one for those executed by stoning or burning and the other for those who had suffered decapitation or strangulation. Thus, even in death, there was a separation between the crimes of more or less severity. Only the bones of the executed man could later be reinterred in the family grave. After the interment, the kinsmen of the executed came before the judges and the witnesses to show that they held nothing against them, then went home to observe the period of private mourning.

Burning was the second most severe capital punishment. Ten offenses were so punished: nine different types of incest and one type of adultery. One type of incest consisted of having sexual relations with a woman *and* her daughter, interpreted as meaning a man's mother-in-law and her daughter. Although the law demanded that the man and both women were to be burned, certain Amoraim opposed such a procedure, since one of the women was the man's legitimate wife. The special adultery referred to here is that of having relations with a priest's daughter if she is a married woman. The Mosaic law expressly indicates this type of execution (Lev. 21: 9), stating that "she shall be burnt with fire."

There are no accounts in the Bible as to the procedure in this form of execution, aside from references to burning the condemned together with his home or surrounding him with burning vine shoots until the flames consumed him. The postbiblical mode of burning—tantamount to a direct abrogation of the Mosaic law—determined that the condemned was to be strangled and if and when he opened his mouth, a burning torch was to be thrown into it "to burn his intestines." Of course, the convict might die before the torch could enter his mouth. This technique was considered more humane, more dignified, and less painful, and it preserved the body for burial.

The prescribed mode of burning was as follows: The condemned man was placed in dung up to his knees in order to prevent him from moving, so that hot lead should not drip on any other part of the body. A twisted scarf of coarse material within another scarf of soft material (because the former alone could scratch his neck, causing unnecessary additional pain) was wrapped around his neck. One of the witnesses pulled one end, while the other pulled in the opposite direction until the individual opened his mouth. At this point, a molten stream of lead was poured down his throat—thus burning the internal organs and leaving the body intact.

Decapitation, wich was regarded as the swiftest and cleanest of all punishments, had no record of foreign sources. It was applied only to the willful murderer and to those convicted of communal apostacy.

In the Jewish system of jurisprudence, it was essential to prove intent to kill for the accused to be convicted of murder. In addition, it had to be shown that the instrument used was sufficient to cause death and that the blow was directed at a spot capable of causing death. In addition, capital punishment was imposed only when there had been intent to kill the person who actually became the victim. For example, some Amoraim did not consider it a capital crime if someone accidentally killed a man when trying to kill an animal or killed an Israelite thinking that he was an idolator. Murder was only a direct action; a man could not be convicted of murder if he set a dog on the victim, only if he himself delivered the blow.

A man who had killed with a stone or an iron rod was convicted of willful murder only if the instrument was of a weight and size calculated to cause death. But if the murder was done with an iron instrument with a point or an edge, no matter what size, he was guilty of a capital offense.

There was a certain amount of dispute regarding the method of decapitation. Some Amoraim were of the opinion that decapitation was done by cutting off the head of the condemned with a sword while he was standing, as the Romans did. Other Talmudists claimed that it was done differently. The condemned man rested his head on a block and it was cut off with an ax. In no case was the culprit ever put to death by being stabbed with a dagger or cut in two with a sword; these were considered unnecessarily harsh modes of execution.

Whenever the Mosaic law failed to determine the method of execution, the Talmud established that the culprit should be executed by the most lenient process: *strangulation.* It was applied in the following cases: striking one's father or mother if the blow produced a wound; kidnapping an Israelite; an elder or judge rebelling against a decision of a court; a false prophet; one who prophesies in the name of a strange god; having sexual relations with another man's wife; and a witness who falsely testifies against the daughter of a priest for having a paramour. Kidnapping was considered a capital crime only if the kidnapper brought the victim into his domain and then sold him to a third party. Kidnapping a slave was not a capital offense, as the slave had already been deprived of his liberty; rather, it was considered theft. A "rebellious judge" was one whose ruling had been overruled by the Great Sanhedrin but who persisted in carrying out his decision. He was brought before the Great Sanhedrin in Jerusalem and was put to death during one of the three feasts: Passover, Pentecost, or Tabernacles. The delay of the execution was assumed to have a deterrent effect.

In execution by strangulation, both witnesses pulled the ends of the scarf, as described earlier, in opposite directions until life departed. The Amoraim never considered adopting strangulation by hanging. Perhaps because the Jews were then under Roman rule, a death sentence had to be carried out in secret, and hanging was necessarily more public than strangulation. Hanging was also considered an affront to human dignity and was among the practices of other nations that the Jews did not follow.

Crucifixion was not among the capital punishments applied by the Israelites. It was mainly used by the Romans during the period they ruled in Palestine. Many thousands died on the cross in the Roman period, but the nails were extracted before the body was buried. They were treasured, even among the Jews, for their alleged healing qualities. The idea of crucifixion was to prolong the agony as long as possible and make it serve as a deterrent. There is ample evidence in the ancient sources that in some cases, the condemned fellow was hanged upside down—a cruel way of hanging or crucifying. In other cases, they tied his arms and feet. It is reasonable to assume that the scarcity of wood may have been expressed in the economies of crucifixion.

The Gospels are silent on whether Jesus was nailed to the cross or bound to it. The fact that he expired after some six hours forcefully sustains the tradition that he was nailed, because through nailing there was a great amount of blood loss, leading to rapid death. Otherwise, crucifixion victims are known to have lived for a day or more.

Noncapital Crimes and Their Punishment

Crimes Punishable by Imprisonment. Imprisonment was indicated in only three cases, two related to the incorrigible offender and one to the willful murderer who has twice been convicted and commits the same crime a third time or who has been warned three times and has disregarded the warnings. Broadly speaking, he would be what is understood today as a recidivist.

According to Maimonides, imprisonment was reserved for cases in which the offender had committed a capital crime but the punishment could not be carried out. That is, if the court was convinced that the offender was guilty but, because of technicalities, the death sentence could not be applied, then the murderer would be sentenced to life imprisonment. There is also mention of another case—murder committed by a hired assassin, which is not punishable by death according to the talmudic law. Here, too, the convicted murderer was sentenced to life imprisonment.

Whether incarceration was ever practiced is not known, since in the Scriptures there is no mention of penal institutions. In biblical times, there was a place of detention for the accused before he was brought to justice (mentioned in Num. 15: 32–36 and Lev. 24: 10–23). During the first commonwealth, imprisonment seems to have been an established legal punishment, used by several of the kings of Judah and Israel, although whether these prisons were solely for political prisoners or for other violators of the law is unknown. The Amoraim reserved imprisonment for a few serious crimes; essentially, it was a sentence of slow torture and death. The prisoner was fed first on bread and water until his intestines shrank and then only on barley until his stomach burst (Mishnah Sanhedrin 9: 5).

Crimes Punishable by Karet, or Divine Punishments. Mosaic law punishes a number of offenses by condemning the guilty party to be "cut off from among the people" (Lev. 18: 29 and 20: 3–5, 18). This rather vague definition leaves a great deal of room for speculation as to the precise nature of the punishment. What appears to be a relatively merciful form of punishment was considered so severe by talmudic scholars that they abolished it, substituting flogging in its stead. Some scholars considered *karet* a valid form of capital punishment, but others regarded it as a form of punishment that was in divine rather than human hands. As in so many cases of interpretation, no single solution was reached. Certain talmudic scholars felt that sincere repentance would exempt the guilty party from divine punishment, whereas others felt that even while no longer liable to divine punishment, the guilty man remained subject to man's judicial system and its punishments.

There were twenty-one offenses punishable by *karet:* seven were for forbidden sexual relations which were not considered capital offenses; one for eating forbidden fat; another for eating blood; one for eating leaven on Passover; one for partaking of food during a fast; one for performing manual labor on the Day of Atonement; and nine for violations of levitical laws.

Crimes Punishable by "Death at the Hand of Heaven." The distinction between "death at the Hand of Heaven" and *karet* is unclear; some Amoraim defined *karet* as death before the age of fifty and "death at the Hand of Heaven" as death before the age of sixty. For others, the former was before sixty and the latter before seventy. In *karet,* the offender's children are exempt from punishment, whereas the offender who dies at the Hand of Heaven dies with no children to survive him. Some Amoraim maintained that in "death at the Hand of Heaven," premature death acts as an expiation for the crime, and the punishment does not affect the offender's eternal life; whereas in *karet,* premature death does not act as an expiation unless it is coupled with flagellation and repentance.

This punishment was applied in eighteen cases of abuses against the levitical role, either by a layman, a Levite, or a priest.

Crimes Punishable by the Mob or Zealous Persons. It seems strange that the ancient Hebrew laws that recognized the right of all men to due process of law justified, in certain exceptional cases, the taking of a man's life by lynching. These were cases in which there were many witnesses to the actual crime and a spontaneous decision to kill the offender. These cases were not mentioned among the capital crimes and punishments.

Crimes Punishable by Banishment. Under Mosaic law and the talmudic legal system, the only crime punishable by banishment was that of unitentional homicide or manslaughter. This form of punishment is mentioned several times in the Scripture, including God's sentencing of Cain to a life of incessant wandering for killing his brother Abel (Gen. 4: 3–16). The culprit is banished to one of the six designated cities of refuge, where he must remain until the death of the high priest. Exile outside the country does not appear, as it would force the exile to worship foreign gods. The Israelite version of banishment or exile was enforced exile of the guilty party from his hometown to a city of refuge.

The Talmud goes into tremendous detail about how judges may determine whether or not there was intent to kill. If a man was rolling his roof with a roller and it fell on a man and killed him, or if he was letting down a casket from the roof or coming down a ladder and it or he fell on a man and killed him, he was guilty of unintentional homicide and sentenced to banishment. In the same three cases, if he were pulling up the roller or the casket or going up the ladder and he fell and killed a man, he was not to be banished because the cases were considered accidents. The general rule of law was that a crime committed during descent ends in banishment, for in descent the possibility of causing injury is greater, whereas the chance of injuring someone while ascending is somewhat less and therefore is considered an accident.

The legal principle seems to have been that no man can be held guilty unless his act was homicidal *ab initio*—from the very beginning. Someone throwing a stone into a public place must make all the necessary precautions to affirm that there is no one in the missile's path. The thrower cannot then be held responsible if someone falls within the stone's range and is killed. If, on the other hand, a man throws a stone into his own courtyard and kills a man, he is held responsible only if the victim had a right to be there.

If someone unintentionally causes the death of another while carrying out his lawful duty, he is not held responsible. This includes cases in which death is caused when a father chastises or instructs his son or when a teacher punishes his pupil. This rule also holds true in the case of a court officer who causes the death of a convict while administering the punishment of flagellation. On the other hand, a father would be banished for killing his son if the murder could not be connected to "instruction."

An act committed by a blind person bordered on the accidental, and he was not condemned to be banished.

The earliest form of sanctuary was that of touching God's altar. However, even the altar was not a completely secure place; in Exodus 21: 14, it is stated that "the murderer is to be taken away for execution even from the altar." A more permanent form of sanctuary was needed; thus, cities of refuge, where the criminal was free from persecution, came into being. In fact, they provided refuge only from the wrath of the mob, from being lynched. The real object of these cities was to protect one who had committed an unintentional murder from the goel ha-dam, the "blood-avenger," who could kill without due process of law. After a court ruling, it was possible to extradite a man from a city of refuge.

However, according to the Amoraim, even the man who killed unintentionally was not entirely guiltless. No amount of money could ransom his freedom. The man was detained until the death of the high priest in order to expiate his guilt. The death of the high priest caused such grief that it was thought to drown even the grief of the blood-avenger. Were the killer to leave the city, the goel ha-dam had the right to kill him on sight. Even if the killer were slain by someone other than the *goel* while outside the city of refuge, this killing would be considered justifiable. Inasmuch as the entire community had banished the killer, the punishment for escape could be meted out by any citizen.

The roads leading to the cities of refuge were kept in perfect condition and clearly designated; the word *sanctuary* was posted on signs at crossroads in order to assist the fugitive, who might be pursued by the avenger. Upon reaching the city of refuge, the fugitive stood at the entrance or the gate of the city and explained his situation to its elders, who decided if it was a *prima facie* case of manslaughter. In this case, they assigned a place within the city where the fugitive was held until his case was returned to his hometown and tried by a tribunal. If he were found innocent of willful murder but guilty of manslaughter, he was to return to the city of refuge until the death of the high priest. The court would appoint two of its members to accompany him, in order to rescue him from possible attack by the blood-avenger. Thus, cities of refuge served two purposes: as temporary asylums for unintentional murderers, protecting them from blood-avengers, and as permanent asylums for the convicted who had been sentenced to banishment. There is no doubt that these cities of refuge were both asylums and prisons.

If the fugitive were to die during the high priest's lifetime, he would be buried in the city of refuge and his body removed only after the death of the high priest.

At the death of the high priest, the banished manslayer must be released from his *miklat* (refuge) and may return to his home. (Indeed, relatives of the high priest used to provide the fugitive with food and clothing so that he should not pray for the death of the high priest.) If the high priest were to die immediately following a court decision of banishment, the convicted man would be set free. But if the high priest were to die during the trial and another priest replace him before the sentence was passed, then the banishment would be valid until the death of the new high priest or until the high priest is murdered or commits a murder. A man sentenced to banishment at a time when there was no high priest in office could never return to his home and was to remain in the city of refuge until his death. While in the city of refuge, he was bound to inform the residents of his status and to refuse any honors wished to grant him. He was not required to pay rent, however, as he resided in the city against his will.

A banished man who committed another act of manslaughter while in the city of refuge was transferred to another quarter of the same city. He could not be banished to another city (because of the sentence for his first crime) unless he killed a Levite.

The concept of sanctuary, with all the complexities it entails, shows an important progression from the institution of blood-avenger to that of trial by due process. Rather than surrender the murdered to the highly subjective "justice" of the victim's family, biblical and talmudic precepts attempted to transform murder from a private to a public crime, for which the suspect was liable to trial before a court of justice.

Crimes Punishable by Flagellation. *Makkot* ("blows" in Hebrew), the fifth treatise in the order of *Nezikin* ("torts" in Hebrew), deals with the law and procedure of corporal punishment known as flagellation or flogging.

There are 168 offenses for which an offender is liable to flogging. These include, among others, three types of marital sins committed by priests; four types of prohibited marriages; seven types of incestuous sexual relations; eight types of violations of dietary laws; twelve types of violations of other prohibitions; twenty-five types of violations of Levitical laws; and a number of violations of agrarian and Passover laws. Among the most serious offenses were incest with one's sister, one's mother's sister, one's wife's sister, or one's brother's wife; having sexual relations with a menstrually unclean woman; a high priest marrying a widow who is also a divorcee or who had performed the ceremony of *halitzah,* an Israelite marrying a bastard (a woman born of illegitimate relations) or a descendant of the Gibeonites; and a daughter of an Israelite marrying a descendant of a bastard or a Gibeonite.

The following six precepts were intended to limit the use of flogging:

1. Whenever the transgression of a prohibitory law was not accompanied by another violation (such as slander), flogging was applied only in the following cases: (a) one who swears falsely; (b) one who exchanges an animal brought by its owner as an offering to God for another animal; and (c) one who curses by using the name of God.

2. Should anyone transgress a law generally punishable by death but because of a legal technicality escapes punishment, he may not be subject to flogging.

3. Theft, robbery, and similar offenses, for which the Mosaic law prescribes retribution, are not punishable by flogging.

4. The transgression of a prohibitive law requiring reparation is punishable by flogging only if reparation is not made.

5. Flogging is not administered for the infraction of a prohibitory law that is only part of a general law. For instance, the general biblical injunction against eating blood (Lev. 19:26) includes several specific dietary laws, such as not partaking of the meat of an animal before it is actually dead, not eating meat that has blood in it, and so forth. Flogging was not inflicted for the transgression of any one of the specific laws derived from general biblical injunction.

6. The transgression of a prohibitory law that is not expressly mentioned in the Pentateuch but is derived only by implication or analogy is not punishable by flogging. Some Amoraim prescribed flogging for crimes that were also punishable by divine justice (*karet* or "death at the Hand of Heaven") in order to exact repentance that might absolve the criminal of his guilt before God.

"If the wicked man deserves to be beaten, it will be done before the judges according to his fault but not to exceed forty stripes" (Deut. 25:2–3). The Amoraim reduced the maximum number of lashes to thirty-nine so that even if there was an accidental error in the counting, the number should never exceed the biblical forty.

Talmudic scholars introduced a new concept regarding flogging. They felt that the body of the offender, rather than his guilt, should be the determining factor. Thus, a man was flogged "according to his strength"; he would receive only as many lashes as he could bear. Contemporary judicial systems have yet to reach this level of humanitarianism.

The procedure for the administration of lashes was as follows: The chief judge read a number of biblical verses, another judge counted the number of lashes, and a third one gave the order: "Strike!" If the officer gave just one lash too many and the man died, the officer was to be banished. If there was an error in counting and the man died, the officer responsible for the error was banished. If extra lashes were administered and the guilty party did not die, the court officer responsible for the mistake would be punished with lashes. However, these punishments were applied only when the "mistake" was intentional.

Flogging was administered thus: The hands of the condemned were tied to pillars on either side, and the minister or the court officer bared his chest, because the lashes had to be administered upon the bare body. The officer stood behind him on a stone, with a doubled strap of calf hide in his hands. The strap was long enough to reach the navel and was the width of one hand. One third of the lashes were given on the front of the chest and two thirds on the back of the bared shoulders. The man could not be given his punishment in a standing position, only when he was bending down. The court officer raised the strap with both hands but struck with only one, with all his might.

Whoever administered the lashes was required to possess less than ordinary physical strength but more than ordinary knowledge.

Crimes Punishable by Talionic Measures. Offenses committed against the person and gross violations of God's will were crimes against God and society. If the crime did not call for capital punishment, the court sentenced the offender to a talionic punishment—that is, the same injury he caused his victim: "Eye for eye, tooth for tooth, hand for hand, foot for foot, burning for burning, wound for wound, stripe for stripe" (Exod. 21: 24–25 and Lev. 24: 19–20). It is possible that the Mosaic law was influenced by Hammurabi's code. Though the biblical injunction may seem rather cruel, the talionic principle established a fixed limit to retaliatory punishment. It substituted a legal punishment commensurate with the injury for limitless revenge. In the Talmud (Baba Kama: 84a), "eye for eye and life for life" does not mean life and eye for one eye—a warning that while the offender is being blinded, "his soul may depart from him." The Amoraim were not particularly happy with the literal interpretation of the biblical text. They pointed out that in cases of bodily injury, compensation proved to be more humane.

Crimes Punishable by Fines. In most legal systems, ancient and modern, offenses against property are serious crimes. Sumerian and Babylonian laws considered larceny, under certain circumstances, to be a crime punishable by death. In Athens, Draco made theft a capital crime, as it was in England until abolished by George IV.

Under the Mosaic and talmudic legal systems, offenses against property were punishable only by fines. In cases of larceny, the offender had to pay two, four, or five times the stolen amount (Exod. 22: 3). On the other hand, if the thief admitted his guilt and repented, he was not required to pay the fine; in cases of robbery, it was enough for the offender to make restitution to the victim (Leviticus 5: 21–26).

However, the ancient Hebrews had the highest regard for the sanctity of private property. Stealing was strictly forbidden, whether it was done with the intention of retaining the stolen property or with the declared intention of benefiting the victim. Theft was dealt with in remarkably lenient terms, however; indeed, no crime against property was punishable by death.

Certain crimes entailing bodily injury were also punishable by fines. If a man were to harm another during a quarrel, and the victim had to remain in bed, the offender was obliged to pay back his lost days' wages and the medical expenses incurred. If a pregnant woman were to suffer a miscarriage as a result of a blow, the offender would have to provide remuneration according to the husband's demands or the judgment of arbitrators. If a man were to blind a slave or cause him to lose a tooth, the slave was to be freed immediately.

Even the rape of a maiden was not considered a capital offense, since restitution could be made by payment of a fine and a forced marriage (Deut. 22: 28–29). In cases of seduction, the offender paid the woman's dowry and married her (Deut. 20: 16). Afterward, he could not divorce her—the only case in which a husband could not divorce his wife. The dowry of a virgin was evidently a fixed sum of money, which explains the fact that the biblical text does not mention the amount to be paid by the seducer.

Crimes Punishable by Penal Servitude. Penal servitude was not adopted by the Jews as a legal punishment for crime until very late in the development of their criminal law. When an offender was unable to make restitution for stolen property, he was sold into slavery by the court for as long as deemed necessary, but in no event for more than six years (Exod. 22: 2). If he had repaid the amount stolen but was unable to pay the additional fine determined by the court, he could not be sold into slavery. Under no circumstances could women be sold into penal slavery.

Haim H. Cohn was right in stating that "the humanization of punishment is the fundamental concept of talmudic penology. It shines throughout the centuries as a monument of penological insight and humanitarian orientation, hardly paralleled in the history of law." This has not prevented anti-Semitism, an expression chosen to suggest that it was against not the Jewish religion, but the Jewish people. Whatever the case, the continuity of this phenomenon, combining both aspects, is still very much alive today despite the tremendous progress achieved by humanity. Nevertheless, the Jewish people have preserved their identity against all kinds of tragic circumstances, including the conquering empires of ancient times, the corrosive influence of Hellenism, the arrogant power of imperial Rome, the evangelization trends of Christianity, the proselitizing fervor of Islam, the savage torments of the Inquisition, the systematic and industrialized annihilation planned by the Nazis, and the permanent seduction of assimilation. According to Abba Eban, this may have been due to the Jewish emphasis on the emotional, passionate, mystical, and metaphysical aspects of national idiosyncracies, compensated by a strong inclination to rationality.

5
The Law of the Medes
and the Persians

Historical Background

Our knowledge of the Persians has been assembled from a variety of sources, few of them direct, for the Persians left a very limited number of written records. There are a few monumental inscriptions and some tablets inscribed in Elamite, an ancient language still poorly understood; but Egyptian and Hittite archives, Assyrian and Babylonian chronicles, the Old Testament (particularly the books of Esther and Daniel), the classical Greek historians, and archaeological evidence are of greater value in the reconstruction of Persian history.

On the basis of these sources, general consensus regards the original Persians as an integral part of the Indo-European family known as the Iranians, who were members of a still larger group of barbarians, the Aryans—a nomadic tribe who probably came from the Eurasian steppes of southern Russia or Central Asia somewhere between 2000 and 1800 B.C. This was possibly the first contact between people from certain European regions and those of the Near and Middle East. The Aryans were one of the peoples who crossed the Kabul passes, continued southward to the Indian subcontinent, and occupied the Hindustan area. They easily dominated the autochthonous Hindu population and developed the Vedic civilization, based on a vague form of pantheism. In order to remain the rulers of the vast area that they had conquered, they established a rigid social caste system.

Another group of Aryans, which included peoples of different ethnic backgrounds—the Medes and the Persians—came from the northwest and moved gradually to the southwest, entering the Iranian plateau and the Persian Gulf sometime between 1400 and 1000 B.C. The Medes, who chose the northern part of the plateau, with its rich soil and fertile valleys, had to combat the Mannaeans and other settled populations. Eventually, they established themselves as the ruling power. The Persians in the south, on the borders of the Persian Gulf, settled in a rather harsh and desolate region. They encountered almost no opposition, but the difficult conditions under which they lived forged a people of sober, frugal, and austere character who were also fierce warriors.

The early Medes and Persians were separate, independent clans and tribes. The Persians are first mentioned in the Assyrian records of king Shalmaneser III (c. 859 to 824 B.C.). According to Herodotus, the Persians submitted to the Medes in about the middle of the seventh century B.C. The capital of the Medes was established in Ecbatana, and their rise to power coincides with the decline of Assyria. In fact, in 612 B.C., Cyarxares, king of the Medes, with his ally Nabopolassar, king of Babylon, conquered Nineveh, the Assyrian capital, thus toppling the Assyrian empire. Cyrus I, a Persian vassal, led a successful uprising against the Median ruler Astyages in 550 B.C. He captured Ecbatana and established the kingdom of the Medes and the Persians. Foreigners such as Herodotus continued to speak of "Medians" while meaning Persians, for Media had been the greater power, whereas Persia was almost unknown. Cyrus, the founder of the Persian empire, reigned from 555 to 529 B.C. and established the Achaemenid dynasty. In 547 B.C., he conquered Lydia, in the western region of Anatolia, on the Aegean coast of Asia Minor in modern Turkey—the kingdom of Croesus, famous in Greek tradition for his enormous wealth—and destroyed Sardis, its capital. Then he conquered the cities of Greek Ionia as well as the lands of Central Asia to the Jaxartes river, on the Indian border. A few years later, in 539 B.C., he added the kingdom of Babylon to his already vast realm. When he died in 529 B.C., he had carved out a Persian empire that stretched from India to Lydia, a distance of some 2,600 miles.

Cyrus I was succeeded by Cambyses II, who added Egypt to Persia's domain, which thus extended from the Nile to the Indus rivers. All this was achieved in less than thirty years, from approximately 550 B.C. to 522 B.C. After the civil war that followed Cambyses's death, Darius I, also known as Darius the Great, took the throne. He is perhaps best known as the author of the famous trilingual inscription of the Rock of Behistun. The inscription, written in Old Persian, with Median and Babylonian translations, is a landmark in the deciphering of ancient languages and the most important direct source regarding Persian history during the Achaemenian period (555 to 330 B.C.). The inscription, carved into the face of a mountain cliff on the main road between modern Baghdad and Tehran, reads, in part, as follows:

> I am Darius, the Great King, the King of Kings, the King of Persia, the King of the Provinces, the son of Hystaspes, the grandson of Arsames, the Achaemenian. The father of Arsames was Ariyaramnes, and this father was Achaemenes, so we are called Achaemenians. Eight of my race were kings before me. I am the ninth. By the grace of Ahuramazda I am king. Twenty-three lands or provinces are subject unto me: Persia, Susiana, Babylonia, Assyria, Arabia, Egypt, the Islands of the Sea, Sparda, Ionia, Media, Armenia, Cappadocia, Phartia, Drangiana, Aria, Chorasmia, Bactria, Sogdiana, Gandara, Scythia, Sattagydia, Arachosia and Maka. Cambyses, the

son of Cyrus, one of our race, was king before me. He had a brother Smerdis, whom he slew, but the people did not know, and Cambyses went into Egypt. After his departure the people became hostile and the lie multiplied in the land, in Persia, Media, and other provinces. Afterward there was a Magian, Gaumata by name, who raised a rebellion, pretending to be Smerdis, and seized the kingdom. Afterward Cambyses dies by his own hand and Gaumata was king. The people feared him, for he slew many who had known the former Smerdis. There was none who dared say against him, until I came and with the help of a few men I slew Gaumata and his chief followers and I became king. . . . Whoever helped my house, him I favoured, he who was hostile, him I destroyed.

He concluded with the following admonition:

Thou, who shalt hereafter see this inscription which I have written, or these sculptures, destroy them not, preserve them so long as thou livest. Then may Ahuramazda be thy friend, may thy house be numerous. Live long and may Ahuramazda make fortunate whatsoever thou doest. But shalt thou destroy them and not preserve them then may Ahuramazda slay thee, and may thy race come to nought, and whatever thou doest may Ahuramazda destroy.

Notice the similarity to the epilogues of the early cuneiform codes.

The Persian Religion

We are not certain as to when the Achaeminid kings embraced Zoroastrianism (or Parsiism, as their religion is also known). There is little evidence regarding the situation among the predecessors of Darius, but there is no doubt of his devotion to Ahuramazda, as stated in the inscription on the Rock of Behistun. From about 480 B.C., the time of Xerxes I, Darius's son and successor, Zoroastrianism became the official religion in Persia. Xerxes's tomb is inscribed with the words: "By the will of Ahuramazda I uprooted the cult of the '*daevas*,' who shall not be worshipped, and only Ahuramazda should be worshipped, in accordance with the Truth, and using the proper rites."

As there is no documentation regarding pre-Zoroastrian religion, the scant available data are grounds for educated speculation alone. More important than the archaeological findings is the *Avesta,* which was originally inscribed during Zoroaster's lifetime. Actually, the Avesta is a collection of texts that comprise a body of traditions transmitted by word of mouth over many centuries. It was probably completed, arranged, and inscribed for the first time about the third or fourth century A.D. Perhaps even more revealing is the Rig-Veda of India, part of the Vedas, the sacred books of India. This book (which is actually divided into ten books) contains some 1,028 hymns or songs that reveal the roots of brahamanic mythology, cosmogony, philosophy and ritual, and forms the principal source for the study of Hinduism. In the earlier polytheistic religion, the numerous gods were of two types: the Ahuras (the lofty deities, concerned mainly with the order of the universe) and the Daevas (related to worldly considerations, personifying such elements as earth, fire, water, and winds). Zoroastrianism, the major ancient pre-Islamic religion of Iran, represented a complete break with Iran's religious past. Conceived by one man, Zarathustra (or Zoroaster, as he is known in the Western world), as an almost pure form of monotheism, Zoroastrianism centered around one supreme god, known as Ahuramazda, the "Wise Lord," the omnipotent creator and preserver of the universe, the sovereign lawgiver and judge. Assisting Ahuramazda were a number of holy but subordinate spirits through whom the god expressed his will. These were not really separate divinities but different manifestations of the one true god. Among these subordinate spirits were two opposing forces: one representing truth and similar virtues, known as Spenta Mainyu, the "holy spirits," and the other, Angra Mainyu, the "destructive spirits," embodying the principles of evil. Both influenced man, whose moral responsibility it was to choose between them. The antagonism between good and evil existed in the earlier Iranian religion, but in Zoroastrianism the struggle took on the dimensions of a universal conflict. According to Zoroastrianism, man possessed the free will to choose between the kingdom of justice and truth and that of evil and lies. Man's soul was immortal, and three days after death it appeared before a divine tribunal that judged the individual according to his choice. He who had chosen good was granted an afterlife of joy; he who had chosen evil was condemned to everlasting torment. Thus, man is ultimately responsible for his own fate. It is here, as well as in the ancient Jewish penal philosophy, that we find the roots of the "free will" doctrine of the classical school of criminal law of Beccaria, established during the eighteenth century.

Such a structured doctrine—with one god, based on ethical dualism, free will, and posthumous reward or punishment—constituted a radical departure from the polytheistic faith of the early Medes and Persians and their predecessors in Iran. Indeed, the rulers were forced to modify it to make it more acceptable to a populace who continued to adhere to the old beliefs. By the time of the Achaemenid rule, some old pagan and primitive concepts—rejected by Zoroaster—had begun to reassert themselves. Nevertheless, some of Zoroastrianism's fundamental principles survived and may even have influenced other major faiths such as Judaism, Christianity, and Islam, as well as some Greek philosophers, such as Aristotle.

The sacred book of Zoroastrianism, the Avesta, assumed to contain Zoroaster's original teachings, was written in an eastern Iranian dialect, the Avestan or Zend, which is very similar to the Sanskrit of the Indians' Vedas but still defies complete comprehension. Perhaps the most important text is the Videvdat or Vendidad, which consists of two introductory sections recounting how law was given to man, followed by eighteen sections of rules, which represent the only original legal material surviving from ancient Persia.

Zoroastrianism had three basic rites: the lighting and maintaining of sacred fires (Ahuramazda's gift to man, which symbolized truth, since it dispels the darkness of the evil and lies); the concocting of an intoxicating drink from a sacred plant called *haoma* (a species of ephedra, a mydriatic alkaloid); and the sacrifice of bulls. The remains of five fire tower temples have been found, built during the Achaemenid period between 600 and 400 B.C. At the center of these temples were three hollowed altars where the magi (priests) held the eternal sacred flames. In the walls were fire ovens and pits containing bone fragments, evidence of the animal sacrifice rituals. The magi did not blow the flame with their breath but fanned it, in order not to contaminate the sacred fire. Whoever dared to blow the flame or throw anything dead or unclean upon it was put to death. According to Strabo (a Greek geographer of the first century B.C.), the priests themselves wore mouth coverings to keep their breath from polluting the flame.

There is no description of the haoma ceremony, but from suggestions in the Avesta and from later Zoroastrian practices, it is possible to form some idea of this ritual. The ceremony took place in the fire temple and was centered around the sacred flames. It was conducted twice—once for the priests only and immediately afterward for the holy men and the laity together. One of the first acts was the slaying of a bull; and since Zoroaster regarded cutting the fully conscious animal's throat as cruel, it was first mercifully stunned with a club. Following the sacrifice, the priests prepared the haoma to be consumed during the ritual. Some of the juice of the crushed plant was sprinkled around the altar, where the invisible gods were believed to sit. Another part of it was mixed with the raw flesh of the sacrificed bull; after the meat was cooked, some of it was divided among the faithful and some was offered to the gods. The rest of the haoma juice was mixed with milk and water, which the priests and worshippers drank after reciting hymns in praise of Ahuramazda. The effect of the drug was to induce (supposedly, in all good men) a state of euphoria and to impart a sense of physical and spiritual immortality. The ceremony lasted from dawn to dusk, and the congregation spent the rest of the day listening to recitations of the Gathas and other hymns.

Because fire, air, earth, and water were considered the four sacred elements of Zoroastrinism, the Persians did not cremate or bury their dead. The naked corpses were left on "towers of silence" and, within a few hours, were stripped of their flesh by vultures. When the bones had been dried by the sun, they were swept into the central well.

The evolution of Zoroastrianism is a much debated subject, but it is clear that it was radically transformed by later generations. Elements of the old polytheism began to creep in, and the abstractions used by Zoroaster to describe the attributes or characteristics of the "Wise Lord" were soon personified and later became separate deities. By the time of Artaxerxes I, who included some of the old gods in his Persian calendar of 441 B.C., the monotheistic core of the religion had certainly atrophied. Zoroastrianism, in some form or other, was the official religion of the Persian empire until the last of the Achaemenid kings. After Alexander's conquest and during the Macedonian rule, the religion lost its official status. The Parthian dynasty that followed (from 250 B.C. until 220 A.D.) showed little interest in this faith, which remained dormant for about five centuries. With the advent of the Sassanian kings, in 226 A.D., Zoroastrianism gained royal favor and again became the official religion, yet it bore little resemblance to Zoroaster's original teachings. Moreover, the Sassanian priests who attempted to restore the pure doctrine of Zoroastrianism were able to understand the language of the ancient texts, and their interpretations were often inaccurate. Zoroastrianism suffered a telling blow when the Muslims overran Iran in 642; but it is estimated that it is still practiced by some 10,000 believers in Iran. Zoroastrianism has survived among the descendents of a small group of believers who preferred exile to Islam. Known as the Parsees of India, they still practice the ancient Iranian rituals and number some 100,000, mainly in Bombay. If Zoroastrianism holds a relatively insignificant place among the world's main religions, it is perhaps because it was adopted primarily by the Persian ruling class and never by the populace at large.

Sociopolitical Organization

The role of the Persians was as important in the political history of the world as it was almost insignificant in the history of civilization. In the two centuries during which they were in power (from 550 to 330 BIC.), the Persians forged a gigantic empire but contributed relatively little to the fields of philosophy or law, literature or technology, science or the arts. However, they did play a significant role in the political evolution of Western civilization. The Persians rapidly absorbed the political and administrative patterns of the city-states as well as other characteristics of the more ancient people of the Middle and Near East. These elements became an integral part of the sociopolitical structure of their vast empire. Thus, they served as a living bridge between East and West—Egypt, Mesopotamia, and Palestine on one side and Greece, Europe, and Africa on the other. For the first time in history, the monarchical, hierarchical, and priestly East faced the republican, egalitarian, and secular West, creating a civilization that was, in fact, an amalgamation of the two basically different systems. The Persians transmitted a vast accumulation of Oriental culture to Western civilization, which was evolving on the islands of the Aegean Sea and would reach its height in classical Greece. In such a way, the Persians forged a vital link between the ancient civilizations and the builders of the modern world.

The original ten or more Persian tribes presumably elected their leaders for the specific purpose of leading them into battle. When Assyria became a serious threat to their independence, they appointed such a leader, who became what would later be known as king. In later generations, it became customary among the nomadic Persians for the son or grandson of a popular headman to succeed him, a practice that created a dominant clan within each tribe. However, the tribe retained the right to reject such heirs. Although the principle of a ruling class was strongly established by the time Cyrus came to power, he was nevertheless required to win the support of a number of other tribal leaders. Cyrus utilized diplomacy rather than force, presenting himself not as an "absolute ruler" but as "first among equals." Cambyses had not the energy and charisma of his father Cyrus. During the eight years of his reign, he almost forfeited the newly founded empire to various claimants who challenged the Achaemenid's overlordship. Darius, his second cousin, had to depose a pretender before he could restore the monarchy to the Achaemenid family. The problem of succession continued after Darius's thirty-six year reign, for there was not yet a written, clear law of succession. The king was expected to announce his heir before going to battle, in case he was killed. Darius had to decide between two of his sons: Artabazanes, the elder, and Xerxes, the younger. The succession problem was further complicated by the royal harem, which housed the king's wife, his concubines, the queen mother, the king's unmarried sisters, a throng of royal offspring (including the crown prince), and a contingent of eunuchs. The king was subject to the intrigues instigated by his harem; indeed, a preferred concubine might try to influence the king to appoint one of her children as crown prince.

The royal office as an administrative institution began to take shape under the Persians. Cyrus proved to be a pragmatic, though unoriginal, administrator who subjected all the Persian tribes (to whom monarchy was a relatively new concept) to his rule. The imperial administrative mechanism actually developed under Darius. He inherited the basic institutional proto-types from his kinsmen and former overlords, the Medes, as well as from various Middle Eastern kingdoms. The political accomplishments of the Persian rulers can be at least partially attributed to the adaptability of these prototypes to the requirements of Persia's enormous empire.

Royal authority was exerted through a rather sophisticated system of government: The bureaucracy was headed by Persian nobles, with a school of scribes that not only kept records but also adapted the cuneiform scripture to their own needs. The treasury collected revenues and made the necessary disbursements; and most important, there was efficient network of communications. The grand vizier, in charge of the empire's administration, was directly beneath the king in the hierarchy of power. The king also received the advice of the royal council which was made up of seven members appointed by the king.

Darius's rule was characterized by religious and political tolerance toward the many peoples of his empire. He cleverly attributed the divine sanction of his rule to the authority of Marduk while in Babylon or to Ra while in Egypt, thus honoring the local divinity of the conquered nation. Each people was permitted a certain amount of autonomy; indeed, an attempt to subject some one hundred nations who spoke twenty different languages to the same rule would have been not only absurd but dangerous.

Darius's regime became a symbol of imperial strength; his authority was exercised through a pyramidal structure controlled, under the monarch's rule, by the *satraps*—the governors of the Persian provinces. The satrap was, in a sense, a king himself: He was responsible for the province's administration, commanding his own local military force, collecting taxes, and so forth. Indeed, the high degree of autonomy granted to the satraps proved a double-edged sword, permitting the empire to function smoothly while paving the way for numerous rebellions.

Darius was also known as the "merchant," a name that signified admiration for his abilities in the economic sphere. Indeed, under his reign, the empire enjoyed unprecedented prosperity for a period of some fifty years. Darius systematized taxation; standardized weights, measures, and a monetary system in order to simplify commercial exchange; extended and improved transportation networks (including an early version of the Suez Canal); founded a royal merchant marine; developed agriculture, the basis of Persian internal economy; encouraged the growth of a banking system; and promoted international trade.

In traditional Indo-Iranian society, there were no organized social classes, but it was possible to distinguish four classes or estates: the warriors or aristocracy; the priests; the officials or civil servants; and the people—the "fourth estate"—farmers and herdsmen. Slaves were a separate group. A small circle or aristocratic families formed the ruling class from which the Achaemenid dynasty chose their wives and successors. Most of the satraps were also appointed from the ranks of these families. Indeed, without the support of what later came to be known as the "seven families," a ruler would have been hard-pressed to retain his throne. Just below the "seven families" was another elite category of hereditary landholders—chief among them high-ranking military officers, priests, and government administrators—who oversaw the running of the imperial treasury, enforced the king's law, and controlled trade, irrigation, and agriculture.

Family and property were the pillars of Persian society. The Avesta recommended marriage between next of kin; indeed, marriages between brother and sister were common, because it was thought that they would be granted divine splendor. Polygamy was prohibited by the Avesta, but concubines—particularly among female slaves and prisoners of war—were tolerated.

After Darius, there was a conscious trend to "Persianize" all the satrapies and provinces. Persians played a larger role in administering the empire's colonies as well as filling judicial and military posts.

The lower class was made up of agricultural laborers, artisans, and free laborers, or hired men. At the bottom of the social scale were the bondsmen, or serfs and slaves, who were bought and sold along with the land. Although the slave was the property of his owner, no cruel punishment could be inflicted for a slave's first misdeed. Bondsmen came from many segments of society: prisoners of war, slaves bought in foreign markets, children sold by parents, freemen whose debts or crimes had reduced them to servitude. In certain parts of the realm, notably Babylon, slaves were living in even greater comfort than poor freemen in Persia. Certain classes of slaves—skilled workers such as builders, bakers, and barbers—enjoyed advantages not even granted to all freemen. Some were allowed to receive payment for their work or to go into business for themselves. In some parts of the realm, such as Mesopotamia, they even gained the right to own and dispose of property, including slaves. Thus, an industrious slave could often attain a degree of influence and social status that put him above his free counterparts.

The size of Darius's kingdom necessitated an efficient system of communications. To ensure that his messages would reach their destination swiftly, Darius established an empirewide pony-express service. In seven days, a message could be sent from Sardis, in Lydia, to Susa, 1,677 miles away—a distance that took three months for a caravan to cover. There was also an even more rapid "postal system," based on a chain of hilltop fire towers that used a visual flashed code—similar to the modern Morse code. This system remained in use in Iran until the appearance of the telegraph in the nineteenth century.

The large size of some of the satrapies (Egypt, for instance) posed obvious administrative difficulties. The trend was toward smaller and more manageable political units, which entailed changing the boundaries of some satrapies. According to Herodotus, whereas Cyrus had only twenty satrapies, by the end of the Persian empire there were at least twenty-eight.

The distance, wealth, and power of the satrapies often put them in a position in which they could become a very real threat to the empire's central government. As a safeguard against ambitions of governors and satraps, Darius maintained a network of his own agents in every satrapy. The treasurer and the secretary of each satrapy were directly responsible to him. In addition, regular investigations were carried out by special roving officers—known as "the king's eyes and ears"—who checked the accounts, examined records of lawsuits, and interviewed staff and public in order to verify that the king's will was being obeyed by his "viceroys." They also reported to the king any signs of disaffection or intrigue. Many of these administrative techniques were later adopted by the Greeks and Romans.

The eventual economic demise of the Persian empire seems to have been brought about, at least in part, by a modern ailment: inflation. Privately owned banks, managed by wealthy families, charged higher and higher interest rates; the standard of living was eaten away by ever-rising prices. Taxes became more and more burdensome, and because of the Achaemenids' tendency to hoard money, there was less and less currency available. People eventually began to revert to the barter system, abandoning the currency of the realm. When Alexander of Macedonia conquered Susa, he found an imperial treasury that contained 270 tons of gold coins and 1,200 tons of silver cast into ingots.

Legal and Judicial System

The available information regarding the Persian legal system is too scant to enable us to draw precise conclusions about its most basic characteristics or its influence on the evolution of criminal law and criminological thought. We do know that a new word for *law* appeared in the Near East in Achaemenid times: the Iranian word *data,* which seems to have been borrowed from a Semitic language used in the empire. Persian judges were sometimes called *data-bar,* a term that probably referred to the judges of the imperial courts.

The Persian king, who ruled "by the grace of Ahuramazda," possessed unlimited power, and he alone determined the verdict in crimes committed against himself or the state. Although he was the supreme judge, the king was bound by tradition to consult with his high officials before arriving at crucial decisions. Court judges, called *law bearers,* were supposed to advise the monarch regarding customary law as it applied to a particular situation, but their suggestions were not binding, and their decisions were considered final only when they received the king's approval. Therefore, the judges avoided bending the law, delivering a verdict that might displease the king. Indeed, they may have preferred to deliver an ambiguous verdict, leaving its interpretation to the king himself. It seems that the magi were also trained in matters of law and acted as judges in civil matters since the times of Cambyses.

If the law was flexible in relation to the king, it was otherwise immutable and irrevocable. The Achaemenid Persian kings, particularly Darius, distinguished themselves by their devotion to the legal system. Persians and foreigners alike called Darius "the Lawgiver," and the inscription he chose for his tomb stated: "my law . . . of that they feel fear, so that the stronger does not smite nor destroy the weak." However, no actual code of Persian law has ever been discovered, and what we know about the outlines of the Persian law was assembled from a variety of nonlegal sources, including the Avesta, the Greek historians, and the later books of the Old Testament. Modern scholars believe that the Persians did not advance the underlying philosophy of the law as much as they extended and developed the use of ancient Mesopotamian law and other existing Middle Eastern legal concepts and codes.

The first recorded Middle Eastern law codes, as indicated earlier, tried to systematize the custom within the framework of acceptable social behavior. The precedent—the actual case rather than the general rule—was the basis for deciding each and every legal issue. The actual codification, aside from contributing a certain logical order to the legal concepts of preliterate times, had the advantage of being written and thus durable and relatively easy to circulate, providing a certain uniformity. It is generally believed that the Code of Hammurabi was the ancestor of Persian laws, which were disseminated throughout the empire and, eventually, throughout the Western world. Even the language of the Persian law seems to have been borrowed directly from the Babylonians. Darius used phrases that appear to have been copied verbatim from Hammurabi's case books. For the Persians, who regarded "truth" and "lie" as sacred definitions of "good" and "evil," the law was held to be unalterable. Therefore, it is not surprising that in one of Darius's inscriptions, it is stated: "What is right I love and what is not right I hate." He particularly wished to be remembered as the great lawgiver, and law reform was one of the cornerstones of his program for the organization of the empire.

The Old Testament Book of Esther relates how the advisors of king Xerxes urged him to banish his queen, who had disobeyed him, lest "the great ladies of Persia and Media" imitate her independence. They also recommended that the banishment order "be inscribed in the Laws of the Medes and the Persians, never to be revoked."

To judge from certain Babylonian evidence, two sets of law—possibly administered by two different sets of courts—were enforced in the satrapies. One was the local law, undoubtedly based on custom and previous local codifications; the other was the Persian or imperial law, based on the ultimate authority of the king.

Persian justice was also dispensed through a system of courts, but little is known of their structure or of how they functioned. It is probable that there were two courts of law in each jurisdiction. One dealt with cases involving family, inheritance, and property; the other was concerned with such state issues as taxation and transgressions against the king, the government, its officers, and its property.

Royal judges were appointed for life or until they were disqualified on the grounds of unacceptable behavior. It seems that ordeals were used to determine the innocence or guilt of the accused. The death penalty was usually not inflicted for a first offense.

Broadly speaking, there were three types of crimes: (1) those committed against Ahuramazda (blasphemy or transgression of basic religious norms); (2) those committed against the king (treason, rebellion, deserting the battlefield, etc.), and (3) those committed against a fellowman. For the first two types, the penalty was death; for the third type of crimes, the talionic principle was applied. Recidivist thieves were hanged, in order to deter frequent stealing.

Punishments were rather harsh: the death penalty and corporal punishments were inflicted for both civil and political crimes. Beheading, impalement, and crucifixion were common—and no penalties were more severe than those inflicted on erring magistrates. Sisamness, a royal Persian judge during Cambyses's times, was caught accepting a bribe to fix a case. The king ordered that the judge's skin be removed in strips and used to upholster the judge's own courtroom chair. His son was appointed to the same judicial post and thus received a constant reminder of his father's crime. Artaxerxes established the same punishment for judges who delivered "wicked sentences." Mutilations of the nose, hands, ears, tongue, and so forth, were common. High treason and rebellion were severely punished: After being blinded, the guilty party's hands and ears were severed. The condemned man was then exhibited in public before his execution. Sometimes, vicarious punishments were inflicted; and because of Persian's strong familial feelings, these punishments were considered particularly dreadful.

Once the king's decision was fixed in a certain prescribed form, even he could not revoke it, as stated in the biblical Book of Daniel. When the court officials convinced Darius that he must punish Daniel, they told him: "Now, O King, establish the interdict, according to the law of the Medes and the Persians, which cannot be revoked" (Dan. 6:8). "Therefore king Darius signed the document and interdict" (Dan. 6:9).

According to Greek historians, the Persians practiced "condemnation of the memory of the dead people." They mention the case of Dareio and his followers, who plotted against Artaxerxes. Their memories were damned; their images, statutes, or medals destroyed; their names erased from official records; their houses demolished; and their interment forbidden. Their heirs lost all rights, honors, and social positions that they would have inherited, so that the dishonor was passed on to future generations. Animals were also put on trial. According to Venidad, the first time a dog bit a man, it was to be punished with the amputation of the right ear; the second time, the left ear; the third time, one of its legs; and the fourth time, its tail. The Persians also tortured those who had been condemned to death. This was not done to obtain a confession, but only to increase the suffering of the condemned. The limbs of the offender were cut off—a punishment meant to show the disdain of the court for his behavior. Greek prisoners of war, as well as those convicted of witchcraft and similar crimes (who were regarded as the devil's allies), were subjected to the ignominious fate of having their noses and ears cut off.

Aelianus, cited by Thot, describes one of the first cases of *conditional remission of a sentence*. It refers to a citizen by the name of Rhacone, who surrendered his own son for punishment to king Artaxerxes "for having caused a lot of damage to the 'magi' and the wise men of the community." Rhacone had tried to discipline his son, but to no avail. Finally, when the judges approached Rhacone's home, he took his son, with his hands bound, accused him before the judges of his persistent misbehavior, and asked them to sentence him to death. The shocked judges advised the father to go directly to the king. The father did so and repeated his request. After listening to him, the king appointed the father as a member of the College of the Royal Judges, stating that someone who was so severe with his son would certainly become the perfect judge—strong and incorruptible. Then he pardoned the son but told him that if he were to commit another crime similar to his previous ones, he would be put to death in the most terrible fashion.

If "the Laws of the Medes and Persians that altereth not" became proverbial through the biblical book of Daniel, the Persians' other remarkable works have been obscured by the biased interpretations of the Greek and Roman historians, who provided so much of the surviving information. Because they emphasized the period of decline, the often melodramatic story of Persia's fall served to conceal its finest hours.

Archaeological digs, started some fifty years ago, provide compelling evidence that behind its traditional malevolent image, the ancient Persian Empire had worn a much more attractive and benign face. The testimony of such incomparable human witnesses as Herodotus and Xenophon, combined with the cumulative findings of modern archaeology, evoke a people no less remarkable than the better-known ancient Egyptians and Babylonians, whom the Persians conquered, and equally as interesting as the Greeks, who conquered the Persians and learned so much from them and their former vassals in the process.

6

Ancient India and the Laws of Manu

Only that person is a saint who serves the whole of Mankind.
—Guru Nanak

Early Developments

The geographic unit known as ancient India covers the entire subcontinent from the Hindu Kush and the Himalaya mountains in the north to the Bay of Bengal and is surrounded by the Indian Ocean and the Arabian Sea, including territories that now comprise the states of India, Pakistan, Nepal, Bangladesh, and part of Afghanistan.

Unlike Mesopotamia and Egypt, India's archaeological remains had not been extensively explored until the last few decades, so their contribution to our understanding of the history of the subcontinent is rather poor. Original written sources are also insufficient to provide an understanding of ancient India. The inability to separate fact and fancy, truth and legend, makes the construction of a chronological record of this ancient civilization more difficult than others, and many dates are accurate only within one or more centuries. Since antiquity, the Hindus have used two kinds of chronological systems: One requires that the years be reckoned from some historical event; the other starts the reckoning from the position of some heavenly body. The historical system—the more common in modern times—exists side by side with Muslim and other international systems that were successively introduced.

The vast majority of the classical Indian texts—many of whose authors are anonymous or of doubtful identity— were transmitted by word of mouth from master to pupil, from one generation to the next. The oral recitation through many generations undoubtedly changed and reshaped the original, and the resulting texts were recorded centuries after their oral circulation. Kings' annals, so frequent in Near Eastern documents, are practically non-existent in India, where politics and warfare were considered unworthy of being recorded. The majority of dates in Indian history have been established upon the evidence of early Greek and Chinese travelers and, later, Moslem merchants, Buddhist pilgrims, and European writers. Indian history prior to the twelfth century A.D. had to be compiled from scattered allusions in religious or literary works, inscriptions on rock or copper plates, coins, travelers' reports, and the like. Thanks to the Moslems' interest in history, India's background became far more detailed after their conquest of the subcontinent.

At first glance, it is difficult to understand how the first inhabitants reached the interior of India. The towering Himalaya and the Hindu Kush mountain range seem to seal off the subcontinent from the rest of the world. Nevertheless, there are a number of natural gorges, such as the Khyber Pass, that facilitated infiltration.

Some scholars believe that the oldest primitive inhabitants of India might have been the Nagas, snake worshippers, whom the later Aryan invaders found in the northern provinces. Others assume that they were a negroid people, related to the aborigines of Ceylon, Sumatra, or even Australia. They were dark-skinned, similar to the negroes of Africa, who settled on the Vindhya plateau, between northern India and the Deccan. Afterward, quickly or slowly, an enormous number of invaders and their descendants, all different in ethnic origin and cultural background, were forced to find a way of living together—coexistence, not merger—and they became an integral part of historic India. Whatever the case, the oldest Indian civilization is considered to be that of the Dravidians, also a negroid people, who went south of the Deccan and established themselves in the temperate coastal plain that they found in their migration. They came, perhaps, from Western Asia, through Baluchistan, and reached Cape Comorin, the southernmost tip of India. They were followed by waves of other invaders and conquerors of six different ethnic prototypes and nine racial subdivisions, who also reached the southern Indian plains but never outnumbered or overwhelmed the Dravidians. They were black, white, and yellow races, nomads, traders, and armies. Some were already refined people, whereas others were still primitive root-grubbers, but India found room for all of them.

The pre-Indus civilization, which archaeologists and anthropologists discovered only within the last century, is as old as human civilization itself. About 4000 B.C., during the Early Bronze Age, soon after the appearance of the first farming communities in Mesopotamia, man made the transition from nomadic to settled life in the northwest corner of India. A millenium later, he developed a primitive village culture, which, 500 years later, became one of the world's great civilizations— the Indus Valley or Harrapan culture, which flourished over a period of 1,000 years, from about 2500 to 1500 B.C. Although there are still important gaps in our current knowledge (the first evidence of this culture was unearthed only in 1924), there is no doubt that this civilization is as old as that of Egypt or the Sumerians and extended over an area far greater than that of Egypt and Sumer together. This area, in the shape of an enormous triangle, has its apex at the Indus river system and its base along the coast, from the end of the Arabian Sea (today the border between Iran and Pakistan) to a site near modern Bombay.

More than fifty Harrapan communities have been discovered, ranging from farming villages to large seaports and including two great capitals: Mohenjo Daro, on the left bank of the lower Indus river, and Harappa, some 400 miles to the northeast, on the Ravi river, one of the Indus tributaries. Both capitals were masterpieces of urban planning, with wide streets and avenues in a rigid mathematical grid pattern. From their well-structured public and private edifices, sophisticated drainage and sewer systems, and the artifacts found within these cities, it is clear that their cultural level was equal to that of Egypt and Mesopotamia. Archaeological findings in these two cities—as well as recent excavations at Chankudado, Ropar, Rangpur, and Lothal, still in progress—have proved that their inhabitants were Aryans ("noble ones" in their own language), Indo-European–speaking tribes who began to invade India just before 2000 B.C. The phallus symbol, the bull (sign of faith), the goddess, and the dresses found there, all belong to the Aryan cult. These excavations have also proved that, within a radius of 800 miles from northern to western modern Gujarat, there was the same civilization as in Mohenjo Daro and Harappa; coins, toys, beads, weights, measurements, and animals were all the same. It is possible that the original Aryans came from the Arctic region and that the Vedas came into existence in the same area. They settled on the "seven river" land of Punjab and Sind.

Their arrival contributed to the downfall of the Indus Valley civilization and signified the earliest and perhaps the greatest of all Indian ethnical fusions during the many centuries of India's evolution. Although they did not leave much for archaeologists to reconstruct their civilization, their heritage includes religious concepts, first transmitted through oral tradition and later collected in writing. These scriptures, known as the Vedas, are collected in a number of books that have given their name to an entire period of Indian history—the Vedic Age, which lasted from about 1500 to 600 B.C., during which the fundamental principles of Hinduism were laid. They introduced a pattern of life that, to some extent, persists to this very day. It is impossible to establish when the first Veda, the Rig Veda, was written, fluctuating between about 6000 to 1000 B.C., according to the different scholars. Varma is of the opinion that the Vedas were not "composed" but "perceived." The Vedas are contained in a number of volumes, one of the main being called *Samhita,* which is accompanied by appendages and exploratory passages known as the *Brahmins,* all with different authors. The Vedas have 760 *Suktas* (main couplets) and 6,000 *Mantras* (hymns). Every couplet or hymn has an author, whose name is given with it. It would be strange to find in any other literature every line with another author, whose name is tagged to it, so that his personal responsibility is related to a specific part. On the other hand, to explain the intricacies of the hymns and couplets, there are 120 Upnishads (some scholars have counted 1,080 of them), which mean "sit and listen carefully." And besides the Vedas, there are the *Vedangas,* which are special sections of the Vedas.

The Vedas also contain historical chronologies of ruling families and republican governments. At different times, there were more than eighty republics, some of them better organized than the Greek republics of later days. The Vedas provide a good description of their systems of government and the political problems of those days, even including a geographic description. The Vedas also have some references to astronomy, some of them so perfect that in spite of modern scientific achievements, they are still valid today. Thus, it may be stated that the Vedas, with their hymns, prayers, rituals, incantations, and poems, reveal a great deal about the Aryan religion and social structure as well as the religious foundations of the Indian culture.

The Indus Valley civilization seems to have disappeared after about 1500 B.C. The quality of workmanship and materials in the artifacts declined, and the cities appear to have been finally abandoned. Archaeologists have found no evidence of a slow decline, as in other civilizations. Life simply stopped at the peak of prosperity, and despite learned conjectures, the cause remains a mystery. The Aryans' civilization left a clear and lasting mark on Indian society, both in its language and in its caste system, which is based on ethnic origin and color (*varna*). It was succeeded by a plethora of different peoples, dynasties, and states, all of which would be later united under the Mauryan Empire. Among them, Darius of Persia claimed the northwestern region of India as part of his empire, and even Alexander the Great attempted to conquer the subcontinent. In 327 B.C., he smashed through Afghanistan, down to the Punjab. Although he was largely unsuccessful and left India three years later, he brought with him the influence of Hellenism and Greek humanism.

In about 320 B.C., a young Indian warrior-king of a noble family, Chandragupta Maurya, began to build the Mauryan Empire, which would reign over Hindustan and Afghanistan for 137 years. Little is known regarding his origins, but he was indeed the first real political leader of India. After gaining control of his native state, the kingdom of Magadha in northeastern India, he extended his authority over all of northern India, from the Bay of Bengal to the Arabian Sea. Within a decade, he also became the ruler of the Indus Valley and the Punjab region and established his capital in Pataliputra, in modern Patna. When his empire was at its peak, his army numbered 700,000 men, 9,000 elephants, and 10,000 chariots. Tradition has it that he abdicated his throne after twenty-four years of absolute rule. He adopted the new religion known as Jainism, founded by Mahariva a couple of centuries earlier; became a monk; and fasted to death. Some scholars contend that he committed suicide in 298 B.C.

His son and grandson inherited his empire. The forty-year reign of his grandson Asoka, during the second third of the third century B.C., is considered one of the golden ages in Indian history. After witnessing the suffering brought about by his military campaigns, he renounced his throne and became a Buddhist—a religion already well established with temples in many places of northern India. He preached it and devoted himself to serving his subjects, annulling oppressive laws, pardoning prisoners, and instituting a number of public welfare services. His teachings were engraved on stones and pillars throughout his kingdom, and he himself toured the region to preach to the people compassion, nonviolence, honesty, and modest living. Unfortunately, his pacifist doctrine may have undermined the strength of his empire, for only fifty years after his death, the empire disintegrated. Asoka, who had been responsible for spreading Buddha's teachings throughout India and even beyond its frontiers, was forgotten for centuries, and reappeared much later in India's history.

Little is known of some 600 years of Indian history that followed the end of the Mauryan Empire. Invaders from Persia, Afghanistan, and Central Asia seem to have contributed to the internal disorder of India's small kingdoms and principalities. The first invaders, in the second century B.C., were Greeks coming from Bactria, in Central Asia, north of the Hindu Kush mountains, where the generals of Alexander the Great had founded some kingdoms. Then came the Parthians, or Pahlavas, who probably migrated from the Iranian plateau. They later were able to establish the Pahlava kingdom in southern India, which lasted for over 500 years. Afterward appeared the Shakas, or Scythians—barbaric nomadic tribesmen from the steppes of southern Russia and the northern area of Pont-Euxin, the ancient name of the Black Sea. India's population was further augmented by a number of other migrating peoples, including Indo-Europeans, Medes and Persians, Huns, Turks, Mongols, and Arabs. The vast majority of them settled in the fertile plains along the Indu and Ganges rivers, and their descendants remained in India. Some of them were nomads, while others were traders or part of invading armies; some had reached a certain degree of civilization, while others were still primitive, but India absorbed them all. Each group lived according to its own customs and traditions and remained separate and distinct, later forming a separate caste. The fundamental difference between the Indo-Europeans who invaded Egypt and the Aryans who came to India was that the former were absorbed by the people of the older civilization they encountered in the Valley of the Nile, whereas the latter, retaining their distinctiveness, contributed a greal deal to Indian culture.

The only ones of all these invaders who were able to establish an extensive and lasting kingdom were the Kushans, descendants of some other Central Asian nomads. The Scythians controlled a lucrative overland trade with Central Asia, and the Bactrian Greeks developed a maritime trade between India and Persia and Arabia. They were not interested in building political units, kingdoms, or empires. The Kushans ruled a vast area from the Arabian Sea to the Himalayas in the north and the Ganges River in the east. They ruled the Punjab for some 200 years but never penetrated into southern India. But as the vast majority of the invaders had done, they stopped at the Narmada River and the Vindhya Mountains, remaining in the north of the country.

For many centuries, southern India remained apart from northern turmoil. It also had three independent kingdoms—the Cholas, the Pandyas, and the Cheras—whose peoples were descendants of the Dravidians, not the Aryans. Even their language, Tamil, was not related to the northern languages. "Tamil land" was quite different from Aryan India. Only the Kushans were able to infiltrate deeper into India, from the Indo-Gangetic plain to Varanasi (modern Banaras) and later to the Deccan plateau. This was possible only after they learned to grow crops of their own.

The Kushans are important not only for their political power but also for their impact on Buddhism and Hinduism. Kanishka, the greatest of Kushan kings, became a patron of Buddhism and helped spread that faith through the entire Far East. The early Buddhist cult became the complex religious system called Mahayana Buddhism, which reveres Buddha as a saviour god, and Indian sculptors started to carve the figure of Buddha as supreme god. This was the starting point of the masses of iconographic sculpture so important to Hinduism.

After the fall of the Kushans, a power vacuum was created—like the one that preceded the rise of the Mauryan Empire. And once again, it was the kingdom of Magadha that gave birth to a new empire. A man of obsure origin, Gupta, drove out the invaders and established the Gupta dynasty in 320 A.D., calling himself Chandragupta I. When he died in 335 A.D., he controlled a large part of northern India. The empire reached its height under Gupta's grandson, Chandragupta II, who died in 415 A.D. after a reign of thirty-five years. Like Asoka, he was a devout Buddhist and a patron of the arts. There was a tremendous development in literature as well as in poetry and drama. Evidence of the Gupta dynasty's contribution to art was discovered in the frescos of the Ajanta Caves, where murals covering the walls of this Buddhist shrine colorfully depict the life of the Gupta court. The University of Nalanda, with eight colleges and three libraries, was also established. Indian scholars developed Arabic numerals as well as the symbol zero. The advances made in the fields of astronomy and mathematics were yet unparalelled in the Western world. The Indian lack of interest in recording historical events is the reason so little is actually known about Gupta's empire and its rulers. Fa-Hsien, a Chinese Buddhist monk who visited a great number of Indian shrines and monasteries between the years 401 and 410, is perhaps the best source of Indian history during this period.

For the Hindus of India, the greatest of all ages of their country took place between 320 and 467 A.D., when the Gupta dynasty ruled the northern part of the subcontinent. Peace, unity, prosperity, and well-being prevailed to a degree unmatched in India before or since, when the arts and sciences reached creative peaks.

This exceptional era came to an end when the Guptas were overthrown by the White Huns, who came from Central Asia and occupied a great part of northern India. By the sixth century, the Gupta dynasty had come to an end, and its palaces, temples, paintings, and sculptures were in ruins. The Huns' rule was short and brutal, ending in 528 A.D. After a period of chaos, a descendant of the Guptas regained the throne for a short while, but his death in 647 was followed by 200 years of upheaval. A group of militant aristocrats, the Rajputs, dominated Indian history during the 400 years that preceded the Arab invasion of India. The Moslem conquerors, unlike the people who had preceded them, did not adopt India's caste system or her religious beliefs. They confronted Hinduism's polytheism with a stern, unbending monotheism, and they countered the rigid caste system with the egalitarian belief that all Moslems were brothers, regardless of social class or color.

The Moslems invaded India in three different waves: the Arabs in the eighth century, the Turks in the twelfth century, and the Turkish-Afghans in the sixteenth century. The Arab Moslems came from the far western regions of Arabia, via Persia, soon after the death of the Prophet Mohammed in 632. A century later, they overran the Sind and the lower Indus Valley, on the western side of the Thon Desert. They dominated the entire northwestern border regions of India, which became strongholds of Islam. Settling in the Sind, they converted many Hindus and Buddhists to Islam. They ruled for some 300 years.

The Turkish Islamic invasion occurred 150 years later. The leader, Mohammed Ghuri, moved down from Afghanistan and by 1186 had defeated the Arab Moslem rulers of Sind, occupied Lahore, and marched on Delhi, at the center of the Indo-Gangetic plain. Ghuri continued his conquest despite the resistance of the Rajput armies, plundered the holy city of Varanasi, and ransacked the capital of Bengal; by 1206, his successors controlled nearly all India north of the Decccan. One of his generals, Qutr-ud-din-Aibak, proclaimed an independent Moslem kingdom, the Sultanate of Delhi, where his successors ruled until the sixteenth century.

In the early thirteenth century, the Mongols of Central Asia swept through an area of over 1,000 miles, from Japan to Hungary. Genghis Khan (1162–1227) and his troops rampaged through all the lands as far as Baghdad, where they massacred scholars and burned libraries. Northern India escaped such a fate, probably because of its mountain barriers, and thus became a sanctuary for refugees, including Moslem scholars and artists. The combination of Islamic scholarship and the artistic roots of ancient Persia and classical Greece created a civilization of greatness. The Mongol armies conquered the entire Indo-Gangetic plain and even large areas of the Deccan, but they were unable to control such a vast area. A number of their governors proclaimed independence, and India became a conglomeration of Moslem and Hindu states. The last of these independent sultans was defeated by Tamerlane (1336?–1405), the famous Tartar conqueror, who crossed the Indus River in 1398.

The third wave of Moslem conquerors were Turkish-Afghans, who were Persian in culture and Moslem in religion and came to be known as *Mughals* or *Moguls* (corruptions of Mongols). The Moguls ruled for seven generations, from the sixteenth to the eighteenth centuries, and their empire reached its height under Akbar (1542–1605), whose vast domain stretched from the Bay of Bengal to Kabul and from Lahore, in the north, into the Deccan, in the south. He reigned for forty-nine years (from 1556, when he was a child of thirteen years, until his death), and his three heirs remained in power for another century.

His grandfather Babur was the founder of the dynasty, but he died barely four years after his arrival in India. He was succeeded by his son Humayun, who promptly lost the control of the territories his father had won. Ousted from his throne and pursued by his enemies, he escaped to the desert as a refugee. In his desert tent, his son Akbar was born; he became the greatest of the great Moguls. His story is full of drama and love, pomp and pageantry, a glittering court, palace intrigues, a large harem, and military and political power. He was among the first Indian rulers to have a vision of a united India. Despite his lack of formal education, he was an important patron of the arts. And thanks to his prodigious memory, he was able to have discussions with scholars, intellectuals, and holy men. He was also the first of the great Mogul builders. At the age of twenty-nine, he ordered the construction of a new capital at the dusty village of Sikri, in northern India, twenty-four miles from the earlier capital at Agra. He renamed his capital Fatehpur-Sikri (City of Victory), and he ruled from there from 1571 to 1585, when he left for Lahore, troubled by revolts in other parts of the country. At his capital, he encouraged draftsmen and artisans, builders and singers, poets and mystics, so it was full of paintings and miniatures, carpets and sculptures. He was the first ruler in northern India to mint gold coins. Fatehpur-Sikri had palaces, halls for public audiences, marble tombs, and mosques, combining Hindu style with Mogul geometry. In his later years, Akbar relocated his court at nearby Agra. Even after his death, his capital continued to hold an important place in the Mogul empire. Under the last Mogul emperor, the bigot and ascetic Aurangzeb, the city lost its significance and became the isolated place it is today. But even so, it reflects, perhaps, Akbar's unique place in history—peerless among his contemporaries and a legend to the generations that followed him.

It is interesting that the 600 years of Moslem rule did not bring about mass conversion. When their empires fell, less than a fifth of the Indian population was Moslem. Hinduism's passivity proved its strength; it was never vanquished by its many rulers.

The Religions of India

India's history is inexorably linked with the Indian religion—Hinduism—and it is almost impossible to study one without the other. Its continuity has been unbroken from ancient times to the present. The oldest religion was an animistic and totemic cult whose worshippers believed in the soul as a separate entity and spirits who dwelt in stones, reptiles and other animals, trees, rivers, mountains, stars, and the like. Later Indian religions are customarily divided into four periods, each based on a specific religious tenet: the Vedic, Brahmanic, Buddhist, and Neo-Brahmanic or Hinduist.

During the Vedic Age, from about 1500 to 600 B.C., Indian life was based on the great religious encyclopaedia known as the Vedas—the famous psalmodies in homage of the gods. They are vaguely dated about the second millenium B.C. There are four Vedas: the Rig Veda, the most important, is a collection of 1,028 hymns addressed to the many deities of the Indian pantheon (*Veda* has been translated as "science" and *Rig* as "praise"—thus "the science of praise"); the Sama Veda "the science of melodies"; the Yajur Veda, "the science of sacrifices"; and the Atarva Veda, "the science of magic." Other Vedic literature consists of the Samhitas, which contain the Mantras (hymns and poems for the people); the Brahmanas (rituals and prayers for the priests); the Aranyakas (text of the forests, for the hermit saints); and the Upanishads, speeches and commentaries for philosophers. These belong to a later period, from about 800 to 600 B.C. The Vedas were written in Sanskrit, considered a sacred language.

Vedic divinities were many, but the principals among them were Agni, the goddess of fire; Varuna, the god of the skies; Vayu, of the air; Maruts, of the sun; Soma, of the liquor. The supreme deity was Indra, the god of storms and wars.

In contrast to ancient Egypt, in India, the living or dead body had no significance whatsoever. No monuments were built to house embalmed bodies, which were even regarded with a certain amount of contempt, because the people were absorbed by a metaphysical reality.

The Brahmanic Age, which lasted from about 600 to 200 B.C., reaching its heights between the fourth and the third centuries B.C. Whereas the Vedic Age centered in the Indus Valley, the Brahmanic Age centered in the Ganges Plain. It was during this age that the brahmans became the most important of the castes. According to tradition, they approached divinity and were the representatives of the gods on earth, in charge of performing religious rituals, interpreting divine omens, and tutoring the royal children.

During this age of wars and conquests, the priests raised themselves above the nobles and even above the king. They claimed responsibility for the preservation of the cosmic order (*Rita*) through the performance of complex rituals—rituals that were in their hands alone. This was a period of absolute theocracy, yet it produced the Laws of Manu, also known as the Manava-Dharma-Sutra, the basis for political government and justice. This period is also known as the Age of the Sutras ("strings" or "manuals of instruction"), dating from about the fifth century B.C. The Sutras were brief maxims meant to define, teach, and codify the proper conduct of every man at each moment of his life. For such a purpose, the brahmans elaborated upon these maxims in manuals containing detailed instructions: the Shrauta Sutras, concerned with sacrificial rituals, and the Grihya Sutras, concerned with conduct in domestic relations. The Dharma Sutras, which appeared in about 300 B.C., contain the sacred quasi-legal material, similar to the Hebrew Torah: divine teaching as to individual and social conduct. It is common for the Sutras to devote a chapter to the duties of the king. They are supposedly invested with divine authority and contain the claim that at the time of creation, human society was divided into four classes: the brahmans (priests) the kshatriyas (kings and warriors), the vaishyas (farmers and merchants); and the shudras (serfs). Each member of the three upper classes went through four stages during his lifetime: the student stage, during which he lived and studied in the home of a guru (teacher); the householder stage, during which he married and raised a family; the hermit stage, a period of retirement and meditation during which he gave up his worldly responsibilities and lived simply; and finally, the complete withdrawal and ascetic stage, during which he became a Sannyasi, gave up all material possessions, and lived as a homeless wanderer, with no physical needs or earthly ties. During these stages, man was to strive toward four goals, in ascending order of importance: (1) acquiring material wealth; (2) self-gratification through enjoyment of physical pleasures; (3) performing men's duties according to what is right and to the law; and (4) transcending the earthly world through the cleansing of the soul from desires and passions. Having attained the fourth goal, man was freed from the cycle of reincarnation.

The Buddhist Age originated in India in the sixth century B.C. but reached its peak between the second century B.C. and the second century A.D. In a sense, it was an expression of the inevitable reaction to the severity of the Brahmanic Age. The young Siddhartha Guatama, who came to be known as Buddha, supposedly came of a noble and wealthy family of northern India. Dissatisfied with the teachings of his guru, he sought his own truth—and a new religion was born. The popularity of Buddhism might be attributed to a number of factors: Buddha taught in the vernacular instead of in Sanskrit, thus making teachings available to a wider segment of the population. Buddhism contained no elaborate rituals; anyone with the necessary self-discipline could follow its teachings. Buddhism did not concern itself with metaphysical speculations about the universe. In other words, it was a religion without a god and without a prescribed system of worship; and Buddha's five moral rules (not to kill any living creature; not to take anything that has not been given to us; not to lie; not to drink inebriating liquors; and to lead a chaste life) were so widely accepted because of their basic humanity and because they contributed to bettering the relationship between man and his fellows. Buddha ignored the distinction between castes; he was concerned with relieving the suffering of all human beings rather than emphasizing the differences between them.

Buddhism was the major civilizing force throughout southeast Asia from the second to the ninth centuries A.D. In spite of the fact that Buddha himself resisted deification, after his death his successors split his movement into sects—the Greater and Lesser Vehicles, both claiming to lead man to salvation. The Greater Vehicle, with 250 million followers in Asia, not only deified Buddha, the "Illuminated," but introduced a cosmology of heavens and hells, peopled it with saints, and even embellished religious practice with ritual use of incense, candles, and holy water—all of which Buddha had opposed. Afterward, Buddha's teachings underwent significant changes and became a complex religion system called Mahayana Buddhism, which also reveres Buddha as a savior and, for the first time, introduced a carved figure depicting Buddha as a supreme deity. Buddhism flourished in India for more than a millennium after the death of Buddha. In spite of the fact that it was accepted by the entire Eastern world, it almost completely disappeared in India by the fifth century A.D., perhaps because it gradually fused with India's new religion: neo-Brahmanism, or Hinduism.

Among the surviving remainders of Buddhism are the *stupas,* or memorial shrines. The most impressive of them still standing is the one at Sanchi, in central India, which was decorated during the first century B.C. Its main symbols are the Bodhi tree, under which Buddah was enlightened, and the wheel, representing the doctrine itself. Buddhist temples are found almost everywhere in the Middle East. In 1984, archaeologists in Kabul unearthed a "majestic" temple, 1,600 years old, containing, among many other items, terracotta statues as well as bronze and copper coins.

By the middle of the sixth century B.C., the brahmans' predominance was challenged by other than Buddha. Of the many cults that sprang up, only Jainism survived. Founded by a young man named Nataputta Vardhamana, Jainism accepted *Karma* (one of whose several definitions is the ethical law of cause and effect, which evaluates all spiritual and physical acts in life and determines which types deserve reincarnation), and *reincarnation,* as well as the concept of *Brahma* (the neutral and impersonal spirit) and *Atman* (the internal ego of every man) but provided new interpretations. For Jains, all creatures and objects had souls—man, trees, stones, and so on. Violence against any of these creatures was forbidden. Jainist monks carried whisk brooms to brush aside insects and wore masks over their noses and mouths to avoid accidentally breathing in a living creature. Jains could not be farmers, because plowing destroys creatures living in the soil. They normally dealt with trade and commerce. They were vegetarians and ate only in the daytime, to avoid harming insects in the dark. They walked naked and wore a loincloth. Despite their veneration of life, they took a paradoxical delight in death; Suicide by starvation was considered a supreme accomplishment.

Although Buddhism and Jainism all but disappeared, many of their principles remain deep-rooted in the Indian soul. They helped contribute to the reformation of Hinduism, a reformation that was to bring about the fourth and last period of religious development in India: *Neo-Brahmanism* or *Hinduism,* which flourished between the second and ninth centuries A.D. Hinduism gradually became more flexible until it could accommodate the more primitive deities, the philosophical speculations of the brahmans, the nonviolence of Jainism, and the ethics of Buddhism, which ignored the traditional Indian caste distinctions. The Hinduism that evolved and that remains the prevalent religion on the subcontinent has millions of gods, no fixed system of worship, and no clergy, organization, or established creed. There is no single prophet or founding father. However, Hinduism provides a solid foundation from which to achieve unity within India's diversity. This faculty for accommodating differences enabled Hinduism to prevail over the other religions of India.

Out of the millions of deities in the Hindu pantheon, five are most significant, and most Hindus worship one of the five. These gods are Brahma, the Vedic Indra, the supreme masculine god, creator of the universe; Shiva, destroyer and regenerator; Vishnu, preserver of the universe created by Brahma; Shiva's wife, a mother-goddess known by many names, including Kali, Durga, Parvati, and Uma; and Krishna, one of several human reincarnations of Vishnu.

Hinduism recognized four basic types of man in the material world, known as *Maya* ("illusion" in Sanskrit). They are the meditative, emotional, active, and experimental. Each type has its own yoga: a system of mental and physical self-discipline, including a number of exercises and postures, that brings man closer to god.

The Hindu belief is essentially based on three fundamental concepts: reincarnation, Karma, and Dharma. The human soul is caught in a cycle of reincarnation; the soul is born and reborn in a new body, until it achieves its destiny—an understanding of bliss. The cycle of reincarnation is governed by Karma, a law that judges all man's physical and spiritual actions. A good life will be rewarded by a reincarnation of a higher order; an evil life will be punished by a reincarnation of a lower order—a worm, a reptile, an insect. Man is bound by Dharma, the moral code that determines the right way of life. Each man's Dharma is different, according to his role in life, his caste. A man who lives according to his Dharma will have a good Karma; thus, his next reincarnation will be in a better life. This system is inexorably intertwined with the caste system and justifies the inequalities inherent in Indian society. Sri Paripurnanand Varma, the former president of the All India Crime Prevention Society, wrote the following in a personal letter dated August 9, 1985:

How can there be a total eclipse of the Soul after death? I am not questioning the wisdom of any Faith or Religion, but I am simply asking about the rationale of the matter. If one day, the Day of Judgment will come, will the sinner remain in purgatory till eternity and the good man in heaven for an eternal period? Thus, it is more scientific to accept that there is a constant change and continuation of existence, by rebirth—a rotation of life—and death and suffering for past sins in the life itself. So, we are to be born again, and who knows we may meet again!

The brahmans (priests) were Hinduism's most privileged caste, since the Laws of Manu determined that everything in the universe belonged to them. The source of their power lay in their monopoly on learning. As the sole experts in the Vedas, they were stronger than the king. A brahman who committed the most heinous crime imaginable would not be sentenced to death, but would only be banished, under conditions that allowed him to retain his wealth. And the *shudras,* or "untouchables," were the lowest of the low— beneath even women, who were considered the source of all mortal woes. A shudra who heard the reading of the Vedas would have his ears filled with molten lead; if he recited them, his tongue was to be split; and if he learned them by heart, he was split in two. One who seduced the wife of a brahman was emasculated and all his property confiscated.

Social Structure

The earliest Indian tribes were herdsmen, and even after they settled in small agricultural villages, the cow remained their most valued possession. Later, as communities grew and land became limited because of the growth of the population, a kind of feudalism became evident. The land laborer became a feudal tenant and sometimes even a serf. Absolute monarchies were established—yet empires were often short-lived, and few rulers had the strength or influence to leave a lasting mark.

The Aryans who first came to India had a rather simple social system, loosely divided into three classes, that later developed into the caste system. Besides the king (*raja*), and the nobles (*rajanyas*), there were the priests (brahmans), and the commoners (*vis*)—tenders of cattle, farmers, artisans, and tradesmen. The prisoners of war constituted the fourth class—menial laborers, serfs and slaves, inferior to all the other classes. However, it was not impossible to move from one class to another. Family and tribal life were patriarchal but open and informal. The chief, like the Roman *pater familias,* did not have absolute authority and was subject to the dictates of old traditions.

Thousands of years later, when crafts and manual occupations became more diversified, the caste system began to crystallize. The brahmans became the arbiters of Indian life; the social classes became gradually more complex, hereditary, and rigid because of religious rules and tenets; the segregation came to dominate Indian society. The castes prevented the mixture of blood in order to preserve ethnic purity; Aryans and Hindus could not mix with foreigners. During the Buddhic Age, the caste system persisted, and even the protests of Buddha could not alter the fundamentals of Indian society.

To meet the threat of revolts from within and attacks from without, the kings recruited standing armies, which allowed them to claim a rank far above all the other rajanyas. However, the priests succeeded in maintaining the perennial covenant between the altar and the sword; while the kings protected the priests, the priests reciprocated by giving them religious support. The priest who became *purohita* (the domestic priest of the ruler) enjoyed an even greater influence.

The original basic four castes included the Kshatriyas, who, according to a Vedic hymn, came from the arms of the gods and were thus the most important. Within this caste were the kings and the noblemen as well as the soldiers. The increasing importance of religion gave a great deal of power to the priests, the brahmans, born from the mouth of the gods. The third class was formed by the vaishyas—merchants, farmers, traders, and other freemen— thought to be born from the thighs of gods. Finally came the shudras, or serfs, who constituted the majority of the indigenous population and came from the feet of the gods. They were also known as the "untouchables" and were regarded by all other classes as something less than human. A shudra could never be free of his status, because, like all caste divisions, it was inherited.

The Aryans were also unwilling to mix with the descendants of the primitive tribes—some forty or more types of "impure" human beings. One of the most despised was the chandala or pariah (from the Tamil word *paraiyan,* meaning "low caste"), mentioned in the Laws of Manu. These pariahs could not leave their villages, located far from populated areas, without striking a wooden clapper to warn of their "contaminating" approach. Their touch, sight, or breath was considered a tragedy by those of other castes.

During the Vedic Age, this system of segregated groups was known as *varna,* meaning "color"; afterward, it was known as *jati* (birth). From the sixteenth century, Portuguese travelers applied their own word for clan or family—*casta,* from the Latin *castus,* meaning "pure."

Each of the many Indian castes has its own traditional rules for cooking and eating, marriage, and occupations. Cooking is of paramount importance, perhaps out of fear of spiritual pollution through food—one of mankind's oldest known beliefs. Each caste had its own prescribed diet; the upper classes were usually vegetarians. There was also a strict ban on intercaste marriages. Each caste had its own specialized occupation, a fact that strengthened the caste system by emphasizing the interdependence of the castes. This interdependence also created an economically viable society among groups of people who had contact only at the trade and occupational level.

Indeed, the caste system gave its members a sense of security, since the caste assumed all financial responsibilities for every one of its members, from the cradle to the grave. Each caste had its own legal machinery to punish wrongdoers within the caste and to defend caste honor regarding offenses for which the offender was not subject to trial. If a merchant was insulted by his landlord, the merchant caste could close their shops until the injury had been atoned for and the landlord punished by his own caste.

The caste system is indeed a distinctive social arrangement. Caste is the living enactment of *difference* in every detail: life and death, truth and lie, karma and dharma. Here the unit is not the individual but the group to which he belongs.

The Sikh of the Punjab

Historian Khushwant Singh describes the Sikh religion as a reformist movement, founded by a Hindu called Nanak Chand about 1500 A.D. He sought to do away with Hinduism's caste distinctions and its many gods. Guru Nanak, as he was known, distilled Hindu and Moslem beliefs and drew converts from both religions. Arjun, the fifth guru, compiled the *Adi Granth,* the Sikhs' holy book, with more than 6,000 verses written in a simple language understood by every Punjabi, Hindu, or Sikh. He also founded the Sikh holy city of Amritsar. His execution by the Mogul Emperor Jehangir in 1606 produced the first stirrings of Sikh militancy. But it was Gobind Singh, the last of the gurus, who gave the Sikhs their martial tradition and the characteristics of unshorn hair and turbans. Stung by Mogul persecution, in 1699 he forged the Sikhs into a fighting fraternity called *Khalsa,* a Persian word meaning "pure." He stipulated that the names of his followers should include the word *Singh* (lion), as a way of avoiding the caste distinctions of Hindu surnames, and that they should observe the five *k*'s: *kesh,* hair and beard unshorn; *kangha,* a comb worn in the hair; *kuchha,* a pair of shorts worn by all Sikh men and women; *kara,* a steel bracelet worn on the right wrist; and *kirpan,* a holy sabre carried by all Sikhs. Finally, he decreed that he was the last guru and that after his death, Sikhs should worship only their holy books.

Hindu-Sikh links remained strong until Punjab was partitioned in 1947, when India and Pakistan gained their independence. At least 2.5 million Sikhs poured into Indian Punjab from the Pakistani side during the partition. Since then, the Sikhs have had a feeling of suffocation—the real origin of the communal violence between Hindu and Sikh—aggravated by the establishment by the Indian government of the new states at Haryana and Himachal within Punjab. And in 1984, the Golden Temple of Amritsar was the site of the bloody Indian army invasion. The dome of the building was blasted, and the facade of the Akal Takht, "the immortal seat of power," was badly damaged; but the Kotha Sahib, the *sanctum sanctorum* where the holy books are kept at night, was practically intact. It is still not known how many people were killed then, although it is assumed that 1,000 Sikh extremists and at least 200 Indian troops died during the June 1984 fighting. From then on, there have been frequent clashes between Hindus and Sikhs, and they may last for a long time to come.

Political Framework, Family, and Economic Status

During the three Indian empires, the king was the supreme military, legislative, and judicial authority. He controlled a centralized and rigid bureaucracy, with separate departments for trade and commerce, agriculture, forestry, public works, and so on. The bureaucracy's head offices were in the capital, with branches at local centers. The smallest social unit was the village, followed by the district (a group of villages), each with a governor, and finally the province, each headed by a viceroy who reported directly to the central government. Only four of these provinces have been identified, with their capitals in Taxila, Ujjain, Dhauli, and Suvarnargia.

The seventh book of the Laws of Manu deals with the rights and duties of the king, stating that he should be devoted to the welfare of the community and to setting a personal example. The government was nothing but an indirect brahman theocracy, since the king existed mainly to maintain the divine order of the castes. If it were true that a brahman could never be appointed king (who had to be a kshatriya), it was also true that the king was supposed to act only after consulting the brahman council.

Monogamy was the general practice, except among the king and nobles. Marriage was for life, but a sick, rebellious, wasteful, or quarrelsome woman could be replaced by another wife. The Laws of Manu opposed marriages between people suffering from tuberculosis, epilepsy, leprosy, chronic dyspepsia, hemorrhoids, frigidity or lack of virility, and extreme talkativeness. No one could marry outside his own caste. If a man married a shudra, his children would be pariahs.

The father was the head of the family and owner of all its property. When he died, the elder son (if he was worthy) would take the entire inheritance for himself, but he had to care for the welfare of his family. If the elder son misbehaved or resigned his rights, the other brothers would divide the inheritance, in equal parts, among themselves. Family property was kept in common, if possible, and passed to the male descendants from generation to generation (Manu IX, 104 f). Wives, children, and slaves could not possess goods; whatever they earned was the property of the head of the family (Manu VIII, 416, and Narada V, 39).

The impact of the Moslem philosophy brought about a change in women's status. In the north of the country, they began to use the *purdah* (veil) and married women were required to avoid all social contact. The wives of the *rajputana,* the king's sons, accompanied their husbands to their tombs, in accordance with the rite of *suttee*—the custom of burning the wife on the funeral pyre of her husband. The suttee is not mentioned in the Laws of Manu.

With the exception of the three imperial periods, when India was more or less united, India has always remained a strange mixture of peoples. Political disunity proliferated to such a degree that the fragmented Europe of medieval times looks positively monolithic. But in spite of unending dynastic wars, revolts, and all kinds of uprisings, there never was a war involving the entire country, and the pattern of small states prevailed until India won her independence in 1947.

Poverty is so extended in India, and was so since immemorial times, that the selling of children as slaves, bonded laborers, or prostitutes—for no more than 1,000 to 2,000 rupees (US$100–200)—is an established racket, particularly in Uttar Pradesh. Today, it is a well-organized business, with its own schedule of supply and demand and price fixing.

The Meanings of Some Ancient Indian Psychological, Legal, and Penological Expressions

Vidhi denotes a rule, formula, ordinance, precept, or statute that governs human conduct. *Pāpa* is any action against socioreligious, cultural, or moral vidhis, usually recognized as a sin. *Aparādha* or crime, is any action against the throne, administration, or legal vidhi. Any action may be perfectly legal but it may be sinful; therefore, society needs to be protected from both possibilities. *Vidhāna* is the proper interpretation and consecutive action in relation to a particular vidhi. *Ācarana* signifies a person's mode of behaving in accordance with his mental dispositions. *Vyāvahāra,* in the context of law and justice, is everything related to the legal procedure in a court of law. *Jadabuddhi* (mental deficiency), *unmāda* (madness, insanity), and *smrtibhramsa* (psychopathy) are states that affect the consciousness of one's *ācarana,* needing special examination before assigning criminal responsibility. *Manobhūmi* represents the mental plane—the cognitive field or mind—which depends on both *prārabdhājna* (congenital predisposition) and *ārabdhajnāna* (environmental factors). *Danda* is a force that stands against any undesirable move, but in penology it represents justice, punishment, chastisement, imprisonment, reprimand, and fine. If properly administered, it would facilitate expiation. *Dharma* is a term widely used in different contexts in social and religious fields. From the sociolegal point of view, it means strictly performing all prescribed duties and responsibilities of an individual in relation to the basic purposes of life. *Sāsti,* meaning punishment, was the only prescription for an offender, varying according to the gravity of the offense. It was understood that there are undetected offenses due to obvious human limitations or lapses; *viveka,* a highly critical faculty for self-evaluation, guides human behavior toward ideal conduct, free from egotism and parochialism and respecting all creatures. Only then do a person's actions become free from the elements of harm, hatred, and malice. *Buddhi* is the mind as an inner instrument that reaches out to the external environment, creating sensations and impressions and unifying them into a coherent knowledge. After the mind has perceived a certain object, situation, or incident, it is the buddhi that guides man's action. It is the primary entity that guides man's behavior, and *sadācāra* is the ideal conduct.

Ancient Indian law was a precept based on ethics and piety, on social needs and propriety. It was an ordinance for the conduct of daily life, based on minimum requirements; therefore, its evasion was a sin or crime that had to be expiated. Indian life is still governed by the old concepts of dharma and sadācāra, although they are slowly disappearing in the wave of modernity.

What is important to note is the fact that ancient Indian scholars attributed human conduct to mental peculiarities—buddhi. Therefore, human behavior has to be judged from a psychological point of view; this was the basic assumption for the formulation of law codes and jurisprudence.

Legal Philosophy in Ancient India

It seems doubtful that the ancient Hindus had any written legislation. No written inscriptions have been discovered prior to the Mauryan Dynasty. The earliest surviving Indian literature is purely religious. Legal matters are mentioned only after the brahmans came to take an active role in the administration of justice. Information regarding the early Indian laws has been gleaned from a variety of sources: the *Arthashastra,* a secular treatise on the political and economic framework, written at the end of the fourth century B.C. and attributed to Chandragupta's chief-minister—a brahman known as Kautilya Chanakya, the "Indian Macchiavelli," because of his cold-blooded aphorisms about politics of his time; reports written by Megasthenes, a Greek ambassador to the Mauryan court; the Laws of Manu, and subsequent documents. The Arthashastra cannot be considered a book of law, but neither is it a text of religious law; its third book deals with the administration of justice and starts declaring that the royal power, when exercised with impartiality and responsibility, is the binding force of the entire world. Its first chapter enumerates the four elements that form the foundations of the proper administration of justice: royal edicts (*rajasasana*), the history of precedents (*charitra*), the evidence of witnesses (*vyāvahāra*), and religious law (*dharma*). The four are given in descending order of importance; if a conflict arose between the king's law and the religious one, the former prevailed.

The brahman's role in the administration of justice was the inevitable outcome of their monopoly on literacy. Although not all brahmans could read or write, scribes were educated only within the temples. There were no legal text per se, but religious sources, which became a mixture of religious and moral tenets, gradually developed into "proper" legal texts.

The most important texts of the Vedic Age were the dharma shastras (law books), which, as religious texts, included certain main aspects of brahmanic teaching. The Manava Dharma Shastra, the Laws of Manu, were followed by the law books of the Institutes of Vishnu in the third century A.D.; the law code of Yajnavalkya, a century later; and the Code of Narada, of the fifth century A.D. The latter is free of religious matters and is a valuable treatise of a specific legal system. However, it retains a religious echo of the brahmans, who contributed a great deal toward drafting the text. If the first legal documents are awkward and even contradictory, the Code of Narada is just the opposite, being the first code to distinguish between civil and criminal law. Finally, there are the brhaspati smrti, of the eighth century A.D.

The Laws of Manu include a number of rules that were never actually administered in India. To a large extent, they represent the brahmans' ideal picture of what the law ought to be. It is difficult to date the Laws of Manu with any precision; scholars place them between 1280 and 880 B.C. and believe that they were transmitted orally from one generation to the next until they were put into writing at a date which is also open to speculation—anywhere between the first century B.C. and the fourth century A.D. Whatever the case, the laws are, in fact, from the Brahmanic Age, composed by the brahmans, and from a strictly brahmanic point of view that glorifies their caste.

The first six books of Manu refer exclusively to the way a brahman must live as well as his rights and duties. The seventh book is devoted to the rights and duties of the king. Much of the eighth and some of the ninth books refer to the duties of the judges and to criminal and civil matters. The tenth and eleventh books deal with the lives of the hermits and other ascetics, who voluntarily live in isolation and dedicate their lives to meditation. They also touch upon the situation of the "untouchables"—their penitence and expiation of their sins. The twelfth and last book is dedicated to the transmigration of the soul.

In the opening verses, the great sages approach the divine Manu (the father of man) and pray to him to declare the sacred laws, the rights and duties of each of the castes—particularly that of the brahmans. He consents to do so, gives them an account of Creation as well as of his own origin, and declares that having learned the sacred laws from the Creator, he has brought them to the sages. Basically, it is an instructional text with which the brahmans were to teach the Aryans. The chapters referring to law and justice comprise only a third of the whole, and only a third of this is actually law, since much of the law is unstated, as the code itself is subject to local customs and practices. According to these chapters, the king is invested with supreme moral authority and is to decide all cases according to the principles drawn from local custom and from the sacred Laws of Manu. The learned brahman is the legal adviser of the king and his deputy in the decision of lawsuits. If the king does not personally investigate the suit, he is to appoint a learned brahman to try them (Manu VIII: 9).

The Laws of Manu are more an ethical code than a system of applied legislation. They constitute a complete and authoritative statement of the Hindu religion and social norms, describing an ideal system of justice. Given the political structure of the subcontinent, no legal code could be applied to the entire expanse that was India. Since the caste system was considered to be the ideal structure of a perfect society, the code determines the rights and duties of the different castes. Manu himself is the mythical ancestor of the brahman caste and is represented as the son of god who receives the laws of Brahma himself. The brahmans' 2,685 verses, which originally were considered the specific caste's manual of behavior, were gradually accepted as the behavioral code of the entire Indian community.

The legal philosophy of the Laws of Manu is based on eighteen basic points, which are the source of all unrest and conflict that affect the human race:

1. The payment of debts (loans of money at interest was the common practice)

2. The payment of pledges and trust deposits

3. The selling of something by someone who is not the proper owner

4. Public works executed by trusts, partnerships, or companies

5. The recuperation of loaned objects and the reclamation of gifts

6. The nonpayment of salaries or other similar pledges

7. Nonfulfillment of contracts

8. The annulment of purchases

9. Disputes regarding cattle or between masters and servants

10. Problems of boundaries

11. Insults, slanders, and defamations

12. Ill treatment of people

13. Stealing

14. Violence

15. Adultery and kidnapping of women

16. Rights and duties of husbands and wives
17. The partition of inheritances
18. Bettings during animal fights

In ancient India, sins were punished by expiation, as ordained in the sacred books, whereas crimes and other similar deviations were punishable by punishments inflicted by the court and the king. Punishment was considered a religious duty, but extreme precautions were taken before determining guilt and inflicting any punishment, because the ancient lawgivers were anxious to avoid miscarriages of justice. The law was to be interpreted according to individual circumstances, and the king had to be most careful in his decisions.

Manu held that the state's ultimate tool of enforcement was force, called *rajdharm* in the Mahabharata Epic (Mahab. XII-I: 58–3) and *dandniti* in the Laws of Manu. *Danda* differs from expiation, because it utilizes physical punishment: "*Danda* protects all subjects. When they are sleeping, *Danda* keeps awake. Law is nothing but *Danda* itself" (Manu VIII: 14). But the Laws of Manu, the Arthashastra of Kautilya Chanakya, and the Mahabharata (Mahab. XII: 58, 78, and 79), all state that danda must be wielded with maximum discretion: "If it is not used, there is the law of the jungle (*matsyanyava*), the strong devouring the weaker; if it is used too harshly, the subjects will be distressed; if it is used too lightly, the king will not be held in awe; and if it is used in the proper manner, the subjects are happy and the realm progresses." They agree that the proper use of the science of punishment establishes law and order in society and "indirectly brings about a natural tendency in the average individual to obey the law of the land, which renders the frequent use of force unnecessary. It ultimately secures proper progress in religion, philosophy and economic well-being" (Arth. Chana. I:4).

Crime is defined in these ancient scriptures as an act contrary to either the divine code or the state laws. Deviation from the code or the laws was considered an antisocial act. *Dharma* was not a legislated measure. If religious in nature, it was of superhuman origin; if secular, it was based on universally valid customs. Therefore, law governed even the king. According to the Laws of Manu, the king's scepter symbolized justice, which he was to dispense with discrimination and moderation. Were the king to break the laws, the same scepter would destroy him. Emperor Asoka, in the thirteenth Rock-Edict wrote:

And even [the inhabitants of] the forests which are [included] in the dominions of *Devanampriya* [the expression *deva* originally meant "brilliant" but afterward was also used as "divine"] even those he pacifies [and] converts, they are all told of the power [to punish them] which *Devanampriya* [possesses] in spite of his repentence, in order that they may be ashamed [of their crimes] and not be killed. For *Devanampriya* desires towards all beings abstention from hurting, self-control [and] impartiality in [cases of] violence. (*Shabazgarhi* version)

It is not difficult, therefore, to grasp that a development of the law similar to that of the cuneiform laws can also be detected in the laws of ancient India, with a trend toward talionic remunerative laws.

The Administration of Justice

In ancient India, the administration of justice was one of the primary functions of the state. The king, the ruler, or the head of state—whatever he might be—was the fountain of justice and equity. His foremost duty was to protect his subjects from every harm or devaluation of human worth. Such a protection was twofold: (1) protection from internal antisocial forces affecting one's personal and social life and (2) protection from the military aggression of invaders. It is no wonder, therefore, that there are no references to any judicial organization of the Vedic Age, which was at least 1,000 years before the Laws of Manu. Vedic literature nowhere refers to the king as a judge, either in civil or criminal cases. In other words, the Indian classical four phases of individual life (mentioned earlier) are maintained in proper order because of a proper danda—the administration of justice by the king.

The king named the members (*sabhya*) of a court of law (*vicārasabhā*), but he himself could judge a lawsuit in accordance with the directives given in the authentic texts (*sāstra*) and in consultation with a virtuous and wise brahman, who must have a proven ability to treat both friend and foe with an impartial attitude for adjudication purposes. If there is no one at hand, the king may select any person with such qualities from any social stratum. If any member of the court should be found guilty of corrupt practices, the king must impose a fine—double the amount usually prescribed to punish such an offense. On the other hand, the chief magistrate must not remain bound to uphold the personal view of the king and has to reach independent decisions. Court members and their assessors are not paid officers, but the king pays honorarium (*dāna*) and special recognition for their services. Their number should be either three, five, or seven.

The Hindu, Buddhist, and Jainist lawgivers had linked criminal behavior to the moral conduct of daily life. Lord Buddha prescribed 227 rules to control criminal behavior through different types of punishments. Therefore, courts were open to the public, and full opportunities were given to the plaintiff and the defendant. Proceedings were recorded in writing. The court usually had local known members, whose knowledge of the place and its people were beyond question. Cases were disposed of without delay. Court members should not divulge any *sub judice* information to any outsider. And the chief judge had to revise the case proceedings and advise the king about the right judgment. The king was the highest authority for appeals, and his throne was the supreme court. During the Gupta period, the system of using the seal of a court was introduced. In civil matters, most of the judicial work was undertaken by a board of five wise men of a village. The administration of justice was not entirely free: 5 percent of the cost was charged to the parties involved in a suit.

Regarding the nature of the offenses—such as murdering a brahman, theft, murder, drunkenness, adultery, abduction, and treason—no complaint was necessary. It was enough that someone should appear before the king and state what had happened. This led to the presumption that there was a system of "lawyers," but if they were paid or not is not clear. Written statements were preferred so that no side could change them. Perjury was a crime, and if anyone, belonging to any caste, was found speaking ill of the king, his tongue would be cut off and he would be exiled. In the code of Narada, it was ordained that if a brahman had committed a crime for which he deserved capital punishment, he should not be executed, but his head should be shaved; his forehead should be given a nonerasable mark (mostly by fire); and he should be seated on an ass and turned out of the town.

There were three tiers of courts: the lowest, on the local level; the district court; and then the high court, where the matter would come before the king. He used to execute the sentences awarded, as well as their reduction, postponement, or remission. He had the prerogative of pardon: He could exercise his clemency and even let off the accused if he so wished. He usually celebrated the birth of a son by releasing the prisoners, or he did so in celebration of victory in war or on the occasion of the coronation of a crown prince. Asoka granted pardons twenty-five times during his reign of twenty-six years. But there were also a few restrictions in this matter. For instance, the king would not pardon a prisoner convicted of serious offenses, such as robbery, rape, forcible destruction of property, and similar offenses. If he pardoned these offenders, the king would get their sins to his credit. Usually, pardon was granted to first offenders. As a rule, the king heard cases each morning, and when he was unable to personally deal with a given case, a wise brahman, assisted by three advisers, took his place. This constituted the Assembly of Brahma, equivalent to a district court. Some of the judgments that were considered outstanding were inscribed in golden plates, and so judge-made laws grew up.

The *sutras* include certain maxims advising the king regarding his behavior in criminal and civil trials, but it is doubtful that they should be regarded as law rather than religious teaching. The few instances in which crimes and punishments are mentioned are capriciously arranged; there are some references to inheritance customs, gambling debts, debtor slaves, the equivalent of compensation, incest as a crime, and so forth. The chief offenses were theft (for which men were put in the stock), robbery, and burglary. In the case of an unjust verdict, the offender suffered only one-quarter of the crime's consequences; a false witness suffered another quarter; the judge the third quarter; and the king the last one. When the verdict was just and proper, the consequences of the crime rested upon the offender alone. It was also thought that a king who punished the innocent and allowed the culprit to go free would suffer the worst sort of ignominies and would go to hell. It should be mentioned that in the Laws of Manu (VIII: 229 ff., 293, and 409) there is undoubtedly the early manifestation of the notion of *negligence*.

Centuries later, in the Liechavi tribe (settled in some areas of present Bihar and Uttar Pradesh states during the fifth and fourth centuries B.C.), the final judgment was delivered after seven stages of trial, the king being the eighth and final stage. These stages were (1) arrest, at which time the accused was brought before "rulers"; (2) interrogation by the *Winichchiya Maham-atta,* the prosecuting elders; (3) interrogation by the *Woharikas,* the judicial magistrates; (4) interrogation by the *Suttadharas,* the high court of judges; (5) interrogation by the *Atthkulakas,* the eight judges; (6) bringing the accused before the *Senapati,* the commander-in-chief; (7) bringing the accused before the *Up-Raja,* the regent; and (8) final judgment by the *Raja,* who is bound to follow fixed written rules in determining the penalty. The historian Jayaswal has interpreted the terms of this complicated procedure in the following way: The second stage was a court for civil matters and minor offenses; the third was one of "lawyer" judges; the fourth was constituted by "doctors of law"; and the fifth was the council of final appeals.

Immense care was taken to avoid a miscarriage of justice. Even the king was warned to be just and to abide by the rules, since "law's adminis-tration is the real king, the ruling authority, providing security to the people. The king who properly employs it prospers, but if he is selfish, abnormal and deceitful, Danda destroys him. Danda cannot be held by despots. It strikes down the king who swerves from the law, together with his relatives" (Jayaswal, cited by Varma).

During the Mauryan rule, there were three local courts. The first con-sisted of the kindred of the accused; the second was the guild to which he belonged; and the third was the village assembly. Great importance was attached to these local courts, since it was felt that a more valid verdict could be reached in the place where the dispute had arisen. Brhaspati, another law-maker, advised that court should be held in the forests for people dwelling in the forest, in the market for those dealing with the market, in the military camp for warriors, and so on. There were also central courts, and the chief justice was called *Pradvivak.* The high court consisted of four or five judges, chosen for their character and legal erudition.

During the Buddhist Age, confessions—sometimes exacted under tor-ture—played an important role in determining punishment. An individual who confessed his guilt was usually treated with leniency and would "suffer" only expiation. Even the Buddhist monks put a great emphasis on confession. During the regular assemblies of the *Bhikshus* (as these monks were known), a learned monk recited the *Patimokkha*, a treatise containing a list of crimes and offenses that were to be avoided by the monks. The assembled monks and nuns were asked if they were guilty of any of the specified offenses; if so, their case was treated according to established rules (*Majumdar*, cited by Varma).

Punishment was never retributory; it was meant to absolve the soul of guilt through phsyical or mental suffering. Kautilya Chanakya advised that prisoners be kept in roadside lockups, so as to serve as an example to passersby.

The criminal law of the Mogul Empire was based on precepts of the Holy Koran, which punished the wrongdoer in order to teach him righteousness. During the reign of Akbar, provincial governors were asked to exercise foresight and to interrogate witnesses with care. Judges were expected to discover and understand the innermost thoughts and feelings of offenders and witnesses, through a study of their physiognomy, their body language, and so forth. In other words, legal functionaries were expected to use a form of judicial psychology—indeed, a pioneer form of this discipline.

The administration of justice was relatively simple, and the uncodified laws were based on custom. Any honest person other than a shudra could be a judge. Witnesses were required to tell the truth, on pain of severe punishment. Both sides of the dispute could present witnesses chosen from the best landlords, fathers of male children, and males born and living in the same district, whether they were kshatryas or vaishyas. The most honorable members of these castes should be preferred. All important transactions were conducted before a substantial number of witnesses to avoid the possibility that a third person or the seller might claim that the property was his and had been stolen from him.

People who could not serve as witnesses were those having a personal interest in the matter (friends, enemies, or servants); those whose bad faith was manifest; sick people; those previously convicted of a crime; cooks, actors, theologists, students, or hermits who had lost contact with human beings and feelings; men who were known to be completely subject to other men or have a bad reputation; those dealing with forbidden occupations; the very old, infants, bachelors, mestizos, crazy people, drunkards, the hungry or thirsty, those exhausted with fatigue or sex, the furious, or the thief. Women could act as witnesses in matters related to women and shudras in matters related to shudras. An eyewitness to a homicide had to serve as a witness (no matter what his caste status), but his testimony was to be regarded in a doubtful light and carefully examined. The king could not act as a witness, no matter what the subject of litigation might be.

Witnesses who told the truth retained their virtue and property and enjoyed eternal happiness in future reincarnations. But those who lied, led a miserable life and were cursed with equally miserable reincarnations. Only after 100 transmigrations would the false witness be able to cleanse himself.

He was condemned to an afterlife in the "mansions of torment" as were the murderer of a brahman, a woman, or a child and he who injured a friend or had been ungrateful. When there were no witnesses, judges tried to discover the truth through oaths or ordeals. The oath of a brahman would be based on the truth and nothing but the truth; that of a kshatriya on his arms and war chariots; that of a vaishya on his cows, grains, and gold; and that of a shudra on the basis of all the sins. If the house of a witness who swore to the description of an event was burned within a week of his oath, it meant that he had perjured himself.

The Laws of Manu prescribed a number of trials by ordeal, particularly in cases where witnesses were not available or were considered unreliable (VIII: 109f, 190). The employer played a prominent part, whatever the nature of the issue to be tried. The earliest ordeals recognized by Manu were those of fire and water. Originally, the ordeal by fire consisted of walking through fire; later, the witness or the accused had to carry a hot iron ball, and if he was not burned, he was judged innocent. In the ordeal by water, the accused was thrown into water, where he was to remain for as long as it took for a dart to reach its goal. If he did not drown, he was judged innocent. Later types of ordeal included the ordeal by balance, in which the accused was weighed twice, and if he weighed more the second time, he was found guilty because the weight of the sin had gone against him; the ordeal by ploughshare, which was reserved for those accused of theft of cattle; and the ordeal by hot gold piece, for cases of theft. The ordeal by dharma and adharma consisted of painting a picture of justice (right) and injustice (wrong) upon two leaves (one painted white, the other black). Then, unobserved by the accused, the leaves were rolled in balls of earth and put in a jar. The accused was then asked to draw out one of these balls. If he drew dharma, he was held innocent; if the other, he was considered guilty and was punished. The ordeal by poison consisted of putting a very poisonous snake in a basket into which a coin or a ring was also placed. The accused had to remove the object with his eyes covered. If he was not bitten, his innocence was proved. The ordeal of the cow dung consisted of putting boiling oil mixed with cow dung in a big jar. The accused put his arm in up to the elbow, and if he was not burned, he was considered innocent. In the family ordeal, the accused was to touch, separately, the heads of his wife and every one of his children; if he did not soon suffer a family misfortune, he was considered to have delivered truthful statements. Oaths by the grains of rice and the sacred libation are also mentioned but never clearly defined.

Law Enforcement Services

Restoration of stolen property and investigation of crimes were the two most obvious procedures under the law enforcement service program. If the king failed to restore any stolen property of his subjects, he had to meet the cost of such property from the state treasury. Therefore, the ruler used to appoint honest and trustworthy people in villages and towns for the protection of the people. They, in turn, appointed other persons with the same personal qualities to serve under them. These officers were held responsible for thefts committed in their respective areas and for the recovery of stolen goods within their jurisdictions. In the times of Kautilya, there was a police station (*sthāna*) at the center of 800 villages; under each *sthāna* and for each group of 400 villages, there was a zonal police office and under each of them, and for every 200 villages, there was a district police office, with twenty local police officers. The police officers could arrest a thief if he had stolen goods with him, if the footprints coincided, if the suspect was a jailbird, or if the suspect failed to prove his identity and purpose of his stay on the spot at the time of the incident. Police officers in those days were expected to be very honest, since they were severely punished for the slightest dereliction.

In the ancient scriptures, there is evidence of the existence of an espionage system for collecting information regarding criminal acts, detecting criminals, acting as agent provocateurs, assuming other functions of an intelligence department, and reporting to the king so that he could take direct legal action. The king used to appoint informers (*sūcaka*) or authorize volunteers (*stobhaka*) for these functions. They used to work under the guise of scholars, widowers, householders, merchants, ascetics, priests, physicians, female mendicants, and so forth, in their respective well-defined jurisdictions. Among them were dwarfs, mutes, hunchbacks, pseudohermaphrodites, and similar characters that the Hindus generally avoided. The "merchants" among them would work inside the forts and cities; saints and ascetics in the suburbs; cultivators in the countryside, and so on. Cypher writing was used by the spies to pass on information or instructions. They also used trained pigeons to carry secret messages from one place to another.

Police investigation was not a dreadful affair in those days, since there were prescribed rules of procedures for the interrogation of suspects, free of physical torture. In cases of homicide, they had to try to establish if it was a case of homicide or suicide, if there were direct witnesses, who was with the victim before he died, what kind of circumstantial evidence could be made available to detect who might be the culprit, and so forth. The investigating officer had to make detailed inquiries among the people living near the place where the homicide was discovered: Had there been a quarrel with someone? What were his relations with his wife and other women? (this being, perhaps, the origin of the famous criminological dictum *"Cherchez la femme"*)? Was he abnormally greedy for money? Who were his business associates? Did he have relations with strangers? Who were they? And many other related questions.

For the detection of cases of theft, the investigating officer had to question the witnesses in the presence of the individual whose property had been stolen and his relatives. He had to inquire about their domicile, caste, clan, name, profession, property, and economic situation. Afterward, the officer had to ask about where the suspect had spent the day preceding the theft and the night till the time of this arrest. If the answers were satisfactory, the suspect could be released; otherwise, he had to be held and sent for trial. No one was to be arrested on suspicion after three days since the theft, except when stolen property or other incriminating factors had been found in his house. In such a case, the officer had to ask about the implements used for his action, whether he had advisers or helpers, to whom he delivered the stolen goods, and so forth. A person whose footprints were identical to those found in the dust near the scene of the theft could be considered the possible thief. Information could also be gathered from known thieves, prostitutes, spies, and similar characters to complete the case before the trial.

Regarding the detection of a corrupt judge, spies could act as agents provocateurs. They might become aquainted with the judge and then, in a friendly conversation, say, for instance: "The accused is my relative, and his case is pending before you. Please acquit him, and here is the money, please accept it." If the judge acceded and received the money, he could be declared as a receiver of bribes and punished accordingly. Similar methods were employed to detect all kinds of wicked people and to investigate sexual offenses, such as rape and adultery, which were regarded as offenses not only against the person but also against matrimonial rights and public morality. Forced sexual intercourse with a woman, whether married or not, mature or immature, chaste or unchaste, with or without her consent, was punishable by law, with only a few exceptions.

There were also elaborate guiding principles for the *prevention of crime* as much as possible. As a preventive measure, the following persons could be arrested on suspicion: (1) one whose hereditary property of a great amount has been significantly diminished without an acceptable cause; (2) people who live with faked names or domiciles and without any ostensible means of livelihood; (3) habitual drunkards, extravagants, hard-core gamblers, and spendthrifts; (4) those who visit solitary houses or gardens at unusual times; (5) those who consult with other people in secret places or visit medical men for secret treatment of wounds; (6) those who are notorious for their bad tendencies, who have police records of theft and other misdemeanors, and who privately sell suspected articles; (7) those who keep regular contacts with habitual offenders and antisocial elements; (8) those who avoid being seen by police officers because they are always in fear and are frightened at the sight of their arms; (9) those who practice the use of weapons, probably for reprehensible purposes, under the shadow of walls or in other secluded places; and (10) those who are addicted to women and are particularly inquisitive about their ornaments or wealth. Special attention was also given to trappers, archers, hunters, and wild tribes. Managers of institutions or masters of private houses were required to report the times of arrival and departure of all strangers who stayed with them for the night.

To prevent fires or arson, kindling fires at noon or during the night was prohibited. Every house had to keep five waterpots, and many more were in the main streets and in front of royal buildings. Thatched roofs were to be removed. Every house owner had to be in his house after the trumpet was sounded to indicate the curfew. Transgressors were punished. Physicians and other state officers had special passes while on duty. And besides all these precautions, policemen and spies frequently patrolled the streets and public buildings, uninhabited houses, and artisans' shops.

Spies were also employed to examine secretly the behavior of state officers. If the reports were favorable, the officers were to be honored; otherwise, they were to be punished, by confiscation of all their property, and then banished.

The Objectives and Modalities of Punishment

Because the mind was considered the main source of human behavior, major consideration in the treatment of offenders was given to expiation through the process of inculcating a deep sense of repentance and a spontaneous effort for self-reformation. The straight admission of guilt by an offender was encouraged in ancient times; for his frank confession, he got due appreciation by the judge or the king during his trial. Fines were usually imposed for ordinary offenses, and physical punishment was the last resort for heinous crimes. Sympathetic punishment was the extreme corporal punishment, frequently replaced by exile for the rest of the offender's life.

King Harsavardhan of the Gupta period (606–48 A.D.) was a strict dispenser of justice, but he was very charitable with his subjects. People were so happy that hardly any crimes were committed. Extremely rarely, in very serious cases, a nose, ear, hand, or foot was amputated. Even a traitor was sentenced to life imprisonment but no physical punishment.

The basic aim of punishment was to deter abnormal tendencies and transform them into healthy social urges for the benefit of the security and safety of the society. There was no trace of any motive of revenge or retribution. Punishment was the righteousness emanating from the divine right of the king and was based on four important principles: *prevention, correction, purification* and, only lastly, *eradication. Deterrence* was also considered. Prevention was the most important and was considered as a social prophylactic. Only when an eradicative measure was unavoidable for a recidivist was life imprisonment or amputation of some part of the body resorted to. Punishment registered society's disapproval of the offender's transgression, but it was effective only if justly and properly inflicted. It was felt that the fear of pain was a decisive deterrent instrument.

Before an award of punishment, the court scrutinized some relevant facts about the accused: his family background, motives for the crime, age, ability, profession, and so on. There was always ample provision for social rehabilitation through counseling and prayers. Because prayer was thought to purify the mind, the offender could "pray and be purified." Punishment was awarded to help the offender repent and get rid of his guilt sense; but if it was unjustly or disproportionately inflicted, its effects were ruinous for the entire community. Once the punishment had been accomplished or the offender had been pardoned by the king, the sin of the commitment of the crime was automatically washed away, and the offender was given a clean slate in life. It should be remembered that pardon was not an exception but a rule. Moreover, according to the code of Narada, once an offender was pardoned or received his punishment, anyone who even casually referred to his past record, would be guilty of defamation and had to pay a fine, half of which went to the state and the other half to the aggrieved party.

In ancient times, the impact of the environment on human behavior was appreciated by both the Hindu and Jaina schools. For them, the environmental complex of place, time, motives, and particular situations was of the utmost importance. Therefore, pardoning was the greatest virtue to be observed by all people, since every human being might, under situational adversities, deviate from the path of *dharma* and commit wrongs or even the most inhuman offenses, but he would still remain pardonable until all efforts of expiation had failed.

Crime was defined then as a "violation of right affecting the community at large." It was the community that had to be compensated for the damage caused. Therefore, the code of Brhaspati indicated fourfold punitive measures: *abomination, reproof, fine,* and *corporal,* which was the last resort to be undertaken. And because some individuals had a propensity to repeat criminal acts, they had to perform penance for the sake of purification and to restore their good sense. Such a penance had to include restraint, ablutions, the practice of silence, fasting, sacrifices, controlling of passions, and the like. As punishment was an act of divinity, retribution or revenge were quite remote from the ancient Indian mind. But even the king and the sages could commit deplorable acts; therefore, they had to receive a punishment that was apt for them. The king, for instance, would have to pay a thousand times greater fine than an ordinary subject would have to pay for a similar offense. The code of Manu prescribed only a warning for a first offender, a heavy fine for a third-time recidivist, and mutilation of limb or body only for a genuinely incorrigible offender.

Individualization of punishment was also considered in ancient India: "Punishment should be accorded to the merits of each case, after due consideration of the mind of the offender and the circumstances under which the offense was committed" (Manu VIII: 126). And Kautilya warned that if a punishment is too severe, it alarms the people; if it is too mild, it frustrates them; so proper punishments were to be encouraged. For that purpose, penal science had to be studied with reference to the past, the present, and the future, taking into consideration the four orders of Indian society. Ancient lawgivers were never in favor of rigidity of the penal law.

The code of Narada classified criminal offenses into six categories: homicide, theft, sexual offenses, two kinds of violence, and miscellaneous. This is the best proof that all kinds of crime existed in ancient India, when offenders were treated through expiatory methods, so that "men who have committed crimes and have been punished by the king go to heaven, being pure like those who are in the right track" (Manu, VIII:318).

Summing up, it may be stated that there were many different punishments in ancient India—*death, imprisonment, banishment, corporal punishments,* and *fines*—but broadly speaking, punishments were never sadistic. Most crimes were punished by fines, with the purpose of compensating the victim.

Capital offenses included murder of a brahman, stealing gold from a brahman, drinking intoxicating liquors, treason, and soiling one's parents' bed (incest) or that of spiritual preceptors. The death penalty was also inflicted on people who did not obey the king or stole from his treasury, incorrigible imposters, rogues, and those who stole valuable jewels from the noblemen. Thieves who broke in through the wall of their victim's house at night were impaled after having both hands severed. An untier of knots (a kind of pickpocketing) had his fingers cut if it was a first offense, his hands and feet if he was a multiple recidivist; he would be put to death after the fifth offense of the same type.

The death penalty could be imposed by fire, strangulation, hanging, drowning, crucifixion, decapitation, or being torn by dogs or crushed by elephants. The convicted man had three days before his execution to pray for his soul's redemption and thus get a place in the world-to-come. In pre-Buddhist India, the condemned was dragged a long distance, chained and whipped, and, only after being exhibited in public, ultimately put to death. The execution itself was quick and simple.

Robbery was considered the illegal and violent appropriation of another man's property in his presence. If the owner was not present, and no violence was used, it was considered *theft*. In both cases, the offender was considered "purified" after suffering his punishment and might still reach a better reincarnation in his next life. If he were not punished, he would carry the burden of responsibility for the crime for the rest of his life. The sanctions for these offenses varied in proportion to the value of the stolen property and the status of the offender. The victim might be doubly compensated for the stolen property (the value of the property plus a fine for an equal amount) or even multiply compensated, and the offender might be sentenced to imprisonment, amputation of the offending hand, or even death (Manu VIII: 319ff). Stealing was considered so disgraceful that the higher the offender's status, the greater the compensatory sum he was required to pay his victim. Whereas a commoner would be fined one karshapana, the king would be fined a thousand (Manu VIII: 336). The guilt of a brahman was put at sixty-four or a hundred times the value of the property and at four times sixtyfold if he knew the nature of the offense. A *kshatrya* was fined thirty-two times the value of the property, a *vaishya* sixteen times, and a *shudra* only eight times (Manu VIII: 338). Broadly speaking, the theft of property of substantial value was considered a capital crime, whether or not the thief was caught in the act (Brhaspati XXI: 2 and Manu VIII: 320); if the property was of less value, the thief might be subjected to a severe whipping. Thieves and robbers were classified as either "open" or "concealed," according to the "skills" and methods they employed. Thieves were rarely condemned to death, and then only if they were apprehended with the stolen goods and the tools with which they committed the crime. The death penalty was also inflicted on those who abetted robbers by providing them with food, shelter, or the tools for committing their crime. Indeed, provincial governors or officials who did not interfere while robbers attacked a community were punished by the king as if they themselves were the criminals. Any citizen who was able to but did not attempt to prevent or repulse bandits attacking his town would be exiled with his entire family.

According to the basic rule that a member of a higher caste who committed an offense would be punished more severely than a member of an inferior caste, a *shudra* who killed another *shudra* could expiate his crime by giving 10 cows to the brahmans; if he killed a *vaishya* the fine was 100 cows, and if he killed a *kshatrya*, the fine was 1,000 cows. If he killed a brahman, he had to be killed, for the killing of a brahman was the highest degree of homicide. According to Brhaspati, there were four kinds of violent crimes: homicide, theft, assaulting another's wife, and injuring someone through either assault or abuse. The penalty for intentional homicide was not expressly stated but must have been capital (Manu VIII: 350, 351) for everyone except a brahman, unless he was convicted of treason. Then he could be branded or even blinded, fined and tonsured, but more frequently he would be banished (Manu VIII: 379, 380). Sympathetic punishments were inflicted on those who wounded an equal; the "guilty" limb was to be cut off (Manu VIII: 279, 283). During the Gupta dynasty, capital or corporal punishment was rare. Fines were much more common. However, rebellion, was punished severely; the culprit's right hand was cut off. Although murder was regarded as a sin, killing in self-defense was not considered a transgression of the law, because "wrath indeed touches wrath" (Code of Narada).

The Indian scriptures' treatment of sex is thorough and explicit; the *Kama-Sutra* of *Vatsyayana* (44 B.C.) and the works of *Kuttanimatam* (fourth century A.D.) provide a beautiful, scientific analysis of sex, sexual behavior, and the sex act. However, the *Kama-Sutra* closes with the following statement: "Those who read this book shall realize the importance and significance of celibacy." In other words, one may find in the book the way to master over sex and thus never be a victim to the pranks of loose women and never lead a demoralized life. He would be able to enjoy the aesthetics of erotica in a truly monogamus and happy conjugal life, full of devotion and charm. This is why the sexual ethics of ancient India was so different from those of other civilizations of those days.

According to the Laws of Manu (VIII: 317), a fallen woman's fault lies not only with her but also with her husband, who, under sacred oath, had taken charge of her. She can also be purified through expiation. And no law in ancient India gave complete authority to a husband to decide punishment for his fallen wife.

Prostitution existed in ancient India and was regulated by the state. These women were trained in sixteen different kinds of fine arts. Nevertheless, Brhaspati and others were against this state patronage. They stated that the police should be authorized to raid the houses of prostitution. Virginity was considered then the most sacred thing to be honored, and there were severe penalties for spoiling a virgin girl. Ramayana wrote: "A woman, a pearl, and water are never impure" (12/165: 32).

The *Rig-Veda* mentions cases of incest; seduction; prostitution (in those days, mainly confined to temples housing Devadasis, "god's servants," who were in fact prostitutes, giving part of their earnings to the brahmans, who acted as a kind of procurers); abortion (punished as a crime similar to the killing of a brahman); infanticide (rare occurrences); adultery; homosexuality, and so forth. Rape and adultery were severely punished because they facilitated the mixture of castes. Rape of a maiden was punished by emasculation (Manu VIII: 364, 367), but if the maiden consented and both parties were of the same caste, they were merely fined (Manu VIII: 368). A *shudra* who had intercourse with a woman of one of the higher castes was punished either by castration or death (Manu VIII: 374). In other cases, the rapist was exiled, after being branded. The Laws of Manu mention, only once (VIII: 371), that the offended husband could react against his wife and her paramour, but he could not do so against the man alone, since that would savor of conspiracy between husband and wife. Because the pair was not usually caught *in flagrante,* and direct evidence was not available, the wife was tried by ordeal. She could prove her chastity by going through the ordeal of fire. In theory, at least, adultery was punishable by death: she was torn to pieces by wild dogs in a square or other public place, and her lover was burned in an iron bed, beneath which pieces of wood were added until the offender was completely consumed (Manu VIII: 359, 372). In practice, male offenders were fined and females were liable to have their hair cut off and thereafter be treated with contempt.

Betting and gambling were forbidden and were severely punished by corporal punishment, because they were two vices that might cause the king to lose his kingdom. Betting was putting money on the fighting of live animals, such as peacocks, goats, turkeys; gambling was using certain inanimate objects—such as chips, cards, or dice—as a means of entertainment.

Prisons in India, as in many other places of the ancient world, were places where capital punishments were inflicted or where people sentenced to death or to be tortured were incarcerated. Kautilya wrote that prison houses should be located in the main road or other public places, so that the passersby could witness the result of bad behavior and take a lesson; that is, they were meant to intimidate others. He mentioned separate prison houses for males and females. To accept a bribe from a prisoner or to steal from his ration was a punishable offense; the jail superintendent was also held responsible. Prisoners were chained hand and foot, subject to hunger and thirst, and left with their hair, nails, and beard uncut. The Chinese traveler Yuang Chwang, who spent many years in India during the seventh century A.D., mentioned the prison established by Asoka to the north of Pataliputra, known in Hindu tradition as "Asoka's Hell." Here, in the beginning, the inmates were subjected to unimaginable tortures; Asoka even proclaimed that no one entering this prison should leave it alive. Afterward, he himself ordered the demolition of the prison and the mitigation of the penal practices. Prisons that restricted liberty as a means of punishment did not appear until the end of the sixteenth century. From another point of view, short sentences could be served under "house arrest."

Except in the case of treason, for which the penalty was death, punishment of any crime depended on the social status of the offender. A warrior who defamed a priest was fined 100 panas, but a slave was sentenced to corporal punishment for the same crime. For crimes that called for such a penalty, a priest suffered banishment.

For murder, the offender had to give compensation to the relatives of the deceased or to the king or to both. During the Vedic or Sutra age, compensation was treated as a "royal right," but as it was regarded as a penance, the money was given to the priests. Damage to property was also settled through an agreed compensation (Manu VIII: 288, 298).

When a member of an inferior caste wounded or mistreated someone of a higher caste, he was sentenced to a talionic punishment, which was often sympathetic or symbolic: the part of the body with which the offense had been committed would be cut off. For blows causing pain, the fine had to be proportional to the pain.

The king could impose the following fines: for false testimony, from 100 panas to 250, 500, or even 2,500 panas. For a mild offense, the king might content himself with a warning or an admonition, a severe reprimand, or a fine. The king could level more than one punishment for a single crime if necessary.

Members of the three superior castes who were convicted of slander or insulting behavior were fined a sum that depended on the seriousness of the crime. For a similar crime, the shudra suffered sympathetic punishment: his tongue was cut out. If he was convicted of mocking a member of the superior castes, a burning iron torch some ten centimeters long was put into his mouth. And if he was imprudent enough to insult a brahman, the king could order that boiling oil should be poured into his mouth and ears.

The king could pardon any criminal. Even a murderer—except in later laws—could expiate his crime by risking his life for his king in battle; a murderer who took part in three battles was freed. The sentence passed and the pardon granted by the king were supposed to purify the offender.

A special reference should be made to the criminal tribes, known today as "scheduled tribes." Some 4 million people, living mainly in the north of the subcontinent (mainly in the states of Madhya Pradesh, Bihar, Bengal, Orissa, Andhra Pradesh, and Maharashtra) are engaged in systematic robbery, pimping and prostitution, assault, frauds, and the like. The guilty hands of such robbers (*dacoits*) were amputated. In order of their numerical size, the main tribes are Gond, Santal, Bhil, Oraon, Khond, Munda, Bhuiya, Ho, Savara, Kol, Korku, Maler, Baiga, and the Assam tribes of the northeast.

Laws regarding crimes and punishments, as well as judicial procedures, appeared in India only after the brahmans began to take a practical interest in the country's administration. Until then, Indian literature was only religious and moralistic in nature. It was sufficient, according the Laws of Manu, to accept and to live according to one basic philosophical principle: "Nobody causes happiness or misery to anyone. It is wrong to think that pain and pleasure had been caused by others. It is you alone and your actions which are responsible for both these conditions."

The genius of India, said Jawaharlal Nehru, consists of synthesis. Successive cultural influences have fused together to form the intricate way of life we know as India and Hinduism. India's society, in spite of its peculiar characteristics, is one of the most closely knit in world history. Through a combination of worship, ritual, and religion, Indians have succeeded in synthesizing diverse forces and influences. India's creative power was first seen in religion, with the development of three great creeds—Buddhism, Jainism, and Hinduism—a record that no other culture has ever matched. This creativity was next seen in art, architecture, and literature. In its social order, India created elaborate structures of caste and class, which can be explained—if not justified—by its overall world view. Even in such a limited field as crime and punishment, Indians were among the first to develop the notions of "negligence" and "judicial psychology."

7

Crime and Punishment in Imperial China

> Art is what everyone knows it to be.
> —Benedetto Croce

Historical Evolution

Western knowledge about China was quite scanty before this century; existing knowledge was based primarily on old-time legends and myths, preconceptions, and misinformation. Therefore, it seems worthwhile to open this chapter with a description of certain fundamental issues about this huge country.

From the earliest recorded times, the Chinese have shown a great interest in and respect for their own historical past. Historians and chroniclers have always been an important part of Chinese intellectual life, and like the Hebrews and the Greeks, they developed a sophisticated historiographical tradition, reaching back to the ninth and seventh centuries B.C. Before then, Chinese sources disagree, and lack of basic material makes it impossible to reach a consensus.

However, archaeologists have unearthed remains that reveal something of prehistoric China. The earliest remains have been discovered in the northeastern regions, especially around Lake Baikal in northern Mongolia and Manchuria, in the sites of Djalai-nor (c. 6000 B.C.), Ang-ang-shi (c. 5000 B.C.) Lin-shi (c. 4000 B.C.), and Hung-shan-hou (c. 2500 B.C.). These sites are no more than 550 miles apart. In 1921 and 1928, two late Neolithic cultures were discovered in northern China: the earliest, the Yang-shao culture, on the plateau; the other, the Lung-shan culture, on the plain. These were undoubtedly purely Chinese cultures, as evidenced by elaborately painted pottery discovered at excavation sites. Recently discovered cliff carvings found in the south China Yunnan province, which picture people hunting and gathering food, date back some 3,000 years.

The earliest Chinese historical documents are contained in the *Book of History*. The texts within this book deal with the deeds of kings and nobles, their sacrifices to the gods, military expeditions, and the organization of their government. The book concentrates on a description of the founders of dynasties (paragons of virtue) and their opponents (models of wickedness).

Although Confucius is reputed to have edited the book, at least forty of the fifty-four documents it contains could not have existed during Confucius's lifetime. Only fifteen of these documents are probably genuine, written shortly after the events they relate; another thirteen were probably written several centuries after Confucius. The remainder are considered to be forgeries dating from the third century B.C. The book is more a treatise on ethics than a history in the accepted sense; many of the documents are speeches on moral issues, and those that deal with the questions of proper government are presented as speeches of historical personages.

Though tradition is vague regarding the origin of the Chinese people, it is generally accepted that advanced societies lived in north China well before the historical period. The usual account begins with the Creator—P'an-ku—followed by twelve Celestial Sovereigns, eleven Terrestrial Sovereigns, and nine Human Sovereigns, representing the triad of heaven, earth, and man. These were followed by the five Ti, among whom are the legendary Yellow Emperors, Yao, and Shun. These ancient emperors, particularly Yao and Shun, exemplified royal virtue and reigned for some 150 years at the dawn of Chinese history, just prior to the foundation of the first dynasty—the Hsia. The authenticity of Yao and Shun was generally accepted until the twentieth century, when scholars established that they were purely mythological personages that appeared in Chinese legends shortly before Confucius. The opening document of the *Book of History,* known as the "Canon of Yao," appears to have been written in the late fifth or fourth centuries B.C. and expresses the political ideals of its authors. Part I is the complete "Canon of Yao"; Part II is the "Canon of Shun."

Archaeologists have yet to discover proof that the first dynasty, the Hsia, ever existed. However, the name *Hsia* was used not only as the name of the dynasty but to designate Chinese culture proper, based on common social, political, and linguistic elements. As a matter of fact, the expression *chu Hsia* (all of the Hsia), refers to the superiority and exclusivity of Chinese society in contrast to that of the barbarians.

On the other hand, there is ample evidence that the second dynasty, the Shang, did exist. The archaeological site of An-yang, which revealed a treasure of hundreds of finely cast bronze vessels, seems to have been occupied by the nineteenth Shang sovereign, P'an Kêng, some 273 years before the end of the dynasty.

"The Numerous Regions" (*To Fang*) is considered one of the fifteen genuine pre-Confucian documents in the *Book of History*. It deals primarily with the Chou military conquest of the Shang State. The object of "To Fang" is to justify the establishment of the third dynasty, the Chou, and it is here that the famous theory of the "mandate of Heaven" first appears in writing. This mandate—the right to rule conferred by Heaven—was the accepted basis for the rule of all Chinese emperors. Since Heaven prefers virtue to vice, it withdraws its mandate from an evil ruler and bestows it upon a more worthy one. If the nation functions well, this is proof that the reigning dynasty holds the "mandate of Heaven"; but if it is overthrown, it has lost Heaven's favor. The "To Fang" paints the last of the Shang sovereigns in the darkest possible light, while praising the modesty and forbearance of the Chou conqueror. In the same vein, the last of the Hsias are described as evil and depraved; therefore, Heaven transferred its mandate first to the Shang and later to the Chou kings Wen and Yu, the founders of the imperial Chou dynasty. No matter how large the actual area controlled by a given dynasty, the "mandate of Heaven" was regarded as applying to the entire country. Throughout their history, even in periods of political fragmentation, the Chinese regarded the unity of their country under a single government as the natural and rightful state of affairs. This was the case even during the late Chou period, when the centers of Chinese society were scattered, separated from one another by barbarian tribes. The area of effective Chou rule was never very extensive; and within the last three centuries of the dynasty, it was reduced to a tiny royal domain surrounded by powerful independent states, fiefs that the Chou had granted to its military aristocracy. However, there was a certain amount of centralized leadership under the Chung Kuo, the "Central States," whose traditions and institutions were older. Chung Kuo has come to mean *China*.

The Chou dynasty was followed by the "period of the spring and autumn annals," an age of continual armed conflicts, which were limited to the noble class and were conducted according to a knightly code: no massacre of noncombatants; no pursuing elderly men or killing wounded opponents; no deceptive tactics or ambushes. Most issues were decided in a single battle, and victory was not exploited; the winning prince was not expected to destroy his enemy or to annex his territory. This era of knightly warfare ended when iron weaponry came into general use (about 400 B.C.). The "annals" are in fact the chronicle of Confucius's own state of Lu and of the other many states from 770 to 481 B.C.

The conflicts of the ensuing "period of the warring states" (480–222 B.C.) were much more "professional," with more complex battles, less localized and more destructive. In 221 B.C., an aggressor state in the northwest, Ch'in, succeeded for a short time (221–207 B.C.) in bringing all China north of the Yangtze under one rule.

Prior to the advent of European sea power in the nineteenth century, the main threat to China came from beyond her northern frontiers. The steppes of Manchuria, Inner Mongolia, and Chinese Turkestan (Kashgaria, in central Sinkiang) were populated by a number of nomadic people who lived in an uneasy relationship with the Chinese. The "barbarians" gradually acquired a taste for the luxuries of civilization and became progressively less nomadic. The first Ch'in emperor, Shih Huang-Ti, attempted to deter barbarian incursions by combining a series of walls, built in the fourth and third centuries

B.C. by individual border states. The Great Wall of China served as a viable defense system only when it was constantly patrolled by troops loyal to the central government. Apart from its potential military value, the Great Wall had important political consequences, emphasizing the contrast between the peoples living within the wall and the nomads who lived beyond. This helped unify both the Chinese and the Mongolian tribes who surrounded them, who eventually became a great political power.

Seu-ma Ch'ien (c. 145–90 B.C.) was the founder of the Chinese tradition of historical scholarship. He was the "regulator of the calendar" (court astronomer), but his title was the "grand historian." He served the Han emperor Wu Ti (140–87 B.C.), and his master work—the *Historical Records* (*Shih Chi*)—covers Chinese history from its earliest period to his own. It also includes chapters on the principal lands and peoples beyond the Chinese frontiers. In contrast to the morally didactic narratives of the *Book of History* and *The Spring and Autumn Annals*, the *Historical Records* emphasized historical accuracy (although Seu-ma Ch'ien accepted traditional mythological accounts of the early Chinese dynasties). He invented the "Chronological Tables," which dated important events, and was the first historian to create a unified chronological framework for Chinese history as a whole (not a small achievement, considering that each of the Chinese states had its own system of reckoning time).

During Ch'ien's time, the Chinese world stopped, more or less, at the Yangtze River. The Han dynasty (206 B.C.–219 A.D.) established the maximum borders of China proper, borders that no Chinese ruler was to surpass. During the Ch'in and Han dynasties, the principal threat came from the Hsiung-Nu, groups of Turkic-speaking people of the steppes north of the great bend of the Yellow River. It was only during the seventeenth century A.D. that the nomad's military importance declined; with the introduction of the railroads in the nineteenth century and the consequent opening of Manchuria and Inner Mongolia, nomadism as a way of life was doomed.

The other great Chinese historian of the Han dynasty was Pan Ku (32–92 A.D.). He is the principal author of a 100-chapter work covering the period from the founding of the Han dynasty to the death of the usurper Wang Mang (23 A.D.), known as the *History of the Former Han Dynasty*. His work was based on the Confucian notion that human character is the chief moving force behind history; thus, the rise and fall of a historical house was considered one historical unit.

The reign of Wang Mang (9–23 A.D.) was an extraordinary episode in Chinese history, since it was the first attempt of an emperor to rule according to strictly Confucian principles. Unfortunately, the image of a modest Confucianist gentleman that he cultivated during his rise to power was inconsistent with his love of luxury and power—a fact that eventually contributed to his downfall. His growing unpopularity, coupled with a series of natural disasters that plagued his kingdom, led his subjects to believe that he had lost the "mandate of Heaven." Eventually, he was murdered in his palace by common soldiers.

However, Imperial China's decline is attributed not to the follies of one emperor or the excesses of a particular dynasty but to the principles of Confucianism itself. It was during the Ming dynasty that Confucianism took hold, and by the end of the seventeenth century, the principles of maintaining stability, order, and peace had become utmost in the priorities of China's rulers. This approach ruled out economic expansion and military growth—in short, any change. Thus, it was stagnation that eventually felled Imperial China.

In the last few decades, there has been a tremendous amount of archaeological work in modern China. For instance, in the area of the Ting village, in Shansi province, tourists can now visit a site where human fossils dating back 100,000 years and implements of the middle old Stone Age have been found. They may also visit China's oldest and highest wooden tower, built in 1056 A.D.—69 meters high and 30 meters in diameter. It is one of the ten ancient buildings in the area put up between 618 and 1234, among them a glazed pagoda, the biggest and best preserved in China.

The tomb of Emperor Ch'ien Lung of the Ch'ing dynasty, who reigned between 1736 and 1795, is located in Tsun-hua County, about 100 kilometers east of Peking. It opened to the public in 1978. It is one of the fifteen tombs of Ch'ing emperors in the area. The tomb, built in 1743 at a cost of ninety tons of silver, is, in fact, an underground palace based on the architectural style of the imperial tombs of the preceding Ming dynasty (1368–1644).

The museum established at Deshanpu, near Zigong City, is located atop a dinosaur burial ground, where 180 skeletons of seventeen different species have been found. They are dated about 150 million years ago and are among the best preserved in the world. Finally, Chinese archaeologists have found three pieces of paper that may date back to between 73 and 49 B.C., about 150 years earlier than the world's first discovery of paper. They were made of hemp and the texture was finer than the previously discovered Han dynasty paper.

Politics and Government: Civil and Military Administration

Although China never evolved democratic institutions in the Western sense—elections, parliaments, an independent judiciary, and the like—it did follow the Confucian philosophy that government must exist only for the people's welfare. The Confucianist theory of the "mandate of Heaven" made the ruler's divine right contingent upon popular satisfaction with his conduct. This mandate is discussed in the oldest parts of the *Book of History* and was constantly reiterated by the Confucianists. It must have had a profound effect on everything and everyone concerned with government in China.

Despite the monarchial form of government in pre-Republican China, there was a great deal of effective democracy in practice, as evidenced by imperial institutions such as civil service examinations and a Board of Censors. The existence of such institutions may help to explain why China's subjects remained loyal to the empire for thousands of years—a loyalty that was not necessarily the result of coercion.

According to the Confucian school, the quality of a government depends primarily on the ruler's moral character; an upright, benevolent ruler who observed the proper rituals would automatically act for the general welfare, and the people would be satisfied with his government. A fixed body of laws was therefore unnecessary. It is almost impossible to know whether Confucius refers merely to government by example (if the upper classes perform the proper rituals, the masses will follow) or whether rituals, as practiced by the ruler, had a magical effect.

All major Chinese dynasties since the time of Han have recognized China's need for a well-organized, efficient system of administration. Indeed, the stability of the Chinese empire over a period of more than two millenia must be ascribed, to a large extent, to the quality of its civil service. Civil servants were recruited, at least partially, through a series of periodic examinations—a system that represented the practical application of the Confucian political theory. China's civil service was based on basically egalitarian principles, according to which the humblest citizen might conceivably rise to the highest position of honor and influence. From the middle of the T'ang period (618–906), these scholar officials constituted the highest social class.

An important safeguard that existed within the civil service was the Board of Censors, or Censorate. The censors served as a kind of ombudsmen whose function it was to expose faulty or corrupt administrative practices, even on the highest state levels. The chief censors enjoyed direct access to the emperor, but they could be dismissed, demoted, or even executed for their frankness.

Whereas civil servants belonged to a social class that enjoyed prestige and honor, members of the military establishment were regarded with contempt. By the middle of the T'ang dynasty, the Chinese had come to despise the art of war; soldiering was considered a career fit only for the dregs of society or for barbarians in Chinese service. Even the highest army officers lacked the education and culture level of the civil servants. War had its place in Chinese history, but in no other civilization have the military arts been less cultivated. Chinese literature contains very little that tends to glorify military prowess or to present war in heroic guise. Law and order in imperial China were maintained not by a police force or by the military but by the strength of the Chinese. The weight of the entire body of Chinese literature, without exception, condemns all kinds of unprovoked aggression, sustaining the dictum that "right is stronger than might." Even the military literature stresses the superiority of intelligence over physical force, underlining the difficulties in conquering a well-governed state.

Chinese Society

Chinese aristocracy was roughly divided into four classes: the "sons of Heaven," the feudal lords, the high ministers (*ta-fu*), and the officials of the bureaucracy. The four classes of common people were scholars, farmers, artisans, and merchants. The members of these classes were not supposed to compete with those beneath them socially for the purpose of making a profit. Moreover, a decree of the year 624 A.D., during the T'ang dynasty, forbade farmers, artisans, merchants, and members of various other occupations from fraternizing with scholars. From the fourth century B.C., guilds were established, and members paid dues to the heads of their particular guild.

Chinese believe that the name of a person affects his fate. In choosing a name, it is important to know the exact time of birth and to which of the five elements—metal, wood, water, fire, and earth—a person belongs. Therefore, there have been schools specializing in Chinese astrology almost since times immemorial because of the strong belief in the power of symbols in man's destiny. A good name was considered to give, at least, a good start in life. The same belief spills over to arithmetic, in which some numbers sound better than others: three rhymes with a good character, and eight rhymes with prosperity.

Writing was not a common practice in ancient China, not only because of the complicated caligraphy of most of the symbols but mainly because it was taught only in the schools of the temples and was the particular possession of the scribes, who were not priests but functioned on the fringe of the religious orders. The present Chinese government has been trying to simplify the language and has been periodically presenting more Chinese characters for popular use; it has indicated that its ultimate aim is the Romanization of the language with a phonetic alphabet. By the end of 1977, the number of simplified characters reached 3,091 with a target of 4,500. The logic of this official policy can be better understood if we take into consideration that written Chinese has at least 50,000 ideographs originating from pictorial representations, each of them using a varying number of strokes.

One of China's most serious socioeconomic problems was, and still is, how to cope with its ever-increasing population. It seems that by 156 A.D., during the Han dynasty, China's population had already reached 50 million, and the average small village had about 300 residents. Nowadays, China has 1 billion mouths to feed and expect to have 1.2 billion by the year 2000. These are only estimates; the exact numbers are not known. The late chairman Mao Tse-tung once said: "Every time you breathe a Chinese is born or dies." To control such a massive problem, in 1979 the government promulgated the "one-child-family" policy, which produced, almost immediately, a spectacular outbreak of female infanticide, because parents were frightened that without a grown son to look after them, they would face a bleak old age.

Women's liberation still has a long way to go in China. Almost half of Chinese women are illiterate or semiliterate, and nearly all Chinese women aged sixty and above cannot read or write adequately. Some 45 percent of the adult women population belong to this category, more than double the men's rate of 19 percent. Illiteracy is more than twice as widespread in the countryside—where 80 percent of the population lives—than in towns and cities. Of course, there are exceptions, as was the case with the famous Soong sisters, whose husbands shaped the course of modern Chinese history: the older of the three married H.H. Kung, a prominent financier and Nationalist Chinese politician; Soong Ching-ling was the wife of Sun Yat-sen, the founding father of modern China; and the younger sister, Soong Mei-ling, married Chiang Kai-shek.

Even today, battered wives might appear before a judge who will excuse the husband on the grounds that he was a victim of the "old tradition of thinking" in China. Although a man can admit in private that he behaved improperly toward his wife, he cannot do so in public. Moreover, lately, with the rising living standards in China, there is a rise in bigamy and a revival of the old custom of matchmaking. The slaying of wives and slaves to accompany their royal or noble masters in the hereafter was practiced in China until the seventeenth century A.D. This practice is now at an end, but in many country districts it is still considered scandalous, though legal, for a widow to remarry.

The Chinese began to use jade for female jewelry, religious symbols, and many other purposes in the Neolithic period; they still do today. Jade has always been considered a beautiful stone, embodying the main qualities of the Chinese civilization: durability, venerability, and mystique. The substance itself seems to have formed a bond that links prehistoric and dynastic China, differentiating the Chinese ethnic origin from the rest of mankind.

Ethics and Religion

Ancient China is more profoundly alien to the Western mind than any of the other great classical civilizations of the East. Vast distances separated the cradle of Chinese civilization in the Yellow River valley from the centers of culture in western Asia. Our understanding of ancient China is handicapped by the fact that much of our knowledge depends on translations of Chinese classical texts, which present difficulties even for modern Chinese scholars.

Confucius (Kung Fu Tzu—Tzu being a title of respect meaning "master"), or Master Kung, was born in Tsou, a small village in the small state of Lu (the present-day province of Shantung) in approximately 550 B.C. He is supposed to have been a contemporary of Buddha. Of humble background but well educated, it is assumed that he devoted his life to study and teaching. He described himself as a transmitter rather than a creator of ideas, but he was both. He had the reverence for antiquity that was characteristic of the Chinese, but his primary concern was to improve the society of his time. During this period, the emperor's actual authority extended over only a small area around his capital; his vassals—the real rulers of the various Chinese states—were constantly at war with each other and with the semibarbarian states on their borders. The north China plain was, in fact, a vast battleground. Confucius was convinced that more warfare would not put an end to the chaotic state, but he refused to look to the supernatural for assistance. The basis of Confucian thought was *tao,* "the way," a "golden rule of ethics in human affairs"; faithfulness, loyalty, moderation, and respect for the feelings and rights of others. His insistence on an intrinsic regulator of conduct, as opposed to the extrinsic demands of religious dogma, represented a major shift in emphasis. His message was to cultivate human character instead of worshiping the supernatural. Righteousness, in the broadest possible sense, was his standard for private and public morals. He interpreted the ancient religious rituals—which he respected—as a means to reach the propriety and decorum that lead to harmony in human relations and prevent extremes of emotion.

Legend has made of Confucius a formidable scholar and has assigned him an important role in the composition or editing of the five Confucian classics, known to the majority of educated Chinese. Two of these are historical works: the *Book of History (Shu Ching),* also known as the *Book of Documents,* is a selection of speeches and pronouncements allegedly made by the rulers or important officials of the three earliest Chinese dynasties; and the *Spring and Autumn Annals (Ch'un Ch'iu)* is a year-by-year account of the events in the state of Lu between the years 722 and 481 B.C. The *Book of Songs (Shih Ching),* also known as the *Book of Poetry* or the *Book of Odes,* and the *Book of Rites (Li Chi),* or *Records of Ceremonials and Rituals,* were both regarded as moral treatises because of their discussions of rituals, propriety, family relations, and political ethics. Finally, the *Book of Changes (I Ching)* provides formulas for determining suitable times to engage in various types of activities. A *Book of Music,* sometimes considered a sixth classic, no longer exists as a separate work but survives as a chapter in the *Book of Rites.* All these books became "classics" under the former Han dynasty (206 B.C.–8 A.D.). Modern scholars have ascertained that most of the materials contained in these classics are as old as they are supposed to be. With a very few exceptions, all of them were composed in the period between the death of Confucius and the first century B.C. Only the *Book of Songs* existed in the sixth century B.C., but Confucius probably had nothing to do with selecting its contents (305 poems from an existing collection of more than 3,000).

The only work that is properly attributed to Confucius is the *Analects* (*Lun Yu*), or *Selected Sayings*. This small book is a compilation (from the fourth century B.C.) of the Master's sayings as remembered and transmitted by his followers; despite its possible inaccuracies, it remains the best source of his opinions. As Confucius's ideas gained popularity under the patronage of the Han dynasty, an increasing number of ideas deriving from Taoism, Legalism, and other rival schools came to be presented under a Confucian label. Thus, Confucianism ceased to be a system created by a rather obscure individual and became a vast intellectual edifice embodying all major trends of Chinese thought; it remained the dominant philosophical system of China until well into this century.

The two other great thinkers of classical Confucianism were Hsün Tzu and Mencius. Master Hsün (c. 298–238 B.C.) was a native of the state of Chao, now South Hopei and Shansi, considerably west of the main centers of Chinese culture. His basic ideas are included in a book titled with his name, part of which was probably written by Hsün himself, the rest by his disciples. Moreover, the *Book of Rites* was most certainly compiled by men of his school. Hsün was convinced that not all people can conform to a single standard of behavior; therefore, "goodness" depends not only on human nature but also on culture and training. According to him, human beings are barbaric, unjust, and given to extremes of passion in their natural state (something similar to the basic principles of the Scholastics of the Middle Ages) and may become righteous and wise only through a process of acculturation. He was against a belief in supernatural spirits, considering it superstitious and illogical, but he was in favor of maintaining traditional rituals as a measure of social control. His reputation declined after his death because of the basically unpopular notion that human nature is basically evil. Nevertheless, his ideas were largely incorporated in the *Book of Rites,* perhaps the most influential of the five Confucian classics. His assertion of the equality of men at birth and the belief that their differences are due to training rather than inborn traits became the basis of the Chinese belief in social mobility through education.

Mencius (Meng Tzu, or Master Meng) lived between about 372 and 289 B.C. His book, one of the central texts of Confucianism and still considered a Chinese classic, is a record of some of his conversations both with rulers of states and with philosophical opponents. The book, most probably compiled by his disciples rather than by himself, appears to be a reasonably accurate account of his ideas and also serves as a reliable source of information regarding the fundamental opinions of Confucius. Because Confucian ideas were under attack during the fourth century B.C., Mencius's chief purpose was to defend these traditions. He expanded and explicated certain ideas that Confucius has vaguely suggested.

Confucianism's main opponents were the Legalists and Mo Tzu, or Mo Ti (c. 480–390 B.C.), one of the protagonists of the renaissance of Chinese philosophy during the "period of the warring states." His book, *Mo Tzu,* probably written by him or his disciples, in which he criticizes Confucian philosophy, seems to be a reasonable presentation of his doctrine. He and his followers seem to have been soldiers, since the chief of the Mohists was called "Great Master," held office for life, and had absolute power over his members. His basic concept of "universal love" was based not on pure emotion but on a strictly utilitarian principle that aimed to create a well-organized society, free from war. In his opinion, the Confucian stress on filial piety and loyalty to relatives led to useless and hypocritical distinctions, jealousies, and discords. According to Mo Tzu, the ruler who loved all his subjects equally, would be loved in return, and his kingdom would enjoy social harmony. He did agree with the Confucians on many important matters, however. For instance, he valued the Confucian virtues of goodness (*jen*) and righteousness (*li*) but interpreted them in his own way: the good and righteous man is one who practices universal love, making no distinctions between himself and others. He also revered traditional ways: hereditary rulers should govern their states through ministers selected on the basis of character and talent rather than ancestral ties. Mo Tzu argued that the opinion of one's immediate superior must always be accepted (a notion most probably derived from his military background). Whereas Confucius wanted to regulate emotions through rituals and music, Master Mo considered them a waste of time and energy. Whereas Confucius ignored the world of spirits, Mo Tzu (probably reflecting popular beliefs) thought that it should be properly served and respected.

With the unification of China and the Han dynasty's support of Confucianism, Mohism found itself at a serious disadvantage. Except for Taoism—basically a private doctrine—all the non-Confucian schools ceased to exist as separate entities during the Han period. Their basic concepts were forgotten or were swallowed up in the conglomeration of contradictory subjects that assumed the name of *Confucianism.*

Confucianism, as an all-inclusive philosophy, centered on every aspect of human existence, regarding man in light of his membership in society rather than his relationship to the beyond. It had no supreme, personal deity. Heaven (*t'ien*) was the highest power of the universe, an impersonal force closely resembling the Western concept of nature. The "way of Heaven"—an ethical standard of goodness, righteousness, and propriety—was not achieved through blind obedience to the will of any god. The numerous ancestral spirits (who had once been human themselves) demanded respect—but not the worship required by a deity. Confucius categorically rejected the popular opinion that ghostlike beings—spirits of the deceased—inhabited trees, rocks, rivers, and so on. Master Hsün denied even the power of the spirits, but he valued the rituals of worship as a sign of respect. In spite of the great influence of the Confucian philosophers, magic, occultism, divination, and supernatural spirits retained their importance in the people's mind. In Han times, such practices were followed even by the educated who saw themselves as Confucianists.

Confucianism was eclipsed by both Taoism and Buddhism in the centuries following the fall of the Han dynasty. With the reunification of China under the Sui (589–618) and the T'ang (618–907) dynasties, Confucianism again rose to favor primarily in government circles, where it was studied mainly as a means of official advancement (since the Confucian classics remained the basic texts of the Chinese educational system and civil service examinations). Under the Sung dynasty (960–1279), Confucianism acquired a new lease on life; a number of its followers—dominated by the great synthesizer Chu Hsi (1130–1200)—created the school of thought known as Neo-Confucianism, emphasizing devotion to parents, family, and friends, ancestor worship, justice, and peace. Whereas Buddhism and Taoism tended to regard earthly activities as insignificant, the new school reaffirmed the traditional notion of the ultimate meaningfulness of human existence. Neo-Confucianism remained the dominant intellectual influence in China until this century.

Taoism, or the Taoist school of thought (Tao-chia) was a philosophy, a religion, and a science; it was outranked only by Confucianism in its influence upon the Chinese mind. Philosophical Taoism—as expressed in its two great classics, the *Tao Te Ching* (by Lao Tzu) and the *Chuang Tzu*—is concerned with questions regarding the origin and meaning of life and the nature of the universe. It culminates in the mystic union of the individual with Tao, the impersonal law of the universe—a word denoting "the way" to reach the inner principle of a thing. Classical Taoism provided a more individualistic philosophy of life than the socially oriented ethics of Confucianism did, and its adherents were members of an educated elite, with the means and leisure for contemplation.

Religious or popular Taoism—an organized church with wide popular appeal—was a technique for attaining salvation. It became an important force in the decades before the fall of the Han dynasty and was at its height during the centuries of disunion known as the "six dynasties period" (222–589 A.D.).

Tao, the guiding principle of Taoism, is the law that governs all change; it is eternal and immutable. Natural disasters are the result of man's interference with this cosmic order. In human affairs, Tao means the absence of all effort, defined by the word *wu-wei*—"nonaction." The Confucianist ideal meant an active involvement in community welfare; the Taoist ideal was one of passivity. Taoism stresses the simple life, close to nature, and regards all man-made institutions as artificial. Striving for wealth and fame brings only misery; the quest for knowledge is essentially a quest for power and alienates man from Tao. The impersonal Tao was succeeded by a more personal deity, known as "Lord of Tao" or "Lord Huang-Lo," in the third or fourth centuries.

By the end of the second century A.D., Taoism had become the first large-scale organized religion in Chinese history. The parish, locally supported by the contribution of members, was the fundamental unit of the Taoist church. Its head, called Instructor, held a hereditary position linked to the families of the original Taoist missionaries to the district, and he conducted the religious services. The middle ranks of the church were open to both sexes. Believers were classed as initiates (sufficiently advanced in the faith to aspire to eternal life) and ordinary laymen. Later, the Taoist church adopted many of Buddhism's rites and ceremonies, the Taoist scriptures became mere imitations of Buddhist texts, and the distinction between Buddhism and Taoism faded. Confucianism and Taoism were never regarded as mutually exclusive, despite the contrast of Confucianism's common sense and Taoism's mysticism. Indeed, many Chinese practiced Confucianism in public and Taoism in private.

The supremacy of the concrete and the practical in northern China and of the speculative and abstract in the southern regions layed the ground for the appearance of Buddhism. The first adherents of Buddhism in China appeared in the first century A.D., more than half a millennium after the death of Gautama, its Indian founder. Buddhism's theology and ritual were far more complex and sophisticated than those of any other religious system in China. Most of the first Chinese Buddhists were Taoists, perhaps because of the apparent similarity between the two religions: both were religions of salvation; both had an enormous pantheon of supernatural beings but no supreme deity; both rejected earthly pleasures and cultivated an intense regard for nature and all living creatures; and both worshipped in formal religious services, public ceremonies, and festivals.

But the contrast between Buddhism and Confucianism was total. Whereas the former placed all mankind on nearly equal terms, the latter accepted a hierarchy of birth. According to Buddhism, future reincarnations were determined by *Karma,* whereas Confucianism centered on an ideal of an upright individual, fulfilling his proper place in society. Buddhism was indifferent to human history, whereas Confucianism had a deep respect for human achievements and the past. Instead of attempting to attain *nirvana,* Confucianists aspired to win the respect of their fellowmen in life and stressed the continuity of the ancestral line. Given these fundamental differences, it is not surprising that Buddhism's acceptance in China coincided with the decline of Confucianism during the six dynasties period, after the collapse of the Han dynasty. Indeed, it was several centuries before Buddhism was understood in China in something similar to Indian terms.

Chinese Buddhism, perhaps because its early preachers could not read Sanskrit, often has connotations quite different from those contained in original Indian texts. The predominance of Chinese Buddhism during the fifth and sixth centuries was followed by its gradual decline in the ninth century

A.D. During this period, many of the original objections to Buddhism were revived: it was of foreign origin; its universalistic ethic was contrary to traditional Chinese doctrine; its temples were extravagant; and its clergy were often idle and unproductive. Nevertheless Buddhism left quite a number of impressive relics in China. One of the most famous was Dun-Huang, in Gansu Province in remote western China. There, during the fifth century A.D., flourished a Buddhist religious center, noted for its many cave temples housing a great number of statues, wall paintings, and Buddhist scriptures and relics. It was the last Chinese town on the road to India and an oasis for caravans on the famous East–West trade route, the "Silk Road." It was also a meeting place for Buddhist pilgrims, scholars, artists, and merchants. Travelers returning from the holy sites of India brought back many foreign ideas and influences; the wall paintings at Dun-huang reflect this mixture of styles and concepts.

In spite of all these different religions, Chinese society is remarkable in its religious tolerance and allows for the coexistence of all of them. It was quite common, for instance, for one person to be a Confucianist, a Taoist, and a Buddhist at the same time—something inconceivable to Westerners, who have fought so many wars for religious motives.

Legal Philosophy and Penal Codes

Until the beginning of the Christian Era, China's relative isolation—created by desert expanses, frozen plateaus, and the natural border of the Pacific Ocean—contributed to the development of a culture in no way related to those of Europe and Mesopotamia. It is this factor that must be remembered when examining ancient Chinese law, which evolved independently, free from outside influence.

Law and religion were intimately linked in every one of the codes of the primitive Western civilizations. These early societies attributed their laws to a divine source. In contrast, old Chinese penal codes were absolutely secular.

Whereas Western codes were always directly related to economic developments and the early recognition of private property as well as the rights of the individual in society, ancient Chinese law had no direct relationship to the country's economic evolution. Although economic growth must have played an important role in transforming feudal China to the point where it needed written law, the law itself had a primarily political aim: imposing tighter political controls on an anomic society that was losing its old cultural values while new ones had yet to be established.

There are two conflicting viewpoints regarding the relationship between religion and law. Sir Henry Maine, in his book *Ancient Law,* is convinced that law derives from preexisting rules of conduct that are, at the same time, legal, moral, and religious in nature. It is his belief that every system of recorded law is initially entangled with religious rituals and observance. But A.S. Diamond, in his book *Primitive Law, Past and Present,* while accepting the fact that law and religion often intertwine (sacral crimes as sacrilege and the administration of oaths and ordeals during litigation) and keeping in mind that the ancient scribes were priests or were very closely attached to the temple, claims that surprisingly little religion appears in the early laws.

The first Chinese imperial code, known as the Code of Li k'vei, appeared in the fourth century B.C. and was based on still more ancient laws, some of which were in force at least three centuries earlier. It consisted of six chapters dealing mainly with theft, robbery, prison, arrest, miscellaneous items, and general rules. Later, each dynasty issued its own code, usually adapted from a previous one. The Code of Li k'vei, for instance, served as a model for the code of the Ch'in dynasty (221–207 B.C.). The first real revision was conducted during the Han dynasty (206 B.C.–219 A.D.), when corporal punishments were abolished. In the early seventh century A.D., the T'ang dynasty (618–906 A.D.) conducted an important code revision. It provided for five kinds of punishments, and the death penalty was restricted to only two methods: hanging and beheading. The Code of Emperor Yung Lo (1403–1424 A.D.) of the Ming dynasty (1368–1644), published in 1430, is the most modern of these ancient codes; it became the basis of the statutes of the Ch'ing dynasty (1644–1912).

If Roman law was civil-oriented, Chinese law was penal-oriented. In fact, civil matters (marriages, inheritance, property and commercial transactions, etc.) were entirely ignored or were given only a limited treatment. Basically, Chinese laws were codifications of the ethical norms long prevailing in primitive Chinese society. They were rarely invoked, except when less punitive measures had failed. Traditional Chinese society was by no means a legally oriented one, despite the fact that it produced an impressive body of codified law. The law was mainly concerned with acts of moral impropriety or of criminal violence, behavior considered to violate or disrupt the social order; in order to restore harmony, punishment had to be inflicted. In accordance with the Taoist concept, a disturbance of the social order meant, in fact, a disruption of the total cosmic order.

The differences between ancient Chinese law and Western legislation serve to emphasize the differences between these two civilizations. For instance, China has various extralegal institutions for social control—such as the clan, the guild, and the group of elders—that are almost nonexistent in the West.

Before T'ang's code of 653 A.D., with its 501 articles, no code survives except for a few quotations in other works. Therefore, there are no other sources for the earlier laws than the ancient annals and books of history. Among these laws, the best known is the code and judicial procedure of the first long imperial dynasty, that of Han. But it is during this preimperial age, the "period of the spring and autumn annals" and the "period of the warring states"—often called Chinese feudalism—that the formative beginnings of Chinese written law are to be found. The earliest real evidence of such written law dates from 536 B.C., the *Book of Punishments*. The *Hsing Shu* (*Hsing* = punishment and *Shu* = book) dealt specifically with corporal punishment. As a matter of fact, the five punishments mentioned (tattooing the forehead or face, cutting off the nose, amputation of one or both feet, castration, and death) were enforced in China long before the enactment of any system of written law. Once such a system came into existence, other punishments were added.

Chinese codes deal with the world in secular terms; perhaps this is why they were initially received with hostility. A myth dating from about 950 B.C. attributed the invention of *Fa* (the usual term for a model, pattern, or standard imposed by a superior authority) not to a king or even to a Chinese but to a "barbarian" people known as the Miao. Chinese thinking attributes the creation of civilization to the wisdom of their ancient sages but never suggests divine revelation. In later centuries, when the need for written law became more pressing, "sociological" explanations of its origin spoke of the sages' understanding of the people's needs. This may explain the opposition to the early codes on moral and political grounds.

The Confucians were staunch upholders of the traditional "feudal" scale of values, called *li*, a term that embraces both religious and secular rules of conduct. Thus, the Confucian at first opposed written laws; only when they realized that law had come to stay did they accept it as a necessary evil. Government by law, they claimed, should always be secondary to government by moral precepts and examples.

The Confucians were opposed by the Legalists, whose philosophy emphasized the importance of fixed standards as opposed to personal ethics in government. They were concerned not so much with the letter of the law as with increasing the power of state governments. Whereas Confucianism dealt mainly with ethical norms, Legalism was interested in studying the realities of power. In contrast to other philosophies, Legalism has no recognized founder and no school, in the classical sense of a teacher and students. It was a product of the fourth and third centuries B.C., when the tendency was to consolidate power: the absorption of small states by their larger neighbors, elimination of the authority of noblemen over their peasants (feudalism), direct administration of justice by officials of the central government, centralized collection of taxes, and so forth. The Legalists' attempt to provide the means toward achieving what had seemed impossible—"a united China"— had a particular appeal for men in positions of power. Most of the Legalists were not thinkers but tough-minded men of affairs, practical administrators, and usually close to the ruling circles. They were not unscrupulous power-hungry politicians, but they sincerely believed that only a strong hand could bring peace and unity to their war-torn world. The state of Ch'in, which finally unified China in 221 B.C., was notable for its Legalistic policies.

The principal dispute between Confucians and Legalists concerned the scope of law enforcement. The Confucians pointed out that even the best of laws must be enforced by men, so if the ruler of a state and his officials were upright, a permanent body of law was unnecessary. In contrast, the Legalists, for whom laws were an objective matter, were convinced that a uniform set of standards ought to apply to the entire population of a country. The ruler was to publish his decrees so that no one could remain ignorant of them, and a precise penalty was to be fixed for each offense, regardless of rank or extenuating circumstances.

Whereas the Legalists appear more concerned with law per se than with social welfare, Confucianism's approach was based on a social system that was rapidly becoming obsolete. The ethical principles by which a feudal lord supposedly governed peasants, whom he knew personally may have sufficed within the specific context of that society, but by the fourth and third centuries B.C., the old social structure, based on rigid class distinctions, was slowly breaking down, and men of humble background sometimes obtained positions of power. Bureaucrats representing the central government gradually replaced the aristocracy as tax collectors and judges over the peasantry, and the interests of the government required uniform standards in order to attain unity. In many respects, Legalism was a philosophy for a new and more complex age. Nevertheless, it quickly acquired an evil reputation because of the harsh government of the state of Ch'in, and later of the Ch'in dynasty, which united China. Moreover, the concept of law was never linked to any lofty principle, and the idea that the law was a guarantor of civil rights was nonexistent. To the Chinese mind, law was merely a set of fines and penalties imposed for transgressing a more or less arbitrary list of regulations, and it was decidedly inferior to *li*, the code of morals and manners observed by gentlemen. *Li*, an unwritten law, had nothing to do with government, and the penalties for transgressions were, at most, the disapproval of or ostracism by one's peers. Legalism was not a philosophy to win popular support and allegiance; therefore, the rulers never espoused it openly. Thus, from Han's time, Confucianism was the official doctrine of the empire. Nevertheless, Legalism had considerable influence on governmental policies. The attempt to centralize control of large geographic areas necessitated the adoption of a number of Legalistic measures, such as a uniform currency, uniform weights and measurements, the abolition of independent political authorities, and the development of a bureaucratic framework. Despite their professions to Confucianism, no Chinese government could afford to ignore the realities of political power, and Legalist ideas were frequently camouflaged as Confucianism or even integrated within Confucian classics. Eventually, the distinction between the two philosophies became blurred, and Legalism emerged as an important element in eclectic Confucianism, which prevailed under the Han dynasty.

The basis for the power of the Ch'in dynasty is attributed to Kun-Sun Yang (later, Lord Shang), who died in 338 B.C. In 361 B.C., he joined the court of the Duke Hsia of the state of Ch'in and later became his prime minister. The duke's policy was Legalistic in orientation, and his primary goal was to enhance his own power within his own state. He abolished the almost complete authority of the feudal lords over the peasants, restricted the scope of municipal governmental authority, and broke up the extended family groups in which the eldest male governed his relatives. By 350 B.C., he had divided the territory of the state of Ch'in into thirty-one districts (*hsien*), each governed by a prefect (*ling*), appointed by the duke, who replaced the lords in collecting taxes and administering justice among the peasants.

As a Legalist, Yang believed that laws should be so strict and penalties so harsh that no one would dare to commit crime. He even established a system of collective responsibility, dividing the population into groups of five or ten persons in which each individual had to report any illegal behavior by the others. The entire group was considered guilty of a crime committed by one of its members. This severity seems to have achieved results, since documents of that period show that the population of Ch'in was exceptionally orderly and law-abiding.

Yang also imposed an important land reform by granting the peasant ownership of the land he tilled and the right to sell or buy more land. This reform was probably responsible for a substantial increase in agricultural production.

Legalist theory regarded certain occupations as having priority over others; agriculture, weaving, and tool production, for example, were considered more important than trade. Yang imposed heavy tolls on trade, fixing high prices for luxuries such as meat and wine, and forbade trade in grain, since full graneries were the best guarantee of the prosperity and security of the state. This was another means by which he weakened the position of the nobility, the chief patrons of trade and artisanry.

After establishing these internal reforms, he began to increase Ch'in's influence beyond its own borders. He cultivated the military by granting office and rank only for military accomplishments. He also took severe measures against brigandage and the private wars of the nobility. In 352 and again in 340 B.C., he obtained decisive victories over the state of Wei, significantly increasing the territory of Ch'in. His reward—a personal fief of 15 towns and the title of Lord of Shang—was actually in contradiction of his own decree banning titles derived from landholding. Eventually, his many enemies brought about his downfall; the new Duke accepted rumors that he was plotting rebellion, and he was sentenced to be torn to pieces by chariots, and his entire family was executed.

From the Legalist standpoint, his policies—as stated in the so called *Book of Lord Shang,* were an unqualified success. His centralized political system proved to be the most efficient in China, giving Ch'in a great advantage over the other states, where the landed nobility was still far more powerful. Lord Shang's system of centralized government was, to a large extent, later applied throughout the entire Chinese empire.

Han Fei Tzu, who died in 233 B.C., was the leading theoretician of Legalism. He was a prince of the state of Han, and his close ties with the ruling class colored his political outlook. His book, also known as the *Han Fei Tzu,* is the fullest and most mature surviving exposition of the Legalistic philosophy. There is no doubt that a number of its essays were written by Han Fei Tzu himself. He had authoritarian views and regarded human nature as fundamentally evil, without believing in the redeeming power of education and culture. While Confucius insisted that government ministers should be chosen for their upright character, he was convinced that all officials were potentially dishonest, and should be encouraged to spy upon their colleagues. The masses were ignorant, acting only in their own interests; therefore, a strict set of laws and penalties, impartially enforced, was indispensable in order to keep public order. His analyses of government aims and practices are coolly rational, and many of his ideas, while publicly abhorred, were nonetheless practiced by Chinese governments. His book ranks among the major works of Chinese literature.

If for the Confucians the key term was *li,* for the Legalists it was *fa* (law), from which comes the expression *fa chia* (school of law). If the former believed in the paramount importance of the individual, the family, and the local community, the latter were ardent advocates of the supreme value of law. According to the Confucians, disorder is due only to man's failure to understand or live according to *li,* which represents what man instinctively feels is right. Therefore, *li* might be compared to the western concept of "natural law," while *fa* can be compared to its notion of "positive law."

The classical debate between Confucianism and Legalism can be summarized as follows:

Confucianism	*Legalism*
1. Man is basically good by nature or at least capable of being taught to be so. *Li*'s teaching, therefore, is preventive, whereas *fa* is merely punitive.	1. Most men are motivated purely by self-interest. Therefore, the law must prescribe firm punishments.
2. A virtuous government, based on *li,* can win the hearts of its subjects. Law is the tool of tyranny. An unwritten law is flexible and therefore can be adapted to any situation.	2. The impartiality of law is the basis of stable, effective government. *Li,* which is unwritten and subjective, is always open to interpretation, whereas law is precise and fixed.

<table>
<tr><td>

Confucianism

3. A stable social order is based on the five major hierarchical relationships: father–son, ruler–subject, husband–wife, older–younger brother, friend–friend. By enforcing uniformity, *fa* obliterates these relationships.

4. *Li,* created by the sages, is of universal and eternal validity.

5. Laws are only as good as those who create and execute them; thus, the moral tenor of the kingdom is determined by the morality of the rulers and officials.

</td><td>

Legalism

3. One of the basic principles of social order is that of *collective responsibility*. Every individual is equally responsible for the wrongdoings of others and equally subject to punishment. A strong state maintains a uniform system of morality; individual standards are to be suppressed.

4. Law must change to suit the times; all human institutions must adapt to changing conditions.

5. Even a mediocre ruler can stand at the head of a strong state if he has an efficient legal framework that maintains a high standard of morality.

</td></tr>
</table>

The universalism of the Legalistic *fa* and the particularism of the Confucian *li* have been perpetuated in the imperial codes according to four basic principles. The first of these is based on the Legalistic principle that *the punishment must fit the crime*. In fact, all Chinese imperial codes try to foresee each possible variation of a given offense, providing specific penalties for each of them. The basis for such differentiation was to be established according to three major principles: (1) *motivation,* such as premeditated homicide, intentional but not premeditated homicide, homicide during a fight, homicide by accident, homicide by inducing the victim to commit suicide, homicide for the purpose of witchcraft (with the intention to use the organs for magical ends), killing an adulterous wife, her paramour, or both, and so on; (2) the *status* of the killer vis-à-vis his victim, such as patricide, the killing of an official, the killing of a senior by a junior member of the same family or vice versa, the killing of a child by his father, the killing of a husband by his wife or vice versa, the killing of a slave by his master or the other way round, the assassination of three or more persons belonging to the same family, and so on; (3) the *means* by which the offense was committed, such as the use of poison, the improper administration of a medicine, the introduction of harmful objects into the nostrils, ears, or other openings of the victim's body, deprivation of food or clothing, the use of vehicles or animals, killing in the course of hunting, and so on. These three criteria are not specifically mentioned in the codes but were always used for the purpose of analyzing a given case. Although these distinctions may have been intended to enable the judge to take into consideration every foreseeable circumstance, they actually made the administration of justice more difficult by compelling judges who were faced with a case not covered by existing statutes to apply the statute most nearly applicable—that is, to judge by analogy.

The second principle was *differentiation by social status.* In accordance with the spirit of *li,* the codes prescribe different penalties according to the status of the offender and his victims; slaves, commoners, and officials were the three main categories differentiated by law. Beating another person by hand or foot, resulting in no wound, when occurring between equals, was punishable by twenty blows of the light bamboo; if a slave beat a commoner, the penalty was increased by ten blows; but if a commoner beat a slave, it was decreased by ten blows. A slave who struck his master was decapitated, whether or not there were injuries. No penalty was applied in the opposite case unless the injuries led to death. For beating the official in charge of one's own district, three years of penal servitude were prescribed, but if the offender was from another district, the penalty was only two years or even less, depending on the official's rank.

The third basic principle was that relating to *privileged groups.* There were eight different groups: (1) members of the imperial family; (2) descendants of former imperial houses; (3) persons of great merit; (4) high officials (mandarins); (5) the immediate family members of high officials; (6) lower officials; (7) commoners; and (8) slaves. Members of officialdom could not be arrested, investigated, or tortured without the emperor's orders. If they were found guilty of a crime, their sentences were subject to the emperor's consideration, with a view toward possible mitigation in the case of a member of one of the privileged groups. The usual punishments for commoners (caning, penal servitude from one to three years, exile for life, and death) were commutable to monetary fines, reduction in official rank, or dismissal from the civil service. Officials who violated a given rule were punished by 100 blows of a heavy bamboo cane, whereas the punishment for nonofficials in a similar case was only 50 blows. An official who seduced a woman under his jurisdiction received a punishment two degrees greater than the usual punishment for this offense. Officials who frequented prostitutes were subject to punishment, whereas commoners were not.

The fourth and last major principle recognized *differentiations within the family,* based on sex, seniority, and degree of kinship, especially within extended families. The best example of this is the five degrees of mourning (*wu fu*), which, in descending order of duration and severity, are to be observed by any given member of a family upon the death of any other member. The first degree is that of a son or unmarried daughter mourning his or her parents; the second degree is that of a wife mourning her husband or her husband's parents or a concubine mourning her master. In the lesser degrees of mourning, the circle of relationship widens; the fifth degree relates to more than forty relatives.

The system of intrafamily hierarchy also applied to penal questions. For instance, if a son beat one of his parents, he was to suffer decapitation; but a parent who beat his son suffered no punishment unless the son died. In this case, the parent received 100 blows if the beating was provoked by the son's disobedience or one year of penal servitude and 60 blows if the beating was unprovoked. A wife striking her husband received 100 blows, but in the opposite case, the husband was punished only if he inflicted serious injury, such as breaking her nose, a tooth, a limb, and so forth.

Distinctions were also made according to the ages of the parties involved. If a younger brother beat an older one, he was sentenced to two and a half years of penal servitude and received ninety blows, even if no injury was inflicted. In the opposite case, there was no penalty at all.

Theft within the family was an exception to the general rule; the severity of punishment was in inverse proportion to the closeness of relationship and consistently lower than punishment for theft outside the family. The explanation lies in the ancient concept that within the family, property exists for the joint use of all its members.

The emphasis placed on filial peity (*hsiao*) and loyalty to one's superior (*chung*)—with the father and family taking precedence over the ruler and state—was illustrated by the T'ang code requirement that all officials retire from office during the mourning period for the death of a parent (this period was later reduced to one year instead of twenty-seven months). Another of the code's rules calls for one year of penal servitude for a couple that conceives a child during the mourning period. The Confucian *Analects* states: "The father conceals the son, and the son the father"; that is, a man was not required to reveal his knowledge of a crime committed by a close relative, nor was he compelled to testify against a relative in court.

Another provision, enforced since the time of the Han dynasty, determined that a son who accused his parent of a wrongdoing was condemned to death by strangulation if the accusation was false and to three years of penal servitude and 100 blows with a heavy bamboo cane if the accusation was true. The same terms applied to a wife who accused her husband or parents-in-law of a crime.

A remarkable example of the principle of *hsiao* was that if a criminal was sentenced to death or to a long term of penal servitude, and he was the sole support of aged or infirm parents, his sentence would be commuted to a beating, monetary compensation, or wearing the "cangue"—a heavy wooden yoke worn by a criminal exposed to public mockery.

Death penalties and other major sentences had to be approved by the highest judicial body—sometimes even by the emperor himself—and could be reduced in severity. In fact, harsh punishments and low taxes were regarded as the major characteristics of a benevolent government. In the *Book of History,* a chapter entitled "The Marquis of Lu on Punishments" states that justice must be uniform, though punishments vary according to circumstances. According to Chinese philosophy, particularly Taoism, violations of the social order constituted a disruption of the entire cosmic order; thus, serious penal procedures—especially death sentences—were to be carried out only during the autumn and winter months (which represented decay and death) and were avoided during spring and summer (symbolic of rebirth and growth).

Confucian humanitarianism was expressed in a number of ways. Amnesties were granted frequently, and there were special exemptions and reductions of sentences for the aged (seventy years and above), the young (fifteen years and below), and the physically or mentally infirm. Women enjoyed the privilege of monetary redemption for a number of crimes. Anonymous accusations were severely punished: The accuser was sentenced to death by strangulation even if the accusation was true, and an official acting on the basis of such an accusation was sentenced to 100 blows with a heavy bamboo cane.

Very little is known regarding the administration of justice in imperial China—the selection of judges, the constitution of courts, criminal procedure, and so forth. However, it is quite clear that the emperor had the final word in dealing with serious criminal cases. There was no classification of offenses or sanctions; these were cited according to legal texts of different dynasties and emperors.

The refined brutality of the primitive Chinese punishments is unspeakable. The traditional sanctions were full of cruel and refined techniques, especially those sympathetic in nature: cutting off a man's lower lip for kissing a married woman or his finger for indecent assault. Buddhism, with emphasis on the virtue of compassion, was probably responsible for mitigating the harshness of the penalties for certain crimes.

Intentional homicide was a capital offense, as was adultery. A priest was not put to death for any capital offense, except treason. He could be branded or even blinded, but more frequently he was banished.

The husband of an adulterous wife was entitled to put both his wife and her lover to death or to mutilate them, but not the lover alone, for that would savor of conspiracy between husband and wife (similar to the ancient Hebrew law and the Laws of Manu). Other capital offenses included treason, witchcraft, black magic, incest, blasphemy, suicide, and forgery. An offender convicted of any one of these crimes could be beaten to death, buried alive, impaled, cut to pieces, hanged, burned to death, drowned, or thrown from a cliff, but the emperor could lighten the sentence. Theft of an object of substantial value was considered a capital offense whether or not the thief was caught in the act.

For years, the conventional wisdom was that the Chinese masses were so honest and so purged of human greed that even a discarded razor blade would be returned to a startled foreign visitor. At least, everyone knew that in China, one was safe. This is not so today. Crime, once confidently ascribed to the decadent, capitalistic West, is flourishing in frantically modernizing China. Despite the outward appearance of an established and generally accepted order, there is a subculture of criminality more like the Western example than a model of Marxism. China is experiencing today a wave of violent crimes—murder, rape, and robbery—together with theft, official corruption (one of China's oldest traditions), embezzlement, and general lawlessness to an unprecedented degree. The government is reacting with a nationwide network of measures for dealing with offenders, one of the most important of which is the highly publicized executions of dozens of criminals of a given city on a single day. A spectacular lesson that crime does not pay came in Peking in August 1983, when thirty people were publicly executed in the Workers' Stadium, near the Marco Polo Bridge, before a cheering, highly agitated crowd estimated at 60,000 onlookers. Ranging in age from eighteen to thirty-four, the offenders had been tried and convicted of murder, rape, robbery, and arson. They were handcuffed and shot in the modern Chinese method: one single bullet to the back of the head. This was the largest execution in one day in recent memory. The pattern has been repeated in a number of cities, and some observers believe that between 1,000 and 2,000, or perhaps more, have been executed since then. The new policy is "democratically" applied, including among the executed relatives of national heroes, such as the grandson of Marshal Ye Jianying, a member of the standing committee of the Communist Party Politburo, and the grandson of Chu Teh, China's most illustrious general. Amnesty International has charged that since the purge of the "Gang of Four" in October 1976, many executions have been carried out, not only for such crimes as murder, rape, and robbery, but also—sometimes—for political offenders. Other dissidents have been starved, beaten, and virtually enslaved or sent into solitary confinement. These charges were presented in June 1978 but received no reply.

In order to deal with the situation, particularly the problem of juvenile delinquency, the Chinese government decided to increase education facilities; reform schools have been reopened "in order to educate and save the younger generation." In July 1979, the "Law of Criminal Procedure" was officially enacted; it stresses the rights of the individual, similar to Western law and political philosophy, as the best means to control the recent problem of criminality.

In conclusion, it can be stated that China's legal development differs sharply from that of other civilizations. From the beginning, China's law was viewed in purely secular terms, and the controversy between *li* and *fa* is remarkable in its relevance to modern questions. If the Confucian concern for mankind's moral development is indeed democratic, its insistence on a hierarchical society is aristocratic. In the same vein, the Legalistic wish to control the masses was totalitarian, but the basic aphorism that "all men are equal with respect to the law" was undoubtedly an egalitarian concept.

8

Ancient and Classical Greece

Captive Greece took Rome captive.
—Horace

T he nineteenth-century French historian Ernest Renan termed Greek
civilization "a miracle," in that it seemed to have appeared suddenly,
on a very high cultural level, without having passed through the rudimentary stages of evolution. Indeed, the roots of this magnificient culture
remained a mystery until the end of the nineteenth century, when the discovery of the Aegean-Cretan civilization shed light on what must have served as
a prologue to the Hellenic culture. The civilization that existed on Crete,
known as the Minoan or Minoic civilization, was a bureaucratic monarchy—
a government centered on a king and administered by civil and military functionaries. The Dorian invasion of 1180 B.C. signaled the beginning of an age
of colonization—a confrontation and blending of cultures: The Eolians, Ion-
ians, and Dorians came together to form city-states, which were the central
characteristic of the Greek sociopolitical structure.

Sparta

Greek history revolves almost entirely around the rivalry between its two
great cities: Athens and Sparta. Whereas the Athenian was completely dedicated to politics, arts, and commerce, the Spartan was basically a military
man, devoted to the administration of his state. No more than about 9,000
Dorian families overall populated Sparta. They constituted the first social
class, enjoying all the civil and political rights. The second social class, that
of the Laconians or Lacedemonians, lived outside the city in the nearby mountainous region. They constituted some 30,000 altogether and, as freemen,
had civil but not political rights. They could not participate in the popular
Assembly, so they were entirely dedicated to industry, agriculture, and commerce. They paid tribute to the Dorians and had to serve in their army. The
third class, constituted by some 200,000 Ilotes, were more servants than
slaves. They had no civil rights but were not completely subject to their landlords. In a sense, they were slaves of the community, and no one was entitled

to harm their persons or property. They had to obey but were not the property of anyone. They worked the land, and they could not be sold or given away as a gift. Their duty was to pay their landlords the stipulated amount of wheat but nothing more. Because they were sometimes treated harshly, they frequently rebelled, but without success. Foreigners had no rights whatsoever in Sparta.

Xenophon (c. 457–355 B.C.), the Greek historian and military figure, attributed the great success of Sparta to the legislation introduced by Lycurgus, the Spartan lawgiver who abolished the old Dorian laws and established a new sociopolitical system. His legislation was a kind of educational discipline, meant to preserve the existing aristocratic government of the state and to facilitate the development of the military establishment. He never recorded the laws; they were transmitted orally. He was sure that social harmony could be achieved only by respecting traditional customs and by directing the education of the citizens from cradle to grave. This educational system even dealt with the procreation of children, considered the basic right and duty of women. There were also eugenic practices, such as killing every child born with some deformity. Family life was organized for the good of the state: Women were required to do physical exercises; and at the age of seven, children began training for their military service. (They were not supposed to use shoes, in order to develop strong feet.) All people—men, women, and children—wore one simple dress during the entire year, so that they would become accustomed to both the winter and summer climates.

Education was in the hands of the pedonomes—a kind of magistrate—whose authority encompassed all realms of pupils' behavior. Childrens' diets were planned in order to teach them to know and tolerate hunger and thirst. Lycurgus was particularly severe with adolescents, setting them numerous difficult tasks. He established communal dining halls and ordered the closure of all taverns in the city—measures that helped raise a generation of excellent soldiers. They had great respect for the law, which forbade them to flee the field of battle; only victory in death released them. Cowardice was so shameful that it was grounds for suicide. Paradoxically, it was the very rigidity of Sparta's system of education that created an inability to adjust to new situations and contributed to its eventual downfall.

The kingdom of Sparta had two kings, one in charge of the army and the other in charge of religious ceremonies. These rulers acted as judges in cases regarding family matters as well as crimes. It was customary to stand in the presence of the king, with the exception of the five ephors (the ancient Spartan magistrates having power over the kings). Each month, the kings and the ephors swore oaths of loyalty—the former to reign according to the laws, the latter to the city.

Spartan institutions were of an aristocratic and oligarchic character. The Senate—Gerousia (from the Greek root *geront,* "elder"), or Council of

Elders—consisted of twenty-eight members—some, related to the kings, elected by the people's Assembly. They were at least sixty years of age, and their appointments were for life. Their duties were mainly of a legislative nature (preparing the drafts of laws to be presented to the Assembly), but they also made decisions regarding war and peace and tried all cases of homicide as well as other serious crimes against the state. This was also the only tribunal that could inflict the death penalty upon a citizen.

The Assembly, or Apella, consisted of citizens who were over the age of thirty. It met once a month and dealt with political issues; it discussed and either accepted or rejected the drafts presented to it by the Senate. Its decisions in matters of war and peace could be vetoed by the Senate. The Assembly elected the geronts or senators, as well as the ephors. The candidates walked back and forth through the Assembly, and the candidate who received the loudest acclamation was elected and approved by a commission of elders, who, in order to retain their impartiality, remained hidden, without seeing the candidates.

The ephors, who were in fact the political heads of Sparta during much of the fifth century B.C., and all of the fourth century B.C., were elected annually by the Assembly. In time of war, two ephors accompanied the king, who marched at the head of the army. They and the senators held the most powerful positions in the state. In certain cases, they were even more powerful than the kings, who were under their strict vigilance. It was they who held the political reins and had control over the magistrates. They convened the Assembly, ordered the mobilization of the army, and had some judicial functions. They dealt with all civil and some criminal cases, such as homicide and theft of public funds. The most severe crime was treason—for which the offender and all members of his family were executed. The ephors' decisions were final and had to be unanimous. It is important to note that there is no reliable information regarding which matters were considered civil and which criminal. The ephors also ruled in cases of crimes that violated social mores, such as abortion, and could fine the criminal. They had the power to depose magistrates, put them in jail, and even indict them for capital offenses. However, if one of the ephors behaved improperly, he too could be punished. To a certain extent they were a kind of tribune of the people, protecting the lower classes from arbitrary actions of the magistrates or other officials.

The life of Sparta's citizens was regulated to the most minute detail by a great number of ancient laws, strictly enforced by magistrates with the power to punish transgressors. Any violation of these rules was regarded as an offense against the state, and any citizen was entitled to denounce such violations. Indeed, for the Spartans, respect for the law was not an end in itself but a means for the preservation of the state, its efficiency at war, and the retention of power by the oligarchy. As a consequence, criminal procedure in Sparta, unlike that in Athens, tended to be inquisitorial rather than litigious.

The Cultural and Sociopolitical Structure
of Athens from Homer to Pericles

The ancient Greeks absorbed Mesopotamian culture and funneled it westward. Unlike the Hebrews, they had no direct contacts with Mesopotamia itself, but during the Greek Mycenaean age (from about 1600 to 1100 B.C.), they did have political and commercial ties with Mesopotamian neighbors such as the Hittites and the Canaanites. Through the coastal towns of southern Anatolia, Canaan, Cyprus, and Crete flowed not only material goods but also thoughts and ideas, a number of them undoubtedly taking root in Greek soil. The discovery, only a few years ago, of an important cache of Babylonian cylinder seals was not surprising to the archaeological world, and the future will no doubt reveal many such finds on Greek soil.

The early contacts came to an end when the Mycenaean culture collapsed. Not until the eighth century B.C., when the Greeks began to emerge from the "Dark Age," were they again stimulated and inspired by their eastern neighbors. During this later period, the Canaanite-Phoenicians gave the Greek the alphabet that eventually became that of the entire Western world. Also during this period, pre-Socratic philosophers in Anatolia discovered the work of Babylonian astronomers and began the cosmological studies that culminated in the great philosophical schools of Athens. And by the time Greece entered its "Golden Age," in the fifth century B.C., not a few of its achievements in art, architecture, philosophy, and literature showed vestiges of Mesopotamian origin.

Nevertheless, the Greeks realized that the fundamental difference between these foreign cultures and their own basic culture was that the people of Mesopotamia were slaves while their own were freemen, particularly in the political sense. In Mesopotamia the head of state was everything and the citizen nothing, because the former personified divinity, and his orders were an absolute command to be blindly obeyed. For the Greeks, their own government, no matter which government, respected the basic rights of the people, who never lived under the dictatorship of absolute monarchs except in very few instances. It is interesting that Mesopotamia had no philosophers and no theater.

The *polis*—the city—is the essence of Greek culture. It is difficult to imagine a Greek outside his polis. All Greeks participated in their public Assembly to discuss the needs of their poleis. Anyone who was more interested in his own problem than in those of his polis was despised. For Aristotle, man was a "political animal"; that is, he could never be understood outside his polis. The main outcome of this devotion to the polis was democracy, with justice applied equally to all citizens according to laws they had approved themselves.

Although law in the vast majority of Eastern civilizations was always intimately linked to religion, the legal development of Greece cannot be separated from its sociopolitical evolution. During the "heroic age," there were four different types of kingdoms in the Greek world. The last one was hereditary and legal, exercised over willing subjects. The king took command in war, presided over sacrifices, and decided disputes among the people. The social structure was based on the clan, with all its members claiming descent from a common ancestor; the phratry, a group of people showing the same religious inclinations and observing the same rites; and the *tribe,* a larger unit, including all the members of a given community, which was considered a military division in times of war. At the head of the state was the basileus, sometimes considered to be of a kind of divine descent, whose function was also that of religious leader. Next in line was a council of less powerful chiefs, also called basileis. Each of these chiefs was a suzerain over a group of even lesser chiefs who were, in turn, suzerains over smaller groups of subordinates. Each chief was more or less important according to the number of basileis subordinate to him. Finally, there was the popular Assembly, constituted by all adult freemen of the community, meeting regularly to hear the plans presented by the basileus.

Attica was then divided into a number of petty principalities that, for defensive purposes, were under the suzerainty of the kings of Athens. Otherwise, each community had its own magistrates and managed its local affairs independently, including the administration of justice. Similarities of language and institutions were unifying forces facilitating the formation of groups of small communities for religious and/or defensive purposes. Athens eventually was chosen by the nobles as the capital city, and all the inhabitants of Attica became Athenians (a unity that was achieved before the fifth century B.C.). The commoners continued to live in the country, coming to Athens only for litigation or for the exercise of their political rights.

As a result of Athens' growing importance, a number of political changes came about. Although the king retained his leadership in war and in legal matters, the nobles took charge of religious rites, the election of magistrates, the teaching of the law, and the interpretation of the "will of heaven." The king was also in charge of foreign affairs—official visits, negotiation of treaties, and so forth.

Although the monarch's authority was beyond question, he would generally follow the advice of the Council of Elders, composed of the subordinate chiefs. The king presented his plans to the council before they were brought for the consideration of the Assembly, but he always made the final decisions. The king was usually the one to call the Assembly, which, at least in principle, was open to all the chieftains and to the common people as well.

As the monarchy weakened, its power was gradually usurped by the aristocracy, through the Council of Elders. The aristocracy consisted of a number of families supposedly related by blood. In contrast to Eastern cultures, where the priestly element was so powerful, in the West (at least in the Indo-European states), the era of the heroic kings was succeeded by that of powerful oligarchies.

Solon, the *archon* (chief magistrate) who served from about 638 to 559 B.C., was responsible for effecting important political changes. Until his time, all the functions of government—executive, legislative, and judicial—were exclusively in the hands of the *eupatrid* class (hereditary aristocracy and landowners), acting through the oligarchic council, later known as the Council of the Areopagus. Its members were selected by lot among retired archons who were at least of fifty years of age. Its executive officers were selected according to the candidates' aristocratic and timocratic (political and civil honors distributed in proportion to the material wealth of each citizen) status.

The lower classes—such as the peasant proprietors, or *georgi,* the artisans, or *demiurgi,* and the soldiers—could have influence in the government only by attaching themselves to some member of the aristocracy. Below them were the lowest class of freemen, those without property: the *thetes, hectomori,* or *pelatae.* Still lower were the slaves proper, who had no rights whatsoever. Each family or phratry with wealth and influence was represented in the aristocratic council. An individual who belonged to one of the kinship groups represented in the council was recognized as a citizen. This recognition was also extended to respectable peasants, farmers, artisans, petty landowners, and similar people who were able to maintain their membership in a given phratry because they could pay their taxes during the public meetings and festivals. They were inducted by the phratries for military service and were entitled to attend the Assembly. The hectomori and hired laborers were not recognized by the phratries and consequently were not considered citizens.

Solon came to power at a time when the people were faced with overwhelming debts and a diminishing supply of arable land. Some even had to sell their children in order to survive. Others were forced to emigrate. Solon attributed the existing civil tensions in Athens to the greed and corruption of the oligarchy. He decreed that all men must be equal before the law, despite the fact that nature has established differences between them—an equality that could be assured only through the written law. He coined the expression *eunomia*—which means "new order," "good government," or "government by law"—which became the slogan of the conservative as well as the progressive citizens of the Greek cities. The basis for eunomia was that the state could not prosper without justice and good order, achieved through a written code of law.

Solon organized the people, granting them the power to maintain and defend their political and economic rights through constitutional means. It is he who created the concept of democracy, later to be established in Athens by Cleisthenes. Solon succeeded in limiting the powers of the aristocratic rulers, assuring the rich that the people would pay back their debts while, at the same time, promising the people that he would redistribute the agricultural lands. The rich did not oppose him because he was one of them, and the people recognized that he was a man of great honesty and integrity. By 594 B.C., Solon was already archon, nomothete, mediator, and lawgiver, with almost absolute powers.

One of his first measures was to abolish slavery for debts, perhaps the main reason for the existing social ferment. He forbade debts that were guaranteed by the person of the debtor, his wife, or his children. He also initiated the redistribution of the agricultural lands held by the eupatrides by decreeing that no citizen could have more than a certain amount of land. He also established official standards of weights, measures, and currency.

Solon retained four social classes but based their divisions on wealth rather than family relationship. Thus, anyone could attain membership in the upper class regardless of birth—provided that his accumulated wealth was equal to 500 silver drachmas. Taxes were progressive and proportional to the wealth of each citizen; the people of the lowest class were exempt. However, the lowest class had no political functions and could participate in government only by attending the meetings of the popular Assembly or acting as judges.

Despite its egalitarian character, the Areopagus was still an aristocratic institution. In order to achieve a balance, Solon established the *Ecclesia,* or popular Assembly, composed of citizens of the four social classes, including the thetes. This assembly had the right to intervene in all political matters. The archons were no longer appointed by the Areopagus but by the people. The Areopagus itself was also changed: instead of being composed of eupatrides, it now consisted of thirty-one archons who no longer served in an official capacity. Finally, Solon also established the Senate, or *Boulé* (because it met at the Bouleuterion), also known as the *Council of the 400,* made up of 100 citizens of each of the four classes. The Senate was in charge of preparing the legal proposals to be presented to the Assembly, since such a massive forum could not effectively function without the guidance of a smaller body. The Senate, closely associated with the Assembly, was an excellent device for maintaining the proper balance between the common people and the rich and powerful. The laws prepared by the Senate and approved by the Assembly were to be controlled by the Areopagus, still basically in the hands of the eupatrides. Solon's own reforms must have been studied by the Boulé, approved by the Ecclesia, and executed by the Areopagus.

Another important measure taken by Solon was to allow judicial decisions to be appealed before the Assembly. Thus, the Assembly exercised both deliberative and judicial functions. Appeals could also be introduced by the Boulé, whose members presided at both judicial and deliberative sessions.

Solon's sociopolitical improvements did not solve all of Athen's social problems. In fact, he had to retain the Areopagus, with its predominantly aristocratic structure. However, his reforms did help safeguard the rights of the people and put an end to the oligarchic monopoly.

Solon's reforms included a number of changes in civil and criminal law. He gradually replaced the judges with popular tribunals, and the functions of the archons became more administrative.

Although there is no exact record of his laws, some have reached us through secondary sources. Plutarch mentions some of his laws: (1) it was forbidden to dishonor the good name of the dead or to insult a citizen during court procedures, ritual sacrifices, Assembly meetings, shows, and pageants; (2) disorder or extreme behavior during feasts, funerals, and the like, was to be repressed; (3) the son who has not been taught a craft or profession is not obliged to care for his father; and (4) lazy people who did not work were to be punished. His law regarding inheritance established that the citizen who had no next of kin could distribute his property at will if he was neither insane nor under the influence of witchcraft, nor acting under a threat of violence.

At the end of Solon's term as archon, he left Athens on a long journey to foreign lands. It was then that Peisistratus (c. 561–527 B.C.), Solon's nephew, became the tyrant of Athens. He was not a despotic ruler, although he came to power by force rather than as a duly elected official. He was a great admirer of Solon and his laws, but he also exploited the existing discontent and declared himself the "defender of the people." Indeed, he enforced Solon's laws only when they did not conflict with his personal rule.

After his death, his two sons, Hipias and Hiparcus, tried to follow in their father's path, but because they lacked his ability to govern, their reigns were short. Peisistratus's rule was a period that paved the way for democracy, during which the people began to accustom themselves to Solon's egalitarian ideals.

Cleisthenes, the true founder of Athenian democracy, was deeply convinced of the ethical value of a democratic form of government. Although a nobleman, he supported the people. Under his rule, everyone had equal rights and duties before the law, the only exception being the slaves and foreigners. The latter were free but had no voice or vote in the Assembly.

The Assembly conferred upon Cleisthenes extraordinary legislative powers, similar to those of Solon, and his reforms were established over a period of years. He eliminated differences based on birth or wealth, thus abolishing Solon's four social classes. The grandchildren of foreigners born in Attica were now citizens. He established little units or communities—*demos*—according to the places where people lived: the urban region, or city, and its immediate surroundings; the coastal region; and the mountainous region. Each demos was presided over by a *demarca*. More than 100 demos were so established, and a number of these demos constituted, for political purposes, a *tritia*. Each region had ten tritias. An urban tritia together with another from the coastal region and a third from the mountains constituted one *tribe*. There was a total of ten tribes, each known by the name of one of the ten heroes of Athens. Each tribe elected its own chief—the *strategos,* or general—who, in times of need, was contributed to the national army. The chief of the army was the *polemarch,* who, early in the fifth century B.C., ceased to be a military official and, as one of the nine archons, took on executive and other functions. The strategoi slowly replaced the archons, who had represented the aristocracy.

Cleisthenes increased the number of members of the Senate to 500—fifty for each Attic tribe. They were chosen by lot from a list of volunteers over the age of thirty. This was the Council of the 500, also known as the Boulé, which met daily and prepared the agenda for the Assembly. Each member took an oath to respect the laws, was paid for his services, and served for one year. After an interval, he could serve a second term, but never more than two. In such a way, about one-third of the citizens must have served at the Boulé at one time or another.

Another of his innovations was the concept of *ostracism*—from the Greek root *ostrakon,* a kind of small potsherd upon which the citizens of the popular Assembly inscribed their vote—a novel and ingenious device to protect the people from tyranny. A ten-year political exile (later reduced to five years), was imposed by the Assembly on any citizen whose political or military prestige might enable him to lead an internal rebellion in order to establish a tyrannical government. A citizen could be ostracized without formal accusation or defense. According to available records, no one was ostracized until 487 B.C. Ostracism did not involve dishonor, loss of rights, or confiscation of property. Upon his return, the citizen regained all his political rights and recovered his property. Once a year, during one of the general assemblies of the Ecclesia—regarded as the true representatives of the Athenian people—its members were asked if they thought there were sufficient reasons for ostracizing a citizen. At a subsequent meeting, the members voted secretly. Only with a majority of votes could ostracism be imposed.

The process begun in 507 B.C. by Cleisthenes was completed by Ephialtes, the Athenian statesman who served from 462 to 461 B.C. Ephialtes stripped the aristocrats of all their powers except for certain judicial functions in matters of homicide and some religious duties. He was murdered by the nobles, but his democracy survived. Thereafter, no political body stood above the popular Assembly.

The basic reforms of Ephialtes consisted of establishing laws delegating authority that had formerly belonged to the Areopagus (such as administrative and judicial functions) to other bodies. Homicide, however, was still dealt with by the Areopagus, because the people felt that its authority was held by divine right. When a murderer could not be removed from the protection of a shrine, a committee of the Areopagus was sent to try him at the shrine. This practice of using committees was adopted very early by the Areopagus. The Areopagus also remained in charge of cases regarding morals and customs, education, and impiety, as well as the supervision of laws on arson (when it endangered life) and a general surveillance of rituals, ceremonies, and similar religious matters. It also supervised the magistrates, but the right to suspend those who behaved unlawfully or improperly was no longer in their power.

Pericles, one of Ephialtes's young associates, was responsible for a new attack against the Areopagus in 452 B.C., after the death of Ephialtes. The only powers he left to the Areopagus were those that had never been shared with any other body.

The Athenian Assembly, or Ecclesia, which usually constituted about 5,000 people more than twenty years of age, met in the Agora (marketplace), and was open to all free male citizens, regardless of income or class. It met forty times a year. In theory, every member of the Assembly could speak about any subject, provided that he could command the attention of the Assembly. For practical reasons, there was an official agenda, prepared by the Council of the 500. The subjects to be discussed were introduced by the Boulé to the Assembly; after they were dealt with and approved, they were returned to the Boulé, which studied them, prepared law drafts, and then went back to the Assembly for final discussion and decision. If approved, the proposal became law. Only the Assembly was entitled to legislate laws, never the Boulé, which could publish a decree, but never a law, in times of emergency. Within the Boulé was a smaller inner council of fifty men, known as the Prytany, which met every day and in fact administered the government of the city. The Prytaneum was the seat of the highest Athenian officials. Its membership changed ten times a year and its chairmanship every day, so that no one could remain in power long enough to entrench himself. Moreover, all magistrates on finishing their official duties had to present a detailed report to ten of these officials.

The first meeting of the Assembly, usually on the tenth of each month, was dedicated to examining the functions of the magistrates and their administration of justice. The Assembly analyzed and evaluated the behavior of each of them and either ratified or revoked their appointments.

Besides its basic legislative functions, the Assembly had some executive functions (ratifying the election of the strategoi, granting citizenships, deciding on ostracism, administering the treasury, etc); others of a judicial nature (appointing magistrates and supervising their behavior); and some municipal duties (the upkeep and beautifying of the city). The chief of the Prytany, appointed by its members, was known as the Epistate. All of the Prytany's members attended the Assembly, over which they presided under the direction of the Epistate.

Unlike modern representative democracies, Athens was a true democracy; every citizen could speak for himself. Women, however, had no voice in government. Under Pericles, their role was limited to the home and family.

Many of Pericles' reforms encountered opposition among the aristocracy. The restriction of the powers of the Areopagus, the provision of payment for jurors introduced by Pericles, and similar measures severely limited their influence and brought about an oligarchic reaction. As a result, a number of legal reforms were introduced in the laws of Ephialtes. Homicide cases were again to be tried by the Areopagus; the Boulé tried the cases related to all types of sycophants, putting them to death in great numbers. Again, the Athenian judicial system led to a reign of terror.

The Boulé, instituted by Cleisthenes before about 508–507 B.C., was of great importance throughout the sixth and the fifth centuries B.C. but underwent important changes during the two oligarchic revolutions of 411 and 404 B.C. Before this time, the Boulé was a sovereign body of the state, subject to no interference. It had important judicial powers and could inflict penalties of death, imprisonment, and fines. There were three periods during which the powers of the Boulé were restricted: soon after the beginning of Cleisthenes' reforms, when much of its powers were transferred to the Assembly; after the downfall of the two oligarchic revolutions, when the rights of the Boulé were redefined; and in 387 B.C., when it was again restricted.

When democracy was restored in 403 B.C., the judicial system in Athens was enlarged by thirty circuit judges, who now held court in Athens, not in the other city-states. Each circuit was made up of forty judges, elected by lot, four from each tribe. In cases related to amounts of less than ten drachmas, their judgment was final. Other cases were transferred to one of the public arbitrators, a post that all men aged sixty or more were obligated to fill unless they held another public office or were sick or abroad. Anyone unwilling to serve could be deprived of his civil rights. An official list of arbitrators was made up each year. If necessary, these arbitrators could be called on to sit in judgment regarding the behavior of one of their group. The penalty for improper behavior in office was a loss of civil rights. The arbitrators' sentences were subject to appeal. In 364 B.C., a law was passed requiring that evidence be put in writing in order to save interrogation time.

During the fourth century B.C., the Areopagus was composed of former archons who had successfully passed their audit. The Areopagus could expel any member on a provisional basis; the expulsion became final after being confirmed by a higher court. To retain their dignified reputation, the members of the Areopagus were not allowed to dine in a public house or to write comedies. They retained their jurisdiction in cases of premeditated homicide, intentional wounding, death by poisoning, and arson. They also were responsible for supervising the way in which public physicians carried out their duties.

Evolution of the Greek Criminal Law

If we accept the basic notion that criminal law is law relating to crimes and their punishment, the definition of *crime* becomes paramount. It may range from general formulas of almost universal validity to others so complex as to suit only a particular legal system. The first few instances in which the members of a community united to stone a wrongdoer or to drive him out of the village did not constitute "law." But when the punishment became customary, this custom became "criminal law" and the acts it punished were "crimes." The way in which these concepts developed in each of the primitive societies depended on their character, cultural contacts and traditions, form of government, religious tenets, and similar factors. By "Greek law" we refer to the total complex of separate law systems, juridical frameworks, and traditions that existed in the Greek world, from the formation of the Greek nation (c. 1200–1100 B.C.) until the Hellenistic period and even until the compilation of the Justinian Code, the Byzantine Law. There was a plurality of laws, since each of the many poleis had their own legislation, but their basic guiding principles were much the same. Athens' supremacy in the political arena—as well as in the arts, philosophy, and literature—made its legislation the most important from at least the fifth century B.C. Indeed, the vast majority of available sources relate to the laws of Athens during the classical age. Greek law is perhaps the oldest of all the juridical systems of continental Europe.

The significance of Greek law in relation to modern juridical or criminological sciences lies not in its structure, but in the fundamental principles of democracy on which it is based. Broadly, two main factors postponed the development of criminal law. One was undoubtedly religion and ritual, which are powerful conservative forces. The other was the fact that the early history of "crime" invariably merged with that of "tort." The precise moment at which these two elements became separate and distinct is difficult to determine. For a long time, many wrongs regarded today as crimes were dealt with as torts and were left to private revenge. The best way to ascertain the primitive concept of crime would be to establish which offenses were punished by the community as a whole and which were dealt with by the individual victim or his family. The former could be regarded as crimes, the latter as tort. According to Homer (*Iliad* XVIII: 497–508), the Greeks arrived at the conclusion that revenge had to be taken out of private hands and put into those of the community.

The forerunners of Greek criminal law were, among others, the cuneiform and the Hebrew laws and especially the law system established during the pre-Hellenic civilizations in Crete and some of the other Aegean islands. Athens was constantly in contact with other states whose legal and political institutions were regarded as greatly superior to its own. Available sources are rather inadequate, since many of the possible sources of information are lost in mythology and in the great epic poems of the "heroic age." Nothing has remained, or has been discovered, of the Achean or Mycenean legal practices.

In the Near Eastern civilizations, the concepts of law and justice were linked to the spiritual, to a subjective morality that made responsibility a personal, not a collective, issue. In Greece, these concepts became autonomous, separate from the mysteries of faith and religion.

During Homer's time (also in the eighth century B.C.), the administration of justice was largely an informal private matter between the perpetrator and the victim. Within his own household, the master punished his servants—and even carried out the death penalty. Adultery, seduction, and rape were punished by the husband or nearest relative in the case of a free woman, by her master if she was a slave. Slaying does not seem to have been customary, or considered justifiable, in cases of adultery. Robbery, cattle stealing, and piracy were extremely common and were matters for which the entire community could exact punishment. When the stolen goods were of less importance, the injured person asked not only for the restitution of the destroyed, stolen, or withheld property but also for substantial damages. Homicide did not yet involve the notion of impurity for both the slayer and those associated with him. This would later be firmly established by the statesman Draco in the seventh century B.C., but it is impossible to tell exactly when this new doctrine appeared. Outside the circle of the victim's kinsmen, there was no popular sentiment against ordinary homicide, but the slaying of parents or a guest met with universal condemnation. Public sentiment not only tolerated blood feuds but even demanded that revenge include the killing of the kinsmen of the offender. Shame and disgrace were the lot of one who failed to take revenge on the slayer, his brother, or his son, whereas honor and glory awaited one who performed his sacred duty. Homicide among relatives was commonly settled by banishment, but in cases of homicide outside the family, the slayer usually tried to flee or paid blood money rather than falling prey to the vengeance of the victim's enraged kinsmen. The acceptance of blood money seems to have been comparatively rare, but the origin of this compensation is unknown. The classification of types of homicide was yet unknown.

The expression of popular sentiments against wrongdoers through community actions was well established in Homer's times, when public opinion was quickly crystallized and easily translated into action through the popular Assembly. Of course, the distinction between a deliberative assembly and a judicial body was still ill defined. Disputes were still settled rather informally, through self-help, community action, or evidentiary oaths. The aristocracy claimed to have a monopoly concerning the principles by which quarrels were decided. The new magistrates were invested not only with judicial privileges but also with military, religious, and civil functions. This era of customary law was also a period during which the prevailing customs of the tribes were preserved by oral transmission.

The basic distinctions between *dolus,* or guilt, negligence, and accident were still not established. Criminal responsibility was collective, including the family of the offender, parents and children. Punishment was even meted out to corpses, a result of the influence of religion. The right to punish, if it was exercised by the king, judges, or members of the priestly castes acting on the king's behalf, was always presented as divine property. When ancient Greece was made up of clans and tribes, there were two main varieties of crime: those related to acts committed by a member of a clan against another of its members and those committed by a foreigner or a stranger. The notion of theft as a public crime was introduced by Solon, and homicide was long considered a private matter.

The origins of the ancient Greek law are to be found in the *Iliad* and the *Odyssey,* in which the king is portrayed as absolute ruler and there is an aristocratic kind of parliament. Marriage and matrimonial relations; guardianship of children; common ownership by the entire family (but also with the first traces of private ownership of movables); a primitive kind of contract known as "harmony"; gifts, loans, and sale of goods; and some elements of criminal law and procedure either appear or are alluded to in those epic poems.

Homer's poems show no sign of the concept that the shedding of human blood was something "impure." They show no distinction between different types of slayings, and all types of homicide were dealt with by the relatives of the victim. Blood feud was an established institution, though the acceptance of blood money sometimes took the place of revenge. If the offense was not avenged, the offender fled into exile. Although the slaying of parents or guests met with general condemnation, there was no popular sentiment against ordinary homicide, because there was nothing sacred about human life. The question of right and wrong seems nonexistent in the Homeric feelings toward homicide.

Other attacks upon person or property were also left to the individual victim to deal with as he saw fit, with or without the aid of his family. There were, however, certain established ways of deciding disputes between individuals, such as voluntary submission to arbitration, but inheritance and guardianship were not regarded as subjects for arbitration. The two parties involved agreed to nominate a distinguished citizen, known for his honesty, impartiality, and intelligence—without regard to his rank or official position—to act as an arbitrator who was guided by divine inspiration. Both parties entered into a solemn agreement, confirmed by oath, to abide by the decision. Popular sentiment supported the man willing to arbitrate differences between fellow citizens, as this function reduced a source of friction within the community and helped to preserve its solidarity. These arbitrations were not, of course, functions of the state, but the distance from a situation in which the king acted as arbitrator to one settled in a court of justice was relatively short. So the state began to lay down certain rules governing the decisions of the arbitrators. For instance, both parties had to agree on the person or persons who were to arbitrate. The arbitrators had to hand down their decisions under oath, and the decisions were binding. Moreover, both parties were barred from raising the same issue again before a court.

The ambitious aristocracy did not fail to recognize the advantages stemming from the establishment of a regular court of arbitration, which would increase its political power and enhance its prestige in the community. In later periods, regular judicial processes were developed from the arbitral functions of chiefs and elders. Instead of waiting for calls for their services as arbitrators, court sessions were held in the Agora, with some degree of regularity, to settle disputes. There is no indication that recourse to such courts was obligatory, and it is very difficult to determine when it became so. By the middle of the seventh century B.C., written codes appeared in various parts of Greece, establishing the exercise of judicial functions by magistrates. These codes simply recorded current practices in dealing with particular cases.

Athens claims credit for establishing the first regular and voluntary legal processes in Greece. When the use of a legal framework later became compulsory, an aggrieved person had the power to force the one who wronged him to appear before a court that held regular meetings. In such a way, the Greek citizen had recourse to a number of possibilities: voluntary arbitration in civil matters, self-help for homicide and other wrongs to person or property, and action by the asembled people against dangerous public offenders. Arbitration was therefore the first known step in developing a systematic, formal administration of justice. There are a number of references to these arbitrations and even a detailed description of a case (*Iliad* XVIII: 497 ff) in which the question was merely whether or not the blood money had been paid; the question of the homicide itself was not the issue. Homicide was simply a wrong against the individual or his family. It was not considered morally reprehensible or against the common welfare. It was a private affair that did not deserve public attention or action. Disputes arising from homicides must have been numerous, but they were not different from other disputes adjusted by voluntary arbitration. It is possible that the earliest notion of justice grew out of disputes between individuals or families over rights of property, whereas acts of violence or homicide were matters for adjudication only when translated into questions of this kind.

During Hesiod's times (eighth century B.C.), private arbitration ceased to be voluntary and became public and compulsory. Judges were appointed to settle disputes. Each male citizen had to serve as a judge during the official year following that in which he reached the age of fifty-nine. Judges' names appeared in the register of their respective demes. Service was compulsory, except for holders of public offices or those who were ill or abroad. Failure to serve was punishable by *atimia*. The judges were assigned by lot, and their pay consisted of one drachma from each of the two litigants, and a further drachma for every day the hearing was prolonged. They took an oath before delivering their decision, and the entire procedure was subject to the control of the courts. The judges' sentences could be appealed before a higher court— the Council of the Areopagus—the first real court that judged the most important criminal cases.

In the *Odyssey,* there are allusions to the fact that the community, not merely the individual or the family, attempted to inflict punishment, especially for acts that threatened the public security and well-being. There was a distinct feeling that justice, good government, and social order were essential to the general welfare and that the opposite invites disaster. Such acts were the concern of the whole community, and the offender was punished by the community. In practice, this was mob rule, since actual legislation was still a matter of the distant future. Nevertheless, it may be concluded that the primordial steps toward real criminal law were taken by the Greeks of the Homeric age. When they refer to death by stoning—"to put on a tunic of stones"—it can only be inferred that this mode of summary execution was an established custom, the first and most elementary stage of criminal law. Even in the seventh century B.C., offenses against the state were punished as crimes by the Council of the Areopagus, while attacks on individuals were dealt with by proceedings instituted by the offended person before a magistrate. Only in the sixth century B.C. would Solon introduce important changes in this state of affairs.

From Hesiod (c. 750–650 B.C.) and from other pre-Socratic lyric poets of the late eighth century B.C., it can be seen that Athens had developed a doctrine of crime and, with it, a system of criminal law and procedure. In cases of homicide, the practice of Homeric banishment was followed without regard to the type of homicide, which was still the concern of the relatives of the victim. But there was a growing feeling that such actions, affecting the order and the well-being of the entire community, should be punished by the state. The idea of "impurity" began to be associated with the shedding of human blood. This concept was later firmly established by Draco, and the tribunals dealt with homicide of the various types.

Although there are no mentions of witnesses in Homeric times, they did exist during Hesiod's time, when the judicial system was considerably more advanced. Litigants usually substantiated their statements with testimonial evidence, as shown in documents referring to the regular administration of justice in Boeotia. There, the petty chiefs of the dominant aristocracy of each district met regularly in the principal city for the purpose of adjudicating disputes. The judicial powers of these magistrates were handed down not by the king but by tradition, customs, and precedent. People from the villages came as litigants or listeners. Foreigners could also take recourse to these courts in accordance with special treaties. The main difficulty was that the magistrates, described as "bribe devouring kings" who frequently oppressed the people by their "crooked decisions," made the recourse to arbitration a comparatively better alternative.

Trials during the time of Hesiod were different from the arbitration of Homer's time and from the highly developed Athenian legal process of the fourth century B.C. It is not known exactly how these proceedings were initiated or how judgments were executed. Perhaps the compelling forces for both were custom and public opinion, which no man of that era could disregard.

Although court trials and compulsory arbitration existed side by side, voluntary arbitration was still in use. An injured party could often gain assistance from kinsmen and neighbors. Hesiod recommended that a man not rely too much on his relatives but always remain on good terms with his neighbors. As in Homeric times, adjudications seemed to have been held more frequently in the Agora, where members of the king's council decided disputes. Considerable advances had been made over the practices of Homer's times: witnesses now played a definite role, and their testimony was given under oath; the magistrates swore that they would not accept bribes, and so forth. There was also a compulsory procedure by which an unwilling opponent could be forced to submit to arbitration.

The nobles, who first restricted and then abolished royalty, were looking for popular support. They achieved it for a time by promising honest government and security of property. No citizen would be deprived of his private property without cause (for instance, subversion). This meant a kind of public trial before the Council of the Areopagus. In a dispute regarding boundaries, the archon asked both parties to appear before him. He directed a "legal process" and reached a verdict. Court fees had to be paid.

Although Hesiod says nothing about "impurity" and little about homicide, he seldom neglects the opportunity to refer to right and wrong. The gods looked with approval upon righteous conduct and punished wickedness. He insisted that wrongdoing by individuals would inevitably bring down the wrath of the gods upon the entire community. He also mentions several types of behavior that would later be included in the category of "crime"—such as maltreatment of orphans, strangers, and beggars; abuse of parents; adultery with a brother's wife; and so forth—for which redress could be obtained by legal proceedings. In cases of adultery, the injured husband could exact satisfaction from his wife's paramour without slaying him, and could force him to pay substantial damages. If he were to slay the offender, he might become involved in a blood feud with his relatives. Litigation was always possible if the compensation was not paid.

But for Hesiod, the one offense that was a menace to the entire social order was the perversion of justice through corrupt judgments and perjury. He left the punishment of the unjust magistrates to the gods, for, as yet, there seemed to be no authority high enough to deal with them.

During this period, the judicial procedure was, more or less, as follows: When the aristocratic Council of the Areopagus met to sit in judgment, its members were called areopagites. In the beginning, they dealt only with cases of homicide. Sentences were pronounced not by a single areopagite but by the entire court. If the vote was equally divided, for and against the accused, he was acquitted. The king, who was the guardian of the laws, had his place among the judges; even during the republic, the magistrate who represented the king had the right to vote with the other areopagites. Since there was no distinction between administrative and judicial functions in those times, it can be assumed that the same court also acted as a permanent council of state, assisting the king in the administration of his many other duties.

The Tribunal or Council of the Areopagus, the main administrator of justice, was one of the oldest Athenian institutions. In cases involving money, the citizens themselves could participate in the proceedings. The people used to applaud to express their approval of one or the other of the litigants, but no oratorical tricks for influencing the judges were permitted. When a homicide was committed, the next of kin tried to avenge himself on the offender, but the offender could claim, in front of the areopagites and the people at the Agora, that he had already paid the blood money. Usually, the problem was not that one claimed to have paid the blood money and the other said that he had not received it, but that one claimed to be willing to pay but the other refused to accept it. Then the question was whether or not the avenger must accept the blood money or if he might claim blood for blood. In fact, *wergeld* was not compulsory, since banishment was the usual fate of the slayer. After each side and its witnesses had delivered their statements, each of the areopagites reached his own conclusions. The two golden talents previously deposited, one by each of the litigants, went to the one whom the majority of the judges considered to have spoken the truth or most justly pleaded his case.

The administration of justice was then part and parcel of the prevailing sociopolitical and economic system. Offenses against the state and other wrongs of an exceptionally flagrant character could be brought to the attention of the aristocratic council by the people who had some power or influence. On the other hand, the right of action in transgressions of individual rights was restricted to the injured party. Only members of the bourgeoisie could sue in the courts. All other citizens had to rely on those whom they asked to represent them. Therefore, only influential citizens could count on any real protection from the law. Such a perversion of justice, among many other evils, aroused Solon's indignation and moved him to introduce his famous reforms.

Regarding punishments, the vast majority of the cases were settled by compensation, the material indemnification of the victim or his next of kin. In early times this was left to the parties to settle, but later, in order to avoid abuses, the tribunal fixed the amount of indemnification. Other punishments were death (only for murderers and offenders against the state, through stoning or poisoning by hemlock); total atimia, equivalent to "civil death"—the loss of all civil rights and a kind of perpetual exile, which was later substituted by a simple and temporal banishment within the country; partial atimia, the loss of only some civil rights; imprisonment, rarely used in Athens; confiscations and fines; ostracism; slavery (a frequent punishment for debtors);

flogging and whipping (only for slaves); deprivation of interment and prohibition to enter the temples, usually inflicted on offenders against religious practices.

If these were the customary ways of dealing with private revenge, where did the jurisdictional competence of the Council of the Areopagus come in, and what was its impact on the development of Greek penal law? The truth is that with their decisions, the areopagites implicitly produced a rule of law. For instance, in the aforementioned case, if they were convinced that the blood money was paid, the wish to carry on with private revenge was illegitimate, and the parties were forbidden to reach its ultimate consequences. However, revenge was legitimate and was authorized to be applied if the blood money was not paid. Thus, revenge was no longer an exclusively private affair. The one who carried it out was not acting on a personal right but as a representative of society. Revenge became the exercise of a public reaction to the victim's relatives. The first step toward a penalty—as a punishment applied by society to one who had violated the fundamental rules of the accepted social behavior—had been given. A century later, the penal law of Greece was established.

The Age of the Lawgivers: Draco

The period of primitive monarchies and aristocracies was followed by the age of the lawgivers, also known as the age of the codes. It began with Lycurgus's constitution in Sparta, which reformed and practically abolished the old Doric laws of the ninth century B.C. but was never put into writing. This trend acquired momentum from 650 B.C. onward, thanks to the popularization of the art of writing—first in the Hellenized western Near East and the Ionian Greek colonies and then in continental Greece. This was because the colonies were not as conservative as Athens and were more inclined to accept social and political reforms. Moreover, as the colonies had different ethnical and cultural backgrounds, no single set of customary laws could satisfy all of them, so codification was imperative. This general trend was also stimulated by the criticism of Hesiod regarding the state of affairs of his time. As mentioned earlier, the magistrates of the Areopagus administered an unwritten customary law. The people were dissatisfied by the uncertainties of the administration and the interpretation of such law and asked for rules that would be binding upon all the judges, instead of the vague customary law, which could be modified and interpreted to suit the interests of the ruling class. Hesiod was a member of the lower classes who had personally suffered from the maladministration of justice. Even a few noblemen expressed, in a written opinion, the need for codified laws. Although some authors, such as Maine, consider the codes a means of protection against the corruptions of the administration of the customary laws, others, such as Pollock (mentioned by Bonner and Smith), thought that the codification arrested the normal development of Greek law.

These new laws were generally recorded on the walls of public buildings or on special steles set up in public places. The laws of Draco and Solon were "published" on pillars of wood (for religious matters) or bronze (for all kinds of other laws).

The popular assemblies in the democratic states and the senates in the oligarchic ones seem to have participated, to some extent, in the administration of the new codes. Since important parts of the known fragments of the laws of Draco and those of Gortys (see below) are devoted to matters of procedure, there is no doubt that this aspect was considered of great importance.

There was no attempt in these new codes to classify the laws according to their subject matter. Civil, criminal, and religious topics were thrown together indiscriminately. The absence of provisions regarding homicide is noteworthy in the known fragments of the codes of most of the lawgivers. It is possible that this matter was dealt with entirely by relatives of the victim and was not yet considered a matter for interference on the part of the state. The Gortian code, the most complete of all, does not refer to homicide, but the mention of blood money in fragments of an earlier code points to the possible loss of parts of the Gortian code. The only homicide laws of which some details are known are those of Draco. In several of the other codes, there are provisions regarding marriage and divorce and the protection of the interests of the children. Many of them refer to slavery, since slaves were considered a valuable asset and the laws tried to protect them. There are also references to the disposition of private property, the trend being to make it almost impossible to dispose of property outside the family. Excess in drinking was discouraged by imposing a greater penalty on those who did wrong while drunk. A new feature of these codes was the fixing of penalties; punishment was no longer left to the arbitrary will of the judges. Punishments were often vindictive. (According to the code of Zaleukos, for instance, the adulterer was blinded.) In contrast, the Gortian code mostly imposed fines. It is worthwhile to remember that in these times, offenders could be dragged by their accusers into the Agora, detained until their fate was determined, and punished on the spot.

Among the most important of these new codes were those of Zaleukos, in the Acheaen Locris Epizefiri in south Italy, who seems to be the first to have introduced predetermined penalties for different offenses; Charondas, in Catania, Sicily, who is also considered to be the author of other laws in Italy and Sicily; Diocles, in Dorian Syracuse; Pittacus, in Mytilene, also about the middle of the seventh century B.C., who established a double penalty for offenders who committed their crimes while drunk; Androdame, in Reggio, who is also thought to have legislated on homicide; Pheidon, in Corinth;

Philolaos, who prepared the legislation of Thebes; Aristides, in Ceos; and the unknown author of the laws of Gortys, in Crete, the best known of all of them. Among these laws we must include those of Draco and Solon, in Athens, certainly the most important of all. Some of these laws were adopted by other city-states of Acheaen, Ionian, and Doric origin. Other cities in Asia Minor, the Aegean islands, southern Italy, and continental Greece produced their own lawgivers, but very little is known about them.

Most of the more significant lawgivers—Lycurgus, Charondas, Zaleukos, and Pittacus—belonged to the middle class. In some cases, the task of preparing a code was entrusted to a citizen chosen for his qualifications or because he held a high office in the state. Draco, for instance, was a special thesmothete in 621 B.C., the year to which we generally attribute his legislation; Solon had been appointed an archon; and Pittacus was the supreme ruler of Mytilene for a period of ten years, during which he was asked to prepare the laws.

All these codes, generally believed to be of divine inspiration (Zeus for the Cretan laws, and Athena appearing in a dream to Zaleukos), appeared during periods that, though chronologically dissimilar, were similar in their sociopolitical and cultural development. Many of the important lawgivers visited foreign countries and studied their basic institutions for the purpose of incorporating the best of them in their own codes. Zaleukos was in Crete, Sparta, and Athens; Lycurgus was in Crete, Ionia, Egypt, and perhaps even Iberia and India; and Charondas studied the laws of many states. These early codes were doubtless based on tradition and customary laws, although Draco, as a thesmothete, may have known and used some written material.

The dependence on customary law was clearest regarding matters of procedure. In cases of homicide, existing practices were adhered to, as religious conservatism prevented innovations. Indeed, the mere fact that a law was ancient and of supposedly divine origin was the best proof of its excellence. Nevertheless, as sociopolitical changes brought new realities, innovations were made. From the fifth century B.C. onward, the law was regarded as of human rather than divine origin, and a new public law and procedure began to be modeled on ideals of independence, freedom, and autonomy.

The codes of Crete and Sparta were among the most important of the early codes. Cretan practices during the fifteen century B.C. were strikingly similar to those of the pre-Solon era in Athens. Crete's government was then purely aristocratic. At the head of the state was the board of magistrates known as Cosmi, chosen from certain privileged kinship groups and presided over by the minos, the king. There was also a Council of Elders, made up of former magistrates. The General Assembly of the citizens had little, if any, power, and met merely to ratify the Cosmi's or council's decisions. During this period, Cretan cities were in a state of anarchy, the outcome of incessant rivalry among their different aristocratic factions. There were no popular courts, and the decisions of the magistrate-judges were final. Slavery for debt was recognized by law of custom, but there were certain measures to secure the enslaved debtor's minimal rights. The use of witnesses was a mere formality, as were the oaths they pledged.

Known as the Code or Laws of Gortys, the first written laws of Crete date from about the year 450 B.C. The name of their originator is unknown, and only fragments survive. The laws represent a transition between the primitive and later codes. They are a kind of restatement of earlier laws, with additions and amendments. The information gained from these laws about the actual administration of justice is rather poor, since they reveal nothing about the structure, jurisdiction, and functioning of the court.

Whatever the case, this code represents the victory of the weaker classes in their struggle against their powerful and abusive rulers. Its democratic character paved the way for the triumph of democracy in Athens during the classical age. If some of the earliest legal systems in Greece were intermingled with myth and legend, the codifications of Draco and Solon and the laws of Gortys are sufficient evidence of the tremendous change in Greek political and legal thought during this period, when absolutism began to collapse and to be replaced by the democratic ideas of *polis,* the Greek city, and its new institutions.

The inscriptions of Gortyna deal with penalties for adultery, rape, and criminal assault, all of which were treated as torts—not as crimes—since right of action was left to the victim or his next of kin for the recovery of pecuniary damages in amounts determined by the nature of the offense, the status of the parties involved, and similar factors. No public action was taken against adultery in the Code of Gortys. It is interesting to note that there were no references to homicide or similar offenses directly affecting the state. It is possible, however, that an undiscovered portion of the code dealt with the subject.

Draco is considered the first legislator of Athens. He adapted his laws to a constitution that already existed and stated that magistrates were to be appointed according to their birth or financial status. At first, they were given life-long terms, which were later shortened to ten years and finally, in Solon's era, to one year. The king's absolute reign was modified by the office of polemarch, who was to replace a king who was feeble at war. Later came the archon, whose function was to record legal decisions and to preserve them for future reference—a kind of recorded jurisprudence. An archon never held office for more than one year.

The Council of the Areopagus was in charge of preserving the laws, but it also administered the most important aspects of government. It was allowed to summarily inflict personal punishments and fines. This council was the only institution that lasted until the time of Aristotle.

Besides their political functions, the archons had also judicial functions, which, in the course of time, came to overshadow their other duties. They did not sit as a body; each archon dealt with the cases assigned to him. They had final jurisdiction until the reforms of Solon, after which their decisions could be appealed to the Tribunal of the Heliaea (see below). The archons dealt mainly with cases related to family and property; and the polemarch was for foreigners what the archons were for citizens. The two highest archons, the basilei, dealt with religious cases, could grant amnesty, and fulfilled certain judicial functions. The first archon—the basileus, for instance—was the presiding officer in homicide courts, which dealt with cases of impiety, including homicide, wounding with intent to kill, arson, and poisoning. The six thesmothetais' duty was reduced to writing the laws of custom and recording all judicial decisions. Afterward, when attempts were made to better systematize the administration of justice, they became exclusively judicial functionaries. Later, during the fifth and fourth centuries B.C., all these magistrates were mainly concerned with criminal cases.

Draco may be considered to represent the end of the primitive period in Greek legal development, because he tried to give the state a given structural order in matters of criminal law. His proverbial severity was reflected in the fact that "criminals" were condemned to death for a variety of offenses, including laziness, theft of fruits or cabbage, sacrilege, or homicide. (Some scholars deny this, claiming that the main penalty was atimia.) Whatever the case, harsh penal measures are still derided as Draconian. Draco also gave a creditor the right to enslave not only the debtor but his entire family.

From its inception, the Areopagus had jurisdiction over a number of offenses, a right that it never entirely lost. From the time of Solon, the Areopagus was deprived of many of its privileges and duties, as were public officials, whose functions were assumed by others. For instance, when the polemarch ceased to be a military officer, military offenses were tried by the generals who succeeded him.

Compared with later legislation, Draco's laws were indeed extremely severe, though still better than private revenge. (It is possible that Draco regulated and improved the system of compensation, which began to replace private revenge.) Whatever the case, Draco's laws were the first written laws of Greece, established by the state, which began to limit the legislative and judicial authority of the eupatrides. After these laws were established, the archons were bound to follow a fixed procedure and to mete out predetermined punishments.

Draco's laws—which appeared at least a century after Homer's epic poems—introduced radically different rules in dealing with homicide. Little remains of these laws other than the law relating to homicide, which was ratified by the king and engraved on a marble stele erected in front of the Royal Gate or Portico. These laws appeared in 621–620 B.C., the year of the archonate of Aristecmo, when Draco was appointed special thesmothete for codifying and writing down laws. His laws, especially those concerning debtors, obviously favored the ruling classes. Thirty years later, the people rose up against the aristocracy, an uprising that culminated when Solon introduced his reforms.

The main dispositions regarding homicide are contained between the tenth and forty-first lines of the existing laws. One of these specifies that the Areopagus had to supervise the archons in their decision making so that they should respect the laws. Any citizen who felt he had been wronged could appear before the Areopagus. This was an important step forward, comparable to the right of petition in modern legislations. Draco thus recognized the right of the injured person to take the initiative. It should be kept in mind that the Areopagus was then an outgrowth of the Council of Elders of the Homeric age.

The homicide laws of Draco contain the earliest mention of the Ephetae, an institution about which little is known. There were fifty-one ephetae, each over fifty years of age, recruited from the Areopagus by lot. In cases of death or illness, new ephetae were appointed in order to preserve an odd number and prevent ties. The archon basileus acted as their chairman but did not vote. Perhaps they were the primordial prototype of the popular court.

During this time, there were five different courts dealing with the various types of homicide: the Areopagus, which dealt with cases of murder, malicious wounding, and arson; the Palladium, where the fifty-one ephetae dealt with cases of unpremeditated homicide; the Delphineum, which was in charge of justifiable homicides; the Phreatto, for premeditated cases; and the Prytaneum, which dealt with cases of unknown murderers as well as with animals and inanimate objects that had caused the death of human beings.

There are differences of opinion among scholars regarding which court dealt with cases of tyranny and other political offenses. Some scholars believe that they were tried at the Areopagus; others think that these cases were brought before the Prytaneum, where the nine archons sat.

The first step in a trial for unpremeditated homicide was a public proclamation in the Agora forbidding the accused to frequent the marketplace and the temples, in order to protect the public from his "contamination." Only the father, brothers, sons, children of brothers and sisters, uncles, and first cousins of the victim were entitled to participate in the accusation. The archon basileus, together with his philobasileis, decided *prima facie* the kind of homicide committed, thus determining before which court the offender would face trial. Banishment for an undetermined period was the penalty for an unpremeditated homicide, but under certain conditions—if all the relatives of the victim agreed on a pardon—the exile could be terminated. While in exile, the offender was protected from violence or blackmail under the penalty of paying double damage, and whoever killed him was liable to punishment; but if he returned to Attica before the banishment was terminated, anyone was permitted to put him to death. The culprit also could be turned over to the proper authorities for execution after a suitable enquiry. In such a case, the citizen who arrested him would also be the prosecutor. The citizen who made the arrest and prosecuted the culprit represented the entire community.

Killing in self-defense was one of the justifiable homicides, including the killing of an adulterer caught in the act. In such cases, there was an investigation to determine the facts. The procedure was the same as that already described.

The laws of Draco show that as early as the seventh century B.C., the state had the exclusive task of punishing everyone convicted of homicide. The concept of "contamination" was firmly established. It seems that all the Greek lawgivers followed the oracle of Delphi and the cult of Apollo, at least in relation to the impurity of the murderer. Even Plato insisted on the need to purify even the involuntary murderer. It is almost impossible to know whether the laws of Draco set a precedent or were preceded by others. What is known is that from the second half of the seventh century B.C., a number of Greek city-states had written laws, and some of them included rules dealing with homicide, as proved by documented testimony from the sixth century B.C.

In the first table of Draco's laws it is stated that if a person kills without premeditation, he will be exiled. The king was to be informed of the case following the archons' decision. Pardon could be granted only by the unanimous agreement of the victim's relatives. The second through the eighth table deal with procedural matters. The ninth refers to the homicide of a slave, which is to be dealt with as that of a freeman. The tenth table deals with cases of homicide in self-defense during a violent robbery, for which the killer would not be punished.

It seems that there were two basic reasons for the intervention of the state in assuming control of the situation in cases of homicide: (1) once the concept of "contamination" was accepted, the state was bound, for its own protection, to find a means for getting rid of the contaminated person; and (2) it was necessary to prevent continued blood feuds, which, in some cases, could develop into civil war.

The main differences between the laws of Draco and what emerges from the examination of the poems of Homer are two. First, under Draconian law, only the state was entitled to use force against the offender, because homicide was punished by exile. After centuries of private revenge, this was regarded as a means of escaping the blood avenger; therefore, the legislator had to establish that he who killed a murderer while he was in exile would be punished as if he had killed a citizen of Athens. Second, the next of kin of the victim could liberate the murderer who paid a fine or compensation.

It seems that there were three types of homicides: voluntary; "impassioned" (killing out of anger or love); and involuntary. According to Draco's laws, the offender was put to death only in cases of voluntary and premeditated homicide; in other cases of homicide, he was exiled.

Although civil law today constitutes perhaps 90 percent of total legislation, this percentage gets smaller and smaller as we delve further into primitive laws, particularly in those civilizations in which the mere notion of contract was still unknown. The penal law of ancient communities was not a law of "crimes" (*crimina*), but of "wrongs" (*delicta*), or torts. Offenses that are now regarded as crimes were treated as torts—not only theft (*furtum*) but also assault, violent robbery, trespassing, libel and slander, and, more frequently than not, even homicide. According to Athenian laws, administered by the Council of the Areopagus, sins were also punished as torts. This was because offenses against the gods were established in the first ordinances; those against another fellow were the second ones, and the idea of an offense against the state was the last to appear within the criminal law, usually in a separate text. Only then did the earliest notion of crime appear.

According to the primitive law of Athens, some offenses were dealt with by the archons, who seem to have punished them as torts, and some by the Areopagus, which considered them sins. Civil, religious, and moral matters were intermingled without regard to the basic differences in their essential character. Later, jurisdiction over both civil and religious matters was transferred to the Tribunal of the Heliaea, and the archons and Areopagus became quite insignificant in matters of the administration of justice.

Solon, the Skillful Lawgiver

Draco's law was followed by the legislation of Solon. The king was replaced by nine archons, six of whom, the thesmothetai, were concerned almost entirely with judicial matters, helping the regular magistrates deal with their daily burden. The thesmothetai never had executive functions. The Areopagus was the most suitable body for taking public action on a great variety of subjects. The jurisdiction of the thesmothetai must have fallen between that of the Areopagus and that of the archon basileus; they dealt with both criminal and civil cases, fixing dates for trials and assigning magistrates to each case. They also dealt with offenses against the state—slaves slandering freemen, perjury, and anyone who illegally returned to the city after having been banished for murder or treason. Before Solon, legal procedure took the following form: Each party had to take an oath, and the trial was a kind of a ritual, with the judge determining the victor according to the accepted rules. Acquittal of the defendant meant that the issue was closed, and any unilateral action taken by the plaintiff would render him liable to punishment.

When the Boulé was created, the Council of Elders took on the name Council of the Areopagus, by which it was known for a long time afterward. Athenians had a marked tendency to attribute their ancient institutions to Solon; this may be why the Areopagus was supposed to have been founded by him, when in fact it was in existence long before Solon's time. Some authors make a distinction between the *Court* of the Areopagus and the *Council* of the Areopagus. It seems that the court existed even before the time of Draco and that the creation of the council might be attributed to Solon. Greek states of this period also closely connected the administration of justice with that of government, so that in addition to judges, public officials also exercised judicial functions. It is even possible that the Court of the Areopagus was also a political body. Whatever the case, it seems that the Council of the Areopagus in pre-Solonian times dealt with cases of premeditated homicide in addition to its other functions.

Solon is traditionally considered to be the first to establish a permanent machinery for the punishment of crimes against the state, although this legend is undocumented. It is possible that he merely enumerated the evils that could threaten disaster to the state and proposed some remedies. He was speaking not of private wrongs to be punished by the victim, by his next of kin, or by a divine retribution, but of crimes against the state. Among these crimes were theft or embezzlement of public or sacred moneys, the perversion of justice, sedition and participation in civil strife, conspiracy against the established authorities, enslavement of poor citizens, and the like. He insisted that lawlessness was the chief source of evil and that the only remedy was *eunomia,* the rule of law, which would bring order and harmony to the state. Only then would a state of justice, in the broadest sense, be established.

There is no doubt that the Greeks of the eighth and seventh centuries B.C. gave little thought to the problem of homicide. The turning point came when the right of prosecution arising from a wrong ceased to be restricted to the immediate victim or his next of kin and was granted (at least for certain offenses) to any citizen who might care to exercise it. According to Aristotle, it was Solon who took this important step, which was intended to protect the lower classes from the aggression of the rich and powerful. Solon was in a position to make this change after he was appointed nomethete, to deal with formulating abstract statements of law and have almost dictatorial powers. There were, however, a few special dispositions regarding homicide, such as taking the life of a freeman in self-defense without the payment of blood money. The same dispensation applied to a victim who was a foreigner. The victim might also be an alien who could not demand compensation, a man who had been expelled or disowned by his family or tribal group, or a man who had committed an offense that the members of his own family would regard as making his life a just forfeit to the injured person. These cases were rather exceptional, and most were not dealt with by the polis itself.

Solon began his program of legal and judicial reforms by prohibiting the seizure of persons for debt and the sale of a child by his relatives, thus returning to their homes all those who had been sold as slaves or escaped from Athens because of their debts and restoring them to their original status. He then established popular courts and the possibility of appealing the decisions of the privileged magistrates before the Tribunal of the Heliaea. Finally, he dictated a new law establishing, in a given number of offenses (attacks upon the right of a citizen and even offenses against the state), the right of prosecution to any citizen. This innovation—granting the right of prosecution to the citizens rather than to a public official—was included in most subsequent criminal legislation in Greece.

The archons, who had been the most important judicial magistrates, gradually became less aristocratic. They held their offices for only one year, and reelection was forbidden. Any male citizen, with the exception of the thetes, was eligible for office. The people elected 500 citizens, of whom nine were selected by lot as archons. On assuming their offices, they had to take an oath to respect the rights of the citizens. In administrative and military matters, the archons were replaced by a board of ten *strategoi,* who could reassume office year after year. The power of the archons was drastically reduced: They were to prepare cases for adjudication, to preside over the popular courts, and to deal only with family problems, such as mistreatment of parents or mismanagement and dissipation of family estates or other properties because of insanity, idleness, or similar causes. In time, the offices of the archons and those of the strategoi lost most of their importance to the new popular institutions of the state, especially the Ecclesia and the Council of the 400.

Before their powers were reduced by the development of the democratic institutions, the magistrates—archons or others—could use their own initiative regarding a variety of cases, particularly those in which people interfered with the discharge of their official duties or in the settlements of disputes brought before them. They had also the power to impose fines up to a certain upper limit (apparently no more than fifty drachmas) for offenses against widows and orphans. After the establishment of the Tribunal of the Heliaea, both as a court of first instance and a court of appeal, the people could oppose the imposition of a fine that they considered too high. In this case, the decision was left to the heliastes, who could even repeal the fine. Nevertheless, the magistrates could still pass final judgment on cases involving ten drachmas or less.

By the middle of the fifth century B.C., when the people won the right to prosecute in a first instance and then to appeal, the Council of the Areopagus lost a great deal of its authority and was reduced to dealing mainly with cases of homicide (particularly intentional homicide). The council was replaced by the Tribunal of the Heliaea, which was, in fact, the representative of the entire population sitting as court of justice. This high court of popular justice was perhaps the first in which the accused was judged by his peers. Its sentences were final and immediately executed. It seems to have been established under Solon, but it reached its peak of importance and influence during Cleisthenes' and Pericles' time. It dealt exclusively with judicial matters, public or private, and acted both as a first instance court and as a court of appeals, depending on the kind of offense. It consisted of no less than 6,000 members, known as the *heliastes,* each of them elected for one year with the possibility of reelection. Every citizen over thirty years of age was eligible, provided that he was not in debt with the state and that he was prepared to take the heliastic oath. The Heliaea was divided into ten *dicasteries,* with no maximum number of members. It could meet with some 100 or 200 heliastes, up to 1,500 or 2,500, or at times even the entire 6,000, but usually 500 heliastes met, depending on the nature and seriousness of the matter. The remaining members served as substitutes according to the needs of each dicastery, which was always constituted by odd numbers in order to avoid ties. Each of the heliastes received, at first, two obols a day, later increased to three obols, as retribution for their services.

These dicasteries originated in a much simpler system, under which the entire population sat as a court of first instance and in some cases as a court of appeals. The Ecclesia and the Boulé had the right to send their recommendations to a dicastery. As a matter of fact, trials for political crimes (attempts to overthrow the constitution, treason, bribing an orator, making deceptive promises to the people, etc.) were initiated before the Boulé and then presented to a dicastery. Such was the procedure during the last part of the fourth century B.C.

As there were not yet lawyers, each party had to state its particular point of view to the heliastes, each of them disposing of an equal amount of time, measured by the *clepsydra,* the water clock. The vote was secret and was expressed with little stones—white for acquittal, black for condemnation. With such a large number of heliastes, it was very difficult to ensure that each of them had cast his vote; and if this was not done, having an odd number of them was no help. In those cases where, despite everything, there was a tie, the verdict was in favor of the defendant.

The appeal to the Heliaea was meant to give the people an opportunity to protect themselves against crooked decisions of the magistrates. The chairmanship of this tribunal was exercised by members of the Boulé, since they were entitled to administer oaths. According to other scholars, the chairman was one of the thesmothetai; still others believe that he merely organized the functioning of the Heliaea and summoned it when necessary, leaving the chair to the magistrate whose decision had been appealed. Little is known of the actual organization and functioning of the Heliaea as a court. It seems that the distinctions between its being a judicial or a deliberative body were the oath and the secret ballot of the judicial functions. There is no direct evidence of whether the members of the Heliaea were sworn when they acted as judges, but it is very possible that they were during Solon's times. Membership in the Heliaea seems to have been selected by lot, without age or wealth qualifications.

The Areopagus continued to participate in the administration of justice according to Solon's constitution. It was still the guardian of the laws and overseer of the constitution. As such, it had full authority to fine or otherwise punish offenders. The responsibility of the magistrates to the community seems to have been enforced by both the Areopagus and the Heliaea. Their judgments continued to be final. Both bodies could also audit the accounts of outgoing magistrates, whereas the expenditures of the Boulé were audited by the Ecclesia. Other scholars are of the opinion that only the Boulé was in charge of checking the expenditures of the magistrates and that it presented its conclusions to the Ecclesia for its analysis and final decision—that is, to ratify or reject the Boulé's recommendations. This division of authority between the two bodies, representing two different political elements, was in accord with Solon's belief in preserving a balance between the two elements.

Between the time of Cleisthenes and that of Pericles, the Heliaea ceased to be a court of appeals but remained a court of first instance through its dicasteries. The other members only prepared the cases for trial and chaired the court sessions. This reorganization is also attributed to Cleisthenes. The Assembly acquired the right to take judicial actions, particularly when existing legal procedures did not afford the community adequate means for redress. The first of such cases occurred in 493 B.C., but the change in the constitution must have been made much earlier. Later, Pericles substituted the dicasteries for commissions of the Areopagus, commissions that previously sat in the building of the ephetae court.

Three measures—the prohibition against lending money on the guarantee of the debtor's person; the institution of popular courts, particularly the creation of the Heliaea who replaced almost all other judicial courts; and the grant of the right of prosecution to any citizen—were Solon's greatest contributions to the process that made Athens the cradle of democracy. Now the polis had the complete and exclusive right of penal repression. No other place in the ancient world possessed a truly independent system that granted political power to its populace.

There were two basic differences between the dicasteries of Draco's and those of Solon's time and the previous system of arbitration: (1) whereas the latter could reach a compromise between the two sides alone, the former could not; and (2) although the arbitrators had a greater latitude, the dicasters were bound by oath to act strictly according to the laws.

In both cases, there was a rather well detailed procedure. According to Aristotle, evidence could be given by means of persuasion (through the art of the orators, for instance); laws, decrees, and private documents, such as contracts and wills, that could be presented by each side; witnesses; extrajudicial agreements that might have been arrived at by the litigants; or torture and oaths. Expert evidence by physicians or other professionals was of no particular importance.

From Solon's times, if not before, to the present, judges and jurors have been faced with the problem of determining the credibility of litigants and their witnesses. There were no witnesses in Homer's time; the judges' decisions were based on their impression of the relative credibility of the parties. Witnesses first appeared in Hesiod's time, certainly before Solon's. Later, they were used at all occasions, the sole exception being when a man borrowed money from a banker, because the books of the banker were considered sufficient evidence.

Only one witness was necessary, but there could be more. Every adult male citizen not disqualified by atimia was competent to appear as a witness. Nevertheless, it is necessary to keep in mind that a male Athenian probably came of age at the end of his seventeenth year. Before this, he could not serve as a witness, except in homicide cases, and he had to be represented by his father or guardian. On reaching maturity, he could testify to things he knew while he was a minor. Women remained "minors" all their lives and could appear as witnesses only in cases of homicide and only if they were against, not in favor of, the accused. With the agreement of both parties, a woman could take an evidentiary oath and testify. A similar situation existed for slaves, but their evidence was admitted when it was given under torture; only a few cases are known in which their testimony was accepted without torture. Though cruel and irrational, this method of obtaining evidence was considered more reliable than obtaining it from a freeman. If the slaves' evidence against their masters or other people was upheld by the court, they were freed. Slaves' evidence under torture was never successfully impugned.

Those who were deprived of citizenship could no longer give evidence in court, although foreigners could. A man twice convicted of giving false evidence could not be compelled to serve as a witness, because a third conviction would render him liable to total atimia. No one was prevented from appearing as a witness unless he was actually a party to the suit.

Hearsay evidence was strictly forbidden, and witnesses were to confine themselves to matters of which they had direct knowledge. Exceptions were made, however, when the original witness was dead or if the witness was considered incompetent.

Only those adult male citizens who had not been deprived of some or all of their civil and legal rights due to partial or total atimia could appear as bona fide witnesses in the Athenian court. If a qualified person could not appear in court because of illness, or if he was abroad, extrajudicial depositions could be taken; the evidence could be taken in writing in the presence of a number of witnesses who could later identify the document in court. Before the use of written evidence, which began in 378 B.C., it was not always easy to distinguish between hearsay and extrajudicial evidence.

Witnesses were not sworn in, but they could voluntarily take an oath in order to render their statements more persuasive. A witness who was related to a litigant, or who was known to be friendly or hostile, could discredit the testimony. In family matters, however, relatives were the best witnesses, and failure to produce them might be used against a litigant. Another of the most effective ways of discrediting a witness was to show that he had a financial interest in the suit. A problem might arise when a vital matter depended on the testimony of a man who, for some reasons of his own, was unwilling to testify. But if the man was already in court, such a situation could be solved without major difficulties.

The state did not summon witnesses by subpoena. If a witness failed to appear or testify in court or did not take the oath if present in court, one of the litigants could ask the court for redress. The unwilling witness could be fined as much as 1,000 drachmas. If he was fined in absentia, he could appeal the fine if he could show sufficient cause for his absence. The question arises whether the obligation to testify was a duty to the state or to the other litigant. In general, the former was the case.

Wealthy men were often suspected of buying testimony and other advantages in litigation. In fact, it might fairly be assumed that in Athens there were no difficulties in securing paid or "voluntary" witnesses. Perjurers ran little risk even if their falsehood was detected, since it seems that there was no legal penalty for giving false witness. However, since the perjurers would suffer public disgrace and, in some cases, even partial atimia, they considered it proper to ask for money for their services. There were also many instances in which the testimony of witnesses was of no importance. For instance, the confession of a defendant was the best evidence. Accepting exile in a case of murder was tantamount to a confession of guilt. Malefactors who boasted of their deeds could be executed immediately, even before a trial. Failure to appear in court was considered sufficient evidence for verdict by default. If the man fled the country, his flight was regarded as a confession of guilt and he was condemned in absentia.

The facts of the case were heard from the litigants themselves, with supporting testimony at various points. In the fifth century B.C., witnesses were questioned by the litigants, with no provisions for cross-examination other than the questions addressed by a litigant to his opponent. The litigant who lost his case had to pay large sums of money in fines and damages. He needed ready cash to save himself from total atimia if he did not pay in time. It should be recalled that litigants might incur heavy fines—as much as 1,000 drachmas—for failure to obtain one-fifth of the votes of the members of the court.

There are indications that during a trial, efforts were made to influence the jurors. The evidentiary character of a forensic speech was well understood in Athens. By the end of the fifth century B.C. litigants began to employ professionals to write their speeches. There were also "advocates" who, with the agreement of the court, could speak on behalf of a given party. Their speeches were taken into account in the time allowed to each of the litigants. These advocates could not officially be paid for their services, but "unofficial" payment was far from rare.

Oaths were of two types: promissory and evidentiary. The first was a promise that something would or would not happen regarding the matter in the hands of the one who takes the oath. This type of oath appeared in various forms, including the oaths of public officials and jurors. The evidentiary oath was a statement that something had or had not happened; it included two varieties—the real evidentiary oath and the ordeal. Both left punishment to the gods, but in the case of the ordeal, the liar was punished on the spot, whereas in the case of the oath, the gods could postpone punishment so that it might fall even on a descendant of the liar. In addition to the real evidentiary oath, there was another oath in support of testimony, which might be called the confirmatory oath—to be taken by litigants or witnesses. The curse was an important feature of the oath: the stronger it was, the more likely the oath taker would keep his oath. Magistrates took an oath on assuming office, promising to perform their duties in accordance with the laws and to refuse bribes. Other governmental and judicial officers, such as the members of the Heliaea, were also required to take the oath.

At the age of eighteen, every youngster was enrolled in his demo's register and took the oath of allegiance, which was of a promissory nature. Another evidentiary oath was the *exomosia,* which served two purposes: a man could swear that he was unable to carry out some act or official duty due to poverty, illness, and so on; and a witness could swear that he knew nothing about the case and therefore could give no evidence. *Automosia* was an affirmation of the truth of the pleadings of both litigants. The *diomosia* was the oath taken by the prosecutor in homicide cases, swearing that he had the right to prosecute, based on his relationship with the deceased; that the defendant was guilty; and that he would confine himself to the matter at hand. In his diomosia, the defendant in a homicide trial swore that he was not guilty. This oath was taken by the prosecutor in all five homicide courts, but not if the defendant was an animal, an inanimate object, or an unknown person and the case was heard before the Prytaneum. The diomosia was also not taken by the defendant in some cases before the Delphineum, since justifiable homicide carried no moral guilt and the killer was not even considered to be impure.

Compurgation, usually treated as an independent institution, was really a development of the evidentiary oath. The witness swore to his confidence in the defendant's word. A slave could not be an oath helper, a function reserved mainly for the relatives of the defendant. Later, it was extended to neighbors and friends. These helpers had to be adult males and were always on the side of the accused, although later the institution was extended to the plaintiff. In Greece, there were two distinct forms of oath helpers: those who swore their confidence in the defendant and those who swore a joint oath with the accused as to the veracity of the facts. A false oath of this type could not be punished by legal means; punishment was left to the gods.

There were some other procedural means, such as the *anakrisis* and the *eisangelia*. The anakrisis was an informal interrogation of the litigants by the magistrate, to enable him to determine whether or not he should accept the case. The eisangelia, meaning "information," was in practice the term applied almost exclusively to actions brought before a political forum, such as the Areopagus in early times and the Council of the 500 or the popular Assembly in later times. It was similar to a modern impeachment procedure for serious crimes against the state when there was no particular law to deal with them and they had to be dealt with very promptly. Later, this recourse was employed for even the most trivial offenses. In order to restrict such abuses, a fine of 1,000 drachmas was imposed on an accuser who failed to obtain at least one-fifth of the votes against the accused. In Draco's times, this procedure was used against misbehaving public officials. Solon limited it to attempts to owerthrow the government. Ephialtes deprived the Areopagus of its authority in such cases, turning them over to the Council of the 500 or to the popular Assembly. For fines over 500 drachmas, they had to turn these cases over to a court. A new law dealing with cases of treachery against the state, which was certainly put into effect before the end of the fifth century B.C. (411 or 403–402 B.C.), had three main clauses: an attempt to overthrow the government, betrayal of the military forces, and an orator accepting bribes. A revision may have been introduced afterward, including such offenses as offering deceptive promises to the people, dishonesty in a Greek embassy, and transactions endangering the Athenian maritime confederation. The eisangelia was used consistently from the times of Draco down to the fourth century B.C.

The earliest notion that homicide was a matter to be settled by the victim's relatives was gradually replaced by the idea that a state court should put an end to blood feuds. The belief that the murderer was contaminated was a later development; it led to the ruling that an exiled murderer who returned from exile or entered forbidden places could be killed by anyone on sight. Exile did not "purify" the killer, and pardon and the return from exile could be granted only by the relatives of the victim, revealing the compensatory nature of exile. In historical times, only premeditated homicide could not be pardoned. Murderers were always excluded from amnesty laws. On the other hand, a man fatally wounded might forgive his slayer and release him from guilt, thus prohibiting his relatives from taking revenge.

The legality of giving blood money to the family of the deceased has been much discussed. The *wergeld* system was recognized in Athens even during the fifth and fourth centuries B.C. A private settlement was permitted by law or custom if a release had been formally granted by the victim of his relatives. Otherwise, private settlement was a sin, a quasi-criminal offense.

The notion of "contamination" in cases of homicide, which must have appeared very shortly after the Homeric period, had a considerable effect on criminal procedure. Only the family and perhaps the phratry (religious group) members of the victim could initiate prosecution for homicide before one of the five homicide courts. A murderer was not legally considered contaminated until these relatives had formally indicted him. Apparently, there was no ban against the slayer until the archon had accepted the case for trial and the interdiction had been proclaimed, at which time the accused was considered contaminated and was barred from public places, despite the fact that he remained at home. The two elements of compensation and contamination did not apply in cases of justifiable homicide. In the laws of Draco, it was expressly stated that if a man killed another in self-defense, there was no punishment and therefore no contamination. The same applied to the slaying of one who attempted to overthrow a democracy, a thief at night, a soldier in battle, a physician slain by his patient, or an adulterer caught *in flagrante.* Doubt remains about whether in these cases, when no punishment was inflicted, the murderer was still considered contaminated and had to undergo some ceremonial purification. The majority of scholars believe that anyone shedding human blood was considered unclean and had to undergo purification.

The early Greeks did not consider homicide nearly as serious a wrong as many other crimes viewed today as far less heinous. It remained fundamentally a matter for the family to handle in one of the Athenian courts. This situation persisted during the fifth and fourth centuries B.C. Sometimes, the state left crimes unpunished for lack of an accuser, but there was no statute of limitations for the prosecution of homicide. Afterward, with Solon's reforms, any citizen could, under certain conditions, prosecute someone for homicide. This was the provision for crimes that could not be tried by the regular procedures. But when the homicide was connected with some other crime—such as robbery or kidnapping—anyone with knowledge of the offense could prosecute.

Any slayer could be pardoned by his potential prosecutors, and no trial would ensue. But if he was not so released, he was allowed to escape into exile if he so chose. If he remained until the completion of the trial and a vote decided in his favor, he could make a thanks offering to the gods. If he was convicted of premeditated homicide, he was put to death. If he was convicted of unpremeditated homicide, he was exiled until he could obtain a pardon. No pardon was given for premeditated homicide. According to Draco's laws, the pardoning power rested entirely with the victim's relatives. With the refusal of even one relative, the pardon was not effective. While the killer remained in exile, he was protected; it was a punishable offense to kill him, and he was treated as any other murderer. But if he was caught in any of the forbidden places, he could be killed with impunity.

Regarding legal pardons and amnesties, the Ecclesia, as the supreme state institution, granted pardons, either rejecting or annulling the verdicts of the dicasteries. Amnesty laws were passed in Athens on rare occasions, but when accepted, they granted amnesty in wholesale fashion, with only a few exceptions, to all who were wholly or partially disenfranchised by the courts. The amnesty restored all the rights and privileges of citizenship as well as private property. The amnesty laws also halted pending suits leading to a possible atimia.

Solon made no attempt to modify the laws regarding homicide, traditionally attributed to Draco. He never defined homicide as a crime, leaving it to the victim's family to claim retribution. During the classical age, the law of homicide was still that of Draco and Solon. Whereas in pre-Solon times, the relatives of the victim had to bring the case before one of the courts dealing with cases of homicide, during the classical age there were public and private suits. The former could be initiated by any person qualified to plead, whereas the latter could be brought only by the wronged person or by his relatives in cases of homicide. Another basic difference lay in the penalties imposed. In the public suits—often dealing with acts of violence—in addition to compensation or restitution to the victim or his relatives, the defendant had to pay a penalty to the state or the prosecutor. In private suits, the compensation money went *in toto* to the wronged plaintiff.

There is no doubt that changes in human institutions are due to evolution quite as much as to the inspiration of gifted lawgivers. Solon's reforms were no exception. An important part of these reforms referred to the section of Draco's laws that dealt with homicide. His Tribunal of the Heliaea was no more than a reorganization of the Homeric Agora. Solon's greatness lies in the fact that he adapted ancient institutions to current needs and practices, his chief concern being the protection of the people's newfound political and economic freedom by providing them with the right of prosecution and the right to appeal to a citizen's assembly, a right that he transferred from the Areopagus to the Ecclesia.

In the heroic age of kinship, the entire population, rather than just the victim, assembled spontaneously in the Agora to deal with individuals whose acts endangered the community's safety. In the aristocratic period that followed, the Council of the Elders (the Areopagus in Athens) acted on behalf of the community, imposing fines and other punishments. Every member of the Areopagus who was aware of the wrongdoing could act as prosecutor. The victim or his relatives had to bring the matter to the attention of a member of the Areopagus. Only after Draco's reforms could the victim or his relatives appear directly before the Areopagus and prosecute the offender or the magistrate who wronged them. But these trials were still considered private suits, since only relatives could prosecute. If the murderer returned unlawfully from exile, any citizen could take action against him, since this was considered a new offense.

According to Draco's legislation, if the victim was unable to take action on his own behalf (for example, if a debtor was already a slave, or if he refused to appear in court as the legal representative of his children whom he had sold into slavery), a third person could represent him. Solon allowed complete freedom of prosecution, particularly in cases of plotting to overthrow the government, in which the entire community was affected, when volunteer prosectuors were needed. Solon empowered the Areopagus to try those accused of such crimes but, as these magistrates were drawn from the aristocracy, he took the precaution of having them swear to protect his new legal system. Every citizen could initiate prosecution against an archon who, in his opinion, had broken his oath. Solon acted on the conviction that injuries inflicted on individuals were harmful to the entire community. In some cases of intervention by a volunteer prosecutor, the victim lost the right to receive damages, since the aggressor was considered to have injured both the state and the victim.

The practice of recording judgments and verdicts—in both public and private cases, from homicide to tyranny—was introduced by the thesmothetai. Solon also introduced the official use of oaths in litigations. When no documentary evidence was available, the magistrate was entitled to administer oaths to both parties to ensure that they answered his questions truthfully. If one party refused to take the oath for fear of divine retribution and the other side agreed to take it, the latter won the case.

Freedom of prosecution and the right to appeal ensured the punishment of offenders. Even the rich could not expect to escape prosecution for bribery or for threatening their victims. The people themselves possessed adequate means of attaining justice, even when the wrongdoer was more powerful than they. Every citizen was a potential prosecutor and a member of the court of appeals.

Although every citizen was now able to present his own case in magistrate court, only those who had been victims of gross injustice would appear before the Heliaea (the court of appeals). Oratory, as an art, was still unknown, and since the people had no experience in public speaking, such an appearance was considered a real ordeal. Later, during the era of the orators, appeals were discouraged because of a provision stating that the unsuccessful appellant would have to pay a heavy fine or could be sold as a slave.

Solon probably followed a simple method, which later—during the fifth and fourth centuries B.C.—was used almost universally in Greece. It was based on incorporating a change granting the right of prosecution to any citizen in each criminal law. Of the many laws attributed to Solon, only two are certainly his own: the abolition of slavery due to debt and the prohibition against selling children as slaves. In both of these cases, he incorporated the right of every citizen to start prosecution. In the so-called *graphé paranomon,* any citizen who thought that a given law or a decree was illegal could institute action against it before someone came to suffer from it.

Solon was indeed limited by the sociopolitical structure of his time, when the process that would eventually culminate in Athenian democracy had just begun. But he was well aware that many acts that affected the individual more than the community were, in the last analysis, crimes that had to be dealt with by the state. Such a conviction moved him to dictate the first criminal code of the Western world, based on the two laws mentioned above, since these issues presented, to his mind, the most immediate threat to Athenian society.

In order to limit the overwhelming power of the Areopagus, he divided its functions between the popular Assembly and the Council of the 400. The Areopagus was now in charge of the control of the constitution and dealing with cases of treason and corruption. It was the Areopagus that convicted Cheronees' deserters in 338 B.C. and supervised the trial of Demosthenes in 324 B.C. The council was in existence until the end of the empire.

When Cleisthenes remodeled the Athenian constitution in 507 B.C., the Ecclesia was composed of all free adult male citizens, regardless of class or income. About a century later, as more people acquired voting rights, the power of the Assembly increased and that of the Areopagus decreased proportionately. Later, in 462–461 B.C., Ephialtes stripped the aristocrats of their power—all but that which permitted them to deal with cases of treason and corruption, homicide, and some religious duties. During this period, the Ecclesia arrived at a number of important decisions, such as the payment of fees for public services, thus making it possible for the poor to hold office; the reconstruction of the temples destroyed by the Persians; and the fateful decision to wage war against Sparta. After the death of Pericles, the leaders of the Assembly, lacking both his authority and his clear judgment, brought about its gradual decline.

From 411 B.C., the Council of the 400 was responsible for the entire administration of the state, including the control of the economy. The functions of the Ecclesia and the Council of the 400 were never clearly determined, depending rather on the political strength and efficiency of their leaders. Jurisdiction regarding state offenders, which had rested almost exclusively with the Areopagus, now belonged largely to whichever body happened to be predominant.

Solon's real contribution to the development of criminal law was the introduction of the criminal process and its democratization. He paved the way for his successors to develop a rational and orderly system of statutory criminal law. Solon introduced a primary classification of penalties: those affecting the person and those affecting property. The penalties for the former were death, imprisonment, exile, and atimia. For the latter, penalties ranged from a simple fine, as a redemption of the different forms of atimia, to the confiscation of the entire estate. He also established a few new penalties, such as malediction, interdiction from public places, and the sacred fine, in which a ransom replaced divine punishment. Only foreigners could be punished by being sold into slavery, never citizens. Atimia could be total (an ancient penalty) or partial, a newer type more frequently used. Total atimia could be absolute or relative. Total and absolute atimia, also called proscriptive atimia, included the loss of all civil and legal rights, total confiscation of property, and permanent exile from the state, with strict prohibition against living within the city. The offender could be killed by anyone who found him there. (Later, only a tribunal could inflict this kind of death penalty.) Proscriptive atimia was applied to those who plotted to institute tyranny; those who proposed law changes without going through proper channels; those who acted as magistrates while being in debt to the state; those who gave a foreign female in matrimony, declaring her a legitimate daughter; those who were in debt to the state (until the debt was paid; if it was not, the atimia passed to their heirs with the same condition); and those who killed a person to whom the polis had granted immunity. This type of atimia was for life, unless some kind of pardon was approved by the Ecclesia.

Total and relative atimia meant the loss of some civil rights, but the convicted person remained in the city and could even attend the Assembly and the Boulé—though he was not permitted to take part in discussion. He was forbidden to come to the Agora, the sanctuaries, and other holy places and to participate in public sacrifices. Partial atimia also limited the legal capacity of the condemned to that possessed by women and children below the age of puberty. Originally, the only known atimia was the proscriptive type, but Solon introduced the less severe types. A person previously convicted on three different occasions, with no regard for the nature of the previous offenses, was automatically punished with proscriptive atimia.

A defendant could be imprisoned before his trial, in order to ensure his appearance on the day fixed by the court (something similar to modern remand in custody); after his conviction, to ensure that he payed his fine; or as a punishment. When the verdict of a court required that the defeated litigant pay anything to the plaintiff in the way of damages or debts, it was the business of the successful litigant to execute the verdict. Confiscations, however, were the business of public officials.

Penalties were either fixed by law or determined by the court. A choice of penalties was given to the jurors in the majority of the cases. The prosecutor and the defendant each proposed a penalty, and the dicasts had to choose between them. Corporal punishments were exacted by the state.

Imprisonment in Athens could be precautionary or penal. The first was used by persons accused of flagrant crimes until the time of their trials. Those condemned to death were imprisoned until execution. Penal imprisonment could be used for people who had been fined, until the fine was paid. A state debtor who failed to pay his debt at the appointed time could be imprisoned and might remain their indefinitely, even for life, if he refused to pay.

The death penalty was mandatory in cases of murder, high treason, temple robbery, and similar serious offenses. Stoning was a natural form of community revenge on a wrongdoer who had openly injured the community.

It was used during the heroic period. There were three other methods of inflicting the death penalty, the most common being to hurl the condemned from a high rock or tower into a chasm. The *barathron* was ensured death; it was a rocky chasm fitted with spikes and hooks, designed to tear and lacerate the body. The second method was interpreted as "beating to death with a club." Some scholars believe that iron bands were fastened around the neck of the condemned man and around his ankles and wrists. Several methods of execution were possible with such implements, including crucifixion (in the Oriental manner, this punishment was inflicted by driving spikes through the hands and feet). One description mentions that the criminal was stripped and fastened to a wide, upright plank by means of five iron bands around his ankles, wrists, and neck. The criminal was thus suspended for days, exposed to heat and cold, hunger and thirst, birds and insects until he expired. Some scholars are convinced that such inhuman punishment would have been uncharacteristic of Athenian civilization in the fifth century B.C.; rather, it belonged to more primitive times. The third method was poisoning by hemlock. Finally, people caught in the act of stealing, betraying their country, or returning from exile without legal permission were executed by *apotympanismos,* an ill-defined mode of execution.

Solon's legislation realized the democratic conception that dispensing justice was the obligation of all citizens and a right to which all were entitled. This democratic machinery of justice gave birth to the legal concepts that formed the foundation of all civilized juridical thought. Nevertheless, the study of law never developed in Greece as a specialized branch of knowledge during the classical age. The most important "lawyers" of the era were, basically, philosophers, orators, and poets. However, after the third century B.C., law schools were established through the eastern part of the empire, particularly in Constantinople, Alexandria, Antioch, and above all Beyrouth. For centuries, these schools were the depositories of Greek legal thought, since they used the Greek language and followed the Greek philosophical outlook. Later, when Egypt became a Roman province in 30 B.C., a struggle ensued between the Greek and Roman legal concepts, culminating in the amalgamation of the Roman rigid, systematic thought and the Greek generalizations and flexibility. Thus, the *jus Romanus* became the *jus Greco-Romanus.* The Justinian legislation of the fourth century A.D. in Constantinople brought about the end of the struggle, when the Greek system of generalization and classification was adopted in the field of legal research.

After Solon's Era:
Peisistratus, Cleisthenes, Ephialtes, and Pericles

As could be expected, Solon's constitution was unacceptable to both conservatives and radicals. Thus, five years after the archonship of Solon, there were bitter new factional struggles and disruptions of constitutional government. No archons were elected for five years—a period known as *anarchia*. Threats of tyranny brought about a compromise in which five eupatrides, two georgoi, and two demiurgoi were elected archons. There were three parties: one that was satisfied with Solon's constitution; another that favored the restoration of the aristocracy; and a third that was convinced that Solon had not gone far enough in satisfying the wishes of the masses. Time was ripe for tyranny, and although Solon was not willing to become the tyrant, Peisistratus was—and had the backing of the common people. Peisistratus seized the government of Athens by force in 561–560 B.C., some thirty years after Solon. He ruled "constitutionally," not "despotically," but his chief officers were his relatives and friends. He kept the people busy and contented, so that they had neither the leisure nor the desire to take part in public affairs. He even strengthened the magistrates in order to offset the opposition of the Areopagus, which was the center of hostility against him. He himself used to revise verdicts considered to be unjust. He traveled around the country settling disputes by arbitration or by rendering a verdict he enforced upon his own authority. He appointed judges to visit the various villages, dealing mainly with civil cases. These judges acted first as arbitrators and only afterward as judges. Peisistratus is credited with establishing one of the more admirable institutions of the Athenian legal system of the fifth century B.C.: public arbitration. The Areopagus continued to function as a homicide court under the tyranny and also tried those charged with plotting to overthrow the government. Peisistratus appointed nine archons each year to the Areopagus; thus, it remained an institution that willingly did his bidding.

Peisistratus was ousted a number of times, returned to power, and finally succeeded in creating an Areopagus that was subservient to his wishes. He frequently interfered in the administration of justice, mitigating or reversing the verdicts of the magistrates. In the final years of his reign, he had many of his enemies executed or banished from Athens.

According to Aristotle, Solon's laws were not repealed by Peisistratus during his fifty years of tyranny. The excellence of Solon's reforms lay in the mere fact that the possibility of appeal acted as a warning to the magistrates. During the years of anarchy, the administration of justice must have been partially suspended, while arbitration enabled the people to deal with the most pressing matters. Solon's laws may have been disregarded and overridden during this period, but they were not altered or repealed. Under Solon's law, the aristocracy had little to fear. In fact, according to Aristotle, Peisistratus made these laws the basis of his administration, taking into consideration the prevailing circumstances. Even later, during the democratic regime of Cleisthenes, there was no need for officially repealing these laws, since they were now being administered in the interest of the people by officials appointed and controlled by the citizens. It is true, however, that he enforced only some of Solon's laws and disregarded others, as necessary.

When Peisistratus controlled the state, he appointed his friends as chief magistrates, but the Areopagus, composed of aristocratic ex-magistrates, could not be so easily remodeled and must have been the principal organ of opposition. Before winning the support of the masses, Peisistratus had no sure majority in the Council of the 400 or in the Assembly, but he was reluctant to destroy or weaken them, as he could use them to his advantage. Thus, Peisistratus had to give as much support as possible to the officials and magistrates, particularly in the field of their jurisdiction in criminal cases involving state offenders. The best way to achieve his ends was to reinstate Solon's laws of public prosecution, allowing him to prosecute his political enemies before his appointed friendly magistrates. Since more magistrates favorable to the tyranny were added to the Areopagus each year, the representation of hostile aristocrats steadily diminished.

After the overthrow of the tyranny, Cleisthenes reorganized the state on a new basis. His reforms belong to the period between the expulsion of the tyrants and the final defeat of Persia—that is, from 510 to 480 B.C.

Cleisthenes did little more than restore Solon's constitution, though some scholars regard him as the virtual founder of democracy. Like Peisistratus, he found his political opponents entrenched in the Areopagus, but he had the advantage of heading a powerful and apparently united popular party, and he could count on the support of the Assembly and the Council of 500, or Boulé. He was committed to a program of democratic reforms, both to satisfy the aspirations of the masses and to secure his own leadership.

The Boulé, as revamped by Cleisthenes, gained some judicial functions at the expense of the magistrates and the Areopagus, which were limited to dealing only with certain cases of homicide and impiety. Through massive banishments and proscriptions, he diminished even more drastically the power of the Areopagus. He also relied on direct support of the people in dealing with his political opponents, as shown by the important political trials that appeared before the Assembly. He did not show any particular interest in criminal legislation, since the customary judicial powers of the parliamentary bodies, especially the Assembly, were more than sufficient for dealing with powerful opponents. Nevertheless, he effectively reorganized the popular courts, reducing the judiciary to the status of mere examining magistrates, constantly reviewing appeals. The Assembly again became the sovereign power of the state and the permanent legislative machinery, which was to become the most important source of future civil and criminal laws. Without the fundamental changes Cleisthenes introduced into existing legislative and judicial spheres of government, the tremendous expansion that the criminal law was soon to undergo would have been impossible.

Cleisthenes seems to have disappeared from public life soon after his reforms. He was not a political reformer, like Solon, but a shrewd politician whose purpose was to secure the goodwill of the masses. To assure his own position, he prevented the return of the tyrants and weakened the aristocracy, putting more power in the hands of the people. His democratic movement lasted for a bit more than twenty-five years. It is not known how long he retained his leadership or when he died, so it is possible that some of his laws could have been legislated by other leaders who shared his democratic approach to government.

The administration of justice was one of the most important functions of government, and Cleisthenes realized that without an independent judicial system, the Ecclesia could not become the sovereign body of the state. This was achieved in 502–501 B.C., when the oath was imposed upon the members of the Council of the 500.

According to known decrees and other documents, only the full Assembly could determine questions of war and peace; inflict the death penalty; and demand a fine of more than 500 drachmas. Ostracism required a majority of the 6,000 votes. It is possible that the attendance at the Assembly never exceeded 5,000 prior to 479 B.C. A definite quorum was never established, and it seems that the 6,000 members were the equivalent of "all Athenians." In the beginning, there was no payment for attending the Assembly, but as many people did not attend, provision was made to pay each of those attending one obol a day. In the same year, the Ecclesia gained the right to elect the ten generals, so the people also gained some control over the military establishment. The majority of the jurors were elderly men, beyond the age of military service. In fact, all members over sixty who volunteered were elected, to avoid reducing the number of men fit for military service.

The smaller court panels normally had 500 jurors, so that ten of these panels could function simultaneously. The remaining thousand served as supernumeraries to fill the vacancies in each panel due to death, illness, and so forth, or to expand the number of a given panel to 1,000 or 1,500 in important cases. The courts opened early in the day, and the jurors had to arrive before daybreak. All those arriving on time were admitted. The average yearly attendance in each panel was around 400. Every panel could function without its full number of jurors, but there was always an odd number in order to avoid ties.

The middle of the fifth century B.C. saw the greatest growth of criminal law in Athens, due once again to the struggle against the Areopagus, culminating in the reforms of Ephialtes in 462 B.C. and the reign of Pericles some thirty years later. In fact, the Areopagus had gradually usurped many important state functions and exercised extensive powers, becoming extremely conservative, as opposed to the more liberal trends in the Assembly and the Council of the 500. Temporarily, the Areopagus had recovered a broad criminal jurisdiction; it ignored Solon's laws of public prosecution and took upon itself the functions of the popular courts. When Ephialtes and his followers considered themselves strong enough to remove these powers from the Areopagus and return them to the popular courts, they had to create new security measures to avoid possible encroachments on these jurisdictions. Therefore, they enacted new statutes, better defining and expanding the criminal jurisdictions of the various magistrates. This trend was marked by the creation of the court of circuit judges in 453 B.C., which presided over most of the cases previously dealt with by the superior magistrates, the thesmothetai. This court was established for the purpose of discouraging rural dwellers from coming into the city for the settlement of their legal differences. These judges—who were also known as "the forty," because they were chosen by lot, four from each tribe—were responsible for dealing with cases that had previously come before arbitrators. From then on, the thesmothetai dealt mainly with other public functions. The creation of this new court made necessary the revision of the entire system of justice. By the beginning of the fourth century B.C., there were other judges, elected by lot, who were to relieve other magistrates of a number of suits and to deliver a decision within thirty days. Among these judges, there were the five *eisagogeis,* who dealt with the monetary litigations of the tribes that did not come before arbitrators; the *nautodikai,* who dealt with disputes among merchants; and the *xenodikai,* who had jurisdiction in matters involving foreigners. Among many other types of street and market officials, there were the *metronomoi,* in charge of controlling the use of correct official weights and measures.

The dicasteries were in existence in 462–461 B.C., when Ephialtes stripped the Areopagus of all its authority as guardian of the constitution, delegating some of its powers to the Assembly, others to the Council of the 500, and still others to the dicasteries. It is difficult to determine whether the dicasteries were instituted because of an increasing frequency of appeals from magisterial judgments or as a result of popular demand for greater participation in the administration of justice. In any case, the tendency of Greek democracy was to concentrate all powers in the hands of the Assembly. When the Heliaea ceased to be a court of appeal and became a court of first resort for all cases except homicide and sacrilege, the entire Heliaea could not possibly sit in judgment in each case, so it was divided into a number of sections (the dicasteries), which could hear a number of cases simultaneously. There is evidence that in 415 B.C., the full number of members of the Heliaea was 6,000. Each dicastery was annually drafted and sworn in as a body. The members' fitness for office was not tested, nor were they accountable for their actions, since they were not the representatives of the people but the people themselves. The 6,000 dicasts were divided into sections or panels, each of them like a little Heliaea. They were sovereign in their functions and their verdicts were final; there was no revision or appeal. Each consisted of 500 ephetai more than thirty years of age, chosen by lot. The credit for introducing jury payment belongs to Pericles; it was introduced not later than 463 B.C. The 6,000 citizens who were to act in judicial matters were chosen annually by lot from citizens over thirty years of age, provided that they were not debtors to the state and had not lost their civil rights; 600 were drawn from each tribe. Those of a higher social status were more interested in serving as jurors than the lower classes were. All of them were volunteers, and while acting as jurors, they could not serve as soldiers. By the middle of the fourth century B.C., the criminal law of Athens may be considered to have attained its maturity.

This situation created some difficulties for the citizens. In Draco's time, it was extremely easy for every citizen to bring his case before the courts and act as his own prosecutor. Solon also permitted any qualified citizen to prosecute wrongdoers, so that members of the lower classes could protect themselves. Athenians became highly conscientious regarding their civil duties. There was no lack of prosecutors, and public opinion approved of those who served the city zealously and was critical of those who failed to do their share. Anyone who so wished could intervene and prosecute a wrongdoer, even if he was not the victim. Athens relied on volunteer accusers, but when public interest was involved, the best advocates were employed. Financial dishonesty of public officials attracted a great deal of public attention, and good advocates were appointed to deal with these cases. Presiding magistrates could not, of course, act as prosecutors; therefore, in public trials the *synegoroi*—the advocates who assisted the *logistai,* or public prosecutors, in presenting their cases—were indispensable.

During the fifth and fourth centuries B.C., citizens had to face large juries and deliver speeches before unusually critical audiences, which presented quite a different situation. With the permission of the jury, a citizen could have the assistance of more experienced people in prosecuting his case in court and to speak either in his stead or after he finished his own speech.

In the fourth century B.C., there was a general dislike of paying public advocates, because it was considered undemocratic and gave the rich an advantage over the poor. However, there were exceptions: the state employed the best advocates in important cases, and advocacy was a common practice. Nevertheless, the right of volunteers to appear in court was always acknowledged. Of course, it was best if the accuser could deliver his own speech, but as many of them were unable to do so, a new profession appeared: the writing of forensic speeches to be recited by litigants in court. The people who wrote these speeches, often teachers, were known as *logographoi*. They were not mere writers of speeches, however; they also advised their clients in many aspects of presenting evidence. In matters of citation, interpretation, and application of the different laws, the services of an experienced logograph were invaluable.

Certain types of offenses—such as slander, robbery, assault, and battery—affected only the individual. In such cases, the victim could bring the offender to justice and use the services of professional speechwriters to assist him in the prosecution.

Prosecution soon became a well-recognized means of taking vengeance on one's enemies, and another "profession" appeared: the *sycophants*. The original meaning of the word is not clear, and there were several definitions, such as "one who brings all kind of charges and proves none," suggesting the false accuser; "they bring charges even against those who have done no wrong"; "they attack men who are entirely innocent"; and the like. The sycophants used calumny and conspiracy, false accusation, and malicious prosecutions, and they abused the legal process for mischievous or fraudulent purposes. The implication, at any rate, is clear. There were laws against these sycophants, usually cited by volunteer prosecutors.

Litigation became the handmaiden of Athenian politics. Everyone with political ambitions sought to advance his fortunes by prosecuting officials regarding their audits as well as other politicians for bribery, corruption, misappropriation of public funds, and other crimes and misdemeanors. Abuses soon appeared, and it was difficult to distinguish between an honest prosecutor and an unscrupulous sycophant. In fact, sycophancy was quite prevalent in Athens in the late fifth century B.C. and became a serious menace to the proper administration of justice, so measures were taken against the sycophants. The sycophants reacted by forming associations to defend themselves, and they began bringing countersuits against the accusers of their clients.

In Athens, the cost of litigation was comparatively modest, but a prosecutor who failed to obtain one-fifth of the votes of the jurors was liable to a fine of 1,000 drachmas. Once a suit was filed and proceedings began, the prosecutor who dropped his case was also liable to a fine of 1,000 drachmas and the loss of the right to bring similar cases in the future. Nevertheless, for the purpose of encouraging prosecution in certain types of suits, no penalty was imposed in cases similar to those mentioned above.

The offenses that appear to have been generally defined and punished as crimes in the various states of Hellas, including both Athens and Sparta, could be classified as follows: (1) treason, including attempts to establish tyranny, betrayal to an enemy, and sedition; (2) attempts by magistrates or other individuals to obstruct lawful process or to procure a law's annulment or repeal in violation of an express prohibition; and (3) offenses against private property, such as theft, robbery, and frauds. Arson was severely punished, as fire was a genuine threat. Thieves caught in flagrante could be killed by the house-owners; in other cases, they had to make restitution of the *res furtiva*. Other punishable offenses included (4) the refusal or failure of an individual to comply with the law, which represented a policy adopted by the state as a whole; (5) the refusal or failure of a magistrate to carry out the provisions of the law; (6) trespassing on public or sacred domain; (7) the violation of sumptuary laws—for example, the evidence of bankruptcy was a presumption of fraud, the bankrupt party seen as having the intention of harming his creditors; and (8) violating custom, sacrilege, blasphemy, and the like.

Prostitution was not illegal, but forced prostitution was severely punished. Prostitutes were usually recruited among foreign slaves, and the Areopagus, through a kind of police force, controlled prostitution in Athens.

There was no law defining and punishing attacks on individuals as crimes. Only later was premeditated homicide severely punished, but negligent manslaughter was punished with temporal exile. The kidnapper of an honest woman was punished by having his eyes put out.

Drastic punishments were also imposed on civil servants who abused their powers or demonstrated a lack of responsibility. Embezzlement was punished with the death penalty. Capital punishment could be inflicted by administering hemlock or by putting the condemned to death by hanging and crucifixion. Another method of execution was hurling the offender into the *barathron,* the pit of death; this was obviously a very ancient method, a convenient substitute for the even earlier stoning. By the fifth century B.C., hemlock poisioning had replaced use of the *barathron,* but the latter was never abolished. Hemlock was used to poison Greek citizens sentenced to capital punishment, as in the case of Socrates. The sword was used in cases of prisoners of war or slaves. Hanging and crucifixion were used in certain cases, as well as against slaves. Solon had already imposed the death penalty in cases of adultery. Suicide was punished by erasing the memory of the suicide himself. The same punishment was applied to certain types of people who committed particularly serious offenses, such as the case of Herostratos, who sought lasting fame by burning the temple of Artemis at Ephesus, one of the wonders of the ancient world. The "punishment" was an empty gesture, since the crime and the name of the criminal are still remembered today. Exile was another type of punishment. Prisons are mentioned in some sources, but there are no available details as to how they functioned. Other penalties usually imposed included atimia, confiscation of property, and fines.

The Eleven were primarily executive officers, elected by lot. They were charged with the execution of the punishments imposed on convicted offenders, including the death penalty. They were also in charge of the city prisons.

In the Attic system, there was criminal proscription as well as amnesty and indult. Amnesty (from the Greek *amnestia,* meaning "forgiveness") was applied for the first time in Athens, approved by the Ecclesia as a law establishing that no one should be prosecuted for political crimes committed during the tyranny, which ought to be forgotten. Later, the regime in power occasionally exercised the sovereign right of amnesty.

The Greek Philosophers: Socrates, Plato, and Aristotle

Plato introduced the first classification of criminal offenses: those against religion (theft within the temple, blasphemy, impiety, or disrespect); those against the state (treason and similar offenses); those against prevailing customs and family (disregarding the obligation to marry, for women between 16 and 20 years, and for men from 25 to 35 years; adultery could only be the husband's crime, because it was inconceivable that a wife should dishonor her family; children had to obey their parents until the age of 30 for men and 40 for women); and those against persons (including the use of drugs and witchcraft, spellbinding, or charms—for example, although poisoning was considered homicide, it was intermingled with witchcraft and sorcery, and homicide was mainly a civil and only partially a criminal offense). There were also distinctions regarding the status of the offender and the victim, such as free citizens and slaves, and the relationship between them in cases of violence and homicide. Some types of murders were excused, such as killing a thief caught at night inside the home of the victim or killing him during the day if he intended to rob the victim; or in cases of rape and similar sex crimes, when not only the victim but also her parents, brothers and sisters, and husband were excused for killing the rapist caught in flagrante; or in cases of criminal assault or unjustified attack in defense of parents, wife, children, brothers and sisters. The final classification was offenses against property (both fraudulent misappropriation of public funds and ordinary theft and robbery). Plato's classification shows not only a clear concept of crime and a precise distinction between different types but also a real progress in judicial development.

To better understand the classification of crimes in ancient Greece, it is important to keep in mind that there were a limited number of clans at the time and that within each of them solidarity was a necessity. Originally, the concept of crime existed only regarding intragroup relationships, and there were no more than two kinds of crimes: those committed by a stranger against a member of the clan and those done by someone of the same clan. The former called for revenge, particularly when the victim had been killed and the killer caught. Later, such distinctions disappeared. In Solon's time, theft and robbery were considered public offenses, whereas homicide remained, for quite a while, mainly a private and civil offense. Homicide was punished through private revenge, and the forgiveness of the victim or his next of kin ruled out any other proceedings.

The Athenians made equally great strides in the development of substantive criminal law and in court procedures, and they were well in advance of their neighbors. Moreover, the criminal law of Athens evolved as an original and independent achievement not equaled by any other Greek state of the classical age.

The basic differences between the Attic laws and those of the Near East and other Eastern countries rest in the fact that the aim and purpose of the Attic laws was "justice" as an end in itself. They established and defined the rights and duties of the individual toward his fellowman and toward the state, trying to reconcile the two when conflicts arose and setting up adequate processes for the protection and enforcement of the rights of the different parties involved. This basic notion made the Attic law, and later the Roman law, preeminent over all other ancient systems of law known today.

There are records of criticisms of the Athenian judicial system. Socrates, for instance, condemned the common practice of bringing weeping children and female relatives into court. He also protested against the practice of allowing popular prejudices to influence verdicts. Some people in Athens were of the opinion that the Athenians were less concerned with justice than with advancing their personal interest—an attitude that is certainly not beyond the realm of imagination.

Any attempt at a critical analysis of the criminal justice system of Athens would find it difficult to determine its effectiveness. Some scholars regard it as poorly suited to the true administration of justice, because a large assembly is not the best tribunal to decide questions of law and easily degenerates into a mob, which is easily swayed. Furthermore, the participation of volunteers creates an atmosphere of suspicion; however, there is no evidence that Athenian judges were often corrupt or dishonest. Because of their number and their representative character, they could not have become an instrument of oppression. They were not likely to treat as criminal acts that were tolerated by public opinion. The speeches of the orators were the best argument to prove the vices inherent in such a system, providing sufficient condemnation of courts that were influenced by passions and political prejudices and that handed down verdicts based on insinuating sophistry and outrageous misinterpretations of the law. Even so, these verdicts did not bind another court, since each was a committee of the sovereign people, supreme and responsible to no other body.

Today, the large popular juries are considered one of the justice system's drawbacks, but in ancient Athens, political democracy and popular juries were inseparable, and service within the courts was considered a mark of good citizenship. Plato distrusted the large popular courts, but Aristotle, with some hesitancy, maintained that the masses, with all their liabilities, were still better judges than a superior few.

Legal and Criminological Implications of Greek Philosophy

The primordial notions of criminogenesis and criminal dynamics, as conceived and applied in different times and places, could and should be considered an indispensable part of the study of modern criminology. The Greek philosophers had already dealt with the issues or crime and punishment. They started with the first hints about imputability and culpability, as well as with the notion of personal criminal responsibility, in order to replace the collective notions. For them, crimes could be voluntary, involuntary, or accidental, so they prepared the basic ground for the concepts of premeditated homicide and involuntary manslaughter. Even the pre-Socratic philosophers dealt with problems related to ethics and law. Protagoras, for instance, was convinced that even the wisest of punishments could not right a wrong but could act only to prevent future wrongdoings. He certainly did not use the term *deterrent,* but to a certain extent, he did conceive the notion of preventive sanctions. Even Hippocrates expressed some ideas on crime causation that were remarkable for his time.

For Socrates, justice was nothing more than learning and wisdom. Criminals were moved by fatalism, but in any case, they were more insane than wicked, and if not insane then at least foolish, for no one would voluntarily do evil. He claimed that criminals suffered from a disease of the soul, being unable to distinguish between just and unjust. He also put a great emphasis on environmental factors in his criminogenetic reasoning. Crime was the direct result of ignorance, poverty, and social deprivation. He emphasized the corrective rather than punitive value of legal sanctions. He was, indeed, the first moralist, always preaching absolute obedience to the laws derived from the divine principle of justice.

The basic ideas of Socrates were further developed by Plato, whose concepts of justice, crime, and punishment are found in his *Dialogues, The Republic, The Laws,* and *Gorgias.* According to Plato, the essence of every law, including the criminal law, is its absolute value as the best tool of goodness, and goodness is the equivalent of divine intelligence. If the offender were able to understand the injustice of his act, he would certainly abstain from committing it. The most prevalent causes of man's injustices to man are his excessive egocentrism or self-esteem (*The Laws* V), which are frequently associated with aggressiveness and violent passions (anger, rage, fury), depressive moods (sorrow, grief, fear), exaggerated hedonism (pleasures, enjoyment), or ignorance.

In the last analysis, there is no doubt that Plato recognized that the personality of every individual was the direct outcome of the interaction of different biological (inheritance, age) and environmental (education, instruction, family, economic situation) factors and that the criminal act should be considered the result of this interaction of a given personality to a given situation. Aristotle was basically in agreement, although he considered an inherited handicap an extenuating circumstance and thus a legal excuse. Plato regarded cases of diminished responsibility as those including insanity, organic diseases, imbecility, infancy, or extreme senility (*The Laws* XI); Aristotle spoke of children, idiots, the mentally diseased, and those in a state of ecstacy as being exempt from criminal responsibility.

Whereas Plato's distinction between different types of acts was a preliminary one, Aristotle developed a precise and definite theory. He stresses the importance of differentiating between voluntary and involuntary acts. Voluntary acts—those consciously and unjustly committed by an individual—were of two types: those committed in ignorance or without a reasonable motive and those consciously committed, with or without premeditation. Involuntary acts were those committed by force but over which man had no control—for example, while demonstrating a catapult, it goes off; trying to save someone's life, poison mistakenly administered. Acts might also be defined as just and unjust. Just acts have to be voluntarily committed, with or without premeditation. In one case, the act is unjust but the person who committed it is not; in the other, both the act and its author are unjust.

Plato defined three different types of homicide: involuntary homicide, homicide committed in a passion, and premeditated homicide. For Aristotle, the classification was somewhat different: unjust homicide committed by mistake, conscious homicide without premeditation, and unjust homicide committed consciously and with premeditation. He expressed precise concepts about criminal determinism: sociological causes (state of need); physiological causes (childhood and senility); and pathological causes (mental diseases), all of them leading to a diminished or absence of responsibility.

For Aristotle, the criminal was not a sick man but someone whose behavior was voluntary, a direct outcome of his desires and appetites. He believed that there was a direct determinism in each case of criminal behavior, be it of a sociological or pathological origin. Moroever, he felt that the majority of voluntary criminal acts derived from man's ambition and cupidity ("Politics"). He also emphasized the importance of economic conditions, since he stated that poverty created crime and sedition. He was convinced that sociocultural factors had a decisive influence on human behavior through the environment in which the offender lived and in which the crime was committed.

Aristotle's position regarding the problem of responsibility was far more developed and refined than that of Plato. He believed that such responsibility should be limited to the individual offender, rather than being considered a collective responsibility. The intention with which the act was committed—*mens rea*—also had to be taken into consideration. The essential elements that determined responsibility were imputability, putting the blame of a deed on a given individual; and culpability, involving condemnation for having committed unlawful acts or omissions.

Plato felt that criminals who had no chance of being reformed had to be eliminated from society through exile, life imprisonment, or capital punishment. Other offenders, who could be reformed, were not evil but should be treated with a kind of "medicine of the soul"—suffering that taught the meaning of truth and justice. However, Plato also thought that if the judge was convinced that the offender had sincerely repented, there was no need to apply a sanction.

Some of Plato's penological measures were indeed exceptional for his time, and some were to be adopted in the nineteenth and twentieth centuries. For instance, when he referred to the need for a "medicine of the soul," he was actually introducing the notion of *pena medicinalis,* which would later be presented by Christian philosophers, from St. Augustine to St. Thomas, as punishment by isolation, prayer, and meditation.

Plato suggested three types of prisons (*Laws* X): one functioning near the Agora, for preventive detention; another known as *sophronister,* a kind of *prison école,* reserved for offenders who might reform and return to society; and the "prison of torture," located in an isolated place, where incurable offenders who have not been exiled or executed should be kept for the rest of their lives.

For Aristotle, the social reaction to crime had a double purpose: preventive and repressive. The former, expressed in his *Politics,* had eugenic, demographic, and deterrent elements. In what might be called a eugenic policy, he stressed the need to have a law forbidding the nourishment of defective children, who should be abandoned to die. His demographic measures consisted in his insistence on having a limited number of births, allowing abortions before the fetus "received the touch of life." He was also in favor of isolating criminals so that they could not hurt again and for severe punishments as a deterrent measure. And regarding repressive punishments, he advocated that they should be more humane.

The Greek philosophers expressed all the doubts and contradictions that were to pave the way for scientific criminological thinking. Socioeconomic, environmental, social, and cultural conditions were high on the list of the Greek philosophers' priorities—an attribute that, in itself, is deserving of admiration. Their contribution culminated in Aristotle's approach, which began to divorce criminology from philosophical speculation in order to enter the world of facts and observation.

9

Roman Criminal Law

Not to know what happened before we were born, is to remain perpetually a child. For what is the worth of a human life unless it is woven into the life of our ancestors by the records of history?

—Cicero

The Original Settlers of the Italian Peninsula

The early Italians consisted of many tribes, each with its own language and culture. Among them were the Latins, who, after crossing the Apennine mountains, established themselves in the Latium valley, where the city of Rome would later be erected. The most important of the Latins would become the Romans.

From the seventh century B.C. onward, the Romans would be influenced by two culturally superior peoples. One was the *Etruscans*. Although the very memory of the Etruscans also fell when the Roman Empire crumbled, they seem to have been of Indo-European origin. Influenced by Greek culture, the Etruscans' art, religion, and social customs had an important impact on the development of Rome.

The other great impact came from the Greeks themselves, who, at the beginning of the seventh century B.C., occupied the southwestern coast of the peninsula and a great part of Sicily. Their impact is easier to detect because of the Etruscans' role as intermediaries. For instance, Roman writing, with the Latin alphabet, derived from the Etruscans, who received it from the Greeks. There was also a Greek influence in the Roman legal field. Much later, of course, Rome would go through a much deeper Hellenization, which would affect its entire material and spiritual culture.

During the seventh and sixth centuries B.C., the Etruscans expanded their domain till it included lands from the south of Venice to the Tyrrhenian Sea. But their most important conquest was the Lazio, the valley of the Tiber, where stood the seven hills called the Septimontium, on which Rome would be established. It was the Etruscans (not the legendary Romulus—the name

Roma is of Etruscan origin) who developed Rome from a cluster of huts to a great city and who evolved the first great civilization of Italy.

The Roman Monarchy and Its Basic Institutions

Of the seven traditional kings (*rex*) of Rome, three who were of Etruscan origin seem to have been historical, reigning before the end of the sixth century B.C. The purple robes they put on after a victorious campaign, the *lictors* (public attendants, later of the Roman magistrates) marching in front of them, and the *sella curulis* (a folding chair with curved legs and inlaid ivory but no back) were all, by the Romans' own admission, appropriated by the Romans and became symbols of their own might. When Sextus, the son of the third of these kings, was accused of raping a virtuous Roman lady, Lucretia, who committed suicide in shame, the outcry that followed her death triggered a revolt. The king, whose power had been declining anyhow, was deposed, putting an end to the dynasty in 509 B.C.; and Rome became a republic. Amid the ensuing hostility between Romans and Etruscans, the Etruscans were expelled from Rome once and for all in 509 B.C.

The Etruscans, however, not only had established the city of Rome but also had created the Roman State. They first divided the city into three different regions, or *tribus* (tribes, meaning a third of the community), each with its own religious cults and priests and each with ten subdivisions of neighborhoods, called *curias*. Afterward, with the expansion of the city, there were four tribes, known as *servias*—a derivation of the name of the Etruscan king Servius Tullius. This remained the basic distribution of the city till the beginning of the empire.

Before and during the monarchy, the steep expansion of Rome's population produced a basic social division into *patricians* (nobles) and *plebeians* (common people). The patricians were thought to be descendants of the original founders of the city. Artificially attached to them were clientes (clients)—dependents who, in return for patronage and protection, gave political support and open shows of loyalty whenever "patron" and "client" met. Although this *patricii–clientes* relationship gradually disappeared, it was replaced by similar bonds of protection and fidelity that always existed in Rome and underlay the entire Roman legal structure. The plebeians were composed of (1) established foreigners—traders, industrialists, and farmers who settled in Rome of their own free will; (2) conquered populations—most importantly an ancient people of Italy, the Sabines, who were northerly neighbors of the Latins; and (3) *clientes* whose patron families among the patricians had died out.

There was yet a third social class, the *slaves*—usually prisoners of war. Their numbers increased considerably with Roman conquests, till they in fact constituted about 30 percent of the population of Rome and 40 percent in the rest of the peninsula. The slaves' lot improved somewhat as Rome went from the monarchy to the republic and to the empire. Roman history registers only one slave rebellion, the famous one led by Spartacus in the first century B.C.

The basic cell of the Roman social organism was the family (*familia*), which included the father, his wife, their children, and the descendants of their male children. The patrician nobility was also divided into groups of families called *gens,* which were united by a common religion and name (Fabius, Cornelius, Julius, etc.) and included clients and other dependents. In early times, it was the chief, or *patres,* of the *gens* who constituted, by right of birth, the Council of Elders, or Senate.

From the very beginning, the state was never an abstract notion for the Romans, and their sense of being participants in it, or citizens, was strong. Therefore, the state was known as the community of citizens, Populus Romanus—a name that remained in use not only during the republic but also during a good part of the empire.

During the Etruscan monarchy, the king had at his disposal, only as consultative bodies, the Council of Elders, or Senate, and the elected Assembly of the Curias (*Comitia Curiata*). The Assembly, constituted only by patricians, elected the king (who then served for life) and the other magistrates, decided about war and peace, and discussed and approved the laws. Once elected, the Assembly had to approve the *Lex Curiata de Imperio,* which defined the king's executive rights and authority. This *imperium* is of great importance throughout Roman history. The Senate also had to approve the Lex Curiata, due to the *autocritas patrum,* the authority of the *patres.* Both the Senate and the Assembly were oligarchic bodies par excellence. Only later, with the establishment of the four serviae—each including patricians and plebeians and divided into *centuriae* (groups of 100 military men each)— would the new type of assembly appear, the important *Comitia Centuriata.*

The Roman Character

The earliest Romans were farmers. From these pioneers, the Romans inherited their respect for strength, discipline, and loyalty, as well as their industry, frugality, tenacity, and self-assuredness.

From cradle to grave, the life of the Romans was determined by position and status and was regulated by traditions and customs. As we have seen, the family was the fundamental unit, and kinship had a tremendous importance, despite the fact that in ancient Rome, the sale of children was rather frequent. The *pater familias* had absolute power and was the virtual owner of the members of his household. Perhaps this underlay the Roman trend toward an authoritarian state and, later, the institution of the all-powerful emperor, the *pater patriae* (head of the country). By the first century A.D., however, the *pater familias* usually consulted with the "family council," which became the chief family authority.

Besides politics or judicial affairs, the army or farming, there were few other proper activities for the Roman gentleman. Major commercial ventures were dealt with by men called *equaestrians,* or knights, whose title derived from old military castes but who were actually merchants, and shopkeeping and crafts were left to the plebeians.

A trait that the Romans admired was *gravitas*—a weightiness, a sober, lofty, and enduring quality. *Gravitas* lay at the heart of the Roman character, with its preference for strength over delicacy, utility over grace. Strength clothed in dignity was the Roman ideal. In his *toga,* a Roman gentleman never gave the impression of being in a hurry. He seemed to be always on parade, conscious of his audience. Pageantries and ceremonials abounded in Roman life, even for the declaration of war or the formal making of peace, which was performed by a special college of priests called *fetialis.*

Some scholars have attributed Rome's success to Roman character: practical, prosaic, prudent, intellectually timid, but bold and aggressive in the conduct of life. The Roman lacked imagination but was endowed with a remarkable strength of mind. Since no historian was able to answer the essential question of whether this character was the expression of ethnic origin or environment, other explanations were sought. Some thought that the Romans believed in their own superiority and pursued the conquest of the world step by step. Others interpreted Roman imperialism in terms of fighting for *lebensraum* (living space) or conquest of new markets. Some explained that such a tremendous expansion was achieved in a fit of absentmindedness—just a series of groping, stumbling, and accidental instances, betraying a nonimperialistic trend. This seems too naive, since accidents that repeat themselves so frequently are likely to suggest that it was really all part of a plan, although this notion is very difficult to prove.

The Romans were also very superstitious and religious people. To satisfy them, something of the ancient monarchy was kept, though only for religious and ceremonial purposes. Even so, these functions were slowly being transferred to the *Pontifex Maximus,* or *Rex Sacrorum*—a "religious king" who would be responsible solely for ritual sacrifices and other religious functions, whereas the consuls would have solely political and military power, not religious powers.

The private life of the Romans was strictly regulated by an unwritten code defining acceptable and forbidden behaviors, though no one had much trouble finding the loopholes he needed to conduct business. Here, as elsewhere, the letter of the law rather than its spirit, outward appearance rather than inner meaning, were always the important considerations. In contrast to the

Greeks, who were so preoccupied with speculative morality, the Romans rarely concerned themselves with theoretical definitions of ethical ideals. They clung to a deep conservatism, justifying their resistance to change by the belief that the old ways were the best ways. The Romans looked down on the more artistic and less inhibited Greeks, considering them frivolous and ineffectual. Therefore, Romans never played musical instruments, participated in gymnasium activities, or wrote philosophy, except a few individuals who expressly considered themselves philosophers. Much later, of course, when the Romans were initiated in the field of philosophy, they followed the Greek tradition, and the echo of the great disputes among the different Greek schools also reached the Roman cities.

The Romans considered themselves models of uprightness, unsentimental makers and doers who were firmly attached to reality. To others, they were thought to have less pleasing characteristics; they were seen as the personification of ruthlessness, enjoying bloody gladiatorial contests—practitioners of debauchery who imitated their own monstrous emperors. Perhaps these negative traits grew out of the long Roman conflict with man and nature. Every one of their generations had to leave, more than once, its civil activities and take part in military adventures, fostering an acceptance of savagery. Even later, when they became more sophisticated, they continued to enjoy entertainments horrifying to present standards.

The Roman authors Suetonius, Juvenal, and Tacitus, among others, wrote in vivid terms of the depravity and corruption of Roman life, especially among the members of the elite. Still, the majority of the Romans conducted themselves responsibly and respectably.

The Development of Rome

Until the beginning of the third century B.C., Rome was no more than another city-state of the ancient period, centered in a fortified area that was the stage for its entire sociopolitical and economic life. Around this area was an agricultural area with some small, open villages, isolated one from another. The state territory was extremely small—no more than a third of present-day Andorra—with a population of some 10,000. By the beginning of the fourth century B.C., when Rome already had an important role in the political life of central Italy, it encompassed an area ten times its original size, but still no more than half of modern Luxembourg.

During the fourth and third centuries B.C., however, Rome continued to grow, and it became one of the most powerful states of the ancient world. Soon afterward, with the successful war against Carthage and Hannibal (264–146 B.C.), Rome gained control of the western half of the Mediterranean; and about 150 years later, it extended its domain as far as the Euphrates and the Black Sea in the east. Thus, Rome became the ruler of the entire Mediterranean; the Roman Empire (*Imperium Romanum*) and the earth globe (*Orbis Terrarum*) were now the same thing.

The Latin expression *colonia* was not entirely unrelated to such a conquest and to what today would be called imperialism, since the *colonia* was one of the Romans' principal instruments for expanding their national territory. *Colonia* was a collective noun meaning a body of peasants who, as settlers in a specified locality, formed a self-administered civic community. Colonization in Rome was always an official act of the state, not something left to the haphazard enterprise of private individuals. In republican times, the decision about when and where to found a colony belonged to the people; therefore, it needed a law passed by the Plebeian Assembly (*Consilium Plebis*). Before 200 B.C., the roman Senate decided about the founding of colonies. Later, in the first century B.C., such decisions were made by political dynasties and military dictators and, under the Empire, by the Roman emperor.

After the victorious Roman legions came governors and civil servants, architects and merchants, building the new colonies in Rome's image. Roman roads facilitated contact with the metropolis. But Rome also changed, becoming the most cosmopolitan of cities. In the words of one of its poets, Rome made one city where once there was a world.

Still, in architecture as in many other spheres, the Romans were avid borrowers: They took over the Doric, Ionic, and Corinthian columns of the Greeks as well as the arch of the Etruscans, building with them their temples, pantheons, and other similar public institutions. They were, however, the first to use concrete to achieve their architectural dreams.

Of all their monumental works, nothing matched the majestic vastness of the open forums, where the Romans met for business or pleasure. The Forum Romanum, the oldest and greatest of these squares, gradually became the center of Rome; here was the Senate where Cicero spoke and where Julius Caesar was murdered.

Despite all this greatness, a walk through Rome at night was a grim adventure. With no lights on the streets, they were usually swarming with vehicles, prostitutes, and rampant criminality. Wise Romans, like many city-dwellers today, stayed home after sunset.

Rome was able to rule its huge and complicated empire thanks to some precise principles. Perhaps the most important was *divide et impera* (divide and reign), which meant that the Romans did not allow political organizations that could endanger their domination. Alliances among conquered peoples were not permitted, and each of these communities had direct contact only with Rome. Another principle was to permit the subject peoples to administer their own internal affairs, including religious matters, for which Rome exercised great tolerance. A third principle was to strongly consolidate the conquered territories, using a network of strategic roads and a great many fortified strongholds.

Rome's career spanned a millenium, during which it assembled the greatest empire the world had seen. But its more enduring claims are two. The first is Rome's marked genius in nourishing and embellishing the intellectual and cultural life of the Greek world that it conquered. Roman architecture, art, literature, and even religion show, in their Greek influence, the aptness of the Roman poet Horace's statement: "Captive Greece took Rome captive." The second achievement was the transformation of a fragmented world into a single great community, thanks to Rome's innovations in political organization, individual liberty, and respect for law. The expressions "natural rights," "equality before the law," and "government for the good of the people" are intimately connected with the Roman heritage.

The Roman Republic

In 509 B.C., the Romans overthrew the Etruscan monarchy in a revolt that was totally patrician, with no participation from the plebeians. Rome then set about trying to find a new political system that would avoid personal despotism. It is possible that the Romans studied the existing systems of neighboring peoples.

At any rate, the transition from the monarchy to the republic was rather easy, because the Romans retained the basic institutions. It seems that for a time, the supreme authority of the state was a collegiate body composed of two or more *praetores*. In 367 B.C., the title *consul* was adopted instead of *praetor*. The consulate was based on two consuls (colleagues) elected simultaneously by the comitia centuriata, which, as we have seen, evolved from the Etruscan-period Senate, and the Comitia Curiata; it included both patricians and plebeians. After the Leges Liciniae Sextiae of 367 B.C., plebeians as well as patricians could be elected consuls. Although each consul enjoyed the supreme authority, the *imperium,* it now had two important limitations: It was vested for only one year (not for life, as with the kings), and both consuls had equal power (*par potestas*) and could nullify each other's measures with the *intercessio,* similar to the modern veto. This created complications, which each Consul could try to overcome by appointing a dictator. The dictator had full civil and military powers, but his tenure lasted only as long as the consul who had appointed him wanted or six months maximum, and he could never be reappointed to this office. Also, in making military decisions, he had to consult with the chief of cavalry, further ensuring that he would not become a dictator.

Besides these two annual and collegiated consuls, the laws of 367 B.C. designated a third kind of magistrate with *imperium*. They were known by the ancient name of *praetor;* although their *imperium* was equal to that of the consuls, in practice they had a lesser status. The praetors were in charge of the *iurisdictio,* but in certain cases they could substitute for a consul in dealing with political or military problems. After the middle of the third century B.C., with a growth in administrative functions, new praetors were created.

There were also a number of other magistrates with more restricted responsibilities. They had the *potestas* (the authority to do their specific tasks), but not the *imperium.* They included the *quaestores,* responsible for the public and military treasury as well as, later, various legal functions such as judge and prosecutor; the *aediles curules* and plebeian *aediles,* a kind of police of streets and markets; and the prestigious *censors,* usually former consuls, responsible for the census and other administrative duties.

The early republican government retained the three basic monarchial institutions: the Senate, the Comitia Curiata and the Comitia Centuriata. The Senate (*Senatus*), originally an assembly of *patres* of noble families, slowly changed during the republic into a council of former magistrates. It was divided into a number of orders: First came the *censorii* and *consularii,* then the *praetorii* and *aedilicii,* and so on. Its members served for life, and this stability explains the tremendous power it exercised over the centuries. Though it never had executive or full legislative powers, it had the real control of the state. The period of its predominance was the most brilliant of Roman history; its decadence brought with it the fall of the republic.

The Comitia Curiata gradually lost its important political functions, becoming a religious and judicial body presided over by the *Pontifex Maximum,* a high priest, with no effective participation of the citizens. Some believe that it may still have retained some political functions, such as intervening in matters of war and peace.

Meanwhile, the other Assembly, the Comitia Centuriata, was gradually losing its early military character and gaining a distinctive political character instead. As mentioned earlier, Rome's citizens were classified according to their wealth into a number of *centuriae.* Since each *centuria* had only one vote—established after computing the votes of all of its members—the majority of the votes decided ever issue. In other words, the poor citizen practically never exercised his right to vote, and the timocracy had a clear predominance in the Assembly.

The Comitia Centuriata did not assemble in the center of Rome but met outside the city, in the so-called Campus Martius. It was this Assembly that elected the consuls, the praetors, the censors, and all other magistrates and executive officials; decided on policies of war and peace; and intervened, as a final court of appeals, in cases involving the death penalty.

Nevertheless, these functions were limited, not absolute. For instance, if the Comitia Centuriata was entitled to elect the consuls and the other magistrates, the consuls had to transmit to the new ones the *auspicium,* the command of office. Thus, the consul convocated and presided over the special meeting of the Assembly at which the new Consuls were to be elected, and in reading out the list of candidates, he could sometimes omit a name that he considered unworthy of the position. Another limitation was that the Senate had to ratify the elections of the Comitia Centuriata; without its approval, the elected candidate could not assume the office of consul. In addition, according to the Lex Curiata of the *imperium,* a new consul had to receive the *potestas* (his official relationship with the people) from the Senate and the *imperium* (his real executive, legislative and judicial powers) from the Comitia Curiata.

All in all, there was no doubt that the patricians kept the keys of power. It was primarily they who could get a seat in the Senate or be elected consul or some other magistrate. They also had some privileges that were never abolished. For instance, the old title of *patres* could be given only to the patrician senators; and they also retained the ancient privilege of the *interregnum,* according to which the patrician senators could act as regents—for no more than five days at a time, but with the charge of electing a new consul as soon as possible. This procedure was in force even during Cicero's time in the first century B.C.

Nevertheless, largely because of the plebeians' crucial role in the military, a relatively small number of plebeian families did reach the consulate and the Senate. These constituted a new class of politicians, the *nobilitas,* who quickly became impervious to the upstarts—the *homines novi,* or new men. The greatest breakthrough occurred in the fifth century B.C. with the creation of the Concilium Plebis. Its members, the *tribuni plebis,* or simply *tribuni,* were elected to the Comitia Curiata from the chiefs of the plebeian tribes (there were by now seventeen rustic tribes, or *tribus,* in Rome, and four urban ones).

Of the seventeen tribuni, only two had the right to attend the meetings of the Comitia Centuriata. Although they could not participate in its debates, they did wield the powerful right of *veto* (I forbid). If one of these two tribuni declared veto, the draft law under discussion would not be approved. On the other hand, once the law was passed, the veto could not be applied. Therefore, these tribuni had to stay alert during the meetings.

The tribuni were also entitled to participate in the meetings of the Senate, which led to a kind of cooperation between patricians and plebeians against certain petulant magistrates. But when the tribuni started to oppose the will of the Senate in the second half of the second century B.C., and even pursued revolutionary purposes through demagogic tricks, it was, as we shall see, the beginning of a very serious political crisis that contributed to the fall of the republic.

Over the years, however, the tribuni were able to gain for the plebeians, through a number of enacted laws, the right to intermarry with patricians, to be appointed consuls and, in 287 B.C., to pass laws at the Concilium without the consent of the Senate.

Meanwhile, Rome slowly extended its influence on the peninsula. Through alliances or conquests, the Romans took control of the nearby areas of the Latium plain, then the more distant Italic tribes, and finally the Etruscans. By the beginning of the fourth century B.C., Rome was already the leading city of central Italy; by late in that century, it had become master of the entire peninsula. By now, Rome was a first-class power, which inevitably brought it into conflict with Carthage, the mistress of the western Mediterranean, as well as with the three great Hellenistic kingdoms that remained after the collapse of the world empire of Alexander the Great: the Seleucid empire in Syria; the Ptolemaic empire in Egypt; and Alexander's original empire of Macedonia. The first of the three wars against Carthage, the Punic Wars, lasted from 264 to 241 B.C., with a Roman victory. In 218 B.C., the second Punic War broke out when Hannibal invaded Italy from the north, only to be defeated in 202 B.C. Two years later, Rome fought successfully against Philip V of Macedon, who had openly sided with Hannibal. After his death, the Romans defeated his son Perseus in 167 B.C. During the same period, Rome also defeated Antiochus III of Syria in the battle of Magnesia in 190 B.C. Finally, in 146 B.C., Rome defeated Carthage in the third Punic War; this time, the city of Carthage was leveled, its site was ploughed and sowed with salt to make it into a wasteland, and the Carthaginians were sold into slavery.

While Rome was extending its domain in so many areas, graft, corruption, economic depression, and excesses increased, and a need was felt for reform. The first of the political reformers were the brothers Tiberius (162–133 B.C.) and Gaius Gracchus (154–121 B.C.). Both served as tribunes, carried out extensive agrarian reforms, and were murdered in office. Besides distributing lands to the landless, they tried to increase the political rights of the people at the expense of the Senate. In 134 B.C., after being elected one of the (then) ten tribunes, Tiberius immediately asked for the redistribution of the big estates, leaving some lands for the use of the common people. The Senate convinced another of the tribunes to veto the movement; but Tiberius high-handedly overrode his fellow tribune, which led to a riot in which he and some 300 of his followers were killed. In 124 B.C., his brother Gaius was elected tribune and proposed even more sweeping land reforms. He also challenged the Senate by extending Roman citizenship to other Italian peoples, a right that was then rarely granted. He even proposed that jurors, traditionally Senators, be selected from the *equaestrian* (middle-class merchant) class. The Senate reacted by provoking violence in the city and declared Gaius a public enemy. To avoid being captured and executed, he had himself killed by a servant. Still the laws of Gaius Gracchus established—among many other items dealing with land distribution and other civil and military matters—that no capital punishment could be applied without the confirmation of the people and that the right to judge, till then exclusively in the hands of Senators and patricians, should also be given to the equaestrians.

Years later, Gaius Marus, an equaestrian supported by the *populares* (the large lower class constituted by plebeians who had remained poor), was elected consul and held this position six times between 107 and 100 B.C. He was able to keep domestic peace, but his principal contributions were military: He defeated some African chieftains and repelled a threatened invasion by Celtic and Germanic tribes. In 99 B.C., the senators again regained control, but in 91 B.C., another one of the populares, Marcus Livius Drusus, was elected tribune and reiterated the proposition to extend Roman citizenship to all people of the Italian peninsula. The Senate resisted, and he was assassinated in the same year of his election. His death touched off a bloody social war that lasted for two years, during which the other cities of the peninsula tried to secede from Rome. The war ended when Rome finally granted citizenship to these allies.

A few years later, the antagonism between the *optimates* (nobility) and the populares flared up once more because of the rivalry of two men: Lucius Cornelius Sulla (138–78 B.C.), an outstanding soldier of aristocratic and conservative views who achieved fame as general, provincial governor, and consul; and Gaius Marus, the old leader of the populares. The outcome of this conflict was Marus's death and true dictatorial rule by Sulla. He gave the Senate more power, packed it with his friends, and curtailed the power of the Tribunes; appointments to the judiciary were limited to senators and patricians. The military also acquired a preponderant role, which contributed to the rapid decline of the republican ideal.

Sulla voluntarily retired in 79 B.C. and died a year later. In 70 B.C., Gnaeus Pompeius, a most successful general who had subjugated Spartacus and his slaves and was also known as Pompey the Great, was elected consul together with another great general, Marius Crassus. Pompey, though he had been one of Sulla's most trusted lieutenants, rescinded the most objectionable of Sulla's laws, restoring to the tribunes much of their former authority. He stepped down after only one term in office, but in 67 B.C. he was granted a three-year *imperium* to fight the Meditarranean pirates, who were devastating all the sea-traveling routes. He accomplished the task in just three months but then turned to the East, where Mithridates of Pontus was again threatening Roman provinces. After defeating Mithridates, Rome again became the absolute power in Asia, from the Mediterranean to the Euphrates.

When Pompey came back to Rome, the Senate gave him a *triumph* of official welcome but rejected the agreements he had made with the eastern monarchs and refused to grant land to his soldiers. He then formed a secret alliance with Crassus and Julius Caesar, which came to be known as the First Triumvirate. Pompey gained recognition for his eastern victories, Caesar became commander of Gaul, and Crassus was able to defeat the Parthians. Crassus died in battle in 53 B.C.; by this time, friction had developed between Caesar and Pompey. Caesar, as proconsul of Gaul, increased his political stature with his military victories beyond the Alps, while Pompey was consolidating his power in Rome. The Senate and the optimates were with Pompey, while the populares, along with other followers of Caesar, were demanding Pompey's overthrow. In 49 B.C., Pompey persuaded the Senate to order Caesar to disband his army, but Caesar, in open violation of the law, crossed the river Rubicon, the southern limit of his military command, and marched on Rome. Pompey withdrew to Greece with his army and most of the Senate, but Caesar defeated him at the battle of Pharsalus in 48 B.C. Pompey then fled to Egypt, with Caesar in pursuit; but as soon as he stepped down from his ship, he was killed by an agent of the boy-king Ptolemy. It was upon Caesar's arrival there that he fell in love with Ptolemy's sister Cleopatra, who soon after became queen of Egypt when her brother was killed in battle against the Romans.

Ater his victory over Pompey, Caesar returned to Rome, where, while keeping the structure of the republican government, he became a real monarch, the sole ruler. On the ides of March in 44 B.C., he was killed in the senate by disaffected conspirators. Still, he had succeeded in beginning to alter fundamentally the political system of Rome, believing that if the republic had been the appropriate system for the period of expansion, there was now a need for some kind of absolute monarchy similar to that of Ptolemy in Egypt.

Caesar did not live to designate a successor, and after his death there was another struggle for power between his grand-nephew and legal heir, Gaius Julius Caesar Octavianus, known simply as Octavian, and Mark Antony, Caesar's co-consul. The Senate supported Octavian but refused to elect him consul, so he occupied the city with his army and forced his election to office. Immediately afterward, he formed an alliance with Antony and Lepidus, another of Caesar's top lieutenants, constituting the Second Triumvirate, with Antony in charge of the East, Octavian in the West, and Lepidus in Africa. This triumvirate—in fact, a dictatorship—fought together in Rome against the armies of Brutus and Cassius, two of the murderers of Caesar but also the last real republicans.

The Roman Empire

The organization of such a gigantic empire was a tremendous task, and it soon became apparent that the juridical structure of Rome was inadequate. By the beginning of the first century B.C., the city-state as such had disappeared, since Rome already included the entire Italian peninsula. Slowly, the change to a monarchy became accepted, despite bitter power struggles.

Sulla, who already had absolute political power, had resigned instead of becoming king. Julius Caesar, who was appointed dictator for life in 44 B.C., was assassinated the same year. Thus, it was Octavian who became, in fact, the creator of the Roman monarchy.

While Octavian remained in Rome, meanwhile getting rid of Lepidus by giving him the honorary religious title of Pontifex Maximus, Antony had gone to Egypt to oversee the oriental sector of the Roman conquests. In Egypt, he, too, fell in love with Cleopatra, rejecting his legal wife—Octavian's sister—and marrying the Egyptian queen. In 32 B.C., the Senate declared war on Cleopatra; two years later, she and Antony committed suicide in despair over Rome's advances.

Upon returning victoriously from Egypt in 27 B.C., Octavian offered to resign, but the Senate instead made him Princeps (first citizen) and gave him the honorific name Augustus (the revered one) as well as a number of important functions. And so the new political system, the Roman Empire, was formally established. Although Octavian never called himself emperor, he became a real monarch, with both civilian and military powers.

In many respects, the state was much better run under Augustus than during the republican age; he organized the government so brilliantly that it served even demented emperors for centuries to come. For the personal protection of the Princeps, he created the important Praetorian Imperial Guard; he also created the Consilium, a kind of council of state, to assist him in his functions as supreme judge. He exercised justice ably and leniently and revised the texts of many laws.

During Augustus's time, Rome had a population of about one million and suffered from housing shortages, traffic congestion, air pollution, high cost of living, unemployment, and rampant crime—a familiar litany. Yet to live in Rome remained the cherished goal of every Roman.

Augustus died in 14 A.D., having in effect appointed his stepson Tiberius (42 B.C.–37 A.D.) as the next Princeps. Tiberius quickly gained a reputation as a depraved and brutal ruler. Although, he, too, was considered an efficient administrator, basically all powers continued to shift to the emperor. He restored legislative functions to the Senate, but reduced it to an approving echo of his wishes. It was also under Tiberius that both the salary and tenure of public functions were increased, so that the growth of the bureaucracy under the empire began. (It is interesting that in October 1985, on the island of Capri, a number of historians held a special ceremony to show the world that Tiberius has been unjustly maligned.)

Tiberius was succeeded by his grand-nephew Caligula, whose cruelty and madness led to his being executed in 41 A.D. by a group of Praetorian guards. Rome then remained without an emperor until the guard found Claudius, the 50-year-old uncle of Caligula, made him emperor and forced the Senate to accept him as such. Semiparalytic and a stutterer, but intelligent, Claudius proved to be a sensible and steady ruler. He included Britain within the frontiers of the empire and provided Roman citizenship to any qualified person under Roman dominion.

Claudius was poisoned by Agrippina, his fourth wife, in 54 A.D., after she persuaded him to adopt Nero, her son from an earlier marriage, and to give him precedence over Claudius's own son as his heir. Nero became emperor at age sixteen. A year later, he poisoned Claudius's son Britannicus and later had his own mother assassinated. The great fire that swept Rome in 64 A.D. may have been started by Nero himself, in order to rebuild Rome to his own glory. He was condemned to death in absentia by the Senate and took his own life the same year, saying: "What an artist the world is losing!"

His death created a period of virtual anarchy, known as "the year of the four emperors"—in quick succession, Galba, Otho, Vitellius, and Vespasian. Vespasian, whose family name was Flavius, began the so-called Flavian dynasty, a new era of peace. He extended Roman citizenship to all people of the provinces who served in his armies. He restored good relations between the Princeps and the Senate, creating the Pax Romana. He was succeeded in 79 A.D. by his son Titus, who reigned for only two years, after which Titus's brother Domitian ruled and terrorized Rome for fifteen years, finally being killed by a member of his own household.

The Senate ordered Domitian's name removed from all public places and refused to give him a state funeral. For the first time in Rome's history, the Senate designated as the new emperor a respectable lawyer, Nerva. With him began the "era of the five good emperors." In his two-year reign (96–98 A.D.), he initiated a rational approach to imperial succession—adopting a qualified candidate and training him for the job. A long period of stability followed, with Trajan (98–117), Hadrian (117–38), Antonius Pius (138–61), and Marcus Aurelius (161–80), who were among the greatest men to govern Rome.

Marcus Ulpius Trajanus (52 or 53–117 A.D.) was a Spanish commander who pushed the boundaries of the empire to their utmost extent, from the Caspian Sea to the Atlantic coast of Spain and from Britain to Egypt. Trajan improved the internal administration of the provincial cities, now in the hands not of a Roman governor but of native magistrates. Public and private philanthropy, an old Roman tradition, flourished under Trajan's bountiful reign.

Trajan adopted as his successor a Spanish kinsman, a brilliant general by the name of Hadrian. Convinced that the empire was overextended, Hadrian gave up Armenia and Mesopotamia as well as part of northern Britain. He built the famous wall separating the Roman-held south of Britain from the unconquered north, similar to but much shorter than the Chinese Great Wall. Under him, the Roman empire was becoming a genuine commonwealth, rather than extended dominions ruled over by a central government. So long as taxes were collected and public order maintained, the provinces were free to deal with their own affairs. Towns were granted the "Latin right"; that is, their magistrates were now Roman citizens. Later, the towns were recognized as *municipia,* and all their people were accepted as citizens of Rome. Moreover, many of these provinces were eager to be known as *colonia,* a term rich in prestige because it connoted adopting the Roman heritage and becoming an integral part of the empire. But more important was the standardization of the Roman law, for which purpose Hadrian charged the great jurist Salvius Julianus to prepare what was known as the Perpetual Edict, the first civil "codification" since the ancient Twelve Tables.

From then on, the Roman Empire developed pacifically for more than two centuries, with a few revolutions and wars. "Romanization" proved more effective in the western provinces than in the eastern ones, where Greek culture still predominated and was admired and cultivated by some emperors, particularly from Hadrian onward. Slowly, the Greek and Roman cultures blended to become a cultural unity for both the Occident and the Orient, with the positive outcome that in 212 A.D., thanks to the famous Constitutio Antoniniana of Marcus Aurelius Antoninus Caracalla (Roman emperor, 211–17 A.D.), Roman citizenship was granted to all free inhabitants of the Roman provinces. This Constitutio marks the definite triumph of the concept of a supernational and universalist empire, replacing the original and narrow frame of the city-state and the old republican order, which disappeared altogether. The Roman emperor was now a universal sovereign of almost unlimited political and military power.

Antoninus Pius and Marcus Aurelius presided over the most majestic days of the empire, when the sense of unity among the different provinces was remarkable and each felt that an attack on Rome was an attack on each and all. Scholars from all over the civilized world now studied Roman law at the great law school established by Rome in Syria. In the last years of Marcus Aurelius, however, the Roman borders on the Rhine, the Danube, and the Euphrates were endangered all at once. Although 200 more years would pass before those borders were breached, the three centuries between the great age of Marcus Aurelius and the overwhelming of Rome by the barbarians in the fifth century A.D. are known as Rome's decline and fall—a "decline" not always felt acutely, as business went on in the Roman Empire as usual. When Marcus Aurelius died, probably from the plague that was ravaging the empire, it marked the end of Nerva's system of succession; the throne went to Aurelius's son Commodus, the first of many tyrants and a greater curse to the Romans than any pestilence or crime wave. He renamed Rome Commodonia and was interested only in chariot races, lion baiting, and executions; after twelve years of misrule he was assassinated.

Three months later, the Praetorian Guard decided to auction the imperial office to the highest bidder; Didius Julianus got it in 193 A.D. Meanwhile, the armies of several provinces proclaimed their own commanders as emperors. One of them, Lucius Septimius Severus (146–211 A.D.), commander on the Danube, marched on Rome and deposed Julianus. During his long reign (193–211), he proved to be a competent administrator and an excellent soldier. He died at York, leading the defense of the British frontiers.

For the next twenty-four years, Lucius's sons and relatives—known as the

Severan dynasty—ruled the empire in brutal succession. The Severan dynasty ended in 235 A.D. with the death of Severus Alexander (208–35), murdered by his own troops on the Rhine frontier. The army proclaimed Maximinus, a rude Thracian soldier, as emperor. With his reign, which lasted only four years, commenced a half-century of civil wars, mixed with barbarian incursions, financial collapse, and military anarchy. After his death and until the advent of Diocletian in 284 A.D., there were some twenty emperors and many usurpers who held parts of the empire for short periods. All but two of them met violent death after an average of two and a half years on the throne. Most of them were assassinated by Roman soldiers for their own profit. During these fifty years of darkness, enemies attacked practically all of the frontiers, the finances of the empire were completely dilapidated, and inflation was rampant. The value of Roman citizenship also declined, and the position of magistrate, once a great honor, was now considered a burden. The Senate retained only a remnant of its ancient prestige.

This sad state of affairs ended when Diocletian took the scepter in 284 A.D. He restored a sense of political order, secured the frontiers, and reorganized the government by introducing a degree of discipline that would remain in force till the end of the empire. He also established the "divine right" of the emperor, even requesting that all who approached him prostrate themselves in adoration! Soon after becoming emperor, however, he grew convinced that it was impossible for a single man to rule such a vast empire. Thus, he divided it by creating a ruling *tetrarchy:* two emperors with the title of Augustus and two heirs-apparent with the title of Caesar to succeed them. He kept for himself the eastern half of the empire, comprising Asia, Asia Minor, Egypt, and Thrace, with the capital in Nicomedia near the Bosphorus; and he left for his co-emperor, a fellow officer by the name of Maximian, all of the western provinces, with the capital of Milan. Rome thereby ceased to be the political center of the empire. Each of the Caesars was also given provincial assignments under his respective emperor: Galerio in the east, with the capital Sirmium on the north of the Balkan peninsula; and Constancius Clorus in the west, with the capital in Augusta Trevirovorum (Treveris). Both of them were masters within their respective jurisdictions, and the empire was now, in fact, divided into four prefectures, resulting in a further swelling of the administrative structure. The unifying factor was that the Roman laws remained the only laws valid throughout the empire, and they could be changed or renewed only by Diocletian, the real absolute ruler. From then on, even the Senate was only in charge of the administration of the city of Rome. Thus, the constitutional order had expired and the autocratic and absolute regime had been established, with no limitations whatsoever.

Diocletian, remarkable in many ways, was also the first Roman emperor to abdicate, even persuading his co-emperor to retire with him. He had planned that the two Caesars would succeed them as Augusti, but in less than one year, this arrangement broke down, and again the army tried to dictate the succession. In 311 A.D., there were already four rival Augusti. One of them was Constantine, one of the outstanding leaders of Rome's declining years, who became known as the first Christian emperor.

In spite of the persecution of the Christians dating from Nero's times, they had been able to increase their numbers and even make some converts among influential families. The conversion of Constantine the Great, who reigned from 306 to 337 A.D., contributed to the fusion of church and state. Under his rule, the government became more autocratic than ever. All the energies of the people were expended in maintaining its huge bureaucracy and its defensive armies. But none of this halted the economic deterioration of the empire; its western half was practically exhausted, and Rome was now no more than a symbol. This decline was accelerated in 324 A.D., when Constantine decided to build a new imperial capital in the eastern part of the empire. Constantinople, established on the site of the old Greek city Byzantium (modern Istanbul), on the Bosporus and the Sea of Marmara, was conceived as a replica of Rome, even with its seven hills. It also became the Christian capital in 330 A.D. Here, Roman emperors would continue to rule for another 1,100 years, long after the western Roman Empire was lost to the barbarians.

Julian the Apostate, emperor from 360 to 363, was in a sense a second Marcus Aurelius in that he ruled with great fairness. He died in a battle against the Persians.

Between 378 and 383 A.D., the empire had three emperors: Gratianus in Britannia, Gallia, and Spain; Valentinian II in Italy and Africa; and Theodosius I, a Spanish soldier, in the eastern provinces. The first was assassinated in 383; the second had to take refuge in Thesaloniki; and the last became the new landlord of the empire till his death in 395. It was he who imposed Christianity as the official religion of the empire. After his death, the Roman Empire was never again the great unitarian organization it used to be. In 376, Germanic tribes had broken through the Danube frontier, while the Visigoths, Suevi, and Vandals set up their own kingdoms within the empire. The city of Rome itself was sacked by the Visigoths in 410 and by the Vandals in 455, without ever being completely destroyed. The last emperors in the west were Honorius, son of Theodosius I (395–423); his nephew Valentinian III (423–55); and Romulus Augustus, deposed in 476 by the Suevi chieftain Odoarcus, which event also marked the definite end of the western Roman Empire.

Rome was not effaced by its fall, because it had ensured its cultural survival by "Romanizing" even the farthest parts of its empire. Today, 1,500 years later, the heritage of Rome remains an important part of Western culture, as can easily be seen, for instance, in the classical facades of so many public buildings and the Latin roots of so many scientific words. The Roman heritage was passed on to the modern world in part, of course, through the eastern Roman Empire and the Roman Catholic Church. But the greatest influences of Rome on later civilizations were its language, literature, architecture, and, perhaps most characteristic, its law.

Roman Penal Law

The term *Roman law* covers the complex of juridical norms that were applied in Rome, from the origins of the city till the death of the emperor Justinian in 565 A.D. In its day, Rome exerted the single greatest legal influence on the world—and it still does today. Yet the evidence of its primitive legal sources is scanty.

Primitive legal sources are made more difficult to understand by the need to isolate criminal acts from others. For instance, in primitive societies, offenses against the ethical-religious order were frequently included in penal codes, whereas behaviors that were later thought to seriously harm society were not. In Rome, this held true not only in archaic times but throughout most of its history. Such acts as theft and corporal injuries were dealt with by civil, not criminal, courts and remained outside the penal frame.

The preeminence of religious values in ancient Roman law is shown, for example, by the fact that capital executions were seen as a sacrifice to the offended gods. The presence of the ax in the fasces of the Roman magistrates suggests that beheading may have been the prevailing method of execution in early times. The ax was also used to sacrifice animals before the altar in ancient Rome.

Ancient Roman law regarded crime in general as an offense against divinity and punishment as a means of expiation. In other words, *fas,* the divine law or command, was a kind of religious immutable principle, the expression of the divine wish, whereas *ius* was a more flexible and humane institution, based, at least in principle, on the will of the people. The word *sanctio* (the legal element defining the penalty) comes from *sanctus*—to consecrate, make sacred or inviolable by a religious act.

Although it was recognized that a number of offenses—such as theft or banditry—affected only men, others—such as blasphemy and similar signs of disrespect—offended the gods; in such cases, the state had to pacify the gods so that their anger would not affect the entire community. Offenses against the gods were dealt with by the *pontifices*—in those times a kind of guild with several members, presided over by the Pontifex Maximum. They were even entitled to impose the death penalty—for example, on vestals (the virgin priestesses of Vesta, the goddess concerned with the hearth fire and domestic life) who violated their sacred vows. In family matters, religious influences were, of course, predominant.

As with many other primitive societies, criminal law developed in Rome from a private to a more public character. For a long time, revenge and religious expiation were the principal aims of the penalties, as shown by the frequency of the death penalty and the cruelty of the punishments—axing; hanging; burning (*vivi combustio*); throwing the culprit, within a sack (*culleum*), from a mountain or into the sea; or having him fight in public with beasts (*bestiis obiectio*) such as in the famous "shows" at the *Colosseum* in Rome and other cities. Later, in some cases, the death penalty was substituted by forced labor in mines and various types of relegation or deportation, temporal or permanent. Flagellation and other punishments, all of them severe but not so atrocious, mark the beginning of a change in the purpose of the penalties, an evolution seen in so many different cultures.

For instance, *parricidium* (the homicide of a free man) was at first considered an offense against the person and not the state, and therefore had to be punished by the relatives of the victim. Only later was homicide considered a very serious act, not only in itself, but also because of the instability and blood feuds it led to. Thus its repression was undertaken by the state through *quaestores parricidii* (homicide investigators). From then on the state directly repressed every act it saw as harming its internal order or stability, particularly those of *parricidium* and *perduellio* (treason, conspiracy or a hostile political attempt against the state). Suspects were dealt with in special courts (*quaestores parricidii* and *duoviri perduellionum*) in which the *supplicium* (death penalty) could be imposed.

The evolution of Roman law was also typical in that at first, responsibility was based on the objective or material aspect. This was only a natural outcome of the notion of revenge. In such a system it is impossible to know if the objective aspect of the offense is related or not to the subjective aspect, since the wrath of the victim or his relatives is only the expression of the suffered loss and is blindly applied. Only much later would the subjective element be taken into account.

As for the Etruscans, their influence on Roman law is not known. Nothing is known of their own laws, since their surviving inscriptions are few and have not yet been successfully translated.

At the beginning of the fifth century B.C., Roman law was still transmitted orally. At this point, however, the plebeians, in addition to their political gains, wanted to have a written law as a better guarantee of their rights. It seems that one of the tribunes, Tarantilius Harsa, requested this; soon afterward, the Decemviral Twelve Tables (from *decemviri*, "ten males") appeared, the first landmark in the history of Roman law, dating from 451–450 B.C., during the early stages of the fight between patricians and plebeians. The Twelve Tables constituted an important new beginning in Roman law, both because they were written and because they clearly distinguished between religion and morals. In the Twelve Tables, *fas* and *ius* are separate elements.

According to tradition, the Twelve Tables were the work of ten people (the *decemviri legibus scribundis*), who, while they were at work, were also in charge of the political powers of the state. Only fragments of the original text are known, thanks to some literary works dating from the end of the republic and the beginning of the empire. The text was originally inscribed on twelve wooden tablets, which disappeared soon afterward, perhaps during the fire caused by the Gauls in 390 B.C. Their juridical interpretation is still a subject of discussion today.

The Twelve Tables were regarded with respect by all Romans, and with veneration by the classical authors of the first century B.C., as the fountain of all public and private law. They represented public ratification of the existing customary law. They also constituted a political and judicial victory for the plebeians, since now there was less abuse of power by the patricians. Until the Code of Justinianus, a millenium later, the evolution of the Roman legal system was greatly influenced by the Twelve Tables.

There is no doubt that Roman law was inspired by Greek philosophy, with its aspiration for a better ethical and political order, and that Greek legislation influenced the preparation of the Twelve Tables. For the first time, an attempt was made to unite the dogmatic element of Roman jurisprudence with the speculative character of Greek philosophy. On the whole, the Twelve Tables are a genuine creation of the Roman spirit, stimulated by its contacts with Greek culture.

The Twelve Tables reflected the basic legal practices in use when they were promulgated. They marked a transition from private revenge to state adjudication, but they showed no distinction between what is known today as civil and penal law. Nevertheless, they allowed the possibility that the injured party might be pacified by some type of compensation from the offender. Such a procedure was accepted and developed by the state, which also induced the parties to submit their case to arbitration. The basic purpose of the Twelve Tables, however, was to provide legal protection for the average citizen against the arbitrariness of the patricians in the judicial process, particularly in relation to the distribution of lands and in matters of personal debt. Yet the patricians also achieved one of their main purposes: the written prohibition of mixed marriages. It was only later, and after many battles, that this prohibition was abolished and plebeians could marry patricians.

Although they were mainly concerned with civil, not penal, matters, the Twelve Tables also dealt with certain specific judicial situations. For instance, they imposed the death penalty on judges who accepted gifts or bribes and on false witnesses for being bribed not to tell the truth. Thieves caught at night *in flagrante* (in the act) received the same punishment, as did those who made a mockery of public affairs, as mentioned in the eight table. On the other hand, the Twelve Tables were rather light in dealing with juvenile offenders.

It is not known whether the Twelve Tables were based on previous legislation. Nevertheless, they contained a number of innovations with a clear social purpose. The established norms were expressed with great concision, uniformity, and simplicity. After a conditional sentence, the basis for every legal rule, followed the imperative imposition. The legal terminology and a number of concepts used by these lawgivers have provided the basis for controversies not only among jurists at the end of the republic but also among modern scholars.

The first two tables dealt with procedural matters. Since the primitive Roman community was mainly rural, matters relating to family inheritance, relations with neighbors, and debts were salient, whereas those connected with trade (contracts) were less so. The third table dealt with the *nexum*, a contract between debtor and creditor by which the debtor pledged his liberty as security for his debt—an institution similar to one that existed in pre-Solon Greece. The fourth and fifth tables dealt with family situations, the sixth and seventh mainly with commercial transactions.

Items of a penal nature were more prevalent in the eighth and ninth tables. For instance, the eighth Table stipulates (VIII: 2) the talio for corporal lesions or mutilations (*membri ruptio*) if the offender has been unable to reach an amicable agreement with the victim or his next of kin. The talio also applied in cases of stealing *in flagrante* (*furtum manifestum*) and other crimes against property, which were severely punished. For certain offenses, fines were established, particularly for cases of physical injury and certain types of stealing. In some cases, the judge could arbitrate the punishment.

Another extremely interesting provision (VIII: 24) deals with the case when the weapon "escaped from the hand" of the offender, instead of having been thrown, and determines that "a sheep should be sacrificed in expiation." This constituted the first distinction between a voluntary and an involuntary act. Items 1 and 2 of the ninth table stated that capital punishment should be applied only during the meetings of the great *comitia*, and item 4 determined that special *quaestores*—the *quaestores parricidii*—should preside in capital cases.

The tenth table dealt with matters of funerals. The eleventh table contained the famous prohibition against marriage between patricians and plebeians. It created instead, a kind of civil marriage by *mancipatio*, based on the meager right of the plebeians, that of property if they had any. The twelfth table dealt with a variety of subjects of a noncriminal nature.

The penal side of the Twelve Tables combined archaic and more progressive aspects. Like all ancient legal systems, the tables started from the basic notion of revenge. The state imposed penalties only in cases of *perduellio* or certain other extremely serious or religious offenses directly affecting the welfare of the community. There is no mention of a penalty for the murderer (*parricidium*), leaving the reaction to the family of the victim. The only exception is the provision in VIII: 24, but this merely substituted one subject of private revenge (the sheep) for the other (the killer).

However, the tables expressly prescribe the death penalty for a number of other crimes, with the type of execution often reflecting the nature of the offense: the arsonist had to be burned; the night thief of crops had to be hanged in the place of the crime, in honor of Ceres, the agricultural goddess; the false witness was thrown into the abyss. Still, none of these constituted a public penalty imposed on the offender; rather, they were the talio of the victim against the offender whose culpability had been established judicially. This was crystal clear in cases of stealing, for which the victim could kill an offender caught during the night or even during the day (if he was armed and resisted detention); the only proviso was that he had to call his neighbors to be witnesses of his right to kill. Alternatively, the victim could bring the thief caught *in flagrante* before the magistrate, who could deliver him back to the victim when the facts were evident. The victim could then kill the thief, keep him or sell him abroad as a slave, or accept ransom for him. However, if the thief was not caught *in flagrante,* the tables forbade private revenge by the victim, who could only demand compensation, usually twice the value of the stolen property.

In cases of private offenses (*delicta*) such as light wounds, the penalties were also of a pecuniary nature. The fracture of a bone (*os fractum,* VIII: 3) required 300 asses in compensation if the victim was a freeman or 150 if he was a slave. For even lighter wounds (*iniuria,* VIII: 4), only 25 assess were stipulated. In serious cases, such as disabling an important limb, when the parties were unable to reach an agreement (*composition*), the law permitted the talio, an equivalent damage in private revenge. For cases of simple stealing, not *in flagrante,* there were also fines, equivalent to two, three, or more times the value of the lost property. These pecuniary penalties for minor offenses were final, established at the magistrate's discretion without the possibility of appeal. They constituted the origin of private criminal law, dealing with *delicta,* established only at the end of the republic and during the empire.

Despite these progressive elements, the Twelve Tables were still of a very primitive character, seriously taking into account the malign powers of magic. For instance, the tables prescribe the death penalty for doing exorcisms to turn another's crops sterile (VIII: 8a) or to take from another's field the mysterious fertilizing powers (VIII: 8b); for saying malicious incantations against another (VIII: 1); and for entering another's house to look for a stolen object, but not in the way prescribed by magic—naked and carrying a rope (VIII: 15a). Similar oddities are also found in other ancient legislations.

The evolution of Roman penal law was determined, during the next two centuries, by the interpretation of the Twelve Tables and by the legislation introduced at the behest of the plebeians. Till the beginning of the third century B.C., the interpretation of the tables was solely in the hands of the pontifices. It was strictly literal, in keeping with the formalism of ancient times. Nevertheless, the pontifices did introduce a number of new developments, perhaps the most important being the emancipation of children (*filius familias*) from the power of the *pater familias* (the head of a household), which previously had been for life.

In early times, only the Comitia Centuriata used to legislate, but after the *Lex Hortensia* of 286 B.C.—which declared obligatory for all citizens the resolutions adopted by the people—the Comitia lost its importance. From then on, most of the laws were adopted by the Concilium Plebis, after being proposed by the Tribuni Plebis. Important new laws that would influence the development of Roman law were always approved by *plebiscitum*. During the four centuries from the creation of the Twelve Tables to the end of the republic, no more than thirty such innovative laws were passed—for example, the *Lex Poetilia Papiria de Nexis* in 326 B.C., which eliminated slavery for debt, and the *Lex Aquilia de damno iniuria dato* of 286 B.C., which changed all the dispositions of the Twelve Tables regarding damages and introduced a completely new set of principles into Roman criminal law.

Many other important laws belong to the period after the Punic Wars. The vast majority of these are known in the original texts, with the exception of the *Lex Aquilia,* whose approximate text is known. Most of them have clear sociopolitical purposes (for example, the protection of debtors, victims of usury, minors, or people suffering from other types of incapacities). To avoid erroneous interpretation, these laws abandoned the simplicity and parsimony of the Twelve Tables for a pedantic minuteness.

It would be almost impossible to explore every single detail of Roman penal law. What follows is only a general outline.

The popular Roman laws are known by the cognomen (surname, family name, or name following the name of the *gens*) of the consul or magistrate who proposed them. Thus, the *Lex Poetilia Papiria de Nexis* was proposed by both consuls, and the *Lex Aquilia* was the outcome of a plebiscite proposed by only one of them or by one of the tribuni.

The private criminal law of the Twelve Tables was appropriate for a community of modest proportions and rural character. It was hardly adequate once Rome became a huge metropolis with violent social tensions. The increase of the Roman proletariat and of the number of slaves brought a serious proliferation of criminality, which required strong measures. Therefore, during the second half of the third century B.C., a kind of police justice was established for dealing with violent delinquents, thieves, arsonists, and poisoners. The easy answer was the death penalty for all of them (for the thief, however, only if he was caught *in flagrante*). The mere fact of being in possession of poisons, or of carrying arms with apparent criminal intent, was enough to warrant such a penalty. If caught, the offender was dealt with directly by the police, but the procedure could also be started by a private citizen, who had to prove that the crime was indeed committed.

During the early republic, the Tribuni Plebis and the quaestores were in charge of preparing the cases of political and serious criminal offenders and bringing them to the Comitia for a final decision. After the second Punic War, such a procedure proved completely inadequate, since by then the Assembly was no longer in the hands of the honest and prudent farmers and peasants, but was run by the masses of Rome, strongly influenced by demagogic politicians. Politics and administration were now so complicated that the average citizen was frequently unable to judge objectively the circumstances of certain offenses, particularly those of a political nature. Thus, it became a normal procedure for the Senate to send cases against provincial governors or other high-ranking officials who had overstepped their legal functions to one of the councils or praetors for them to make the proper investigation and present the results to the consilium, which usually was constituted by senators who were expert in these matters.

Criminal jurisdiction—that is, the infliction of punishment for a public or private offense that infringed on the rights of the Roman people—was exercised in early times by the Comitia, and later by the magistrates, but gradually came to be entrusted to the *quaestiones extraordinarie* (commissions). These special tribunals were initially created for dealing with particular offenses, especially those related to movements against the security of the state, which the existing justice system was unable to deal with through the ordinary criminal procedure.

Till the end of the second century B.C., all these public tribunals—*iudicia publica*—were more or less improvised. The members of the consilium who had to establish the culpability of the accused were selected by the Senate or even by the magistrate who presided over it. Only after the *Lex Calpurnia repetundarum* of 149 B.C. was there established—particularly for cases of misbehavior of magistrates—a special roster of judges, lasting for only one year, from which the members of the consilium could be selected by agreement of the prosecutor and the accused parties. The chairman of these *quaestiones* was usually the *praetor peregrinus*. A seminal piece of legislation, the *Lex Sempronia iudiciaria* (122 B.C.) of Gaius Gracchus, stipulated that permanent courts (*quaestiones perpetuae*), dealing with special kinds of problems, could be established only when given statutes were passed defining certain acts as crimes and when they could be constituted of members who were not necessarily senators. This law, which "democratized" the function of judges, was the beginning of the system of jurors that, during the last years of the republic and the beginning of the empire, constituted the basis for ordinary penal justice in Rome. During the second century B.C., these *quaestiones perpetuae* already had the authority to punish certain acts whenever they were committed, no matter by whom; they mark the initiation of an organized system of laws and courts to deal with crime. They were constituted by a smaller number of citizens—only fifty when it became clear that there was no need to convene all the *populares* for each case—who tended more toward political considerations than impartiality. With these courts, procedure assumed a new importance, and Roman criminal law became *iudicia publica* (public justice).

The offenses dealt with by these *questiones perpetuae* seem always to have been of a serious, political type, usually linked to *perduellio*. Punishments usually involved the *aqua et igni interdictio* (deprivation of the basic necessities of life, such as water and fire) or the *insuere in culleum* (drowning in a sack). The death penalty was extremely cruel in that it could be applied to the entire family of the offender.

In the framework of his constitutional reforms, Sulla reorganized and increased the number of permanent tribunals. From then on, there were courts for crimes of treason and disobedience of the supreme state organs (*quaestio maiestatis*); defrauding state property (*quaestio peculatus*); electoral corruption (*quaestio ambitus*); plundering of public funds in the provinces (*quaestio repetundarum*); assassination, poisoning, and offenses against public security (*quaestio de sicariis et veneficis*); forgery of coins and wills, giving false testimony, and usurpation of names or functions (*quaestio de falsis*); and serious injuries, including violation of private homes (*quaestio de iniuriis*). Later, other courts were established, particularly the *quaestio de vi,* for all crimes of violence, and the *quaestio de adulteriis,* for cases of adultery and seduction of honest women.

By the end of the republic and the beginning of the empire, there was a trend toward improving and enlarging the content of the earlier republican laws and applying harsher punishments. Offenses that were previously considered private (*delicta*) began to be conceived as public penal matters (*crimina*). The concept of *iniuria* was expanded to include such matters as the violation of private homes or the corruption of children and women. Augustus accorded the highest importance to penal matters; the permanent courts and the special laws already mentioned constituted his contribution to penal legislation. With him, the *iudicia publica* reached its highest evolution in the history of Rome. A number of other laws were also approved during his time, such as the *Lex Iulia de adulteriis coercendis* (18 B.C.), dealing with adultery and intercourse with an honorable lady; the *Lex Iulia de Ambitu* (also 18 B.C.), dealing with electoral corruption or violence; the *Lex Iulia de Vis* (c. 17 B.C.), dealing with *vis publica* (port of arms or violence in public; organizing criminal gangs; beating or killing a citizen without provocation, interfering with the administration of justice) and also with *vis privata* (less serious offenses against private property); the *Lex Iulia de maiestatis* (8 B.C.), dealing with offenses against the name or the person of the Princeps; and the *Lex Iulia de peculatus et de sacrilegiis* (perhaps also 8 B.C.), dealing with the illegal appropriation of public or sacred funds, the falsification of coins and public documents, and so forth.

The procedure in the *quaestiones,* well known thanks to the forensic speeches of Cicero, was initiated not by a public prosecutor but by accusation of a citizen (*nominis delatio*). Once such an accusation was accepted by the competent judge or by a *consilium* of judges, the accuser had all the rights and duties of a prosecutor. Every honorable citizen could present an accusation. Here lies the main difference between the private action of the Twelve Tables (according to which only the victim or his relatives could be the accusers) and the new "public" penal procedure.

There is no doubt that the motives of the accusers varied widely. Besides the wish for revenge of the victim or his relatives—who could find satisfaction in the mere fact of a public trial (*iudicium publicum*)—perhaps the most frequent motive was cupidity. The law established substantial monetary rewards for the successful accuser, and in cases of the death penalty, the accuser had the right to an important part of the patrimony of the executed. On the other hand, a public accuser whose case could not be established could be punished on grounds of trickery, base motives, or obstruction of justice.

Once an accusation was accepted, the respective magistrate had to constitute the *consilium* of judges by casting lots from the roster of the corresponding *quaestio*—that is, the tribunal of jurors who had to decide the culpability or innocence of the accused. Both parties had the right to reject a given number of jurors, the total number of whom varied under each regime and for the various *quaestiones*. The accuser introduced and interrogated the witnesses for the prosecution, and the accused did the same with those witnesses he assumed would testify in his favor. Afterward came the cross examination of the witnesses, while the members of the jury listened in silence. They were forbidden to exchange any opinon among themselves. The function of the chairman was mainly to keep order during the sessions—not always an easy task because of the generosity of the Roman procedural laws, according to which the accuser could be represented at any given moment by six advocates.

Evidence of slaves was admitted, but only under torture, administered by the court. In cases of *incestum* (incest, unchastity) with vestal virgins, the *quaesitor* (prosecutor) could seize the slaves of the suspected citizen and try to extract the truth by means of torture. In all other cases, a slave could be put to torture only with the consent of his master.

Later, the *consilium* voted the sentence in little covered tablets deposited in a ballot box. Equality of votes meant absolution. If there were too many abstentions, the procedure was started again. On the basis of the vote of the jurors, the presiding magistrate declared the culpability or innocence of the accused. During the early republican times, the convicted offender was not sentenced to a fixed penalty; this was legally established much later.

Crimes were classified, in relation to their punishment, as capital and noncapital. For capital offenses, punishments included crucifixion, being thrown from the Tarpeian rock, decapitation, gallows, and forced labor (*ad opus*). Noncapital punishments included relegation, exile, fines, prison, and the like. Prisons had only a preventive nature—for the custody of the offender. Exempted from punishment were those who acted by *error facti* (a mistake of facts related to the crime); those under the influence of *furor* (rage, fit of madness, etc.); or those who were minors. Self-defense or being in a state of need also excused the crime. Self-defense was considered a right—a licit and even compulsory reaction. The attempt to commit an offense was punished as a consummated crime, since the intention, not the results, was taken into consideration. There was also a distinction between authors and accomplices.

The execution of the penalty was the responsibility of the presiding magistrate. It seems that during the last century of the republic, the death penalty was usually not applied to a member of the superior classes, since the *quaestiones* were generally upper class themselves. In such cases, the presiding magistrate facilitated the escape of the convicted offender into exile. But it was certainly applied when the convicted were lower class or slaves. The death penalty probably subsisted till the end of the republic, since its criminal law did not yet have the penalty of deprivation of liberty.

Augustus reorganized and increased the *quaestiones* of the late republic. They continued to be the ordinary tribunals of criminal justice (*ordo iudiciorum publicorum*). He also nominated a senator, for an indeterminate period of time, as prefect of the city (*praefectus urbi*); reformed the police and created a strong police army, living in barracks (*cohortes vigilum*); and, to fight delinquency and banditry, established a number of military strongholds, usually under the command of *praetores*. These reforms substantially improved the criminal justice system. The mere fact that police jurisdiction was no more in the hands of annually selected, young, and inferior magistrates but of competent people, even some prominent lawyers, made the sentencing process more constant and egalitarian. Even police justice, now under the *praefectus urbi*, was much quicker and better organized than before. The *consilium* of the *praefectus urbi* not only had greater knowledge and experience than the presiding *praetors* of the former jurors, but because it was constituted of former consuls and senators, it was much more competent than the ordinary criminal courts. Moreover, the court of the *praefectus* could deal with all kinds of crimes, including those against state security and public order, obviating the need for a variety of courts. The *praefectus* even enjoyed the benefit of analogy, because he could punish offenses for which there was no specific penal law. Thus, during the first century B.C., the extraordinary penal system (*cognitio extra ordinem*) of the *praefectus urbi* already began to displace the courts of jurors. The only one of these courts that subsisted longer was the *quaestio de adulteriis,* since these types of offenses were beyond the competence of the *praefectus urbi*.

Besides all the types of tribunals already mentioned, the *princeps* himself and the Senate had also some functions of a criminal justice type. After Tiberius's times, the Senate's jurisdiction was drastically limited to problems relating to the members of the senatorial class—a privilege by which they could avoid being judged by inferior-class jurors. Afterward, when the Senate started to heed the real or supposed wish of the *princeps,* this privilege became a rather sour one, particularly if they were accused of political offenses of the *crimen maiestatis* type.

After Augustus's new legislation, the *princeps* had jurisdictional faculties (usually exercised by his representatives) within his *imperium proconsulare,* extending mainly to the provinces and army under his jurisdiction. It is not certain how and when the tribunal of the *princeps* became an established institution, but it gained importance especially under Claudius and reached its maximum development from Hadrian until the Severan dynasty. The emperors could now bring to their courts any kind of litigation, civil or criminal, including appeals against sentences of other tribunals or by their own decision. Only major legal, social, or political cases ever reached the emperor's court. The available information on these "extraordinary" penal courts is very meager, but it is known that the procedure was more expedient, disciplined, and effective than that in other courts. The accused had enough time for his own defense, and the principle that the *consilium,* not the judge, had to determine the sentence was apparently applied, in all kinds of courts, ordinary and extraordinary. It seems that the emperor's tribunals had greater liberty than the courts of jurors to apply the penalty to offenders who had confessed or had been declared guilty by the *consilium.* Whereas these courts had to adhere to the criminal laws of the republic and those established by Augustus—prescribing pecuniary punishments or the death penalty—the extraordinary courts could apply other punishments, such as remission to a school of *gladiatores* or to forced labor in mines (*condemnatio in metallum*) or other public works (*condemnatio in opus publicum*). All of these penalties were applied only to people of the lower classes; for prestigious citizens, the most severe penalty was exile to an island, with or without internment.

With the elimination of the jurors, the independence of the penal justice system was practically lost, but the extraordinary penal procedure was more efficient, more ductile, and perhaps even more just, particularly for the "little" citizen. Even if he was exposed to more serious penalties than the higher classes, at least he did not have to fear the death penalty, and he had greater possibilities for his defense than he had during the republic. During the second and early third centuries A.D., the extraordinary courts became more careful in determining guilt and in assigning penalties. The famous dictum that it is better to leave a culprit unpunished than to punish an innocent was already established during Trajan's reign.

Although the greatest claim to glory of Roman law lies in its civil rather than its penal institutions, the later stages of Roman penal law constitute definite progress in relation to the laws of other ancient peoples. The Roman legislators and judges were able to analyze the basic elements of the human will with amazing finesse. They were able to distinguish, in the commission of crimes, the purpose, the impetuosity, and the fortuitousness of the act. Guilt could be light or heavy; accidental acts were not punished at all. For the first time, there was a differentiation between the subjective and objective aspects of the criminal act. There was also in Roman penal law the basis for the theory of criminal intent, with the consummated act differentiated from the mere intention, both deserving their respective punishments. It is also of great significance that in Roman criminal law, the correctional purpose precedes all other objectives of the penalties. All these marks of progress are related to the development, toward the end of the republic, of the notion of *ius naturalis,* "natural law."

The two outstanding articulators of the Roman conception of law and justice were Cicero (106–43 B.C.) and Lucius Annaeus Seneca (c.4 B.C.–65 A.D.).

Cicero—a distinguished politician, lawyer, and writer—was at first unable to grasp the new legal developments of his time. Whereas, in the East, the individual was practically submerged by the state and, in Greece, was part of a harmonious political unity, in Rome, he was becoming subordinated to the state only as a citizen, not as an individual. Here was the first opposition between liberty and law, so crucial in the history of human civilization. The more this opposition is solved by a greater adherence of the individual to his society, the more advanced the state and, with it, civilization.

According to Cicero, the respect of the citizen for the law was based on fear and interest, not yet in a real spiritual conviction. He saw power as inhering in the state, and so he concentrated in it his elemental affections. That is why Cicero insisted that everybody must sacrifice himself, whenever necessary, for the benefit of the state.

Yet Cicero was also convinced that every positive, political right had to be based on natural and divine law, which constituted the supreme good. All prohibitions and commandments were derived from it, as well as all laws that punished the wicked and protected the good citizen.

According to Cicero, man was born to behave justly, and if he frequently did the contrary, it was because his simple and natural inclination toward the good required much effort and cultivation. For him, crime was the outcome of placing egoistic considerations of usefulness before those of duty and justice. Yet the criminal, while anticipating the pleasure he expected to derive from his misbehavior, did not consider that—even aside from the legal penalty which could sometimes be avoided—he would have to confront the moral one, which was more painful and was the unavoidable outcome of the act itself.

Regarding penalties, Cicero demanded that they should always be proportionate to the crime—never too severe, because then the culprit might not repent; never applied with fury and resentment; and never involving the abuse of the culprit. Cicero thus showed his basic character as a humanitarian philosopher, more inclined to improve fairness and quality of punishment than to follow blindly the practices in force in his time.

Seneca was an important statesman and philosopher and a precursor of the scientific, psychological approach to crime. He saw crime as the outcome of the submission to passion rather than reason. He also tried to relate the somatic and the psychic aspects of the human being. Starting from the Hippocratic classification of temperaments—choleric, melancholic, phlegmatic, and sanguine—he came to the conclusion that the choleric person is the one most inclined to crime, since he is frequently in the grip of anger, a passion that creates a short and temporal madness. He also pointed to the criminal potential of "collective anger," easily aroused by the speeches of demagogues and leading to mass crimes committed in a state of delirium.

Seneca's views on penalties were inspired by those of Plato. Plato had defined penalties as a "medicine of the soul," which Seneca accepted. A penalty might produce suffering and seem harmful, but when it was imposed in accordance with reason, it would also produce a cure, like medicine. Just as, for a physician, no treatment was too cruel if it saved the life of a patient, so the judge could, if necessary, apply punishments up to and including the death penalty—which, in the last analysis, was for the benefit of the stubborn offender.

Seneca regarded the offender more than the punishment, believing that each should incur the penalty most appropriate to his personality. Some of his concepts remain valid today, and his remarks on crime, penalties, and passions make him perhaps the greatest criminologist of the ancient world.

Long before Roman law reached its peak of development in the early third century A.D., the decline of the empire had already begun. Little was left from the institutions of the early republican democracy, and the imperial wish gradually became the source of new laws. From 284 to 337 A.D., Diocletian and Constantine did restore some order and, for the protection of the empire, divided it between east and west. Yet such measures did not, in the end, prove sufficient.

Still, even with the collapse of the western empire into various barbarian kingdoms, many of these kingdomes drew on Roman law as the basis of their own legal codes. The codes of the Visigoth king Euric and of his successor, Alaric II, who in 506 A.D. promulgated the *Lex Romana Visigothorum* or

Breviarium Alarici, long survived and kept the tradition of Roman law alive over a wide area of Western Europe. The two codes of Euric and Alaric were later replaced by the *Liber Judiciorum* (the law book), an enormous treatise issued by King Recesswinth about 614 A.D.; it was a fine compendium of Visigothic law influenced by that or Rome.

Two great Roman legal codes were also issued by emperors of the eastern empire. The first, the *Codex Theodosianus,* promulgated by Theodosius II in 438 A.D., contains the empirical legislation of the Christian period; it shows a good deal of retrogression, including a number of primitive rules. Almost a century later, however, Justinian completed the great compilation of Roman law, the *Codex Justinianus,* which contains the imperial legislation from the beginning of the empire till Justinianus. The classical legislative compilation proper is to be found in the *Digesta* and in the *Institutiones* and the *Novellae,* which are known by the general term *Corpus Juris Civilis.* This Codex is indeed the cornerstone of jurisprudence: the Napoleonic Code was modeled directly on it; in Germany, the Roman law was applied—whenever it did not run against local legislation—until 1900; and even the English "common law" has many roots in Roman judicial principles. Many of these basic concepts of the Codex remain in force today, such as "The burden of proof is upon the party affirming, not the party denying"; "A father is not a competent witness for a son, nor a son for a father"; and "In inflicting penalties, the age and the experience of the guilty party must be taken into account." The Codex also serves as a textbook today for many law students and even for legal scholars.

Part II
Other Penal Systems

10

The Shari'a: The Legal System of Islam

> Islam grew up in the full light of history.
> —H.A.R. Gibb

Arabia and the Arabs

The people of Arabian origin in the entire Arabian peninsula have been known as Arabs since the first centuries A.D. Some scholars prefer to call them Arabians, claiming that this is the proper name. Arabia was inhabited since prehistoric times by a great variety of tribes, most of them established in small villages. Sometimes, they fought among themselves and anarchy prevailed. At other times, they lived with a certain degree of harmony, even reaching a kind of centralized government—most frequently of a theocratic type—but returning sooner or later to their original anarchy. Agriculture was their main activity, but fishing communities existed in the coastal areas.

The theory that considers the Arabs to be of a single ethnic origin or believes that Arabia was the birthplace and homeland of all Semitic people has never received the support of most main scholars. Because of the trade routes that crossed the peninsula, Arabia had permanent contacts with Egyptian, Greco-Roman, and Indo-Persian civilizations, but Arabian culture is basically a branch of the Semitic civilizations. The geographic and climatological characteristics of the Arabian peninsula, and the isolation in which the people of its interior lived for generations, contributed to the preservation of its basic cultural and religious idiosyncracies.

Arabia eventually became the cradle of Islam, which is therefore essentially Arabian in nature, despite all the possible external influences. Islam is the most important contribution of Arabia to human civilization. Because of its inherent conservatism, the Arabian religion requires total obedience to the Islamic law, or *Shari'a,* and is not at all inclined to accept changes unless they are considered a return to the law's original purity. The Arabic language and the Shari'a have affected, to different degrees, the basic cultures of all of the Moslem countries. The study of the holy book of Islam—the *Qur'an,* or *Koran*—and the annual pilgrimage to Mecca, the *Haj,* are still the basic tenets for all Islamic people.

The basic knowledge of ancient Arabia is based on inscriptions found on slabs of stone, on the walls of temples and public buildings, on rock faces, and on plaques of bronze, but proper archaeological surveys are still to be made, in spite of the many sites to be examined because the links of Arabia with ancient civilizations are well known.

If agriculture was an important element for the prosperity of Arabia, trade was of utmost vitality for the entire peninsula—particularly trade based on frankincense, a fragrant resin used mainly for ritual and similar purposes. The main traders were the people of the state of Ma'in, one of the four known south Arabian kingdoms, the other three being Saba, Qatabān and Hadramawt—all of them occupying an area that roughly corresponds to the present-day two Yemens. Ma'in had a sociopolitical structure similar to that of the city-states of Mesopotamia. Kings ruled and promulgated edicts and orders in collaboration with their counselors and other magistrates, forming a kind of cabinet. Saba had an earlier form of government under the Mukarribs, high priest-princes who combined religious and temporal powers. Later, a kingdom was established, and when the kings became autocratic, the office of the Mukarribs ceased to exist. There were also Mukarribs in Qatabān and Hadramawt, but never in Ma'in, where it seems that all the people belonged to a same tribe.

The kingdom of Saba—with its capital, Ma'rib, on the trade route—had a long militant history. It first benefited but then suffered from the emergence of the state of Himyar, sometime between 115 and 109 B.C., when Saba decided to attack Ma'in and occupied its capital.

When the straits of Bab el Mandeb, at the southern tip of Arabia, were open for direct traffic between Egypt and India, the overland traffic of frankincense practically disappeared within a century. This mainly affected the welfare of the Bedouins—the true Arabs of the inscriptions—who were very much involved in the overland traffic. When this happened, the Bedouins started to participate in the numerous conflicts that raged in the southern part of the peninsula during the first two or three centuries A.D., usually as mercenary fighters. It is worthwhile to mention that Rome sent an expedition to Arabia in 25–24 B.C.—under the leadership of Aelius Gallus, the prefect of Egypt—which ended in failure.

The Emergence of Islam

It was only with the advent of Christianity that Arabia began to emerge from its isolation onto the stage of world history. A little more than a century after the fall of Rome and the western Roman Empire, Islam started to rise against the background of the decline of the Byzantine Empire.

Islam is a concept that covers an immense area in space and in time. It developed differently in response to the various regions and epochs. Western Islam, for instance—which developed in northwest Africa and medieval Spain—differed from the Islam of the Indian subcontinent and Indonesia. Yet all these geographic divisions retained certain easily recognizable Islamic features.

The Islamic movement began in what would seem one of the most unlikely places on earth: a hot and parched stretch of land between Africa and Asia, known as Arabia. At the beginning of the seventh century, Arabia was still a jumble of petty autonomies, with no unifying authority. Many of its inhabitants were nomadic Bedouin tribesmen, often engaged in blood feuds with other tribes, with raiding as their way of life. The pre-Islamic Bedouins worshipped stones, trees, and even pieces of wood. Their supreme human virtue was manliness, expressed in loyalty to the tribe, or *asabiyya;* generosity, which basically took the form of hospitality; and courage, which demanded protecting one's women and participating in many raids, for which men had to be skilled in archery and horsemanship. They also admired eloquence expressed in poetry, which played an important role in their lives.

By the middle of the sixth century, there were three major towns in northern Arabia, all of them located in the mountains of the Hijaz. Yathrib was a fertile oasis spread over some twenty square miles; Taif, some 250 miles south, was a cool summer resort in the mountains frequented by wealthy Arabian families; and near Taif was Mecca, by far the most prosperous and important town, set in a rocky ravine and surrounded by mountains without vegetation. Mecca was at the crossroads of the lucrative caravan trade of spices, perfumes, precious metals, ivory, and silk and also of the pilgrimage trade, for Mecca was the site of Arabia's holiest pagan shrine: a modest, cube-shaped building known as the Kaaba, always covered by a black cloth embroidered in gold, believed to have been erected to God by Abraham and containing, among many other religious objects, a hallowed meteorite, the Black Stone, embedded in a wall on a corner. The chief deity of the Meccans was Allah, the creator of the universe, sharing the place with the statues of some 300 other gods and goddesses.

The leading citizens of Mecca were members of a powerful tribe, the Quraysh, who had built a great financial and military organization and governed Mecca as a simple form of a "republic," with a council made up of representatives of the most influential families of the city.

From this background grew Islam, and Mohammed appeared; or, as Suleiman Bashir, a contemporary Druse historian, claimed, he was invented retroactively. Whatever the case, Islam is the youngest of the world's great civilizations.

Mohammed ibn Abdullah—the Prophet

The accepted traditional history of Islam affirms that Mohammed ibn Abdullah was born in Mecca in about 570, into a cadet branch of the Quraysh, one of Mecca's most important clans. Mecca was then a prosperous and bustling station on the trade route between the Indian Ocean and the Mediterranean. Mohammed's father died shortly before his birth. Following a custom of the aristocracy, the boy was sent into the desert for a couple of years to be wet-nursed by a Bedouin mother, so that he could get a sturdier start in life in the desert climate. When he was six, his mother died, and he was put in the care of Abu Talib, his paternal uncle, who reared him into manhood.

With no fortune of his own, he resorted at first to various minor jobs, such as tending sheep and buying and selling goods in the city. Afterward, he became a commercial agent of a rich widow named Khadija, engaging in the caravan trade and frequently traveling north to Syria, then a part of the Byzantine Empire, where he certainly met many Christians.

Arabia was at this time exposed to a number of powerful religious influences coming from Syria, Palestine, and Ethiopia. Some Arabs had been converted to Christianity, and a few places were partly occupied by tribes of Arabian Jews. There were also Hanifs, followers of Abraham, the Prophet—men dissatisfied with Arabian paganism, who lived ascetic lives and believed in a single God worshipped by both Jews and Christians. Mohammed must have realized that his own people lacked a coherent faith. He was particularly distressed by the arrogance of the rich and powerful, who had forgotten the desert ethos, according to which the rich were expected to share their wealth with the poorer members of their tribes.

Mohammed, also known as al-Amin, "the trustworthy," was highly regarded in Mecca for his intelligence, gentleness, and integrity. Khadija was also impressed by his forceful personality and the way he handled her affairs. When he was about twenty-five, she asked him to marry her, though she had been married twice and was fifteen years older than he. He accepted and was faithful to her for the remaining twenty-five years of her life. Their three sons all died in childhood, but four daughters were able to grow up, of whom only Fatima survived him and bore him descendants, who figured in later Islamic history.

Mecca was a wealthy commercial town. Its citizens kept their native Arab simplicity in manners and institutions yet had acquired a certain cosmopolitan sophistication. There was a darker side, however, to Mecca's prosperity—namely, the city's extremes of wealth and poverty, with slaves and servants, social barriers, and injustice. Mohammed seems to have responded to this with a deep, brooding dissatisfaction. His exceptional heightened sense of social justice impelled him to criticize the inequities of the city.

In 610, when he was about forty, he had an experience that shattered his tranquil existence and put him on the path that would transform the lives of millions of people. There are many traditions relating to this event, the most accepted one being that of Ibn Ishaq, his first biographer, who lived a century after his death. According to Ibn Ishaq, Mohammed, as had been his wont ever since his marriage had relieved him of financial cares, had gone on this eventful day with his family for spiritual contemplation in a cave in the mountains. While he was asleep, an angel appeared, and he awoke in spiritual turmoil, even deciding to kill himself. Then he heard a voice from heaven and saw the angel Gabriel, who told him, "Thou art the apostle of God." He told Khadija what had happened, and she went to see a Hanif, her kinsman, who, after hearing the story, told her that Mohammed had been visited by the same heavenly inspiration that had visited Moses in the Sinai desert and that therefore he was to be the prophet of his people.

Mohammed did not assume this role at once. For a long time, he did not receive further messages from God, and he was full of fears and doubts. Then he had a second revelation, ordering him to begin his work, to rise and warn the people. In 613, he began preaching that Allah was the only god, the sovereign of the universe, and that men must thank him for their existence and worship only him. As all believers were equal before God, the rich must share their wealth with the poor; a day of judgment would come for all men. For those who accepted such a god and Mohammed as his messenger, there would be justice in this world and a glorious life after death; for others, there would be only tortures and hellfire.

The Prophet's first converts were his wife, Khadija, soon followed by three others: Ali, his young cousin; Zayd, his freed slave, and Abu Bakr, a man of substance. Many of his early followers came from the ranks of the poor, but most of the aristocratic Quraysh greeted him with fierce opposition.

Their resistance seems to have been due mainly to political and economic factors; in short, his teachings seemed to threaten their prosperity. Indeed, after the years of preaching in Mecca, during which he garnered only a small band of devoted adherents, the abuse of the Meccans became severe and menacing. During this period, Khadija and Abu Talib had died, making Mohammed's position even more insecure. Ostracized, feared, and hounded by the oligarchies of Mecca, he decided to leave the city. He eventually fled and ended up in Yathrib, later known as Medina, having been asked to come there by some residents to settle a feud between two rival tribes, which, it was also feared, might be exploited by the Jewish tribes living there. Mohammed's migration or accelerated flight to Yathrib, in September 622, is the famous Hijra, or Hegira, seen later as the beginning of the Islamic era.

In Yathrib, he turned his small following into a political movement of which the new religion of Islam was an integral and major part. He began to build around him a large community of Moslem believers, who would become the founders of the Islamic state. Mohammed's two basic purposes were now the internal consolidation of this community and the conquest of Mecca. The latter was not a mere desire for revenge. Mecca, the intellectual and political center of western Arabia, remained hostile, and his young Islamic community was in danger of extinction. Moreover, he earnestly wanted to enlist the talents of the Meccans in the service of Islam.

The feuding tribes of Yathrib gradually submitted to the commands of God, as revealed through his Prophet Mohammed, and became a revolutionary political unity. The city became known as Medinat al Nabi, "the city of the Prophet," or simply Medina, "the city." Now, instead of being the religious leader of a small group, Mohammed was becoming a powerful spiritual and political authority, and his preaching was taking on greater legislative and social content.

One of his main problems in Medina was with the local Jews. Several Jewish clans controlled the richest agricultural lands and were allied with one of the two feuding Arab tribes of the oasis. Mohammed expected them to recognize him as a prophet and to this end even adopted some of their religious practices. A few of the Jews did become Moslems, but the majority opposed him. They criticized and sometimes even mocked him, since many of his revelations contradicted their own scriptures. Thus, Mohammed began to attack them in turn, utilizing, strangely enough, many anti-Jewish themes of the early Christian writers. Later he would engage in comparable polemics with the Christians, so his Islamic community was built primarily among Arabs.

Mohammed also began to attack the enemies of his faith in Mecca. He raided Meccan caravans passing through Medina's territory, although largely for economic motives. One of these raids led to the first serious armed clash between the two cities. Surprisingly, the prophet's small band crushingly defeated the proud Quraysh. Arabs everywhere saw this victory as a sign of God's favor to the Prophet's cause, indicating that he was in fact the "apostle of God." Moreover, as the Moslem warriors shared in the booty from the raids, the word soon spread that the cause of God could bring rewards on earth as well as in heaven. Nearby tribes began to join Islam and to fight under its banner: If they were victorious, they got booty, and if they were killed in battle, they were sure of going to heaven and enjoying the most sensual delights.

As for the Quraysh, they did not accept their defeat lightly. The following year, 3,000 Meccans attacked Medina, inflicting a minor defeat in which the prophet himself was wounded. In 627, encouraged, the Meccans decided to wipe out Mohammed and his followers, mounting a full-scale assault on Medina with 10,000 troops. Mohammed, perhaps on the advice of a Persian convert who was an expert in fortifications, ordered his men to dig a deep, dry moat in front of the exposed portion of the city. This innovation in desert warfare confused the attackers, rendered their 600 cavalry useless, and halted their charge. They camped outside Medina, negotiating with a Jewish clan living inside the oasis to attack the Moslems from within. The negotiations broke down, and after forty days, the Meccans went home demoralized and short of supplies.

Meanwhile, Mohammed had learned about the Jews' negotiations with the Meccans. He dealt harshly with them, decapitating all 600 of the men, enslaving the women and children, and allowing his followers to settle in their lands. By this dramatic and inhumane behavior, Mohammed was perhaps showing to the Jews and to all future opponents of Islam that opposition would no longer be tolerated and to his fellow Arabs that tribal loyalties were at an end, the only loyalty now being to Islam itself. He may also, in the wake of this episode, have first begun contemplating some action against the Byzantine power. The fact that his successor, Abu Bakr, almost immediately launched an expedition toward Syria supports this possibility.

In 628, Mohammed went on a pilgrimage to Mecca with 1,400 followers. The Meccans sent 200 horsemen to stop them, but after a while, both sides agreed to a ten-year truce and agreed that the Moslems would return to Medina on condition that they could come on pilgrimage the following year. This was an important victory for Mohammed, in that he established himself as an equal of the Quraysh by having made a treaty with them. Moreover, by having set out on a pilgrimage—an old pagan custom—he had shown all the Arabs that Islam was a religion with an Arabian character.

In 629, as agreed in the treaty, Mohammed led 2,000 Moslems on the promised pilgrimage to Mecca, but there were clashes, and the truce was finished. Therefore, in 630, he marched on Mecca with a force of 10,000 to settle the issue once and for all. Mecca, weakened by infighting, fell after a token show of resistance. Mohammed then entered the Kaaba in triumph and destroyed the pagan idols that filled the holy place, establishing the purified Kaaba as the spiritual center of Islam. After seven years of struggle, Mecca was incorporated not as a beaten and resentful enemy but as a willing, if not too enthusiastic, partner. Meanwhile, Mohammed's troops began to strike deeper and deeper into Arabia, and soon almost all the tribes of the peninsula had joined Islam. Jews and Christians were permitted to practice their own faith but had to pay taxes, adding to Islam's growing might.

In the twenty-two years of his prophethood, Mohammed achieved a synthesis of Jewish and Christian monotheism and gave the Arabs a cause for which they could unite, fight, and win. As a leader, he abolished many social evils. Slavery was still permitted, but the slaves had to be treated humanely. They were now allowed to marry and could even buy their freedom; indeed, freeing a slave was regarded as meritorious. He also prohibited gambling, usury, and imbibing alcohol as being against the rule of God. In addition, he enhanced the status of women in relation with their situation in pre-Islamic

Arabia, but the Koran still maintains the superior right of father and husband and legalizes polygamy up to four wives. In fact, after the death of Khadija, Mohammed took nine wives, making an exception in his own case. One of these was A'isha, the daugher of Abu Bakr, Mohammed's dearest friend and adviser. And in 632, in his sixty-third year—the tenth of the new era of Islam—Mohammed died in A'isha's arms. His followers were swept by shock and panic, but Abu Bakr convinced the people that though the Prophet was dead, God was alive. Still, veneration of the Prophet has become a kind of necessity for his followers. Islam has never lost touch with the human figure of Mohammed ibn Abdullah, the Man of Mecca. In the last ten years of his life, his movement grew into a force of "Arabic feeling," and his successors almost immediately began to expand their influence, sweeping out of the hitherto isolated peninsula and spreading the word of the Prophet as they went from victory to victory.

It is interesting to note that active in Hejan at the same time as Mohammed was another tribal leader, Mohammed ibn Hanafiya, whose personal history bears an astonishing resemblance to that of the Prophet. Later, the Abbasids would trace their legitimacy to rule precisely on ibn Hanafiya.

Islam the Religion: The Koran

The word *Islam,* adopted by Mohammed as the dintinctive name of the faith that he preached, means "submitting" or "surrendering" oneself to God. The adherent of Islam is usually known as a Muslim, or Moslem as the Western adaptation.

The Koran, a book of some 300 pages (about the same length as the New Testament), is the record of those formal utterances and discourses that Mohammed and his followers accepted as divinely inspired. They are regarded as the literal word of God, mediated through the angel Gabriel, and are quoted with the prefix "God has said." The Koran has 114 chapters, called *suras,* arranged roughly in order of length, so that the earliest ones have almost 300 verses and the final ones only three to five.

Some of the Koran's *suras* are warnings of doom, proclaiming a day of judgment and demanding the worship of one God; others discuss biblical prophets and their importance; and others give detailed regulations concerning family, property, and justice. All are phrased in a hypnotic Arabic, which helped convince the early followers—Arab nomadic tribesmen—that these were the words of God himself.

Although Islam has changed politically and culturally over the centuries, the religion has remained practically the same. Thus, the Koran has molded the lives of millions of people and has contributed to the shaping of the modern world.

Although earlier scholars postulated Judaism as the main influence on Islam, later inquiries suggest Syriac Christianity as the dominant influence. Monotheism was already familiar in Arabia, but it was Mohammed who introduced the doctrine of the Last Judgment, certainly derived from Christian sources. At any rate, as a direct consequence of his conflicts with Jews and Christians, Mohammed developed the so-called historical theory of Islam. Since Judaism claims to be the religion of Moses and Christianity the religion of Jesus, he went back to the figure of Abraham (the Hanif), a pre-Islamic monotheist who, according to him, was neither Jew nor Christian but the last prophet of a pure, undistorted monotheism. Thus, Mohammed was the true heir of Abraham and the purifier of the errors of both Jews and Christians. Abraham, of course, was already associated with the Arabs through the figure of Ishmael, since both of them were regarded as the founders of the Kaaba.

As with all sacred books, the need was soon felt for some guidance in the interpretation and exegesis of the Koran. From the tenth century onward, theologians and historians have applied themselves to this task; their glosses increased greatly in number and complexity and today constitute a vast documentation. It is not easy to find in the Koran a systematic exposition of Moslem beliefs and pratices; yet a consistent body of obligations has remained, in all ages, the core and inspiration of Moslem religious life.

The tenets might be summarized as the Five Pillars of Islam—faith, prayer, alms-giving, fasting, and pilgrimage—which compromise the ritual obligations for all Moslems and have given Islam its unique form since the seventh century.

Faith. The Arabic word *Allah* is the shortened version of la-ilah, "the god." As mentioned, the concept of a supreme God and his Arabic name were already familiar in Mohammed's time, but he purified it from the elements of polytheism still attached to it. According to Mohammed, men must live in constant fear of God alone, yet they also have to adore him because, besides his terrible and majestic aspects as judge and avenger, he is also the protector, the compassionate and merciful, always ready to answer to the repentant sinner. Faith is based on the *Shahada,* the core belief of Islam, which is also a declaration of belief through which a man joins Islam: "There is no God but Allah and Mohammed is the Apostle of God, his Prophet." It is one of the tersest religious slogans and, in Arabic, has a certain musical force: *"la-ilaha illa Allah; Muhammadum rasull Allah."* After this recitation in front of any other Moslem, a man becomes a Moslem—and there is no turning back, since the punishment for apostasy is death.

Besides the Shahada, the newcomer has to accept the three other articles of faith: belief in the Koran as the word of God, through the prophets and Mohammed's revelation; belief in the angels as instruments of God's will; and belief in the final judgment day for all men. In the imagery of the Koran, the angels are generally represented as God's messengers. They are, like all men, his creatures, but they record men's actions, receive their souls when they die, act as witnesses for or against them in the Last Judgment, and are the guardians of the gates of Hell. Gabriel is God's chief messenger. Along with the notion of angels, there is also a doctrine of devils, or *jinns,* who lead men astray.

The doctrine of apostles and prophets is, next to the unity of God, the central concept of the Koran. At all times and to all peoples, including the *jinns,* God has sent prophets to preach the unity of God and to warn men of the Last Judgment. Moslems are required to believe in all of them, including Adam, Noah, Abraham, Moses, and Jesus. The last of the prophets is Mohammed, who is God's apostle to mankind. The doctrine preached by all the prophets is essentially one and the same, differing only in matters of detail, and there has been a gradual evolution in their messages, leading to Mohammed's final and perfect revelation. Thus, to Moses was given, by divine inspiration, the *Tawrah,* the Jewish *Torah,* or Pentateuch; to David the *Za'bur,* identified with the Psalms; to Jesus the *Infil,* the Evangile or Gospel; and to Mohammed the *Qu'ran,* or recital. Mohammed, however, was a mortal man with the sole duty of conveying God's warnings and his message of salvation. He had no miraculous powers, but obeying him is necessary for salvation.

The Last Judgment is a vital aspect of the Moslem faith. When the trumpet will be sounded, all men and *jinns* will be called to account. The blessed ones—the God-fearing, humble, and charitable—will enter the Garden of Paradise, while the unbelieving—the worshippers of other gods—will be cast into the fire and remain their forever. But this process of awful reckoning is lightened by repeated assurances of divine mercy. Nowhere in the Koran is it stated that Mohammed has a power of intercession or that the profession of Islam is, in itself, a sure passport to Paradise. The only promise of Paradise is made to those who repent and are righteous. Therefore, in Islamic orthodoxy, faith is always coupled with works, particularly with "acts of devotion," as prescribed in the Koran.

Prayer. The ritual prayers (*salah*) are an essential religious duty. Neither the ceremonies nor the five set times are stated in the Koran, but it is certain that they were all established before the prophet's death. Two kinds of prayer were recognized: *du'a,* the private or inner prayer, and *salat,* the formal ritual prayer. Prayers are said at daybreak, at noon, in mid-afternoon, after sunset, and in the early part of the night. Prayers should be said by every believer, wherever he may be, preferably in a congregation, in a *masjid* (mosque) under the leadership of an imam, the prayer leader of a mosque. The imam and the worshippers must face toward the sacred mosque in Mecca, a gigantic holy place that can hold as many as 300,000 worshippers, at the center of which is the Kaaba, which was cleansed of idols by the prophet in 630. The noon prayer on Friday is the principal congregational prayer of the week, when the imam delivers his sermon.

The Koran mentions the call to prayer (*adhan*) by the *muezzin* (*mu'adh-dhin*, the reciter of the *adhan*). The *minaret* was unknown in the time of the Prophet, having been first adopted in Syria during the caliphate of the Ummayyads. The Koran also indicates how to perform the duty of ablution before prayers, a hygienic practice that is strictly enjoined.

Alms. The giving of alms, *zakah*, is the outward sign of piety and a means of expiation and salvation. The *zakah* is an obligatory contribution, apparently at a rate of one-fortieth of annual revenue in money or in kind, but it is not seen as a tax per se. It is regarded as a loan made to God that will repay manifold. Free-will offerings, which are also means of expiating offenses, are to be given to orphans and to the needy.

Fasting. It was in Ramadan, the ninth month of the lunar year, that the Koran was first revealed to Mohammed and that the Prophet's followers defeated the Quraysh at Badr. Ramadan is to be observed as a period of fasting, with complete abstinence from food, drink, and sex during daylight hours. Exempted are the young, the sick, and the itinerant, but they must make compensation by fasting later for an equal number of days. The austerity of daylight hours gives way to gay festivities at night, and the end of Ramadan is observed as a joyous climax—a feast lasting up to three days.

Concerning food in general, Islam is closer to Judaism than to Christianity, with similar laws regulating allowable types of meat and methods of slaughter.

Pilgrimage (Hajj). Once in a lifetime, every Moslem who is capable must go on a holy journey to the sacred mosque at Mecca. This was legislated at Medina; and the traditional days in Dhu'l-Hijja (the twelfth month, two months after Ramadan), with their respective ceremonies, were prescribed in the Koran. Before making the pilgrimage, the worshipper must be in a state of ritual consecration (*ihram*), involving the shaving of the head and the discarding of ordinary clothing. After the pilgrimage, the pilgrim may not hunt, cut his hair or nails, use perfume, cover his head, or have sexual relations until after the sacrifices of sheep and camels at Mina, on the way back from Mecca, when he resumes his normal condition of life. The *hajj* gives Moslems a unique sense of brotherhood, since thousands of believers from all corners of Islam come together. Moslems who have made the pilgrimage are known as *hajji*, considered a title of great honor, since the *hajj* is an act of devotion that God will count in their favor on Judgment Day. A woman making the *hajj* has to be accompanied by her husband, her father, or a man to whom she cannot be married.

Besides these Five Pillars of Islam, the Koran also enjoins its believers to do *jihad* (holy war) in order to "strive in the way of God" (Sura II, verses 186 and following) to fight for Islam against those who "fight you," but not to commit aggression. Those who are slain in the "way of God" are not dead but are "living in the presence of their Lord, their needs supplied, rejoicing in the bounty which God hath given them" (Sura II, verses 163–64). The *jihad* should not be done during the sacred months (the first, seventh, eleventh, and twelfth of the Arabian year). In fact, the *jihad* narrowly missed being the sixth pillar of Islam. The Koran imposes certain limitations before fighting can begin: An enemy must be given the chance to embrace Islam or, failing that, to submit to Moslem rule and pay taxes.

The holy war in Judaism and *jihad* in Islam are different because, whereas the Jewish discussions on this subject remained on a theoretical level, in Islam they became very practical, as they are to this day. This exemplifies how the Islamic clergy has maintained its influences, especially on the issue of war, whereas in Judaism, the rabbis focus primarily on issues of a higher spiritual level.

The Koran also contains numerous ethical and legal injunctions that serve as the foundation for the Shari'a, or Islamic law, to be analyzed later.

In pre-Islamic times, tradition already played a key role in Arabian social life. Every tribe prided itself on the customs (*sunna*) of its ancestors. The Koran, however, speaks of the unchanging *sunna* of Allah, and reproaches the Meccans for clinging to the *sunna* of their fathers. *Sunna,* in the Islamic sense, thus designates the "customs of the community," handed down by oral transmission, as distinct from the *kitab,* the "written book." At present, there are still Sunnis (or *Ahl al-Sunna,* the "followers of the *Sunna*"), who remain attached to the "usages of the community," and their opponents, the *Shi'a,* or Shi'ites, who adhere solely to the *sunna* of the Prophet and consider the "usages of the community" illegal. The initial Sunni–Shi'ite schism had, of course, a political dimension, as we shall see later.

The *sunna,* or transmitted actions and sayings, of the Prophet were handed down in the form of short narratives, or *hadith* (statements). The *hadith* is thus the most important body of Islamic textual material aside from the Koran itself. Complex problems often arose with the growth of Islam, and when no solution was found in the Koran, it became customary to consult the *hadith.* Within two or three generations, a large number of *hadith* came into circulation, and the religious and political parties utilized them to defend their particular tenets. What also happened was the Arabization of many myths and traditions common in the region in those days. Legal maxims, Jewish and Christian materials, even aphorisms from Greek philosophy were put into the mouth of the Prophet. This is perhaps one of the reasons why there is a certain Moslem tolerance for the "people of the Book"—Jews and Christians—but only if they accept the sovereignty of Islam and maintain a subservient position. There seemed to be no limit to this process of fabrication of *hadith*. The need for legal sanction often underlay this creativity. One rogue, later executed, confessed to having invented no less than 4,000 *hadith,* and by the third century after the Prophet's death, 600,000 of them were said to be in circulation.

Therefore, a science of *hadith* criticism gradually developed. The basic criterion was the reputation of the people through whom an incident or quotation had allegedly been traced back to a companion of the Prophet.

Doubts and Objections

Some European scholars have severely critized the *hadith* and have favored a radical rejection of the whole system as an artificial creation of later Moslem scholasticism. Nevertheless, according to Islamic scholars, the real justification of the system is twofold: (1) it gives formal approval to the work of the scholars of the second and third centuries of Islam in asserting the genuine Islamic point of view in law and doctrine, and (2) it provides a reasonable guarantee for the future against the infiltration of suspected *hadith.*

Islamic studies and the scientific investigation of the origins and history of Islam are not yet a hundred years old. Until they began, the *hadith*—the oral lore—was the main vehicle for conveying the traditions about Mohammed and his teachings. By 1890, scholars became aware that their research had been based on late and suspiciously partisan sources. However, there were no independent historical sources for the existence of the Prophet. The earliest version of his life is of Abbasid origin. The Abbasids were interested in denying the legitimacy of the Ummayyads, who were, after all, so much closer to Mohammed's times. The Abbasid version was written in the eighth century, and there are three contradictory versions of it.

Suleiman Bashir succeeded in obtaining photocopies of some 250 Ummayyad texts that were in the great mosque in Damascus. By and large, scholars have been denied access to these documents. He also studied the *hadith,* fables, and incidents related in these early texts. All this led him to what he calls "a new scheme of history." He challenged the Shahada, the basic element of Islam, maintaining that Mohammed, as portrayed in the Koran and in much of Islamic literature or accepted history, was probably a fabrication, a myth. Under his critical examination, the foundations of the old traditions dissolved into enigmas and hypotheses. So far, the Koran has emerged unscathed, and the bare historical framework survives, but Bashir threatens to replace it. It is clear for him that Islam arose as a state religion, harnessed, molded, and probably distorted in order to serve the interest of the politicians in power at the time. Or perhaps, as he states, "Islam was the religious expression of a national rebellion by Christian Arabs." He adds, nevertheless, that there is a kernel of historical truth for the existence of Mohammed, but the Abbasids projected this back to detach it from the period of Abd al-Malik. In the process, the figure of Mohammed took on mythical proportions, absorbing local and foreign fables and traditions popular in the area at the time. Academic reaction to Bashir's thesis has been predictably cautious. Few people have read his book—*An Introduction to the Other History: Towards a New Reading of Islamic Tradition,* published only in Arabic—or have studied the Ummayyad's texts firsthand, but his work is considered serious and "potentially explosive." He published his book at his own expense, since no one was willing to publish it. And in some Friday sermons, the imams began to denounce this new *hartaka* (heresy), which was intended to produce a *fitna,* a schism negating the basis of the Islamic faith.

Islam the State: Its Expansion

The early history of Islam is commonly divided according to the dynasties of caliphs, the rulers of Moslem communities after Mohammed: the Rightly Guided, from 632 to 661; the Ummayyad dynasty, from 661 to 750; and the Abbasid dynasty, from 750 to 1258. Afterward, it is impossible to use a single dynastic division of time to cover all the lands of *Dar al-Islam,* the area of Muslim rule, the realm of Islam. The rest of the world is *Dar al-Harb,* the realm of war, and there is no intermediate situation between the two.

The Rightly Guided

In this period, the state was governed by a series of four caliphs, successors of Mohammed. The first of them was Abu Bakr, the father of A'isha, the prophet's favorite wife when he died. When many Arab tribes began to withdraw from Islam after the death of Mohammed, Abu Bakr reacted by vigorously suppressing the renegades. Then, following the Prophet's desire expressed before his death, Abu Bakr sent his troops against the Byzantine and Persian Empires, who were waging war in order to control the entire region, and also to alleviate the chronic food shortage in Arabia, while carrying the word of God to some minor Arab kingdoms on the periphery of these two empires.

By the end of the fifth century, these empires were so devoted to fighting each other that they started to decline, without realizing the greater danger of Islam. Thus the Moslems, constituted mainly by the warlike and recalcitrant tribes of Bedouins and guided by distinguished military leaders with great skill at desert warfare, began their conquests almost simultaneously in three main directions: north, into Palestine and Syria; east, into Persia by way

of Iraq; and west, into Egypt and North Africa and then the Iberian peninsula. The Moslems embarked early on a classical pattern: They assured the
lives, property, and religious institutions of the conquered peoples, so long as
they paid the required taxes.

But despite the brilliant military and political successes that took Islam
and the Arab armies to the doors of India within fifteen years of Mohammed's
death, the movement was ridden with secessions and internal rivalries. Abu
Bakr died of a fever just before the fall of Syria and Palestine to Islam, but
he was able to name Omar as his successor.

Omar ruled for a decade and is considered one of the greatest caliphs.
Under his leadership, Islam made major conquests: Jerusalem fell in 637; in
639 the conquest of Egypt began, paving the way for the domination of North
Africa. The conquered communities, provided that they paid their taxes, were
not forced to become Moslems and could practice their respective religions in
synagogues and churches, but with no external manifestations, such as ring-
ing of bells, processions, or building new places of worship. Still, these people
were treated better by the Moslems than by former rulers.

In 644, while praying in his mosque at dawn, Omar was killed by a Christian slave from Persia. The caliphate then passed to an elder Moslem named
Othman, who belonged to the wealthy and powerful Ummayyad clan. He
ruled for twelve years, and his greatest achievement was the standardization
of the Koran. After a peaceful beginning, Othman faced an Egyptian rebellion, mainly because of his nepotism, and was eventually killed in Medina,
while reading his Koran, by dissidents from Egypt—the first murder of a
caliph by fellow Moslems.

The new caliph elected by the elders was Ali, one of the most respected
of all Moslems—the son of Abu Talib (the Prophet's caretaker uncle) and husband of Fatima (the Prophet's daughter), who bore him two sons. Early in his
rule, Ali had to defeat a rival Moslem army organized by two aspirants to the
caliphate and A'isha, the prophet's widow. The aspirants were killed, and
A'isha lived out her life in retirement. Afterward, Ali established his new
headquarters in Cufa, in Iraq, near where the battle had taken place and now
more central to the empire than Medina. Some time later, he faced opposition
from Mu'awiya, an aggrieved Ummayyad and governor of Syria. In July 657,
the two armies met in the upper Euphrates valley. Eventually, arbitrators
decided that both Ali and Mu'awiya should be removed from office and a new
caliph named. Ali refused but was unable to renew the battle because many
of his men claimed that, by submitting to arbitration, he had violated the
will of God. These extremist dissidents became known as the Kharijites, or
"seceders." Ali now had to confront them, and the two sides fought in July
658 in central Iraq. Ali was victorious but was so weakened that he was
unable to challenge Mu'awiya, who continued to rule Syria as an independent
state within Islam.

In 661, when Ali was entering the mosque of Cufa, he was killed by one of the Kharijites. His followers pledged their loyalty to Hassan, Ali's elder son, who, having no political ambitions, surrendered his claim to the caliphate in return for an immense subsidy from Mu'awiya.

The Ummayyad Dynasty

Having finally been generally recognized as caliph, Mu'awiya shifted the capital of the new Arab empire from Medina to the new Moslem capital established in Damascus. Here he founded his dynasty, which lasted from 661 to 750. Fourteen Ummayyad caliphs were succeeded in office by their sons or some other member of the same clan. The dynasty made sharp departures in secularizing the style of government. Mu'awiya himself reorganized his government very well, and his successors further strengthened the central authority of the caliph and relied on the army to control the empire.

At the same time, a distinctive Islamic culture began to take form, particularly during the caliphate of Abd al-Malik (685–705). He began by consolidating Moslem rule; Arabic became the offical language of the believers, instead of Greek and Persian; he collated the Koran; he erected the major Moslem buildings, such as the Dome of the Rock in Jerusalem, and the great mosque in Damascus; he issued the first Islamic coins (gold *dinars* and silver *dirhams*, bearing Koranic texts), which were minted to replace the standard Byzantine coins and the Persian coins; an extensive communication system was established; numerous public works, particularly irrigation canals and new mosques, were built; ancient Arabic poetry was revived; and the caliphs started to live in luxury palaces.

The Ummayyad rule saw the second great wave of conquests, particularly in the early eighth century. The Moslems reached the Indus Valley to the east and, through North Africa, reached Spain and the Atlantic Ocean to the west. Nevertheless, in 732, the French warrior-lord Charles Martel defeated the advancing Moslem armies at Poitiers, in eastern France, thus turning back the Saracen tide that had already swept up from North Africa through Spain and Portugal. The Spanish Christians who retained their faith but acquired Moorish customs became known as *Mozarabs*, "would be Arabs."

But as usual, internal weaknesses and dissension led to the Ummayyad collapse. The Moslems became divided by bitter disputes, particularly with the *mawali*—people converted to Islam, who were considered inferior to Arab Moslems. The greatest ameliorative effort was made by Omar II, who reigned from 717 to 720. He changed the tax system, exempting the Moslems from paying taxes except the religious compulsory tax. This reform affected Islam's economy, because the great number of conversions to Islam had seriously reduced the tax revenue. Moreover, many people who felt that the Ummayyads had usurped the caliphate from its rightful rulers—the descendants of Ali—joined the anti-Ummayyad ranks, among them the *Kharijites* and the *Shi'ites*.

The Shi'ites, the only major schismatic sect of Islam, began as a political movement to restore the House of Ali to the caliphate. They repudiated as usurpers the first three caliphs (Abu Bakr, Omar, and Othman), which has always remained their chief offense in the eyes of the Sunnis. Broadly speaking, the Hellenistic elements of Islam would attach themselves to the Sunnis, while the more Asiatic beliefs tended to become Shi'a. Whereas, for the Sunnis, the caliph was basically a political and religious leader of the community, for Shi'ites, the imam had a spiritual function as an interpreter and definer of dogma. Gradually, the imam became a superhuman character, sinless and infallible, who incarnated the divine light descended through the generations of prophets from Adam onward.

As early as Mu'awiya's death in 680, the Shi'ites tried to make Ali's younger son, Husayn, the new caliph, but he was murdered by soldiers of Yazid, Mu'awiya's son, who had succeeded him. The anniversary of this crime is still observed in parts of the Islamic world as a day of mourning. Meanwhile, while the Ummayyads were occupied with rebellious Bedouin tribes of Arabia, a new revolutionary force appeared—the Abbasid party. Their leader was Abbas, a descendant of an uncle of the prophet, and they were centered in Persia, where many people resented the Ummayyads for treating them as inferior. Besides, there were many Arab Moslems who had various grievances against the Ummayyads. In June 747, the Abbasids raised the black banner of their revolt, which was to become their emblem, overthrew the Ummayyad governor of Persia, and moved west, overrunning the Ummayyad armies. In 749, Abbas was proclaimed caliph by his followers, although the Ummayyads still held Syria. A year later, the two armies met in a decisive battle at the Great Zab, a branch of the Tigris in northern Iraq. The troops of Marwan II, the last Ummayyad caliph, were destroyed, and Marwan was killed and his head sent as a present to Abbas, the new caliph.

It is important that in the period of the Ummayyads, whose capital was Damascus, Medina remained the center of Moslem religious learning, so that a church–state separation developed. Thus, Byzantine elements were more freely absorbed by the empire, such as the style of court ceremonials, the organization of the navy, the adoption of formal currency, the building of splendid monuments, and even the mode of dynastic succession. In this period, Arabs also began the systematic study not only of the Prophetic traditions but also of philology, history, and above all, law—a remarkable transformation considering the previous intellectual poverty of Medina.

The Abbasid Dynasty

Abbas, the new caliph, brutally wiped out the rest of the Ummayyads, even ordering the desecration of the tombs, of Ummayyad caliphs—except that of Omar II, considered the only pious one among them. He also tried to eliminate all other dissidents, including the Shi'ites, who considered themselves betrayed. Finally, he ruthlessly executed all who had helped him ascend to the throne.

Soon after this, the Abbasid dynasty stabilized, and it lasted 500 years. It was in its first century, however, that it reached its summit under the caliph Harum al-Rashid, who reigned from 786 to 809. The new capital, Baghdad, had already been established by his brother Mansur, with the help of 100,000 workers who, starting in 762, had slaved for four years till the extraordinary city was finished. The empire retained the religion and language of the Arabs yet acquired an international character never known before. Islam promoted fresh interaction among poets, jurists, philosophers, scientists, and artists, all attracted by the marvelous city that was Baghdad. Here, Greek philosophy and science was reborn, with Jews and Christians translating Greek manuscripts into Arabic, while the Moslems studied the works of the Greek physicians, astronomers, mathematicians, and geographers. Persian culture also percolated into the empire, with Persians well represented in its army and government. In fact, Persians even married members of the reigning dynasty, and of the thirty-seven Abbasid caliphs, only a few had Arab mothers. Once they acquired absolute power, the Abbasid caliphs lived in palaces, surrounded by a Persian-like splendor. The throne itself was concealed by a resplendent curtain, and all who stood before it had to prostrate themselves and kiss the floor, a custom completely alien to modest Arabia. The Abbasids also followed the Persian saying: "Religion and government are twin brothers." The mantle they donned in public was supposed to have been used by the Prophet himself, and they considered themselves not mere successors of Mohammed but the deputies of God himself.

For their own reasons, the Abbasids rewrote history to emphasize their connection to the Prophet and minimize the role of the Ummayyads. The distortions are expressed not only in the disputes and the almost total confusion surrounding nearly every historical event or personality, but also in the duplication of identities of people, events, and places during the first fifty years of the Arab millennium.

As the caliphs withdrew more and more from the daily affairs of state, a new and powerful figure appeared: the vizier, who stood between the ruler and the ruled, with an authority second only to that of the caliph himself.

While philosophers and theologians were discussing abstract intellectual questions, a mystical movement called Sufism was growing. The Sufist believed in salvation through simplicity and poverty, and they wore rough undyed robes of wool (*suf* in Arabic—believed to be the derivation of their name). Because many of these great mystics were venerated as saints, the orthodox leaders feared their power and fought them by any means. Later, however, these leaders began to realize the value of the Sufi revivalist mission among the urban proletariat and rural dwellers—a change mainly attributed to the great theologian al-Ghazzali, who demonstrated the true Islamic foundation of Sufism and, without renouncing orthodoxy, made mysticism a respectable element in orthodox Moslem practice. Sufism would continue to have profound effects on Moslem religious, intellectual, and even political life.

Meanwhile, the Abbasid empire was in a process of gradual disintegration. As early as 756, Abd al-Rahman had founded an Ummayyad dynasty in Spain, and soon other dynasties were founded in Morocco and Tunisia. In 820, the governor of Khurasan, in Persia, declared his independence from Baghdad; and within the next century, all of Persia fell under the sway of local rulers. Gradually, the Abbasids began to lose control, particularly during the reign of Mu'tasim, who ruled from 833 to 842. Because of conflict between his Turkish slaves, whom he had put in charge of his personal guard, and the Persian soldiers in his army, he was forced to move his capital to Samarra, sixty miles up the Tigris, in 836.

Samarra remained the capital for the next fifty years, during the reigns of seven caliphs. These caliphs became more and more dependent on their Turkish guards, who finally became able to appoint and remove caliphs at will. Meanwhile, various provinces of the empire continued to break away. In 892, the caliph Mu'tadid returned the capital to Baghdad, but to no avail. In 945, a Persian family, the Buyids, entered Baghdad and dominated the Abbasid caliphs until they were ousted, in 1055, by the Seljuk Turks of Turkestan. The Seljuks retained a figurehead Abbasid ruler, but the Seljuk commander had the actual power. When Genghis Khan's grandson Hulagu took Baghdad in 1258, almost without a fight, thousands of people were massacred, including the caliph and most of his family, and the caliph's palace was reduced to smoking ruins. Thus ended an important chapter in Islamic and world history.

The Later Course of Islam

After the debacle of 1258, the entire eastern Moslem world became tributary to the vast Mongol Empire—except Egypt, Syria, and Arabia. These remnants were saved by the military caste of Turkish and Kipchak "slaves," the Mamluks, who had seized political power in Egypt. Under Mamluk rule, the old Arab-Moslem civilization continued to flourish in the material arts (especially architecture and metalwork) for some 250 more years, but with a gradual decay of spiritual and intellectual vigor.

Meanwhile, a revived and rather brilliant Persian-Moslem civilization grew up in the Mongol domains. It, too, excelled in architecture and the fine arts, especially miniature painting; spiritually, it was rooted in Sufism. Persian culture also molded the life of the two new Islamic empires that emerged in the sixteenth century—in Anatolia, the Balkans, and North Africa, the Ottoman Empire; and in India, the Mogul Empire. Both of these empires put a strong emphasis on Moslem orthodoxy and the sacred law, with a heavy mystical component; in fact, Sufism saw its apogee during the eighteenth and nineteenth centuries.

Also in the sixteenth century, another new dynasty, supported by Turkish tribes from Azerbaijan, conquered Persia, revived the long-decaying Shi'ite heterodoxy, and established it as the religion of the Persian state. Through a long series of wars with the Ottomans, the Turks, and the Moguls, all of whom were Sunnis, Shi'ism became identified with Persian nationalism. Thus, a serious rift occurred that broke the orthodox Moslem world into two separate parts, between which cultural communication was slight and sporadic. Persia went into a self-imposed political and religious isolation, and its declining political strength facilitated the breakaway of the Afghan tribesmen, who formed an independent Sunni state during the eighteenth century.

The eighteenth century also witnessed the decline of the Ottoman and Mogul Empires. The latter was undermined by a Hindu revolt under the Mahrattas; and the former, though it was able to retain its Asiatic territories up to World War I, finally lost the Arab lands in the war and gave way to a new and secularized Turkish republic covering only Anatolia and eastern Thrace.

Yet this decay of Moslem political power did not weaken Islamic society. It even seems to have injected new vitality into the religion, which saw an incredible expansion in Africa, the Malay archipelago, China, and so on. Thus, today, Islam is a dominant religion in a vast area of the world, practiced by perhaps 500 million people from Morocco to China, including Malaysia and Indonesia. In all these lands, men and women of the greatest diversity consider themselves followers of the Prophet. And in our time, Moslem political power has seen a considerable resurgence.

As a contrast to such religious expansion, the civil wars among the Arabs have not diminished at all; perhaps they are worse today. The present tragic situation in Lebanon— already some twelve years of civil war among all kinds of Moslem sects—has had another terrible consequence: it is practically destroying the archaeology of the Greco-Roman and Byzantine periods, roughly some thousand years of ancient history. Selling Lebanon's past has become a popular way of making money. Archaeology professor Leila Badr, curator of the Museum of the American University of Beirut, has complained, saying: "We are selling the past for potatoes."

The Interplay of Religion, Law, and Politics in Islam

Islam came out of Arabia as a coherent doctrine, but its theological formulation was still in a fluid state. Perhaps the vast territory over which it spread, and the many religious modes it came in contact with, helped keep it plastic. With the exception of the fanatical doctrines of the tribesmen, Islam tolerated the practical, unspeculative piety of the first generations in Arabia, the influence of Hellenistic Christian thought in Syria, and the influence of various gnostic doctrines in Iraq. No man or sect who proclaimed the sole divinity of Allah and the prophetic mission of Mohammed was excluded from the Islamic fold; whoever wished such an exclusion had excluded himself.

The establishment of an orthodox system was a gradual process in which political action played an important part; another important factor was the moral preponderance of the Arabs in the Islamic empire. Its center was in Medina, the home of the earliest religious studies in Islam, where the traditions (*hadith*) were first collected. Although the schools in other countries had local significance, Medina alone was the universal school.

Also crucial was that in Islamic religious theory, mosque and state were one and indivisible. This changed in the fourth century, after the *Hijra*, when the authority of the state passed into military hands. Medina never accepted this and became the center of religious opposition. By dissociating the religion from the political organization, Medina kept religion above the sphere of politics. Thus, the religion was not affected when Arab political supremacy was overthrown. And when the Abbasid dynasty established their capital in Baghdad, Medinian orthodoxy became their platform, and they even began active persecution against the gnostic and dualistic perversions. Therefore, once the orthodox definition began to rigidify, the fanatical interpretations of the tribesmen—such as the extreme Kharijite doctrine—and the extreme gnostic and dualisatic interpretations were rejected. It is true that all of them survived, but only as heretical sects.

The Hellenistic interpretation was maintained by the Mu'tazilite school, which waged the basic struggle against Islamic orthodoxy for about two centuries. This school tried to accommodate within Islam the fundamental ideas of justice and philosophy of the Greeks, never really appreciated by the Oriental mind. Whereas for Islam, God is the ultimate power, for the Mu'tazilites, it was infinite justice. Islam saw this view as limiting God's power, since justice is derived from human reason. The problem of free will and determinism lay at the heart of the dispute between these conceptions—always a difficult gap to bridge. The Mu'tazilites reacted not only against the excesses of the fanatical Kharijites but also against the ethical laxity of the political conformists, known as Murji'ites. The Mu'tazilite school eventually acquired an intermediate or eclectic position. At first, the Mu'tazilites had been rather rigid puritans, and their teachings had been compatible with the Koran; they became the most active among the orthodox Sunni teachers in Iraq. During the second century, they became an intense missionary movement, which may have been what brought them into contact with Greek logic and philosophy. The translation of Greek works into Arabic followed, particularly at the beginning of the third century, when, for twenty-five years, their influence was dominant at the court in Baghdad. After the fall of the Ummayyads, the Mu'tazilites started to lose their predominant position.

There are also quite a number of sects—systems of Islamic doctrines and beliefs that are generally repudiated by the orthodox and by one another as heretical. Within the orthodox community itself, however; there are a number of semilegal schools—most important among them the Hanifi, Maliki, Shafi'i, and Hanbali—that are mutually tolerated. Some scholars accept a fifth ortho-dox school—called Ja'fari after the sixth imam, al-Sadiq—whose authority is also accepted by the Sunnis.

There were also organized brotherhoods of "poor men" or "mendicants," known as *faquirs* in Arabic (plural *fuqara*) or *dervishes* in Persian. Even pious, venerable men were attracted by them. In a simple initiation ceremony, the newcomer pledged devotion and from then on lived in close association with his *shaikh* or *pir* (leader) till he reached the higher stages of the art and could go out and teach his master's "way" (*tariqa*) to new disciples in some other place.

These *darwish* orders were extremely pliable and could tolerate the religious customs of other countries and people, provided that their outward adherence was to Islam. In some areas, *darwish* brotherhoods governed cities, organized revolutions, and converted pagan tribes. These orders popularized the teachings of the Sufis (see below) down to the lowest ranks of the pop-ulation. Few world religions have tried or succeeded in teaching mystical techniques to the masses. The brotherhoods also transmitted some of the hypnotic or thaumaturgic rituals of the ecstatic orders, together with elements of astrology, divination, and the cult of saints, dead or alive. Almost every male Moslem belonged to one or more *tariqas*, which were, in fact, a com-bination of social club, night school, masonic lodge, and burial association. The core of the *tariqa*'s life was the collective *dhikrs*, or *tekke*, where the dervishes would chant their liturgies and dance in unison until someone fell into a trance. These *dhikrs* still exist in some areas of the Moslem world. Something similar can be seen today in Haiti—namely, *voodoo*, the native religion stemming from West African cults and with parallels in other parts of the West Indies and Brazil. Voodoo has also influenced magical practices and minor cults among American Negroes. A similar movement is Maraboutism of Berber Islam, the cult of living "holy men" who possess mag-ical powers (*baraka*).

Islam also had a tremendous impact on the Turks, the Mongols, and par-ticularly the people of India, where popular Islam presents the most bewilder-ing diversity of beliefs, rituals and orders. Very often, their connection with Islam is purely nominal or accidental, and the practices of their members have helped bring the term *darwish* into disrepute. Nevertheless, the ritual of the sacred fire (*suttee*) is still kept in several communities. Another sect was the Nizaris, accused of immoderate use of Indian hemp—marijuana or hashish—from which their other name, Hashishim, derived. The careful way in which they planned and executed the murder of the enemies of their imam gave the Western world the word assassin and its derivates.

Worthy of note are the Druses of the Middle East—about half a million strong in Syria, Lebanon and Israel. Their religion, which originated in Egypt, broke away from Islam in the middle of the eleventh century. They left Egypt en masse, but little is known of their exodus, except that soon after, Druse villages began to appear in the aforementioned states. They all live in villages, usually on mountaintops because they are easy to defend. There are practically no Druse towns. They share with the Arabs a language and general culture, but they are proud of their separate religious and ethnic identity. Many Moslems concede Druse religious, though not ethic, separateness.

The growth and development of Sufism display many of the characteristic features of Islamic culture. Sufism began with the spontaneous action of individuals of the urban artisan classes and grew from there. It neither sought nor received formal recognition, and at first it encountered much opposition and even some persecution from the upper, learned classes. It always remained autonomous and personal and only after some centuries of growth began to organize itself in institutional forms. In its tension between rigidity, represented by the sacred law, and flexibility, arising out of the spiritual intuition of the individual, it conformed to the basic pattern that runs through all the spiritual and cultural manifestations of Islam.

The Sufi mystics—in the beginning as individual missionaries but later as members of organized brotherhoods—were the leaders in the task of converting the pagans and the superficially Islamized tribes. They laid the foundations upon which, in later generations, orthodox law and theology could be brought to bear. Thanks to them, the religious frontiers of Islam were steadily extended, in successive centuries, to Africa, India, Indonesia, across central Asia to Turkestan and China, and even to parts of southeastern Europe. Moslem missionary activity was similar to the monastic organizations in northern and central Europe, but it always remained individual and unregulated. The Sufi movement was never fully coordinated with the orthodox scholastic organizations but jealously maintained its independence and was even somewhat antagonistic toward them. The caliphate, however, was no papacy, and from Ummayyad times on, the theologians and legists had refused to give it any spiritual authority. (It is true that the caliphs were the religious and secular heads of the Islamic community, in that they embodied the supremacy of the faith and the sacred law, but attempts by three caliphs of the ninth century to define the orthodox dogma were decisively defeated, and the attempt was never repeated.)

Furthermore, independent rulers, while acknowledging the religious authority of the caliphs, resented and suppressed their intervention in the affairs of their kingdoms. Sometimes, they held their Sufi spiritual directors in higher esteem than the orthodox scholars and legists who, for their part, also found themselves in a somewhat ambiguous relationship with the secular power. Since the tenth century, the state had gradually diverged from the path traced out by the Moslem theorists. It developed an ethic of its own, influenced by the old imperial traditions of Asia but far removed from Islamic values. The struggle of the legists to reconvert the state into an embodiment of the principles of sacred law was not successful, and later, together with Moslem political theorists, they finally accommodated themselves to the changed situation. A distinction was made between a caliphate (denoting any government that recognized and enforced the sacred law) and the sultanate, constituted by kings or sovereigns of Moslem states (indicating a secular despotism that governed by arbitrary or natural law). Attempting to maintain Moslem ideals and prevent stagnation of Islamic spiritual and intellectual life, the legists were fighting a losing battle, since they were unwilling to hold any religious office under the sultans; they thus left the field open to their less scrupulous brethren. On the other hand, the middle classes accepted the Islamic ideals even if they did not always live up to them. In the course of time, these people, together with the theologians and legists, were more and more influenced by Sufism. To some extent, one can say that in the Moslem world—concealed by a common outward profession of Islam—there are two distinct societies living side by side, and interacting to some extent, but opposed to one another in basic principles: the orthodox and the Sufi. Of the two channels of Moslem religious life, the mystical one was broader and deeper. Sufism saw its apogee during the eighteenth and nineteenth centuries.

Finally, what should be stressed is the amazing development of Islam from the simple, rigid, and austere monotheism preached by Mohammed to a small Arab community to an intricate complex of legal schools and theological sects, each with its own rituals, comprising an extraordinary diversity of religious ideas and practices. During the last two centuries Islam has fought for revival and readjustment under the double stimulus of challenge from within and pressing dangers from without, particularly deriving from the political and economic expansion of Western Europe and the United States.

Throughout its history, Islam has been marked by two opposed but complementary tendencies. One is the puritan legacy and traditions of the Medinian community, fighting against innovations that threaten to disrupt the purity of primitive doctrine and practice. The other is the universal tendency that explicitly admits a variety of opinions and usages in secondary matters and accepts the necessity of reinterpretation in order to meet new needs and situations in this changing world. The external pressures of secularism, scientific technology, materialism, and the economic interpretation of history have left their marks on several sections of Moslem society. But even more dangerous is the relaxation of the religious conscience due to the weakening of the universal tradition of Islam. The *ulamas*—orthodox Moslem theologians, scholars, and religious teachers—have a special responsibility in this situation. It is difficult to deny in the majority of them, a certain narrowness of outlook, an inability or unwillingness to face the demands of the present times. Nonetheless, they have done much to protect the causes of their religious tenets. Only in one matter can the *ulamas* brook no compromise of any kind: Islam, for better or worse, must retain the supremacy of the sacred law. Any attempt to dethrone the Shari'a or to weaken its authority will produce, as in the past, open opposition on their part. But unless the *ulamas* can achieve a balance between the demands of the new world and the treasures of the old, they will be unable to safeguard the religious heritage of Islam from the corroding acids of our age.

Islam the Culture

For more than six centuries—from the dawn of Islam until the Mongols sacked Baghdad in 1258—Islam was a most challenging religion, the world's strongest political force, and a vital culture that linked such varied and distant people as Spaniards, black Africans, Persians, Turks, Egyptians, Indians, and even Chinese. In its unifying role, Islam transmitted more than one invention that proved crucial to the development of Western civilization. For instance, Moslems learned the technique of making paper from the Chinese and relayed it to Europe. As we have seen, they also revived Greek science and philosophy for the West through the many translations done by Islamic scholars. The Islamic genius for synthesizing and enlarging upon elements from various cultures also expressed itself in medicine, architecture, chemistry, physics, and mathematics (algebra, geometry, and particularly trigonometry were largely developed by Moslems). The same goes for such "minor arts" as carpet making, textiles, pottery, calligraphy, bookmaking, and ivory and wood carving; Islamic craftsmen created exquisite works. In the ninth and tenth centuries, at the apex of Islamic civilization, industry and commerce also thrived in Dar al-Islam.

Islam's most distinctive architectural achievement was the mosque, with its surface decorations that could include tiles, glass, mosaics, glazed bricks, wall painting, wood paneling, low reliefs in plaster and stucco, and ceramic and metal works. Designs tended to be abstract, decorative, and figurative. A famous style of interlocking designs was the *arabesque*. The best-known mosques include the sacred mosque of Mecca, the great mosque of Damascus, and the Dome of the Rock and al-Aqsa Mosque in Jerusalem. The last two are important because although Jerusalem is the third holiest Moslem city, after Mecca and Medina, Moslem literature abounds with praises written to Jerusalem. The two mosques stand on the main Moslem holy site, known in Arabic as Haram al-Sharif, the Temple Mount. The Dome of the Rock was built by Abd al-Malik in 691, and the other mosque was built two years later. Another shrine of Moslem heritage in modern Israel is the Cave of the Machpela, or Ibrahimi Mosque, in Hebron. The Moslem tradition of the holiness of Jerusalem is based on the belief that Mohammed ascended to heaven (mi'rāj) from the rock within the mosque of the same name, most probably a post-Koranic tradition. The minaret, the tower from which the muezzin calls the faithful to prayer, was a later addition to the mosque.

In the "humanistic" area, religious studies continued to develop in a score of new centers is Samarkand, North Africa, and Spain. Literature and philosophy—drawing upon Greek, Persian, and Indian sources—broke out in new directions, sometimes in a kind of revolt against the narrowness of Moslem orthodoxy. An amazing amount of work was done in other fields, such as history and philology. The interest in Greek philosophy and logic inevitably produced a sharp and bitter conflict; the religious leaders of Islam saw its spiritual foundations endangered by the subtle infidelities of pure rationalism and, although they finally triumphed over the Hellenizing trends, philosophy and logic always remained suspect in their eyes, as did any other secular and intellectual pursuit that went beyond the range of their control. Eventually, the Moslem religious culture would overwhelm all independent cultural activities, converting them into its own instruments.

The contributions of a few cultural figures stand out. Avicenna (980–1037), known as the "prince of philosophers and physicians," wrote some 170 books on varied subjects; his Canon of Medicine was one of the most widely studied works in the late Medieval period. The Persian-born Razi (865–925) also contributed greatly to the field of medicine. In Spain flourished the physician, philosopher, and legal thinker Averroes (1126–1198). The greatest Arab historian was Ibn Khaldun (1332–1406), whose famous Muqadima is the classical history of the Arabs. And the Persian poet Omar Khayyám (1070–1123) won renown for his Rubāiyāt. Another great Islamic literary work—The Thousand and One Nights (Alf Layla wa Layla), or Arabian Nights—cannot be credited to any single author but is a synthesis of Indian, Persian, Arab, and Egyptian legends, romances, love stories, and so on. The period considered to be the Islamic Golden Age or Islamic Renaissance was a rather short one, lasting only from the tenth to the fifteenth centuries.

Shari'a: The Islamic Law

In Islam, the law is considered to be of divine origin; the most characteristic activity of Islamic scholarship has been not theology, as in other religions, but the study and exegesis of the law. The concept of divine law is a very ancient one in the Semitic Orient, and early Islam made no distinction between law and religion. Not until a century after Mohammed did Islamic scholars begin to specialize in one or the other of the two: ilm, "positive knowledge," denoted theology, while fiqh, "understanding," referred to law as based in theology. Later, fiqh would acquire an almost exclusively legal connotation.

A separate term for the legal system of Islam—Shari'a—made its appearance relatively late. Since the Koran gave only some basic guidelines, the Shari'a or *Shar'* ("clear path" or "highway") played a crucial role in stabilizing legal norms and thereby molding the social order of Moslem peoples. Moslem scholars studied their law with an ardor that had a parallel only in Judaism. Shari'a set a standard to which Moslem communities conformed more and more closely as time went on, despite the resistance of some of the nomadic tribes, with their ancient habits. Thus, Islamic law gave practical expression to the Moslem quest for unity. Unlike the more secular Roman law, it was the spiritual regulator, the conscience of the Moslem community in all its parts and activities. These functions of the law acquired still greater significance as Moslem political life swung even further from the theocratic ideas of the prophet and his successors. With the decline of the Abbasid caliphate during the tenth and eleventh centuries, the moral authority of the law only grew, and it held Islam together throughout all its fluctuating political fortunes.

In later times, legists granted the Moslem rulers the right to suspend the application of certain portions of the Shari'a, substituting secular laws, particularly in the area of punishment. Still, since it is divine law, the Shari'a was never revoked or abolished; it was merely not enforced in certain times and places. Much later, the Greek word *kanon* (*qanun* in Arabic) was adopted to denote administrative rule as distinct from revealed law; therefore, "canon law" in Arabic is exactly the opposite of what it is in European usage.

Justice is paramount in Islam, and the ruler's principal task is to administer it. A man is born to fulfill a duty toward God and toward the community, and all are equal in the eyes of God. Nevertheless, freedom is not considered a natural right, and there is no Arabic word that corresponds exactly to the Western concept of freedom.

The Five Pillars of Islam constitute an essential part of the complex system of legislation regulating Moslem behavior. Every exposition of Moslem law begins with religious duties and acts of worship, such as ablutions, prayers, and pilgrimage. As in other Semitic religions, law is seen as a product not of human intelligence but of divine inspiration, based on the Koran and the hadith and hence immutable.

To Moslems, the Koran, as the final revelation, contains the most perfect solution for all questions of belief and conduct. However, as it is comparatively short and its main parts have no direct bearing on legal, political, or social questions, there is a need for elaboration—hence, the *hadith*. According to the Koran itself, the Prophet was possessed not only by the *kitab* (the written "book") but also by the *hikma* (the "wisdom"), whereby the principles can be applied to everyday life. Therefore, his actions and sayings, transmitted by chains of reliable narrators, constitute a kind of commentary and supplement to the Koran. Still, though both the Koran and the *hadith* are held to be infallible, neither really offers a coherent system of legal provisions but provides only the raw materials from which one could be constructed.

Islamic legislation, in fact, relies on a diversity of primary sources. In addition to the Koran and the *hadith,* there are the prophetic teachings, or *sunnah,* supplementing the Koran; analogy, or *kias,* based on principles underlying previous decisions; the consensus of jurists' opinions, or *ijma,* the collective approval of religious scholars representing the entire Moslem community; and the legally unsettled questions of common interest, or *Maslaha al-Mursala.*

Where points of law were not covered by a clear Koranic or *hadith* statement, the majority of jurists had recourse to *kias,* the application to a new problem of the principles of the existing decision. This method, however, was rejected by strict jurists for involving an element of human judgment.

A more important role was played by the principle of *ijma,* "consensus." Though Islam boasts that it has no priesthood, the truth is that as it became more organized, it did produce a clerical class with the same sort of authority and prestige as, say, the Christian clergy. This is the *ulama* class (meaning the "learned"—the plural of *alim,* one who has *ilm,* "religious knowledge"). The principle was established early that the consensus of the community—which in practice meant that of the *ulama*—had binding force. Thus, *ijma* served as a tool for jurists and theologians to fill the gaps in Islamic law. It guaranteed the authenticity of Koran and *hadith* texts and determined their meanings. In fact, *ijma* has been given the status of infallibility, a third channel of revelation. The spiritual prerogatives of the Prophet were inherited, at least according to Sunni doctrine, not by the caliphs but by the community as a whole, by virtue of a special grace bestowed on it by God. Thus, *ijma* intervenes decisively in every branch of Islamic doctrine, law, and statecraft, and though it cannot abrogate a direct text of the Koran or the *hadith,* it may nevertheless indicate when a certain law has fallen into disuse.

When a consensus had been attained by the scholars of the second and third centuries of Islam on a given point, their decisions were irrevocable. Thus, the right of personal reasoning or individual interpretation, *ijtihad,* was confined only to points on which no general agreement had yet been reached. It usually involved applying *kias* to an authoritative text such as the Koran or the *hadith.* But these points of disagreement became less and less frequent; for the majority of Moslem scholars today, the "gates of *itjihad*" were shut a long time ago, so that no one could now qualify as a *mujtahid,* an authoritative interpreter of the law.

Thus, the conception of law in Islam is authoritarian to the last degree. The law cannot be other than the will of God revealed through the Prophet, and to violate the law is not merely an infringement of social order but an act of religious disobedience. The absolute power of God imposes severe limits on the freedom of man, and these limits constitute the law; in fact, Moslems use the term *hadd,* "limit," for legal ordinance. The Western distinction between civil and penal law is not made in the Moslem law books; for Islam, law is the science of man's correct conduct in this world and his preparation for the future life.

The Islamic system designates five classes of actions: (1) obligations, such as praying or paying *zakah;* (2) desirable or recommended actions, such as freeing slaves or giving alms to beggars; (3) indifferent or morally neutral actions, such as going on a pleasure trip; (4) objectionable or disapproved but not forbidden actions, such as gambling, marking the Koran, or eating onion or garlic, which cause bad breath; and (5) prohibited actions, or *haram,* such as murder or drinking prohibited liquors. The basic morality underlying this categorization was similar to that of the Old Testament, enjoining Moslems to be patient, chaste, and kind to the needy.

Every observant Sunni must adhere to one of four accepted schools— Hanafi, Maliki, Shafi'i, or Hanbali. The prescriptions of these schools have remained substantially unchanged over the centuries. Still, despite the closing of the gates of *itjihad* in the third century of Islam, some developments show that Islamic law has not remained in an absolutely petrified state. Secular authorities have intervened in judicial administration to a certain extent by holding courts "for the redress of wrongs" (*mazalim*), where a somewhat arbitrarily modified form of religious law was applied, with or without the collaboration of the official *qadis* (judges). In the religious courts and sometimes in *mazalim* courts, it was a common procedure to submit a summary of an important case to a qualified jurist for his opinion. Such consultants were called *muftis,* and their replies took the form of *fatwas*—statements or opinions on a legal issue. The *muftis* maintained considerable independence from the secular administration. In the Ottoman Empire, however, they were given a place in the official hierarchy, and the chief *mufti* of Constantinople, known as the Shaikh al-Islam, was the highest religious authority of the empire.

Until the last century, the general tendency of the *ulama* was to expand the practical application of the law—in theory, eternal and universal—so as to give religious significance to all spheres of life. One means to attain this "universality of the law " was the legal interpretations of the *muftis. Fatwas* collections constituted legal precedents more important than the *fiqh* books of the different schools, not only for practical application but especially for the study of the law and its development.

Crimes and Punishments

Judaism emerged as a theocracy but experienced so many periods of captivity and dispersion that it administered very few criminal laws. Christianity, for the most part, preferred that secular authorities take the responsibility for the administration of criminal justice. In contrast, Islam emerged within Arab nations with full political power, and from the beginning, crimes and punishment appeared in the Shari'a.

According to the Shari'a, crime is the commission of an act that is legally forbidden and punishable or the omission of a duty that is commanded. Crime is punishable in this world by fixed (*hudoud*) or discretionary (*tazir*) punishments. In classical Islamic law, there is no distinction between religious and secular offenses, since the religious element is present in all types of offenses except administrative ones; and as in almost all ancient law codes, criminal matters in the Shari'a are more developed than civil ones (contracts, property, marriage and divorce, succession, etc.).

Recognizing the principle of personal responsibility, Islamic law classifies offenses by the type of punishment they engender. There are five categories of offenses: (1) those with a specific punishment (*hadd*); (2) those for which the punishment is at the judge's discretion (*ta'zir*); (3) those deserving talio or rataliatory action (*kisas*), inflicted by the victim's kinsmen, or blood money (*diya*), to be paid by the perpetrator or his kinsmen; (4) those against the policy of the state, deserving administrative penalties (*siyasa*); and (5) those that are corrected by acts of personal penance (*kaffara,* "expiation"). The Shari'a deals primarily with the first three types of offenses, which are to be adjudicated before a *qadi,* a Muslim religious judge of a Shari'a court. Secular tribunals handle administrative offenses according to the state's *siyasa* jurisdiction. *Kaffara* is usually undertaken voluntarily, outside any tribunal or court. The fundamental principle is that everything is permissible (*halal*) unless specifically prohibited or even frowned upon.

Specified Punishment (Hadd)

Hudoud crimes are described, and punished by God, in the Koran and the *hadith.* Therefore, they are fixed, without a minimum or maximum limit, and cannot be modified. Some jurists believe that crimes of the *hudoud*—retaliatory and atonement types—cannot be imposed on the basis of analogy (*kias*), since they are specified in the Koran and the *sunnah* as being against Allah. Crimes punishable by *hadd* are (1) adultery and unlawful intercourse; (2) defamation and false accusation; (3) drinking of alcohol; (4) theft; (5) highway robbery; (6) apostasy from Islam; and (7) attempted coup d'état. Also related to *hudoud* are crimes punishable by retaliation and blood money, such as different types of murder (premeditated, semipremeditated, or by error) and premeditated offenses against human life short of murder, such as beating or injuring.

Adultery and Unlawful Intercourse (Zina). *Zina* includes intercourse with any person who is not one's lawful spouse or concubine (a woman not legally capable of becoming one's wife, such as a near relative; a fifth wife while the other four are alive; a girl below the age of puberty; a prostitute, etc.). Adultery is not considered a violation of the marital contract and is not a legal basis for divorce; but any kind of unlawful intercourse, within or outside marriage, is an offense against God. *Zina* is seen to produce many evil consequences: it transmits diseases to the innocent, instills doubts among Moslems, leads to the birth of children who are deformed or who do not know who their fathers are, and so on.

The punishment for *zina*—death by stoning, or flogging with a specific number of lashes—does not appear in the Koran but was inflicted by the first caliphs after the Prophet. It may have been adopted from Mosaic law. It can be applied only to a freeman who has been convicted, not to a minor or a mentally disturbed person. For all others, the punishment is a hundred lashes, reduced to fifty for a slave. In some cases, banishment is added to the flogging.

Since this is such a harsh punishment, Islamic jurists impose so many evidentiary requirements as to make conviction virtually impossible: the accusation must usually be brought within one month of the offense; four eyewitnesses, instead of the normal two, have to declare that the act took place and that it was voluntary; or the accused must confess. Witnesses must be competent, adult, male Moslems (non-Moslems may testify in cases in which the accused is not a Moslem) and have to testify that they all saw the same act at the same time.

Some jurists consider it meritorious for witnesses not to testify, so that the accused may settle the offense privately with God. Another incentive for silence is that if the accusation is dismissed, those who testified are subject to the *hadd* punishment for false accusation of adultery, even if the case was dismissed for a technical reason, such as the minority of one of the witnesses. Moreover, the four witnesses must be present at the execution and must throw the first stones; if not, the death penalty is not carried out. If someone is convicted of *zina* by personal confession, the offender is encouraged to remain silent and to turn to God for forgiveness. Moreover, a retraction at any time will void the confession, and even the magistrate should provide every opportunity for retraction. Any person who is not liable for the *hadd* punishment for *zina,* due to any of these limitations, may still be prosecuted and a discretionary punishment (*ta'zir*) may be applied.

False Accusation of Unlawful Intercourse (Kadhf). Anyone who is competent and adult—male or female, Moslem or not, slave or free—is liable if he falsely accused another person of unlawful intercourse, if and when the slandered party is free, adult, competent, Moslem, and has not been previously convicted for unlawful intercourse. The same *kadhf* occurs in false accusations of illegitimacy. Only those who are slandered or their heirs may bring a charge of *kadhf*.

The *hadd* punishment for *kadhf* is eighty lashes for free persons, forty for slaves. Proof is obtained either by confession (retraction will not be suggested by the judge) or by the testimony of two free, adult, male Moslems. Those slanders that do not fall under *kadhf* are punished by *ta'zir*.

In Islamic law, a husband's direct accusation of his wife's adultery, or his denial of the paternity of her child, requires a special procedure known as *li'an*. It allows a husband to charge his wife with infidelity, without risk to himself, if he swears four times by Allah that he is speaking the truth and at a fifth oath calls a curse upon himself if he is lying. The wife may answer the charge by the same five oaths. If the husband makes his accusation without the *li'an* formula, he is liable to the *hadd* punishment for *kadhf*. He may even be imprisoned until he announces the *li'an;* if he still does not do so, he is declared a liar and is given the lashes. If, after the accusation by *li'an,* the wife does not deny the charge, she is subject to the *hadd* punishment for *zina.*

Alcohol drinking (Shurb). Prohibition of drinking was established by Mohammed, who was scandalized by the drunkenness prevalent among Arabs of his time. He saw alcohol and gambling as agents of physical, social, moral, intellectual, and religious corruption.

The punishment for drunkenness is eighty lashes for a freeman, forty for a slave. It is not prescribed in the Koran but was established later by analogy from the punishment for the *kadhf*. The *Shafi'i* school limits the punishment to forty and twenty lashes, respectively. Besides proof by retractable confession, evidence can be given by two male adults who saw the accused drinking, smelled alcohol on his breath, and saw him in a state of drunkenness. The accused must have acted voluntarily and must be totally competent to stand trial.

Theft (Sariqa). Although the *hadd* punishment for theft is the amputation of a hand, there are severe limitations for applying it. To be declared guilty, the accused must be a competent adult and must have had the mental intention to steal. The act must have been by stealth; that is, the item must have been taken from a private residence or must have been under guard, and the thief must not have been an invited guest. For theft of items in shops, bazaars, or other public places, the Hanafi school does not apply the *hadd* penalty, whereas the Maliki school does. The *hadd* penalty is not applied to pickpockets nor to a thief who leaves a residence openly after stealing, unless he is trying to escape imminent apprehension. One is also not subject to the *hadd* penalty if one has not yet left the residence.

There is also a minimum value of stolen goods, which varies from one jurist to the other. If the thief stole different items, even in the same evening, at least one of these objects must be of the minimum value. If there were accomplices, the value of the items is divided among them but must then equal or exceed the required minimum value. The stolen item must be a legal one;

the theft of wine, for example, does not incur a *hadd* punishment. Since there is no intellectual property in Islamic law, books are not subject to theft, because it is presumed that the thief is not seeking the physical book but its contents. According to the Hanafi school, even the kidnapping of a child is exempt, because a free person cannot be owned. On the other hand, it is not considered theft if one takes something in which he has a part interest. Also excluded is taking property from one's husband, wife, or near relative; theft by a guest from his host or by a slave from his master; or even if one of the accomplices is an ascendant relative of the owner of the stolen property.

Except when the thief confesses, the charge must be brought by the owner of the stolen goods. If the accused is convicted, the owner must be present at the punishment or it will not be performed. If the thief returns the stolen objects before the charge is lodged, he cannot be accused. If someone steals out of need, he is considered not to have had the requisite mental intention to have committed the theft. If a charge of theft cannot be brought under the rules of *hadd* punishment, the offense is then reduced to a discretionary one (*ta'zir*) or to usurpation of another's property, which is only a civil offense. In the relatively unlikely circumstance that someone was convicted of the *hadd* offense for thievery, his right hand would be amputated and the wound cauterized. For another conviction of theft, his left foot would be amputated, then his left hand, and, finally his right foot.

Highway Robbery or Brigandage (Qat'al Tariq). This is considered an extremely serious offense, since it threatens the calm and stability of society itself. There are two kinds of such offenses: the robbery of travelers who are far from aid and armed entrance into a private house with intent to rob. Both Moslems and non-Moslems are protected from these offenses. The punishment is particularly severe: amputation of the right hand and the left foot and of the left hand and the right foot for a second similar offense. If murder also took place, the punishment is death by the sword. In cases of murder and actual theft, the penalty is crucifixion, and the body must hang for three days. Exile from the country may be added to the first mentioned punishments. Unlike the normal case of murder, where the relatives of the victim have a choice of retaliation, blood money, or pardon of the offender, here the death penalty is mandatory. All the accomplices are to be treated in the same way, but if one of them (a minor, for example) cannot be given the *hadd* punishment, neither can any of the others.

Apostasy from Islam. Renouncing Islam by word or deed, disbelieving in monotheism or worshiping other gods, rejecting the Islamic commandments, and making disparaging remarks against the Prophet, the angels, or the Koran are all acts that can damage the faith of others. Therefore, the just punishment for an apostate is execution, whereby the Islamic religion is protected. Some

Islamic schools hold that the apostate may be killed with impunity without a trial; others insist on a trial first. A male apostate is given three days to repent before execution; a female is imprisoned and beaten until she repents. For some schools, apostasy is a *hadd* offense; for others it is only a *siyasa*. Some modern Moslem jurists claim that the penalty for apostasy has no authority from the Koran or any other sources.

Attempted Coup d'État. The Shari'a does not decree penalties for the planning and preparation of a crime unless the preliminary steps, in themselves, constitute a *ta'zir* type of crime. Attempted coup d'état seems to be an exception to this general rule, but the opinions of jurists on this matter vary widely.

Discretionary Punishments (Ta'zir)

Ta'zir punishments are for offenses not punishable by *hudoud* or retaliation (*kisas*); they are determined by the competent secular authority. They are neither derived from customary Arabic law (which provided the basis for the laws of retaliation) nor based on the *hadd* crimes listed in the Koran, but they are meant to deal with new types of offenses without a definite text. Some *ta'zir* punishments were established by analogy from general or specific judgments made in the Koran and the sunnah; some are traced to the Prophet himself or to his successors. They developed during the Ummayyad dynasty and grew from the discretionary punishments imposed by the *qadis*. The lack of a Koranic base has tended to give judges more freedom to devise penalties appropriate to the crime.

Ta'zir punishments embrace almost all crimes mentioned in the Shari'a but give the judge extremely wide discretion for investigating the circumstances of the offense and applying the punishment. Offenses under *ta'zir* include perjury, usury, slander, and many similar others. Many offenses that escape the rigorous rules under the *hadd* punishments can be dealt with under *ta'zir*. For instance, only under *ta'zir* can a non-Moslem be protected from the *kadhf*. *Ta'zir* is therefore the most important area of classical Islamic criminal law, since it includes the bulk of criminal offenses. The flexibility of *ta'zir* has tended to inhibit the development of rigorous penal codes. Islamic states that do have such codes can be seen as less oriented toward *ta'zir*.

Sins that cannot be atoned for include kissing another man's wife or having sexual intercourse with her; eating prohibited things, such as blood or corpses; falsely accusing people of adultery; stealing even paltry objects; betraying people's faith; cheating while selling foodstuffs or garments; giving short weight or measure; giving false testimony; accepting bribes; and so on. All of these are subject to *ta'zir* punishments, depending on the gravity of the sin. Other sins are espionage by a Moslem in favor of a non-Moslem enemy, inducing people to contrivance and witchcraft, and so forth.

Ta'zir punishments were seen as having deterrent or rehabilitative objectives, and judges would try to achieve these objectives by varying punishments according to the circumstances of the case or of the convicted party. Consequently, acts of reparation and repentance are relevant to the judge's sentence. *Ta'zir* punishments also vary widely in severity: exhortation and counseling; private admonition (sometimes by letter); public reprimand and censure in court; publicizing and denunciation of the offender's guilt; a suspended sentence; banishment or exile; fine or confiscation; flogging; imprisonment; and for some offenses, such as espionage, even death. Defamation is punishable with eighty lashes, but cursing is not punishable at all. Some schools consider fines valid; others do not consider them legitimate under Islamic law. Of the four schools, all but the Maliki agree that no *ta'zir* punishment can exceed a *hadd* one, though this does not preclude the death penalty.

Anyone subject to a *ta'zir* punishment must be fully competent, but the standard of proof is less strict than in *hadd* cases: either a confession or the testimony of two witnesses is sufficient for conviction, and some jurists even allow one of them to be a woman. In *ta'zir* cases, confessions are not retractable; some jurists even consider that a judge may proceed on his own knowledge, without a confession or witnesses.

Talio (Kisas) or Blood Money (Diya)

In pre-Islamic Arabia, an attack against a member of a tribe was seen as an attack on the tribe itself; thus, blood feuds were common. Through arbitration, justice could sometimes be secured by retaliation against the specific offender or by the payment of blood money to the victim's tribesmen.

Islamic law treated homicide as an area between tort and crime and modified the traditional Arabian laws of homicide and bodily harm in three basic ways: blood feud was abolished; vengeance could be exacted only after a judicial authority had determined the guilt of the accused; and punishment was scaled according to the degree of culpability of the offender and the harm inflicted on the victim. Moslem scholars reject the contention that the talio increased the number of invalids within society, citing its deterrent effect; and they deny that the talio is pure revenge, since it requires the intervention of the *qadi*, who will prevent abuses.

In cases of proven homicide or bodily harm, Islamic law stipulates three kinds of punishments: retaliation, or talio; blood money; and penitence.

In cases of retaliation (*kisas*), the convicted offender is liable to the same harm suffered by the victim. In cases of homicide, the nearest kinsman of the victim performs the retaliation. When there is only bodily harm, the victim himself is entitled to perform the act of vengeance. The one holding the right of talio may forgive the offender; if not, he will have to follow certain rules: The victim must have been equal or superior to the attacker in terms of freedom and religion; and the offender must have been responsible for his act. If these conditions are absent, the talio is not allowed, and compensation must be arranged; some additional penalty may also be imposed. In no case, however, can a father be killed for murdering his child, though the child can receive the penalty for murdering his father. The same applies between masters and slaves; only the Hanafi school maintains that a freeman may be subjected to retaliation for killing another's slave. If the one having the right of retaliation is a minor or is insane, his guardian or the *qadi* should apply it; some scholars say it should be applied by the governor or his representative. If there are no living relatives of the victim, the right of retaliation falls to the state, which can execute the offender.

In cases of wounding, the victim must demand retaliation, but he has the option of asking someone else to do it, on condition that he be present. The talio should never harm anything other than the specified limb. When a talio on a limb produces death, some authors exculpate the performer of the talio; others believe that he must pay compensation to the family of the dead.

If the victim is a minor or is insane, a tutor who is not his relative cannot apply the talio in cases of homicide but may in cases of injuries, since the limbs are considered part of the property under his care. The favored procedure is to hand over the application of the retaliation to an official executioner.

If the guilty party dies before the talio can be inflicted on him, the case lapses entirely, according to some jurists; others believe that blood money has to be paid by his surviving relatives. If many persons participated in the murder, each and all of them can suffer retaliation.

Scholars also differ on the ways for applying the talio in cases of homicide. Some believe that decapitation by the sword should be applied in all cases; others insist that the punishment should take the same form in which the crime was committed.

In cases of bodily harm, the exact equivalent is inflicted on the perpetrator—a hand for a hand, a tooth for a tooth. However, in cases of loss of a nose or a penis—organs of which there is only one—there is no retaliation; only blood money is permitted as punishment. The Hanafi school does not permit retaliation for wounding between men and women or between slaves. The Maliki school asks that experts inflict all punishments, since any excess is punishable by a *ta'zir* punishment.

The talio must affect only the culprit. If it has to be applied to a pregnant woman, it will be done only after the child has been born and suckled. If someone inflicts the talio before the proper judicial procedure has been completed, he is subject to a *ta'zir* punishment; and if he kills without any legal title, he himself is subject to retaliation.

As already mentioned, the talio is excluded if the offender dies before it can be applied or has been pardoned by the victim. To pardon, however, a few conditions must be satisfied. The pardoning side has to be a senior person and must be entitled to the right of talio. Also, some jurists hold that, in cases of homicide, pardon can be granted only by unanimous consent of the victim's kinsmen. Pardon may be given on the basis of compensation or without it.

The second form of punishment, blood money (*diya*), is an option for the nearest relative of a slain or wounded victim. The traditional *diya,* taken from Arabian customs, can be set at two levels: the heavier one (100 female camels, equally divided among one-, two-, three- and four-year-olds) for more serious cases, and a lighter one (eighty female camels, similarly divided by age, plus twenty one-year-old male camels) for the less serious. The *diya* is paid by the near relatives of the offender to the heirs of the deceased or to the wounded victim. If relatives cannot be found, the state pays it. The full *diya* is due only when the victim is a free male Moslem. If he is a *diami* (a non-Moslem protected by a treaty) or a *musta'min* (a non-Moslem under a safe-conduct pass), the *diya* ranges from a third to a half of that for a Moslem, though here the Hanafi school requires full payment. The *diya* for a woman is half that for a man; the *diya* for a murdered slave is his market value.

The *diya* for bodily injury is a proportion of the payment for loss of life. If the injury is to an organ of which there is only one, the *diya* is the same as for loss of life; if it is to an organ of which there is more than one, the *diya* is proportionately smaller: half for an arm, leg, or eye; one-tenth for a finger; one-thirtieth for each joint of a finger; and one-twentieth for a tooth. If an injury is not one of the fixed examples, compensation is paid on the basis of a formula called "actual harm suffered." The *diya* for a woman in cases of injury is less than that for a man, but in no case is less than one-third of what a man would receive.

The third form of punishment, penitence (*kaffara*) is never the only one required; it is always attached to certain kinds of *diya*. An act of penitence can consist of freeing a Moslem slave or, if there are none, of fasting for two consecutive months during daylight hours.

Before we consider the next category of offenses, it is important to note that most Islamic schools distinguish three types of homicide, though the Hanafi school adds another two. The first type is willful homicide—an action taken with no legal excuse, with the intention to kill or wound by means of an instrument that normally causes death. Only in exceptional cases may the talio be substituted by the heavier *diya*, plus, according to most scholars, loss by the offender of any inheritance from the deceased. The Maliki school requires proof of intent and actual causality, similar to modern Western codes. Some schools accept as willful homicide a death resulting from intentional false testimony during a trial or from intentional withholding of food and water. Death caused by repeated blows, even if no one of them would normally cause death, is also considered willful homicide. And, of course, homicide due to highway robbery is a *hadd* offense and is punished by execution.

In quasi-willful homicide, there is an intent to kill or wound with an instrument not normally known to be fatal. If death results, the punishment is the heavier *diya,* acts of penitence, and loss of inheritance rights. If only bodily harm results, the offense is considered willful wounding, and the punishment is retaliation or, if remitted, *diya.* The Maliki school does not recognize this category, claiming that if death results with the above-mentioned instrument, it should be considered a case of willful homicide.

Accidental homicide occurs when the offender has no intent to kill or did intend to kill but believed that he was acting legally—for example, if one shoots at an animal but hits a person; or believes that one is shooting an animal but shoots a human being; or, during wartime, kills a Moslem believing that he is a non-Moslem; or intends to kill a specific person but kills another by mistake. The punishment is the payment of the lighter *diya,* the performance of acts of penitence, and the loss of inheritance.

The first category added by the Hanafi school is quasi-accidental homicide, in which there is neither intent to harm nor a deadly instrument, as when a sleeping person falls out of a treehouse and kills someone below. The penalty is the same as for accidental homicide. The second addition is indirect homicide, in which some instrument not directly controlled by the killer causes the death of the victim, as when someone falls into a pit dug by the guilty party and dies. Here the penalty is the lighter *diya* or its proper proportion in cases of bodily injury.

In a number of instances, homicide is seen as excusable. There is no culpability if a man kills (or harms) his wife, daughter, or sister if he discovers her in actual intercourse with a lover; he may also kill the lover. The same is true if death or harm is inflicted with the consent of the victim, though the Maliki school contests this. Self-defense is permitted if it is proportionate to the danger, and preemptive action is allowed to forestall an imminent attack. The Hanafi school indicates the heavier *diya* if one uses a deadly weapon to kill a minor or insane person in self-defense. Killing combatants in lawful war is permitted and, in many cases, obligatory. One is also permitted to kill male non-Moslems who refuse to pay the obligatory poll tax or who refuse to convert to Islam.

In conclusion, according to Moslem law, the talio is the most pious and correct of penalties, since everything done by a person to another will revert to the former, so that the one who hurts is hurting himself. Thus, both justice and deterrence are achieved.

Discretionary Administrative Penalties (Siyasa)

Under Islamic law, the secular authorities cannot legislate independently from the Shari'a, but the state may enact and enforce administrative regulations to help fill gaps left by the Shari'a. *Siyasa* regulations are not supposed to conflict with the provisions of Shari'a, yet they have often, in effect, supplanted them.

From the early days, the Islamic states have modified the content and process of criminal law. Much of the ill-defined area of *ta'zir* punishments has been taken over by specific regulations and penalties. Moreover, much of the criminal jurisdiction of the *qadi* in the Shari'a courts has been transferred to secular courts that are staffed by imperial appointees. Even judges have been named by the secular authority; and Islamic jurists have explicitly recognized the right of a ruler to limit the jurisdiction of the *qadi* as much as he wishes. This does not mean, of course, that the Shari'a has not significantly influenced the content of the secular criminal law.

During the last two centuries, in fact, reform movements have taken the law even further from the Shari'a. Virtually every Islamic country has adopted a European-style criminal code, and the Shari'a courts have been abolished or restricted to cases involving personal status. Only in Saudi Arabia, Yemen, and Afghanistan have Shari'a courts with judicial power been maintained; but Pakistan, Sudan, and revolutionary Iran have made important moves toward reestablishing Islamic law. Also, in the Libya of Mu'ammar al-Qadafi, the reimposition of the *hadd* punishment has been proclaimed.

Acts of Penitence (kaffara)

Acts of *kaffara* include freeing a Moslem slave, fasting during daylight hours, abstaining from sexual intercourse, or giving alms to the poor. In rare cases, a goat, sheep, camel, or cow can be sacrificed. *Kaffara* is almost always voluntary; only in exceptional cases may a *qadi* require it. Offenses for which *kaffara* is prescribed include breaking an oath, perjury, breaking the fast during the holy month of Ramadan, or violating religious rules while in a consecrated state for the holy pilgrimage to Mecca.

The Shari'a in Contemporary Islamic States

Arab fundamentalists are pressing for a wider implementation of the Shari'a—the 1,300 year-old legal and personal code by which the Moslems are supposed to live. In the beginning, for a very short time, it seems to have been able to stop the bloodshed for which Arabia had always been known. Nowadays, Saudi Arabia, as well as Oman, the Yemen Republic, and other Arab states claim that ever since the implementation of the Shari'a in their respective countries, security has been established and everyone lives peacefully, without the slightest danger to life and property. It is true that since womenfolk are the living symbols of Arab family honor, sexual crimes, for which the penalty is execution by beheading, seem to be highly uncommon. Islamic law is the basis for capital and corporal punishments for many crimes against persons, property, and the state. Aside from imprisonment, the most visible criminal punishment in contemporary Saudi Arabia is flogging in public, carried out by a policeman wielding thick canes. Flogging, one or more times, may accompany prison sentences for "moral" crimes, such as drinking alcohol and slander. Beheadings—by sword—are not so uncommon as to be considered rare in Saudi Arabia today. They are carried out, by royal decree, after the midday prayers on Friday. They always attract large crowds; and when the head falls, the crowd indicates its approval by clapping. Foreigners in the vicinity are encouraged to watch the performance. Less severe but also less frequent in Saudi Arabia today is amputation of the right hand—also by sword—for theft. It is basically intended for the habitual thief, and there must be witnesses for each of his offenses.

The following examples of these punishments are worthy of mention. In 1975, the deranged assassin of King Faisal—his nephew, Prince Faisal ibn Musa'ad—was beheaded in Riyadh with a golden sword. Soon after, a son of King Abdul-Aziz, Prince Mishari, who in his youth in a drunken rage, had shot and killed a British expatriate in Jeddah, was found guilty of "accidental murder," since the real culprit was the liquor he had consumed.

On the seventh of Rabi al-Awal 1397 (February 25, 1977), Abdul-Aziz ibn Abdul-Rahman and Abdullah ibn Nazer were publicly beheaded for kidnapping and sexually assaulting a young boy. Five months later, a Saudi princess, the granddaughter of King Khaled's eldest brother, was executed by a firing squad in Jeddah as an adulteress. Her lover, a commoner, lost his head. The application of the sentence was insisted upon by the girl's grandfather, the oldest surviving son of Abdul-Aziz, the first Saudi monarch and a Moslem fundamentalist. King Khaled, though he disagreed, could not prevent his older brother's enforcement of the Shari'a. In September 1978, nine men were beheaded in Saudi Arabia: three were executed in Jawami, near Riyadh, for raping a girl; three in Mecca, for sexually assaulting and killing a boy; and three others in Taif, for killing a soldier who tried to arrest them after finding them having sexual intercourse in a tent during the holy month of Ramadan. Finally, in February 1979, three Saudi Arabian sailors were falsely charged with raping a hitchhiker and were discharged. Nevertheless, one of them, a married man, was terrified to return home because he might be buried in the sand to his chin and stoned to death. The two unmarried fellows could also be whipped with thirty lashes and put in jail for two years.

These executions and the methods employed underscore the ruthlessness of criminal justice in Saudi Arabia, the Holy Land of Islam, where punishments for crimes, as interpreted from the Koran, are designed to preserve and protect the social order that, it is claimed, has withstood the influences of more than thirteen centuries. The rationale is that there is permanence and therefore social stability in religiously inspired retribution. "In punishment there is life for you, Oh! people of understanding," says the Koran. Beheading in a place of public executions is reserved for the worst crimes of premeditated murder and rape, although what is described as "brigandage" may also result in capital punishment, including—theoretically, at least—crucifixion.

Punishments carried out in public have an additional and not insignificant deterrent effect. For the proud Saudis, the shame of public exposure would be a punishment quite as painful as the physical one. It is claimed that as a direct result, the Saudis are an unusually law-abiding people. Saudis are loath to release precise statistics on their criminal cases; nevertheless, although robberies do occur and the incidence of theft seems to have increased in recent years, such crimes occur nowhere near as often as they do in Europe and the United States. Hypocrisy—such as that in the case of Prince Mishari—is perhaps not so blatant nowadays in Saudi Arabia; nevertheless, although the *mutawarin* (elderly religious men who wield canes and patrol the streets to ensure that shopkeepers close promptly for prayers and that women are dressed modestly) are working, the homes of many princes and wealthy merchants are well stocked with liquors and other delights.

It is doubtful if Western expatriates (about 100,000 today in Saudi Arabia) would suffer the more extreme penalties imposed by the Shari'a, but several years ago, a young Briton received a fifteen year jail sentence for drug smuggling. Two other Britons were flogged in public for violating the prohibition against alcohol.

The average Saudi on the street or in the *suq* (market) appears to be generally in favor of the severe penalties, especially for such crimes as murder and rape. What does shock him is the prevalence of crime in the Western countries, particularly the frequency of thefts and robberies, financial swindles, and mugging—an incident inconceivable on the streets of Riyadh or Jeddah. And he tends to justify the harshness of penalties in his own country by mentioning the executions in the Western world. Some Western-educated Saudis explain that their country's punishments are now more humane, since those sentenced to lose a hand first receive a local anesthetic injection—and those to be beheaded do not need one.

In other countries that follow the Shari'a, the situation is no better. For instance, in November 1977, a nineteen-year old Arab, born in Baghdad, was executed in Abu-Dhabi for killing the United Arab Emirates' deputy foreign minister. He was beheaded at dawn on a Tuesday.

In September 1983, Sudan introduced the Islamic law and, by the end of that year, sent a delegation to Saudi Arabia, including an orthopedic surgeon, to learn judicial procedures and medical skills for amputating the hands of thieves. In the first nine months of Islamic law in Sudan, four convicts suffered two-limb amputations (right hand and left foot); ten more had their right hands cut off, and scores were publicly flogged. Sudan's new military ruler, General Abdul Rahman Swareddahab, has declared that the Shari'a will remain in force, but with certain unspecified revisions.

Meanwhile, in Iran, which also introduced the Shari'a in 1983, five thieves have had one hand chopped off and two adulterers have been stoned to death. During the last nine months of 1984, 160 people were flogged for such acts as fornication and 440 for burglary; and 19 murderers were executed after relatives of the victims insisted on the application of the talionic principle. In fifty-one other cases, the relatives decided to accept blood money instead. Recently, the invention of an electric guillotine was announced for chopping off the hands of thieves.

Concluding Remarks

Perhaps we have failed to modify our retributive notions because they are still linked to comparable biblical and medieval times, when Judaism and Christianity were more significant as religious exhortations than as criminal law. Punishments were the exception rather than the rule; judging was an extremely cautious affair; forgiveness was considered a virtue; and strict adherence to procedure resulted in few condemnations and sanctions. Until the time of the Industrial Revolution, the crimes most often punished were those against God, religious institutions, or the monarch. Today all this belongs to ancient history more than to present realities. This is not so in Dar al-Islam, as has been shown. Nevertheless, politicians and scholars from Saudi Arabia are continuously praising the Shari'a in the most superlative terms. At a symposium in Riyadh in October 1976, Sheikh Mohammad ibn Ibrahim ibn Jubeir, the president of the court of appeal, said: "Corruption, immorality, decay and crime are common features in most of the so-called civilized societies. Islam is different from this false civilization, and has strived to attain justice, security and real happiness for mankind. Thanks to the divine Islamic legislation that such a glorious civilization was possible." He ended his speech by saying that "Islamic legislation is sublime, perfect and universal. In the Koran there is a solution for every problem no matter how insoluble it may seem to be." On the other hand, His Royal Highness Prince Naif bin Abdul Aziz, minister of the interior in Saudi Arabia, said in his opening statement: "The Islamic legislation, in itself, is complete and whole, with all the fundaments of justice. It covers all aspects of life and behavior. The blame for any flaw in its implementation should be put not on the divine legislation, but on those who implement it." And, if all this may seem exaggerated, Sheikh Saleh ibn Mohammad al-Laheidan, member of the Council of the Supreme Court of Saudi Arabia, declared: "One of the distinctive features of Islamic Law is its ability to solve all the problems of Mankind." No more and no less!

11

The Fetha Nagast: The Law of the Kings (Ethiopia)

> Beset on all sides by foes, the Abyssinians slept for a thousand years, forgetful of the world by which they were forgotten.
>
> —Edward Gibbon

African Background

Ethiopia, the land of the Lion of Judah and the Queen of Sheba, the land of revolution and starving masses, was—for many centuries and like the rest of Africa and its people—considered mysterious and even perverse by the rest of the world. Generations of traders came looking for Africa's gold and ivory, but the continent itself remained a puzzle. Europeans looked upon the people of Africa as savage monsters, and only in this century has this naive conception receded and scholarly interest emerged. Today, Africa is no longer seen as a land of savagery and chaos but is known as a continent with a long and lively history that includes many rich cultures and civilizations.

Moreover, it now seems that Africa may have been the birthplace of mankind. Recent evidence from fossil skulls and bone fragments found at the Olduvai Gorge site, in Tanzania, suggests that man's most remote ancestors inhabited certain regions of eastern Africa almost two million years ago. From about a million years ago to the past 60,000 years, when man first began to use fire, human groups seem to have spread through the greater part of Africa. From 5500 to 2500 B.C., the climate went from dry to wet, transforming the present Sahara Desert into a well-watered prairie where many generations of hunters—later, farmers and herdsmen as well—flourished, leaving behind them the evidence of hundreds of magnificent rock paintings.

Then, about 4,000 years ago, the climate changed again: The grass gave way to scrub and sand, and the forests died. Fish and game disappeared, and the people dispersed in three main directions. Some went north into the Mediterranean coastlands, where they merged with the local people to form the Berber culture; others settled in the fertile lands along the Nile, contributing to the development of Pharaonic Egypt; and still others went slowly southward into the heart of the continent, presumably merging with indigenous populations whose origins are unknown. (Bushmen and Pygmies seem to have been in Africa since earliest times, but the ancestors of the modern Negro apparently emerged much later.)

Those who migrated south into sub-Saharan Africa settled in a land that was isolated and inhospitable to man, marked by climatic and topographic extremes. Yet the Africans were able to develop crops and raise cattle; and they learned to extract metals, refine them, and use them in their iron spears. Roaming across the continent, the migrants soon dominated all of central and southern Africa. They ousted the Bushmen and the Pygmies and provided the continent with a family of related languages, the Bantu, still spoken by most sub-Saharan Africans today. Thus, they created a diversified culture, and some of their societies had standards of living—in terms of food, personal safety, and freedom—similar to those of Europe at the time. In matters of social welfare related to widows and orphaned children, in fact, they were even more sophisticated. If Africa was generally behind Europe in technical knowledge, it was far from a primeval wilderness.

During the last fifty years, with colonialism drawing to a close, scholars have looked into African history and have found treasures there. These include the ancient high civilizations of the Nile; the Kush Empire, the oldest and greatest of inland Africa, which even challenged Egypt and was a precursor of modern Ethiopia; mysterious Zimbabwe, whose massive stone walls enclosed the temple-homes of divine rulers; Kilwa, an island fortress off the coast of Tanganyika, whose bustling port had trading contacts with faraway India and China; Songhai, whose powerful kings encouraged scholarship as well as commerce; Timbuktu, of the kingdom of Mali in western Sudan, the fabled city of wisdom, whose scholars were maintained at the king's cost and were taught at the city's university; and Ashanti and Benin, with their great religious sculptors. But the exalted achievements of Africa rested on a foundation of modest but impressive village life, characterized by egalitarian structure, rules for moral and social behavior, and spiritual beliefs.

Ethiopia: General Introduction

Ethiopia is located in the Horn of Africa. It is bounded on the east by Somalia and the former French territory of Afars and Issas (formerly French Somaliland), on the south by Kenya, on the west by Sudan, and in the north by Eritrea, the Red Sea, and Sudan. The country consists of highlands and plateaus, some of them over 7,500 feet high, as well as low-lying areas and deep valleys, such as the Rift Valley, which runs across the country from southwest to northeast. The central Ethiopian plateau has a temperate climate, but the Rift Valley areas are very hot and humid.

Much of Ethiopia's history is still shrouded in myth and legend, but we know that in the second millenium B.C., it was dominated by the Egyptian

Empire and was known as Kush, its people as Kushites. (*Kushi* is still the Hebrew word for Negro.) The Bible relates how, in the tenth century B.C., the Queen of Sheba visited King Solomon in Jerusalem, an event that also figures in Ethiopian tradition, in which the queen is referred to as Makeda. By this time, the Egyptian domination of Kush had come to an end, and the Kushites were ruled for a time by a line of native kings.

Between 750 and 500 B.C., tribes of Sabaeans—Semites from Southern Arabia—migrated to the area and imposed their more developed culture and language on the Kushites. From one of these tribes, the Habeshat, derives the name Habash, or Abyssinia. Another tribe, the Agazi, gave its name to Ge'ez, one of the oldest languages of Ethiopia. By the second century B.C., Ethiopia was ruled by a dynasty of Arabian origin, who called themselves the Negus-Nagast, or "King of Kings." The seat of this dynasty was at Axum, an Ethiopian city founded almost a millenium earlier by the first of the native Ethiopian emperors.

An interesting feature of Axum was its great stone monoliths, or stelae—a kind of obelisk or pyramid—probably for the worship of the sun and the moon. They were narrow and up to thirty meters high, with decorations in the form of windows, one above the other—an ancient architectural style still used in the churches of northern Ethiopia.

As Greece's power grew, it began to trade with Ethiopia and to influence it culturally as well. Thus, in the beginning of the Christian era, both Greek and Sabaean were spoken in Ethiopia. By the third century A.D., there were texts written in Ethiopic or Ge'ez, the local language, and by the sixth century, Greek and Sabaean were no longer used. Early Ge'ez was written in South Arabian characters; later, it developed its own special script. Eventually, Ge'ez, too, fell into disuse. By the twelfth century, it was no longer spoken and was replaced by Amharic, which rapidly developed into the official language of Ethiopia. Yet classical Ethiopian literature, as well as the Bible and other prayer books, are still printed and studied in Ge'ez.

Ethiopia is the only country, apart from Israel and the Arab states, where a Semitic language is the official one. Amharic is the language of the dominant political ethnic group there, the Amhara, and the rulers are now interested in using it for all modern needs. The language is now undergoing a process of modernization. There are six Semitic languages in Ethiopia: five spoken ones, including Amharic and Tigrinya—the second most common Ethiopian language, spoken by about 20 percent of the population, mainly in the north of the country—and one, Ge'ez, used only for prayer. The five spoken languages—which arrived in Ethiopia with the migration of Semitic peoples to Africa from southern Arabia about 2,500 years ago—share a common alphabet.

In the fourth century, Ethiopia converted to Christianity when one of its kings, Ezana, converted under the influence of two Christian advisers of

Syrian origin, originally foundlings. To this day, the majority of Ethiopians belong to the Monophysite or Ethiopian Orthodox Church. Thus, when, with Moslem expansion in the seventh century, the country was cut off from the sea, it became a totally isolated Christian kingdom, dependent on its own agriculture for subsistence. Because of this Moslem expansion, the capital had to be moved from Axum and was later established in Addis Ababa.

European knowledge of Ethiopia bagan late. It was not until the twelfth century, when rumors began to circulate in Europe about a wise Christian emperor named Prester John, somewhere on the route to "India," that the Western world became intrigued by Ethiopia. This fantasy may have been conceived by the Crusaders, who were looking for an ally to fight the Moslems. During the thirteenth century, Latin monks tried to penetrate the area, but there is no evidence of any success. Venetian merchants were more successful; from the end of the fourteenth century, their records mention real Ethiopian place names. From 1431 onward, the papacy tried to establish a link with the Ethiopian emperor—through Abyssinian monks in Jerusalem—with the hope of forging an alliance to expel the Moslems from Egypt. Later, Franciscan monks finally reached Ethiopia and were able to engage the Negus (Ethiopian king) in fighting, together with the papacy, against the sultan of Cairo. And in 1493, Portugal sent its first ambassador to Ethiopia. In 1509, the Portuguese King Manuel I sent a small expedition to Ethiopia that included organists, artists, a typographer, and the chaplain Francisco Alvarez; it was Alvarez who, in 1540, published the famous *Authentic Report of the Lands of Prester John,* giving Portugal and Europe the first real account of Ethiopia. After that, the interest in Ethiopia spread rapidly, and in 1541 Portugal even sent an army to help the Negus Gelawdeus (known as Claudius in the West) in a war against the Turks and Moslems, which the Ethiopians and Portuguese eventually won.

Meanwhile, the papacy tried to convert Ethiopia to Catholicism, and Jesuit missions were sent there until, in 1633, the Negus Fasiladas prohibited any more such efforts. Still, the writings of some of the Jesuits provided further information about Ethiopia. Of course, the many ancient traditions about the country, such as that the Negus was a descendant of King Solomon and the Queen of Sheba, lived on and seemed corroborated by the fact that Ethiopia itself retained many customs dating from biblical times.

After the Jesuits left Ethiopia, almost 150 years passed before other European travelers came to the country. One of the most important of them was the Scotsman James Bruce, who reached Gondar in 1769 and discovered the source of the Blue Nile in Lake Tana. He also described in detail the monuments of Axum. In the early nineteenth century, European explorers, missionaries, ambassadors, and merchants once again began coming to this exotic land, among them the explorer Henry Salt, who in 1805 studied the ruins of Axum and finally recognized the Sabaean inscriptions there, recording them with great accuracy. After that, true scientific study of Ethiopia began.

The European efforts to colonize Africa in the nineteenth century brought Ethiopians into conflict with Italy. Under the Negus Melenik II, Ethiopia defeated the Italian army at the famous battle of Adua in 1896. Ethiopia was then recognized as a sovereign state and underwent a degree of modernization. Later came the Ethiopian–Italian war of 1936–40, during which the Italians occupied Ethiopia, the only parenthesis in the long Ethiopian history of independence.

With about 25 million inhabitants, Ethiopia is today one of the most densely populated countries of Africa. Along with the majority Monophysite or Coptic Christians, there is a Moslem minority of about 35 percent as well as small communities of pagans and of Jews (most of the latter have now emigrated to or been rescued by Israel). Since Mengistu Haile Mariam wrested control from the last emperor, Haile Selassie I, in 1974, reliable information about Ethiopia has been scant; but it is clear that the still mainly peasant population has undergone severe material hardship.

Origin and Basic Structure of the Fetha Nagast

Until the promulgation of the Ethiopian Penal Code of 1930, the country had no unified or codified legal system. The main sources were Moslem law for the Islamic population and customary law for the pagans—and for the Christians, the Fetha Nagast, the "laws of the kings."

There are conflicting claims concerning the Fetha Nagast's origin. Some believe that it was first compiled and written in Arabic by an Egyptian Coptic churchman of the thirteenth century. Others maintain that it was originally written in Greek, then translated into Arabic and finally into Ge'ez. Another tradition, which enhanced its prestige, held that its real author were the 318 Fathers of Nicaea, an ancient Byzantine city where ecumenical councils were held.

At any rate, if there was a Greek original, it is not extant today. The Arabic version, known as the Nomocanon of Ibn al-'Assal, is regarded as very authoritative by the Coptic Church of Egypt. As for the Ge'ez text, it shows a good deal of disparity from the Arabic version. In 1968, an English translation from the Ge'ez was published.

The first recorded use of the Fetha Nagast in Ethiopia dates from the reign of Sarsa Dengel (1563–97); before that, Mosaic, Christian, and customary sources were used. Rather than a working code for the adjudication of court cases, the Fetha Nagast served as an embellishment of de facto decisions, giving the judge authority by virtue of his almost ritual reference to it. Because it contained, like many other ancient law codes, both religious and secular elements, it was venerated and utilized by both church and government. It did not entirely overthrow the customary legal system of the country and was never applied in toto, but its influence was great.

Thus, the legislators who prepared the 1930 penal code stressed that their work was a mere "revision" of the Fetha Nagast, thereby legitimating the new code. The Fetha Nagast has continued to be referred to as an authoritative source in Ethiopian courts.

The Fetha Nagast has two main sections. The first deals entirely with religious matters and is based primarily on the Old and New Testaments as well as the canons and proceedings of the Councils of Nicaea and Antioch. The second, although it has a few chapters on religious matters, deals mainly with secular matters; it is based somewhat on the aforementioned sources but for the most part on a collection of laws called the Canons of the King, which combines Roman, Islamic, Christian, and Jewish elements. Only penal and criminological subjects will be dealth with here.

Rules of Litigation

It should be noted, first, that peaceful settlements were strongly encouraged in Ethiopia as a way of avoiding litigation. It was a generally recognized duty for any disinterested person to accept the role of reconciler, even if asked to do so by strangers. If he was successful in resolving the issue, he took the disputants, at their request, to the nearest, lowest-ranking judge to report the matter.

There were three types of peaceful settlements: by admission, by denial, or by keeping silent, whereby one does not admit or deny the accusation. In all these cases, arbitrators had to be present. In admission, the debtor admitted his debt but, in turn, claimed a pledge he had given the creditor, who did not want to return it. The arbitrators settled the case by inviting the debtor to pay his debt and the creditor to give back the pledge. The second type, denial, could occur when the creditor accused, claiming his credit, and the accused denied. The arbitrators then asked the debtor, who admitted the debt but, in turn, accused the creditor of having wronged him. The matter was settled by inviting the debtor to pay the debt and the creditor to give due satisfaction for the wrong he did to the debtor. In the third case, keeping silent, the debtor, asked by the arbitrators, admitted the debt but declared that he was unable to pay it. The arbitrators could settle the situation by asking the creditor not to be paid immediately and the debtor to pay at a future, agreed time.

If a claim for an object was to be settled by giving the claimant another object, it was done as in buying and selling; that is, the purchaser gave the money to the seller, and the seller gave the object to the claimant. If the settlement concerned an object that was hired to yield profit, it was done in accordance with the contract between the two parties. Every kind of settlement was allowed, provided that no usury was involved, as when, for instance, one party binds himself to give thirty, after a period of time, to discharge a debt of twenty. But when a given measure of old grain was due when the newly harvested grain had been collected, it was indeed permitted to give the new grain instead of the old.

A transaction regarding a debt before the time fell due was equivalent to the sale of the debt, and a transaction involving the payment of a portion of the debt—due in its kind and at a fixed time—was tantamount to forgiving the remainder of the original debt.

Judges

The rules concerning judges and witnesses—those produced by the litigants or the judges who assisted the king during lawsuits heard in his presence—were taken from the laws thought of as "roots" (i.e., the Old Testament) and "branches" (i.e., the New Testament) and from the collection of appendices arrived at "through perfect reasoning"—probably alluding to the glosses and analogies deduced from the basic laws.

Persons eligible to be judges included the highest priest—that is, the patriarch or bishop—and priests ranking just below him. The appointment of a judge was required by law (Deut. 16: 18, 19)—"In all your cities you shall appoint judges who may deliver just judgments, without yielding to either party or making distinctions between person and person, nor accept bribes, because bribes blind the eyes of the wise and they cannot see justice"—and by nature (because in all communities disputes inevitably arise that cannot be settled without judges).

Thirteen provisions for the appointment of priests and archpriests also applied to judges:

1. A judge must be a man who has attained virility (the requirement of being a male was based on the Apostles' statement that man is "the master of women"—that is, more intelligent and capable).

2. He must have intelligence and knowledge.

3. He must be an Orthodox Christian and a priest conversant with his duties.

4. He must be fair—that is, wise, irreproachable, impartial, mild, and patient.

5. He must be a freeman.

6. He must have sound hearing and sight.

7. He must be able to speak clearly and know the languages used in his jurisdiction.

8. He must be free of any illnesses, especially contagious ones, such as leprosy.

9. He must know the law and the rules of procedure in the "roots" and the "branches" and be able to draw analogies in order to connect the "branches" to the "roots" from which they sprouted.

10. The superior judge who appoints another must learn whether he meets these requirements.

11. The new judge must be duly appointed by a written document, and it must be announced to the people.

12. Once he has received the document, the new judge must accept the appointment and manifest this either in word or by beginning to perform the functions of a judge.

13. All those who are under his jurisdiction or the greater part of them shall not be prevented from coming to him, nor shall they oppose his appointment.

If the jurisdiction of a judge is general, he has the power to rule on seven different matters:

1. He may settle disputes either amicably, upon the parties' agreement, or by force, striking fear into them.

2. He may return property to its owners when their title of property has been proved by the confession of the accused or by the testimony of witnesses.

3. He may appoint a guardian for someone who is incapable of administering his property.

4. He must care for the proper administration of charitable legacies, and supervise the affairs of orphans and those under guardianship.

5. He may execute a will.

6. He may appoint a deputy judge if he is too busy himself.

7. He must know the witnesses well to be assured for their integrity.

A judge began to discharge his function by showing the document of his appointment, which he read to the public. He had to be calm and humble, and he was not to judge under the influence of anything that might agitate his mind, such as anger or fear, grief or joy, hunger or thirst, sickness or evil, sleep, drowsiness, laziness, and weakness. Nor could he judge while he was drunk or light-headed or while he was disgusted and annoyed because of the strain of overwork.

He could not judge cases involving himself or his parents, grandparents, sons, grandsons, brothers, or wife. He could do so if they consented to it, but even then it was preferable that he refuse. They could bring their cases before his deputy, and the judge could not testify for either party. He also was not to give a decision either for or against an enemy. Neither could he be a witness against an enemy, because although judicial decisions were public, the testimony was given in secret. In fact, if he delivered a sentence against an enemy, an appeal could be taken to another judge; but if he testified against him, it was not possible to know whether his testimony was true or false, because that was a secret hidden within his conscience.

The cases of those who were in prison were to be reported to him, and he was to free those who, in his opinion, must be free and keep in prison those who he believed should not be released, as well as those who, on the strength of their own confessions or witnesses' testimony, should not be set free.

The court or tribunal was simple and sober. A pure and clean seat was prepared for the judges; they could not sit in the church or the sanctuary to administer justice. No loud quarrels could take place in court. A little behind the seat occupied by the Afa-Negus (the king's spokesman) sat the reader of the Fetha Nagast and other learned men, with their lecterns before them. When the Fetha Nagast was brought into the court, all present would stand up. Scholars might sit with the judge so that he could consult them, when difficult questions arose.

Witnesses

As stated in the Holy Scriptures: "Every question has to be settled by the voice of two or three witnesses" (Deut. 13:15). The Fetha Nagast's eligibility requirements for witnesses, based on the "roots" and "branches," involve competence, mental balance, and moral uprightness. What was expected from witnesses was the true word; therefore, those whose veracity was not perfect were to be prohibited from testifying.

Anyone who was below twenty years of age or under guardianship; deaf or dumb; a buffon or one who dissipates his property; a poor person or a slave; condemned as a fornicator; or under another authority that could punish him, such as a soldier, could not testify as a witness. Others in the same situation were those who kept a concubine or drank, committed little or big sins, played draughts or chess on the streets, ate in the market or other public places, disguised themselves as priests, tatooed themselves, dressed as a soldier, or wore turbans.

If there were no witnesses, an oath was sufficient or necessary; but when witnesses were available, few oaths were taken. The number of witnesses had to be at least two or three; for greater certainty, the number could be increased. The testimony of only one witness was never accepted. Five witnesses were necessary for the making of a contract of loan, and five or seven were needed for drawing up of a will. A man could not testify on his own behalf nor for his kinsman, slave, partner (in matters concerning their partnership), or one named in his will, unless the one against whom he testified gave his consent or unless the witness was equally related to the accuser and the accused. Never could the testimony of heretics against a bishop be accepted, nor could the testimony of only one other bishop be accepted against him. One who was a witness in the preparation of an invalid will—such as one in which the testator makes it invalid—and was not willing to testify when requested to do so, did not have to be a witness so long as the testator did not render the will valid.

The testimony of persons who were "passing by," or the like, was not valid in any respect; for instance: "I was working near A and I heard another person say that he had taken from B such and such a thing." Never was testimony given under duress valid until the witnesses were identified, the matter inquired into, and the facts ascertained.

If someone bore witness against another so that the latter would be deposed from his rank or punished, and it was later discovered that the witness testifed falsely, he was condemned to the same punishment to which the person against whom he testified was condemned. One could not be a witness regarding testimony given by another unless the first witness said to the second one: "Be a witness to my testimony, which is as follows. . . ." If the witnesses withdrew their testimony before the judge during the proceedings, the proceedings were rendered void, but if they withdrew after the proceedings had ended, the judgment was not annulled.

These and many other provisions regarding witnesses were meant to ensure the proper workings of justice.

Confessions

If a man who was free and independent and had attained majority confessed his fault sincerely, he did not receive the penalty. But if a person was under guardianship because he was a minor or insane, his confession was not valid unless the accuser could produce witnesses to prove that he had attained majority or had the use of reason. If, however, a person was under guardianship for other reasons, such as physical incapability, his confession was valid.

A debtor who confessed his debt had to pay it—even if he was already in debt at the time. In this case, he was to pay the second debt after he had paid the first one. A slave's admission of a money debt was valid. If he was not authorized by his master to contract the debt, he had to pay it after his manumission. But if he was authorized by him, his master had to pay the debt.

Taking oaths in the name of God during lawsuits was considered essential, though they were to be avoided if one could pay his money debt or settle a situation through reconciliation or arbitration. What was important was not to swear in the name of God for trifles or without the presence of a judge or an accuser—and especially not to swear falsely. If one ordered to take an oath had sworn by putting his hand on the Gospel and his lie was then discovered, he was to be punished by cutting his tongue. The oath given with due care refers either to the past—"I swear on God that I did (did not) . . ."— or to the future—"God knows that I shall (shall not) . . ." One was not, however, to keep an oath regarding the future if it enjoined doing a prohibited thing; one who did so was to be punished. A minor or one who had lost his reason could not be required to take an oath.

Coercion and Duress

Compelling a man to deny his faith was absolutely prohibited. If such a man was killed, he was called a martyr; if he endured pain but was spared, he was called a faithful witness. Conversely, if a man is under compulsion, even including the threat of death, to transgress the law or to do evil actions, such as killing or fornication, he must not yield.

If one who used duress to take something from another was a rich man, he had to pay four or five times the value of what he took, as stated in the Mosaic law (Exod. 22). If he was unable to pay such an amount, he payed double. Failing this, the entire stolen object was taken from him; if it could not be found, he was to replace it with a similar one of the same value.

Procedure and Judgments

In addition to the procedural principles for court sessions mentioned earlier, the Fetha Nagast gives more detailed provisions.

Decisions could not be delivered on Sunday, the day of rest. Judicial matters were to be settled starting on Mondays; during the week, the reconciliation of the litigants was to be achieved.

Both litigants had to stand together before the judge at the center of the court. The accuser had to produce witnesses to prove his point, and the accused had to take the oath. Only the actual owner of an allegedly stolen object could make the accusation; and the accused had to have the object in his possession. If both parties appeared as accusers, the one who brought the charge first had priority; when he had finished with his charge, the other accuser was heard.

If the accused admitted the charge, the judge declared him the debtor; then, if the accuser claimed his property, the judge decided in his favor and against the debtor. However, if the accused denied the charge, the judge asked the accuser if he had witnesses; if the accuser said no, the judge then asked the accused if he was ready to swear. If the accused declined to swear, the object was restored to the accuser. If, on the other hand, the accuser said, "I have reliable witnesses," the accused was not obliged to swear until the accuser produced them.

If the accused kept silent, neither admitting nor denying the charge, the judge was to say to him: "Answer! Otherwise you must take an oath or produce a guarantor for the object you are accused of having." If the accused then claimed to have witnesses to prove that he was not guilty, he was given time to produce them. If these witnesses then disagreed among themselves, the judge decided on the basis of the predominant testimony (e.g., two witnesses out of three agreeing); if the witnesses were evenly divided, new ones had to be added. Whatever the case, the oath of the one in possession of the object was to be accepted, unless his adversary could produce witnesses to testify that he had committed perjury. If someone dared to accused a woman who was inexperienced in litigation and did not travel for buying or trading, she was not compelled to appear in court and she could appoint someone to represent her. If she had to take an oath, the judge could send a righteous person to her to take her oath.

The judge had to write a special text about his judgment for submission to a superior judge, bearing the testimony of two or more witnesses in favor of the decision. The superior judge then examined it for its correctness and, if he accepted the witnesses' testimony, confirmed the judgment.

A Christian could never go to a pagan magistrate nor to a magistrate of heretics, so as not to let pagans or heretics know anything of the disputes that occurred among Christians. A case involving priests could be brought only before the bishop or the archpriests, never to a lay judge.

Crimes and Punishments

Homicide

Homicide belongs to the category of great sins and calls for the killing of the perpetrator in turn, unless the kinsmen of the victim have mercy on him, in which case he must do a perpetual penance, to be reduced only if he shows that he merits further forgiveness by turning to God. Execution can be carried out by the blood-avenger, but only after producing the offender in the courtroom and with the testimony of three witnesses. One who falsely accuses another of murder should himself be adjudged and punished as a murderer, since he had full intent to kill. If a murderer is not discovered, he will receive the spiritual punishment of the highest priest or bishop—a total excommunication, which denies him any salvation from eternal punishment in the next world.

Some categories of offenders are spared punishment, such as those who lack the use of reason or are minors under seven years old. The drunkard is considered to have lost his reason, but since, unlike the insane or the feeble-minded, he lost it of his own will, he is given the punishment for "unintentional" homicide—exile. The habitual drunkard must be put to death if he commits homicide more than once, the more so if he had killed before in a state of drunkenness or there was a quarrel between him and the victim.

Whoever is forced to kill by one who has real power over him, such as a judge, is not held responsible; the punishment is due, instead, to the one who gave the order. But if the one who obeyed used treachery—such as poison, sorcery, or fire—both he and whoever provided him such implements are punished in the same way.

If a thief is caught breaking into a house and is beaten and dies, there is no punishment for his killer; however, if the sun was up, the killer must be put to death (taken from Exod. 22:2). Still, anyone has a right to kill the thief if he cannot otherwise avoid suffering harm himself; the same holds for someone who breaks into a house at night intending to commit bodily harm. Enemies who fight face to face, such as in a duel, shall be punished with the sword. One who catches another sinning with his wife and kills him is not punished as a murderer. Or if one suspects a man of staining the purity of his wife, makes him aware of his suspicions three times, and sends someone to admonish him about it in the presence of witnesses, and then finds the man speaking with his wife in his or her house, a tavern, a goldsmith's, or in the fields, despite his warnings, he is not held responsible for killing him at that point. However, if he finds him speaking to his wife in some other place or in a church, the culprit has to be brought before a judge as a fornicator.

If a man beats a slave with a stick and death ensues, he incurs the full punishment; but if the victim lies for a day or two, he goes unpunished, since the slave is his property. If he has killed him with poison or burned him with fire, he must be treated as a murderer. If a slave commits an offense deserving the death penalty, his master must bring him before a judge; if the master himself kills him, he receives the death penalty.

A father must not die for his son's guilt nor a son for his father's (Deut. 24:16). But whoever kills a close relative must be delivered to the judge for punishment.

Whoever intends to kill a certain person but kills another by mistake is judged as if he had killed the one he intended to kill. If there is any doubt as to whether he intended to kill a particular person, he is judged as one who killed unintentionally.

If someone hits another with an instrument that causes death, such as a sword or stone, without intending to kill him but does indeed kill him, he is himself killed with the same kind of instrument. But if the victim does not die, the hand of the striker is cut off. Whoever beats a man to death must be killed; if he seeks refuge at the altar, the Fetha Nagast says to "tear him away from it and kill him." But if a man kills another accidentally, as in a brawl in which he mistakenly strikes someone he did not intend to strike, he may be pardoned if he takes refuge in the house of God.

One who kills another in a hunting accident is given the sentence corresponding to an unintentional murder. A similar sentence is given one who has a leaning wall or ill-tempered slaves or beasts and does not warn people sufficiently so that someone is killed. (The Sumerian and the Hammurabi codes, as well as the Pentateuch, have similar provisions.)

One who imprisons another person deliberately, prevents him from providing for himself, or prevents others from going to him, so that he finally dies from starvation, and one who imprisons a person and knowingly puts him in with something that kills, such as a lion or a snake, which kills the prisoner, is sentenced the same as a person who kills voluntarily.

When a murdered man is found in a deserted place or a field and no one knows who killed him, the judges and the elders determine which city is nearest to the spot; then the elders of that city take an oath and say: "Not ours is the hand that shed this blood; our eyes never saw who killed him" (Deut. 21: 1–3). The judges must then attempt to investigate the case.

Espionage and Treason

Those who consent to harm the life of the king must die, and their property must be confiscated. Death is also the penalty for one who shelters murderers of the faithful or who helps their enemies by providing them information or weapons. Such offenders are to be put to death in the place where they sinned and with the things they sinned with. For example, he who made a gun and sold it to the enemies is killed with a gun.

Theft

If a man steals oxen or sheep and slaughters or sells them, then denies the theft on oath but is found guilty, he must make restitution at the rate of fivefold for each ox and fourfold for each sheep. If he admits his guilt, the rate is less severe. If what he stole is not found with him, and he has no property, he must work for the person he robbed until he compensates him for the value. However, the Arabic text of the Fetha Nagast states that he shall be sold as a slave. If the stolen animals are found alive in his possession, he must make twofold restitution.

The Canons of the King have five sections relating to theft on which the Fetha Nagast basically relies:

1. If a man enters a church by day or night and takes something from it, he is marked with a red-hot iron. If he takes from the land around the church, he is beaten, his head is shaved, and he is then exiled.

2. Those who steal (kidnap) children, male or female, slaves or free, must be killed.

3. If one becomes a chief of robbers, his hands are to be cut off, as well as those of his accomplices. He who steals weapons from a field is beaten with a painful stroke. He who steals something from a city pays double restitution on a first offense, or, if he is too poor, is beaten and sent into exile.

4. Whoever persuades a slave to flee his owner and then sells him must either return him or pay for him in money or with a similar slave. The master of a stealing slave pays back what the slave stole, or, if he does not want to, turns the slave over to the aggrieved party for perpetual possession. He who accepts a stolen thing from a slave must return it fourfold. He who receives a slave who flees from his master shall return him and another like him or twenty dinars. He who carries away objects during a fire from a ruined house or from a shipwreck, and those who, by fraud, receive these objects, must pay fourfold restitution or, if the theft is discovered a year after it occurred, eightfold. And the one who knowingly buys a manumitted slaves and sells or give him away to someone else, as dowry for a woman or as a tribute, shall have his hands cut off.

5. If someone takes the clothes of the dead from their graves, his hands are cut off, but the law forbids the mutilation of both hands and feet simultaneously.

According to certain authors, theft and personal assault were comparatively rare. Theft and highway robbery were, in any case, much less frequent than they were in Europe in those days. Dueling was almost not existent. This was due, perhaps, to the rough and rapid justice and to the use of a law code that was well suited to the society.

Fornication

Those who mix blood with blood or seed with blood, as when a father and his son have intercourse with the same woman successively or in cases of parent–child or brother–sister incest, are all punished with the sword. Those who sin knowingly with other relatives (e.g., in-laws, stepchildren or stepparents, a brother's daughter) are to be beaten and have their noses cut off, along with the woman with whom they have sinned.

Those who are united by marriage—such as father and son united with a woman and her daughter or a brother's son united with the wife of his father's brother—are separated and beaten with painful strokes.

Those who fornicate with nuns, deaconesses, or women in training in a monastery to be nuns shall have their noses cut off, as will the women. The same penalty is applied if a man marries his godmother. If prior to this they had, respectively, a wife and a husband, the punishment of beating should be added. Whoever carries off a virgin by force shall have his nose cut off, and half his possessions will be given to her. If a man carries off the betrothed of another, with her consent, both he and she shall have their noses cut off; but if he compelled her, a third part of his property shall be given to her after he has suffered his punishment.

A slave who dares to carry off his mistress is burned at the stake, as well as anyone who helped him. A slave who was aware of a scheme to kidnap his mistress but did nothing to help her receives the same punishment.

If a woman who has a husband commits adultery with her slave, she is beaten, has her head shaved and her nose cut off, and is expelled from her city; the slave is punished with the sword. If an unmarried woman commits fornication with a slave, the punishment for both is somewhat less severe.

A married man who lies down with his female slave must be beaten and do penance; the female slave is sold to another province. One who sins with someone else's female slave must, if he is rich, give her master thirty-six gold dinars—twelve for violating the commandment "Thou shalt not commit adultery," twelve for disobeying "Thou shalt not covet thy neighbor's wife," and twelve for disregarding "Love thy neighbor as thyself." If he is poor, he is beaten and pays whatever he can. If a woman conceives and gives her consent to abort what is in her womb, she shall be beaten and exiled.

The basic punishment for fornication is beating, having the head shaved, and having the nose cut off. The punishment of a married man who sins with a married woman is even more severe, since his evil deed offends both God and other people (i.e., his spouse and the woman's); whereas sin between unmarried people offends God only.

Those who commit the sins of Gomorrah are punished by the sword. A child under twelve years old upon whom a sin is committed is exonerated. Those who lie down with a beast are to be castrated.

There are also six different categories of spiritual punishment for fornication:

1. The first category deals with clergymen. A bishop guilty of any fornication is deposed permanently. If he does penance, he can still associate with the faithful and receive the Eucharist. An unmarried priest who commits fornication must, as penance, fast and pray for a full year and give alms from his own property; a married priest does double penance and is permanently deposed. Sentencing is in the hands of the chief of the monastery and the judge.

2. The second category deals with fornication between the faithful and the nonfaithful. If a faithful person is led, through fornication with a non-faithful person, to abandon faith, the penance is to stay at the door of the church for three years, wearing sackcloth and lying in the dust. There follows an interim year in which the person may enter the church but may not associate with the other faithful. After that, he is forgiven and may take the Eucharist.

3.   One who fornicates with one whom he is forbidden to marry, such as his wife's daughter, is expelled from the church for fifteen years. One who fornicates with his wife's sister, however, is expelled for twelve years, as is a woman who has fornicated with two brothers.

4.   A fornicatress who wishes to do penance must change her dress and stay for one year at the door of the church. Then, after another eight months of hearing the words of God, she shall go out of the church with the catechumens (converts in training). She must then stay four months with female members of the faithful, after which she may receive the Holy Mysteries.

5.   Those who sin with beasts before attaining twenty years of age are expelled from the church for fifteen years but may then associate with the faithful in prayer.

6.   One who eats with fornicators must cease doing so; if not, he is expelled from the church.

Arson

The punishment for arson is burning. If an arsonist sets fire to a field and the houses around it burn, the owner of the fields is not at fault.

False Accusation

One who accuses another of wrongdoing but cannot prove his accusation, even with witnesses, must pay an amount equal to what the accused would have had to pay him.

Usury

Usury is forbidden by God; offenders must do penance. A priest who takes usury is deposed; a layman is ostracized. (Nonetheless, loans at interest were common in Ethiopia. As late as the 1930s, creditors could be seen in the streets with their debtors shackled to them.)

The Rebellious Son

Such a person is to be separated from the community and disinherited by his parents. If a rebellious son causes damages to his parents, they are permitted to send him away. Both his being sent away and his disinheritance are announced before the magistrate and the community. In this matter, the Fetha Nagast follows the Christian law, not the Old Testament, where it is stated that the rebellious son shall be stoned to death (Exod. 21: 17 and Lev. 20: 9).

Apostasy, Witchcraft, Magicians, Sorcerers,
and Soothsayers

The punishment for apostasy is death, by stoning or sword. Those who practice witchcraft and the like are unclean before God and must be made to abstain, exiled, or executed. If they repent, they may do penance.

Drunkenness

Based on Old and New Testament teachings, drunkenness is seen as deserving spiritual punishment. But moderate wine drinking is commanded, since it is wrong to despise what God has created for the joys of men.

Spiritual Punishments

If a priest fights with someone and strikes him until he dies, he is deposed. If a layman does so, he must be sent into exile, thereby being separated from the faithful. He who murders intentionally must do penance until the end of his life; if it is unintentional, he must do penance for seven years and, in some cases, for three years more. One who kills a woman is expelled from the community of the faithful for twenty years; he must remain outside the door of the church for three years, weeping and watching his co-faithful while they enter. For six years, he must stay with the faithful and for eleven years with the catechumens—that is, those receiving instruction in the basic doctrines of Christianity—before his admission to the membership of the church. The punishment is less severe in these cases, because women are considered to create causes for murder more easily. If, however, a man makes a woman abort with poison and lies with her, he must remain outside the church for the rest of his life. Only at the end of his life, or if he is on the verge of death, is he deemed worthy of receiving the Mysteries, because he has committed the three gravest sins: fornication, homicide, and sorcery. As for women who commit adultery or kill their children and hide their death, they are expelled from the community until the day of their death; but because of God's great mercy, the penalty shall be for only ten years, according to a later provision.

Regulation of Slavery

Although the Fetha Nagast views it as proper to enslave enemies captured in war, it sets certain limitations. For instance, the sale of a believing slave to an unbeliever is not allowed. However, the children of a slave belong to his master, regardless of whether they were born from a freeman or from a slave, by marriage or from fornication by a female slave with someone other than the master. If the mother was freed during her pregnancy, the child is free, and he may be set free without freeing his mother.

The price of a slave is like that of an object; at any given time, it may increase or decrease in proportion to his abilities, his ignorance, or his age.

To manumit a slave is one of the deeds of perfection—an excellent form of charity, since it enables a man to become master of himself. Only a slave's owner can manumit him.

There are seven cases in which a slave must be set free: (1) if he becomes a priest, with his master's permission; (2) if his master makes him a soldier; (3) if he saves his master in a fight or warns him against danger; (4) if a pregnant slave woman is set free, her child is also free; (5) if a slave has been detained by an enemy, then returns to his master of his own free will; (6) if a slave's master dies, leaving no heir except the church or the state; and (7) if a rich and a poor man jointly own a slave, the rich one must buy him entirely and set him free.

A free woman must not marry a slave. Never could she dwell with him in the house of his master, even with the consent of his master. If she did, she would become the slave of his master, like him.

Conclusion

Although the Fetha Nagast has a number of imprecisions, it is nevertheless amazingly detailed, particularly the laws for the appointment of judges, which could provide a basis for quite a few contemporary countries. As Margery Perham has said, "Ethiopia can boast an ancient and highly developed system of law and justice, and the cruelty of some punishments should not blind us to the advancement of the system."

12
The Basques: Fueros and Violence

Geographic Background

The Basque region proper consists of the three Vascongadas provinces—Alava, Vizcaya, and Guipuzcoa—known in the Basque language as Euzkadi. The Alava province, with its capital Vitoria, is the largest of the three, bordered on the north by the other two; with its coal, iron, and lead mines, it has a fairly developed industry. The Vizcaya province, with its capital Bilbao, is limited by the Gulf of Vizcaya (Bay of Biscay) on the north; known for its agriculture and husbandry, it also has important iron, zinc, and copper mines and extensive industry and commerce. Guipuzcoa has the Bay of Biscay and France on the north; its capital, San Sebastian, is a famous summer resort, and the province is the site of much commerce.

The province of Navarra, with its capital Pamplona, is sometimes considered intimately related to the three Basque provinces. It borders with France in the north. Some centuries ago, it was a kingdom with territories on both sides of the Pyrenees. It is a rich agricultural province and is known for its cattle raising and particularly its bullfighting.

The Basconia, a Spanish region centered within and around the province of Tarragona, was once part of the ancient principality of Catalonia. Rich in agricultural and forest lands and possessing active industry and commerce, it used to have a great Basque population, as did other provinces, such as Logroño, Zaragoza, and Huesca.

The Northern Basconia in southwest France, is also known as the Pays Basque. It is populated mainly by Basque people, who still speak the Euskara, the Basque language, and is noted for its summer resorts.

At present there are about one million Basques, 800,000 in Spain and 200,000 in France. Together they occupy the areas bordered by the Bay of Biscay and the foothills of the Pyrenees.

In this chapter, all translations from Spanish texts, ancient or modern, are free translations by the author.

The Basque People: An Overview

The Basques were one of a number of peoples of their region who were never completely subjected to the Visigoths, were never Romanized (except insofar as they later adopted Roman Catholicism), and retained their old laws and traditions. The early history of the Basques is vague, but some Roman authors mention the tribe of Vascones in lands corresponding somewhat to the present-day province of Navarra. They appear to have resisted not only the Visigoths but the Franks, the Normans, and even the Moors, who occupied the valley of the Ebro. By the end of the Middle Ages, their provinces had become united with Castille and Aragon, but they retained, in France as well as Spain, a degree of local autonomy.

The three Vascongadas provinces—excluding Navarra—constitute a minimal part of Spain. The Basques there, strongly Roman Catholic and family oriented, have traditionally been small farmers, shipbuilders, seafarers, and also smugglers of goods across the Franco-Spanish frontier. Indeed, Cardinal Richelieu once remarked that "these Basques of 'hot entrails' draw on the speculative reflections and inspirations of the Holy Spirit as the substance of their passionate temperament." They have rated second only to the Catalonians as separatists; their passion for independence dates back many centuries. This Basque separatism played an important part in the two Carlist wars (1834–39, 1872–76), when the Basques, inspired in part by their vigorous animosity toward the Castilians, supported the claim of the conservative Don Carlos and his descendants to the throne as the legitimate heirs of the Bourbon house.

The advent of the Spanish Republic in 1931 divided the political aspirations of the Basques. The provinces of Guipuzcoa, Vizcaya, and to some extent Alava were prepared to work for relative autonomy within the Republic and so remained loyal to it despite its anti-Catholic policy. Navarra, however, was eager to see the Republic overthrown and contributed much to the rebellion of 1936. The capital of Viscaya, Bilbao—long a stronghold of liberalism—became the center both of the republican government and of Basque separatism. The fighting lasted until September 1937 and outside Spain is remembered mainly for the bombing and burning of Guernica, the traditional assembly place of Vizcaya—a symbol of the Basque nation in Franco's eyes and also famous due to Picasso's painting. After the war, thousands of Basques went into voluntary exile, mainly to Latin American countries.

It is very difficult to generalize about the Basques of the Vascongadas provinces, or Euzkadi, today. Their land is green; they work it hard and eat well; and they preserve their traditions. Although physically they are like other Western Europeans, their traditional language, Euskara, is not of Romance or Indo-European extraction; its origin is uncertain, though it was spoken in much of the peninsula before the Roman conquest. Some scholars believe that Euskara was the original language of the Iberian race, if there ever was such an entity. At any rate, it is an extremely difficult language and is now heard mostly in the countryside and in fishing villages, rarely in Bilbao and San Sebastian or, in fact, anywhere to the south or east of Pamplona in most of Alava and Vizcaya. Basque regionalism, however, has found in the language a vehicle for separatist or autonomist ideals, so there has been a revival of interest in Euskara in Basque intellectual circles.

The Basques are a strange mixture of psychological traits. Although they are profound patriots with a strong sense of religious and family responsibility, they regard smuggling and tricky betting as legitimate pursuits—as crafts. They traditionally abhorred any killing in cold blood, even of an enemy, and saw voluntary abortion as a horrible deed. Much of this changed radically during the Spanish Civil War, when some fighting Basques even boasted of having killed people and of other crimes they might have committed. Today, the humanistic side of the Basque character seems to be in temporary eclipse, and an inclination toward violence has come to the fore—another example of how war changes basic human values.

Background of the Fueros

With the decline of the Roman Empire, which began in the third century, a phenomenon of ruralization appeared in many European regions, with a lot of alterations of the public order, particularly in the intercity highways. This produced a weakness and even destruction of the old cities, together with a return to a rural economy, which lasted practically throughout the Middle Ages. This state of affairs facilitated invasion by a number of primitive peoples, with their own cultures.

About the ninth century, however, with the appearance of Islam on the European scene, there was also a decline in the use of the written Roman law and an emergence of the new-old customary law. Later on, during the Renaissance, with its return to classical antiquity and the ancient Roman law—particularly within the universities—there was a dominant trend, especially in those areas having fueros, or unwritten common laws, to put their legal practices in writing in order to avoid their disappearance.

From the eleventh to the fifteenth century, legal systems flourished in Spain. The Christians had both secular and canonic ordinances; the Spanish Moors followed the Moslem law; and the Jews had their ancient Hebrew legislation.

The foral system seems to have first appeared in Castille during the second half of the tenth century. A century later, it was generalized almost to the entire country. A fuero generally comprised all the advantages and privileges granted by a ruler to certain cities, villages, monasteries, individuals, and peoples. Thus, there were military, ecclesiastic, municipal, and other fueros for this or that town or village; not surprisingly, this sometimes led to antiforal reactions by excluded communities.

There are, of course, many contradictory opinions regarding customary and written law. Law based on customs has the advantage of greater flexibility, but it tends to be less specific. On the other hand, no one denies the advantages of the written law, with its greater precision and accuracy, along with some rigidity; it is also easier to elaborate and to modify. At any rate, not many people during the Middle Ages could show such a vast amount of unique linguistic and juridical documents as the Basques.

In the second half of the thirteenth century, the king of Castille Alfonso X (1252–84), known as "the Wise," tried to collate all the local fueros and similar laws into one great legislative work and produced the Fuero Real (Royal Fuero), based on ancient Castilian as well as Roman law. He also ordered the translation of the Visigoths' *Liber Iudiciorum,* known in Spain as the Fuero Juzgo, to be used in some places as a municipal fuero. But his greatest legislative work was his *Book of Laws,* usually known as *Las Siete Partidas (The Seven Books* or *Parts),* prepared from 1256 to 1265 and considered the great Spanish contribution to late medieval legal science, since it put together, for the first time in Western Europe and in a secular language (Spanish), not only the laws of Castille but the total juridical knowledge of the time, consisting mainly of Roman law. However, because it was more theoretical than practical, it was used only in Castille as a supplementary code of laws, though it greatly contributed to the development of legal science in the entire Iberic peninsula.

Because of the initial lack of unity among the Basque provinces, their fueros originated as separate codes for different communities. During the following centuries these foral codes would coexist with municipal laws, which appeared with the reestablishment of cities. Although some Basque fueros appeared artificially through legislative fiat, they mostly grew naturally from ancient Basque common law.

Thus, even in so small and secluded a place as the Basque country, all the distinctions regarding crime and punishment were present from ancient times. In fact, few peoples in the Middle Ages could boast such extensive and unique linguistic and juridical documents as the Basques. The Basque common law emphasizes the important role of the community in private and public matters; respect for individual rights, including penal and procedural guarantees; and regard for ancestral tradition.

The fueros did not have a smooth life. Those of northern Basconia were abolished in 1789 by the French Revolution and those of Navarra in 1841 and of Alava, Guipuzcoa, and Vizcaya in 1876, as a reaction against rising Basque nationalism and support for the Carlist cause. This situation prevailed till the death of Franco, when, in 1978, the Constitution of the Spanish State recognized the value of Basque criminal law by stating that in criminal, procedural, and penitentiary legislation "the particularities of the substantive Basque laws should be respected and taken into consideration" (Art. 149: 1, 6). In 1979, the Cortes—the Spanish parliament—approved a new Statute of Autonomy for the Basque people.

Today, Basque legal scholars are trying to arrange and systematize a kind of corpus of Basque criminal law. They are drawing, incidentially, on numerous old texts that show how common banditry and robbery were in the Middle Ages despite the severe punishments then applied—further proof, if any is needed, that harsh punishment is not a universal panacea for crime.

The fueros must be viewed in the context of their time. In hindsight, they certainly appear excessively severe; but they were distinguished by respect for individual liberty and dignity, limitations on the judicial authorities (with judicial guarantees more advanced than those of some modern states), and the human focus of new legal innovations.

The Basque Fueros

Numerous *Fueros* were granted to different cities, villages, and other localities of the Basque region, starting from the second half of the eleventh century. Here we shall focus on the most important of them.

Among the characteristics of the penal aspects of all these fueros, the following could be mentioned: If a man from San Sebastian is outside the city and someone has a complaint against him, let them both come to the city, where the matter would be settled according to the fuero of San Sebastian, not with some other foreign one (Art. II: 8); no one should be imprisoned if he gives the guarantees required by law, but if he is unable to do so, he should be put in prison (Art. II: 3); cohabitating with a consenting woman does not deserve a fine, unless she is married, but if he used force he has to answer for it or take her as his wife; if the woman is not worthy to be his wife, he has to give her a husband so that she should be considered as honest as before he had intercourse with her. Such a husband should be selected in agreement with the *alcalde* (the mayor) and twelve honest neighbors, and if they would be unable to find such a husband, he should put his body at the disposal of the family of the woman and remain at its mercy.

The Fuero of San Sebastian

Perhaps the remote source of Basque criminal law, this *fuero* was based on the customary law and applied to San Sebastian as well as other places on the same coast. It was granted by Sancho IV Garces, king of Navarra (1038–76), although the exact date is not known. It was granted for political and economic reasons, specifically to attract newcomers and strengthen the new borders of the kingdom.

Among the interesting civil and penal characteristics of this fuero, besides those already mentioned, are great respect for individual liberty and extensive personal guarantees; the inviolability of the private domicile—that is, no judicial officer could approach the house of a Basque against his will, unless he came unarmed and with a clerk to make an inventory of goods that could be seized, which did not include the house itself, arms, horses, or work tools; and the election of judges by the people of each community. Other judicial guarantees included a prohibition against being judged outside one's own town by foreigners or by people not elected by one's own community and one against being arrested without a judge's order, except when caught in flagrante. Also, no one could be imprisoned for debts; there was a special procedure in relation to false witnesses; and judicial duels and other ordeals, except in a few specific cases, were prohibited.

The fuero also contains a detailed list of punishments. Those related to rape are derived from the earlier Spanish fuero of Logroño, one of the six provinces of the ancient kingdom of Castilla la Vieja (Old Castile). Basically, various types of rape incurred monetary punishments; but the fuero of San Sebastian added some innovations, such as the requirement that the raped woman must accuse the offender, with trustworthy witnesses, within three days of the offense (Art. II:4). The same applied for murder and assault, but the monetary penalties were increased; in some cases, depending on the type of injury, the penalty was amputation of a hand. But as with the fuero of Logroño, the vast majority of criminal offenses had monetary, not corporal punishments—an extremely advanced and humanitarian system, especially for its time.

The king's *merino,* or judge, was not entitled to impose any *caloña* (an ancient pecuniary punishment, usually for slander) on the people of San Sebastian, except with the agreement of twelve honest neighbors (Art. II:7). Whoever had incorrect measures or weights had to pay a fine of sixty *sueldos* (an ancient coin having different values, depending on time and places) for the benefit of the king (Art. II:9). A foreigner who came into San Sebastian after having committed a homicide or other crime, but without any weapon, could not be beaten; but if he was armed, he paid the king 1,000 sueldos, and if, because of being armed, the neighbors attacked and killed him, there was no punishment for it (Art II:11).

Whoever forcefully entered a mill paid twenty-five sueldos, and if the mill belonged to the king, forty sueldos (Art III:2). Whoever cut the tree of a neighbor, standing in an enclosed area, had to pay twenty-five sueldos to the owner, plant a similar tree in the same place, and each year give the owner fruits that the tree would have provided, till the new tree started to give fruits by itself; but if the tree was in an open area, the fine was only five sueldos plus the other arrangements just mentioned. In such cases, if the accused had no valid testimony in his favor, he took the oath; if he did not want to, the accuser could demand a judicial duel.

If one entered a house after its doors had been closed, the lights out, and the people sleeping, but someone of the house was awakened and tried to catch the thief and, in the ensuing fight, killed him, it was not considered homicide. But if the thief was caught alive, he could not be killed afterward; instead, the owner of the house was entitled to *caloña* or could pardon him. If a relative of a killed thief charged that the owner of the house had killed him somewhere outside the house, the accused had to take the oath or the ordeal of the red iron. If he came out sane and unhurt from the ordeal, the relatives had to pay compensation. Or both sides could agree on a judicial duel instead of the ordeal (Art. III:5).

The fuero also had some provisions regarding the payment of procedural costs. But the most interesting aspect is that the death penalty was not mentioned at all.

The dispositions of this fuero served as the basis for other, later fueros, since it contained a number of improvements over the old fuero of Logroño. Its democratic penal dispositions have directly influenced Basque criminal law, particularly from the eleventh to the sixteenth centuries—the same period during which the English common law was established. Some scholars even believe that these democratic concepts of the Basques, particularly the personal guarantees so similar to the *habeas corpus,* were brought to England by Simon Count of Montfort (?–1218), who learned and appreciated them while he was in Northern Basconia as a deputy of the Anglo-Norman kings.

The Fuero of King Sancho of Navarra

This fuero was for the farmers and peasants of Durango, a village in the province of Vizcaya. The date of this fuero, though unknown, has to be between 1065, when the reign of Sancho IV el Bravo (the Fearless) started, and 1234, when the reign of Sancho VII el Fuerte (the Strong) ended. The original text has been lost and there exist only two incomplete texts with a Latin introduction. It has relatively little importance because it contains only a few penal norms related to homicide, fines, and similar matters.

The General Fuero of Navarra and the Amejoramientos

The *amejoramientos* were legislative measures adopted by the Cortes, the Spanish parliament, with the intention of improving the fueros. They also represent the monarchs' readiness to accept as law the customs of the people. The most important of these *amejoramientos* were granted by King Felipe de Evreux in 1330 and Carlos III el Noble in 1418.

This fuero is the first written in the Basque country. It seems to belong to the reign of Teobaldo de Champagne in the thirteenth century. Some scholars have called it a cruel fuero, but Arturo Campion notes that the cruel items are only a few. In fact, this is the fuero that abolished torture—unlike, for instance, even *Las Siete Partidas,* which stated: "Men commit great crimes surreptitiously in order to avoid being detected and captured. Therefore the ancient sages adopted torture to get the truth out of them" (introduction to the Seventh *Partida,* Title XXX). The main emphasis of this general fuero is actually on individual rights and freedom and an expanded system of oaths, ordeals, and bonds. Although witchcraft and sorcery were widely practiced, this fuero had no laws similar to the older Fuero Juzgo, which had adopted torture and stated: "The diviners and fortune tellers; or those who cause stones to fall on vineyards and orchards; or those who speak to the devil and thereby change the minds of men and women; or those who engage in night rituals and make sacrifices to the devils, should be tied up, given 200 strokes, marked ignominiously on their forehead, and taken around ten towns and villages so that the others, on seeing them, will become frightened" (Lib. VI, Title II, Law IV).

The articles of this fuero relating to crimes and punishments are rather limited, dealing mainly with fundamental offenses against life and property.

The Cuaderno Penal of Juan Nuñez de Lara

The Señor (landlord) Juan Nuñez de Lara arrived in Vizcaya at the beginning of 1342, when the country was involved in a cruel war among noble families, with many organized robberies and political assassinations as a side effect. Under such chaotic conditions, Nuñez de Lara summoned the Juntas Generales (General Councils) of Guernica, who were eager to end the chaos for the sake of their own commercial activities, and the *Cuaderno* (writing book) was adopted before the end of that year.

The *Cuaderno*—thirty-five chapters reflecting the tumultuous conditions—deals almost entirely with extensive applications of the death penalty. The majority of the punishments were the common ones already existing in Vizcaya; some others reproduced the cruel practices of the people living in the mountains and the forests.

In spite of all its limitations, the *Cuaderno* is considered to be the first to deal with criminal legislation in Vizcaya. It would have been very interesting to know what the laws were before the *Cuaderno* was adopted, but there are not enough sources. This *Cuaderno* was replaced by a new one fifty years later, in 1394.

The Fuero of the Merindad of Durango

The exact date of the fuero of the *merindad* (the territory of a *merino's* jurisdiction) is also unknown, but it seems to have been drawn up by the middle of the fourteenth century. It deals with civil and penal matters, especially problems arising from struggles among political factions, rights of property, offenses against vineyards and orchards, and so on. Its punishments are rather harsh—the death penalty for cutting trees at night, the cutting off ears in other cases—but it accepts pardons in cases of adultery.

The Fuero de la Tierra de Ayala of 1373 and Its Enlargement of 1469.

The seigniory of Ayala, in the province of Alava, was an independent entity since the eleventh century and was governed by consuetudinary law. The oldest of its fueros—the *Privilegio del Contrato* (Privilege of the Contract), granted by Alfonso XI on 2 April 1332—was based on the same old consuetudinary law as well as on the personal will of the ruler, the latter confirmed even in the written fuero of 1373, which was granted by the Señor Don Fernando Perez de Ayala. Its preamble states that since there are no actuaries or notaries in Ayala, there should be no claims in writing unless the ruler, in certain special cases, is willing to attend to the situation. Since this was a mistake, the *señor* together with the five majors of the seigniory, revised this fuero in 1469. The *aumento* (enlargement) consisted of sixteen chapters; all except the first (which ratifies the people's rights and accepts their customs) and the last three (dealing with some formalities) deal with penal matters. For instance, the punishment for making a false oath during a trial is the removal of one of every five teeth; blasphemies against God, the Virgin, and the saints warrant fines of 300 *maravedies* (an old Spanish coin that had various values and names in different times and places) and sixty days in fetters, 200 *maravedies* and forty days in fetters, and 100 *maravedies* and twenty days in fetters, respectively. Claims in writing were now accepted, but only in matters involving more than 1,000 *maravedies*. In cases of killing, wounding, or robbing a foreigner, the respective authorities acted *ex officio*. The ruler and the merinos also had the power to impose a truce or to stop the fighting among the several armed groups of the noblemen.

This enlargement of 1469, known as the *Capitulacion y Ordenanzas hechas por el Señor de Ayala* (capitulation—in the sense of agreement—and ordinances done by the landlord of Ayala), had its final editing in 1487 and was ratified by the Catholic kings on 30 September 1489. It is one of the oldest and most complete of the existing Basque fueros. Its penal aspects, in fact, closely follow those of the *Cuaderno Penal of Juan Nuñez de Lara of 1342.*

Cuaderno de Hermandad de Guipuzcoa (1375)

This *cuaderno* of 1375 was also known as the *Ordenanzas de Enrique II*. The first statutes of this province were prepared by the Juntas Generales of Guipuzcoa, held in Tolosa in 1375 and later approved by the king.

There seems to have been another *cuaderno* in 1377, but its originals are unknown.

Every seven years, seven majors were appointed to deal with the following five situations: stealing or robbery; the use of force; arson of houses, vineyards, or orchards; cutting of fruit trees; and killing or wounding. The procedure was short and the sentences without appeal. The intention was to allow merchants and traders free travel within the province without fear; in fact, if one even stopped them to ask for something, one was treated as a robber.

Cuaderno de Hermandad de Vizcaya (1394)

A bad security situation at the end of the fourteenth century prompted the people of Vizcaya to appeal to King Enrique III (1379–1406) of Castille, also known as "the Sorrowful," to do something about it. He sent Dr. Gonzalo Moro, a judge of his audience, to meet with two honest neighbors of every *merindad* and one landowner from every town. Together they prepared the *cuaderno* in 1393, and it was ratified by the king in 1394. This work of representatives of the people, without the intervention of legal experts, simply ratified the customs of the province.

The *cuaderno* has fifty-four titles dealing only with punitive measures. These were extremely severe, not only for offenders but also for their accomplices and concealers; nevertheless, torture was forbidden. The members of the community were called on to participate; whoever knew of an offense had to denounce the case or pay a fine of 110 *maravedies*. Moreover, every man from twenty to sixty-five years old was obliged to look after the infractor but was forbidden to implement justice by his own hands. The following crimes received the death penalty: murder, unless acting in self-defense; wounding; robbing a traveler of more than five florins (ancient Spanish golden coin equivalent to ten *reales* and twenty-five *maravedies,* used mainly in the Aragon region); stealing more than ten florins no matter where; giving food or lodging to criminals on three different occasions, and so on.

Cuaderno de Hermandad de Guipuzcoa (1397)

This *cuaderno* was also known as the *Ordenanzas de Guetaria*. Enrique III sent the same Dr. Gonzalo Moro to reform the statutes of this province, using a similar procedure as in Vizcaya three years earlier. This *cuaderno,* with sixty-one disorderly chapters or laws, resulted. It, too, sought to control rampant criminality with harsh punishment, but it required only a few conjectures or guesses, instead of complete proof of the commission of an offense. Duels were forbidden, except in certain cases among noblemen. Many offenses received capital punishment, as in the Cuaderno de Hermandad de Vizcaya of 1394, but also including raping a woman, using force to enter a home or church with the intention of stealing, and arson of any kind. Providing food to criminals deserved the cutting off the ears. The same applied to whoever carried a *rallon* (a deadly iron weapon used in ancient Spain for hunting big game). On the other hand, the house of the blacksmith who made *rallons* was to be burnt, and if he had no home, he was to be hanged.

Cuadernos de Hermandad de Labourdi (1396, 1400)

The first of these *cuadernos* may have been granted by Ricardo II (1333–1400), king of England and duke of Aquitania in southwest France. His son, Enrique IV, who reigned from 1399 till 1413, granted the second, also known as the *Estatutos* (statutes) *de Labourdi,* which remained in force till 1420. These were similar in purpose and nature to the *cuadernos* of Vizcaya and Guipuzcoa, but they also meant to limit abuses by noblemen. Thus, they have a democratic character special to the Basque country.

Both of these *cuadernos* dealt with criminal and penal matters but also, rather uniquely for their times, tackled the problem of the reparation and indemnification of the victim. In fact, one specifically stated: "If the offender runs away but has property or other things in Laburdi, they should serve as a means of restitution and reparation to the victim, and the rest should be confiscated by the Lord, the King." Another item states: "In all cases where a murder or stealing, plunder or any other outrage was committed, and in the absence of the *baile,* the people of the place should capture and bind the offender—without beating or hurting him (if this can be done . . .)—bring him to the *baile* or his deputy, so that justice should be done according to the circumstances."

Cuaderno de Ordenanzas de Guipuzcoa (1415)

This *cuaderno* was granted on 3 March 1415 by Juan II, king of Castille from 1406 to 1454, but it was prepared by Juan Velasquez, his representative. It, too, is very severe, determining, for instance, that people without work or known means of subsistence or domicile must assure, with the backing of a guarantor, that they will live honestly. If they have no guarantor, they are expelled from the province and considered vagrants. Concealing a crime deserved, under certain circumstances, the same punishment as the one given the offender. Dualists were severely punished.

Ordenanzas de Guipuzcoa

During the fifteenth century, these ordinances were rather frequent, all having the same basic purpose of controlling the prevailing anarchy and criminality.

An important one, comprising 207 chapters, was granted on 23 April 1453 to the village of Arevalo in the province of Avila. Then came the *ordenanzas* of 1467 by Enrique IV, consisting of 146 extremely disorderly chapters. Doubtful testimony was admitted as evidence, and there was no appeal of first-instance sentences. Like the Cuaderno de Hemandad of Guipuzcoa of 1397, it sought to curtail abuses by noblemen, with the innovation that the Council of Municipality of every city or village had to pay for all things stolen by unknown offenders up to a value of fifteen gold florins. *Merinos* could exile from their territories any disobeying noblemen or those concealing rioters or criminals. Jews were obliged to wear external signs on their garments, a measure that was later applied everywhere. After 1527, no Jew or his descendants could establish residence within the province, under threat of confiscation of all his possessions and being put at the royal mercy. (In some regards, the Nazis of our century were merely imitators of long-established measures.)

In 1469 three more *ordenanzas* were granted to the province, giving the majors of the *hermandad* the right to impose certain torments when duly empowered by judicial authorities. Elgoibar, another municipality, received other *ordenanzas* in 1470 and 1482. And the last one was the *Carta Patente de los Reyes Catolicos al Juez de Residencia de Guipuzcoa* (the Patent Charter of the Catholic Kings to the Resident Judge of Guipuzcoa), dated 1491.

The Fuero General

This fuero, also known as the Old Fuero of Vizcaya (2 June 1452) was perhaps the first written fuero of Vizcaya. All the previous ones were *de albedrio* (nonwritten judicial customs and practices). Though it contains only a few substantive precepts, it is marked by great respects for the individual, including the offender; a relatively benign jail system (ch. 61–68); procedural guarantees; respect for the family and the home; and so on.

The 219 chapters of this fuero typify, for the first time, such crimes as arson and damages and also contain numerous procedural details. Among the personal guarantees that it postulates—so unusual during the Middle Ages and missing from the legislation of many contemporary countries—are the following: to avoid possible abuses by foreign judges, the people of Vizcaya could be dealt with only by their own magistrates, similar to the much older San Sebastian fuero; no one could be detained without a judicial order unless caught in flagrante or a few other exceptions (not even the English law of 1679, creating the *habeas corpus,* has a similar formulation); the judicial investigation ended with the *llamamiento,* an invitation to the accused to come forward for his own defense "under the tree of Guernica" (an oak symbolizing the liberties of Vizcaya, which disappeared in 1892 but is partially replaced today by one of its own sprouts); and finally, the modern principle of publicity was anticipated, in that the accuser had to present evidence to the accused under the same tree.

The Cuaderno of Laws and Ordinances of Alava (1417, 1463)

The first of these, adopted by the Juntas Generales of the province and approved by Queen Catherine of Lancaster in 1417, is a written recompilation of thirty-four *ordenanzas*, the first corpus of laws of Alava. In October 1463, a royal judge commissioned by Enrique IV prepared a new and definitive text. This *cuaderno* is based mainly on the Cuadernos de Hermandad of Guipuzcoa and Vizcaya. (The text of the third edition of 1623 was published in facsimile in 1978.)

The Fuero of the Encartaciones (1503)

This fuero was approved by the Juntas Generales of 1575. The *encartaciones* were territories that, by virtue of charters of fueros granted to them, had extended the same to an adjacent one. This fuero was prepared and published with the assistance of the aforementioned Dr. Gonzalo Moro. It is considered a fuero despite its similarity to contemporary *cuadernos*. It states that, in the first place, this fuero should be used, and in cases of doubt, the ancient fuero of 1394, which it resembles, should be consulted.

In penal matters, there is indeed a retrogression in this fuero compared with the previous Cuadernos de Hemandad. For instance, the punishment of the *cepo*—stocks—was changed to exile or cutting off of ears; and the death penalty was more frequently applied, even for people asking for money on the highways.

The Reforms of the Fuero de Vizcaya of 1452 (1506, 1526)

These reforms eliminated some previous dispositions and introduced some new concepts; basically, they were better structured and better written.

First Ordenanzas de la Tierra de Ayala (1510)

The Council of Saraube approved these ordinances on 28 December 1510. They contain only a few penal norms in their sixty-eight chapters, dealing more with problems related to elections to public office.

The Fuero de Vizcaya (1526)

This fuero deals in detail with the jail system of those days. There were two jails in the province, one in Guernica and the other where the *corregidor* had his residence. The jails had to provide the inmates reasonable space but had to be well provided with fetters, irons, gyves, shackles, chains, and so on. A sentenced offender could choose the jail he preferred, but he could be taken outside it only to appear before a judge. A jailer who helped a prisoner escape received the same punishment as the fugitive would; but if a prisoner had escaped because of the jailer's negligence, the punishment of the jailer was less. Inmates had to pay for their food and upkeep.

The last fuero of Vizcaya was called *La Union y Concordia entre las Villas, Ciudades y tierra llana del Señorio de Vizcaya* (the Union and Harmony among the villages, cities, and plains of the Seigniory of Vizcaya); it was dated 11 September 1630.

Summary

In sum, several features of the foral system stand out. One is that the fueros gave priority to the indemnification of the victim and only afterward dealt with the punishment of the offender—a situation that has been almost completely reversed in contemporary penal systems (only in the last decade or so, in fact, have things been improving in this regard).

Also, a basic function of the fueros was to help overcome tensions between the Basques and the Spanish king in Castille. It was this need to adjust to changing political situations that gave the Basques their dynamism, their capacity to evolve new forms. The foral system represented a perennial effort for understanding, not for intransigence, and in this sense had a markedly democratic, antitotalitarian character. If an arrangement between the Basque country and Castille was based on an authentic dialogue, it was beneficial for both of them; but if Castille imposed its own conditions, the pact could not survive for long.

Also notable is that although the Cuadernos de Hermandad, imposed severe punishments against the excesses of the *banderizos* (people belonging to one group or faction), with emphasis on the death penalty, such measures did not prove very effective. Thus, the fuero of 1452 had the good sense to eliminate these draconian punishments; and the fuero of 1526, the most advanced of them all, preferred preventive to repressive means. Another positive characteristic of the last fuero is the absence of torture; and perhaps more important than everything else were all the measures taken in defense of human rights and personal liberty—a century and a half before the English law of *habeas corpus*.

Advances were also made regarding penal institutions. In 1569, San Sebastian and other towns of Guipuzcoa decided to have separate cells for inmates who were willing to pay for them or who had been sentenced to minor offenses, to avoid their mixing with more unsavory inmates. And in 1574, the citizens of Azcoitia demanded the separation of men and women in every jail, no matter what their social status. Further advances in this area were made in seventeenth- and eighteenth-century Spain.

The Legal Status of the Basque Country in This Century

In the sixteenth and particularly in the eighteenth centuries, the Basque criminal law changed a good deal, largely because of the centralism imposed by the Bourbon kings in Madrid. The fueros ceased to be enforced in 1789 in Northern Basconia, in 1841 in Navarra, and in 1876 in Alava, Guipuzcoa, and Vizcaya. There was also a gradual cessation in the nomination of the *alcaldes de Hermandad* and their replacement with ordinary judges.

But in the present century, the fueros took another form. On 14 June 1931, the General Assembly of the Basque Municipalities approved the *Estatuto General del Estado Vasco* (General Statutes of the Basque State). It established, among other things, that judicial power would be exercised by the Supreme Court and other competent authorities of the Basque judicial body and that the Basque people were sovereign in all matters except those left to the Spanish state (e.g., coinage, weights and measures, criminal law, intellectual and industrial property, etc.). This left the Basque state free to handle such matters as the judicial system, penitentiary administration, and procedural legislation.

Early in the Spanish Civil War, on 7 October 1936, the republican government granted the *Estatuto de Autonomia del Pais Vasco* (Statutes of Autonomy of the Basque Country), which lasted only till June 1937, when Franco's troops occupied Vizcaya. This *estatuto* also left the judicial system in the Basque country's hands, excepting military and naval matters. Judges and other magistrates within the autonomous region were appointed by the Basque state and were preferentially considered if they had good knowledge of the Basque foral system and the Basque language. The Basque state also had charge of its internal police as well as wide competence in matters related to the judicial system, including the juvenile courts, with the exception of all extraregional matters, such as extradition, border police, immigration, emigration, production and trading of weapons, and similar matters (Art. 5). In conflicts of jurisdiction between the regional courts and those of the Spanish state, the Supreme Court of the state decides (Art. 11).

Finally, the Cortes Generales (Spanish parliament) adopted early in 1979 the *Estatutos de Autonomia de 1979* (Statutes of Autonomy), which was approved on 25 October 1979 by the Basque people in a public referendum and remains in force today. Two aspects of this *estatuto* are of special note.

1. *General competence in penal matters:* The Basque Autonomous Community is given executive competence over fishing in the regional waters,

hunting, juvenile institutions, consumer protection, women's status, juvenile education, and other matters (Art. 10: 10, 14, 28, 39). Within its territory, the Autonomous Community enforces the Spanish state's legislation in ecological and environmental matters (Art. 11) and may also establish additional protective measures in these specific fields. Finally, the Community has sole right of execution of state legislation regarding penitentiary matters, intellectual and industrial property, weights and measures, pharmaceutical products, and a few other matters.

2. *Competence regarding the administration of justice:* The Spanish state has exclusive jurisdiction over the military, the organization and functioning of the prosecution system, and the granting of pardons; the Autonomous Community may exercise only those specific functions that state legislation bestows upon it. The Basque courts have all competence to deal with penal matters, except for the right of repeal (*cassation*), which belongs to the Supreme Court of the state.

The Basque Country and Violence

It is a mistake to see violence as particular to contemporary human society. It has always existed; the pages of world history are full of it, despite the major religions' teachings against it. The main difference today is the role of mass communication in disseminating the reality of violence.

For more than one criminologist, present-day criminology has proved a sad deception. Despite benefiting from the most up-to-date technology, it has achieved not a single positive result, while crime and recidivism rates keep climbing rapidly. Perhaps the role of modern criminology is to help create a new type of penal code, one that eliminates archaic and autocratic elements and provides guidance apposite to modern communities.

At any rate, a prime example of a group engaging in violence today is the Basques. Notwithstanding the degree of formal autonomy they have been granted, they believe that they have been discriminated against in regard to their language, customs and traditions, and rights. Some of them express their frustration passively; others do so in unmitigated violence that has gone on for too long.

The problems in regions such as Euskadi willl never be solved with elegant speeches; debates at the United Nations or in more secluded scientific forums only show how difficult the situation is. The Basques resemble other ethnic groups with a deep-rooted sense of independence who have long lived under dictatorial regimes or as minority groups. The Basques, however, have a strong humanistic tradition, manifested not only in their legal history but also in the work of the *bersolaris,* the Basque poets. Their national festivities have always stressed their inclination for peace, their intolerance for torture and slavery. Thus, there is hope that despite the present somber reality of Euskadi with its ETA terrorist organization and acceptance of violence, especially among young people, the Basque people will achieve an accommodation and return to their normal way of life.

13
Early and Feudal Japan

A Peculiar Geography and National Character

Off the east coast of Asia lies the strange and wonderful "Land of the Rising Sun"—Japan. The name derives from two Chinese characters meaning "sun" and "root," but the word *Japan,* according to tradition, is the outcome of Marco Polo's intention, when he came back from China in the thirteenth century, to translate into Italian, the Chinese pronunciation of those characters, which the Japanese themselves vocalize as *Nihon.*

The country comprises four large islands—Kyushu in the south, Shikoku, Honshu (the largest), and Hokkaido in the north—600 smaller ones, and 8,000 minute islets, often no more than mountain peaks emerging out of the sea. Though it is one-twentieth the size of the United States, it is one and a half times larger than the United Kingdom and as large as both Germanies together. The four main islands form an arch of 2,480 kilometers from northeast to southwest. Most of the land is mountainous, with 192 volcanoes, of which 58 are still active. The Fuji-no-Yama, extinct since 1707, is the highest (12,395 feet) and most beautiful of them. Altogether, only one-fifth of Japan's surface is arable land, but with its temperate climate and dependable rainfall, it is a pleasant place to live. Its volcanoes also make it a violent land, however; every third day there is a slight earth tremor, and once in a while there are devastating earthquakes. Also, almost every year, a great typhoon roars along its coasts, causing much destruction.

Japan's geography has also determined its natural culture. The Straits of Korea, separating Kyushu from the nearest mainland, are only 100 miles wide but were dangerous to cross in ancient times and gave Japan a natural semiisolation. Japan's insular position, far removed from the crossroads of Asia, created a cultural marginality, so that the Japanese tended to lag behind other Asiatic peoples in the development of their civilization. The Chinese were writing by the fifteenth century B.C., but the Japanese did not until about the early fifth century A.D., when they borrowed the Chinese system. Buddhism reached China from India during the first century A.D. but did not come to Japan until the sixth century. Popular drama flourished in China during the Yuan dynasty (1280–1368), but in Japan not before 1700. The same general retardation could be seen in the areas of printing, philosophical schools, and mathematics. Japan was within the Chinese cultural orbit yet nevertheless separate and different, because it always adapted foreign cultural elements to indigenous Japanese patterns. There were times when China's religion, arts, science, and literature flowed to Japan, but at other times, this stream was interrupted and Japan developed on its own.

For Japan, as well as for China and India, Buddhism was essential, yet the different form of Buddhist piety that flourished in each of these countries were indicative of the pervasive divergencies that gave each a style of civilization unique unto itself. The same divergence of response can be seen regarding the arrival of the Europeans (the "south barbarians," as the Chinese called them) and their "discovery," so to speak, of the different Asian cultures. Although the Chinese and Indians reacted with a certain general indifference, in Japan—which had not developed a "classical" culture until the sixth century A.D., after a massive and deliberate importation of skills and knowledge from China and Korea—the arrival of the first Europeans, during the 1540s, provoked a lively reaction.

There is a strange parallel between the way the European intelligentsia were so eager to appropriate the culture of the Greeks and Romans from the twelfth to the sixteenth centuries and the way the Japanese learned with such enthusiasm anything Chinese from the seventh to the ninth century. Nevertheless, Japan can be considered one of the most successful and independent Asian cultures. No matter how faithfully the Japanese Imperial Court sought to duplicate the titles and rituals of China, Japan's political reality always remained different from that prevailing on the mainland. The far greater honor paid to military prowess in Japan was another indication of the profound differences between these two societies. Moreover, the importance of hereditary military clans—for instance, during the Shogunate—and of Shintoism in Japanese life had no parallels in China. On the other hand, the Chinese pattern of recruitment to high office by means of strict examinations (which hindered the development of a hereditary aristocracy in traditional China) never took root in Japan, which always remained itself, reshaping whatever came from external sources, whether Eastern or Western.

According to La Senne, *character* is the mass of congenital dispositions that form one's mental skeleton, while *personality* is the outcome of character plus environmental influences. The Japanese national character—in this sense and to the extent that one can generalize about it—is a combination of three main traits: nervous, sentimental, and irascible, reflecting the contradictory nature of the Japanese landscape. Indeed, the Japanese have been among the most ferocious warriors, yet they are extremely courteous and lovingly devoted to flowers, poetry, and art.

It is also important that until recent times and for over 2,000 years, Japan had an almost exclusively agricultural life, consisting mainly of rice cultivation. This seems to have fostered an additional tendency toward uniform behavior. Furthermore, until recently, the Japanese lived under federal tyranny, so that they have a deeply ingrained disposition toward hierarchy and obedience. The mere word *revolution* is frightening to many of them, particularly the older generations.

The Western world was frequently appalled by some traits of the Japanese; they were considered fanatics and ferocious. Few Europeans perceived that they were conforming to a traditional code of honor, tied to the concept of unwavering loyalty and the mystique of the sword. If the basic Japanese values have changed today, their traditional concepts are still deeply embedded in their culture, as expressed in their classical theater—*Noh, Kabuki,* and *Bunraku*—their films, and their televised sword-operas.

Charles de Secondat, baron de Montesquieu (1689–1755), in his *L'Esprit des Lois* (1748), wrote about Japan and its people: "There, almost all crimes are punished by death, because disobedience to a great potentate such as the Emperor of Japan is conceived to be itself an enormous offence. They are people who naturally despise death and commit suicide by opening their stomach for the slightest fancy. They have a hidden streak of cruelty in their make-up."

Maximilien Robespierre (1758–94), during a debate at the French National Assembly in 1791, also violently criticized the Japanese by saying: "There is no country where the death penalty has been so abused and such cruel punishments adopted as in Japan."

Japanese scholars believe that it is sufficient to correct such statements by mentioning the historical fact that in 792 A.D., Kammu Tenno, after the battle of Husanko, declared the establishment of a "demilitarized peace state" and abolished the death penalty. This abolition continued from 810 to 1157 A.D. No other state, these scholars add, abolished the death penalty for such a long period. They consider their people tolerant by nature, holding that cruelty is extraneous to the Japanese way of thinking. For instance, death by burning was not originally applied in either China or Japan, having been introduced later under the influence of the European Christian practices of the Middle Ages. In addition, Japanese penal legislation incorporated only mild punishments compared with those adopted by other Asian countries, such as China.

Ethnic Origins and Archaeological Data

The Japanese people, with the exception of a very small number of Ainus, are of the same ethnic origin and speak the same language. Therefore, there are practically no racial problems in the country.

These islands were settled by their original inhabitants very early, perhaps during the Neolithic era, but the exact origins of the Japanese are still unknown. The prehistoric inhabitants had a highly developed stone and bone tool culture, with implements for everything from hunting elephants to carving magic talismans. In March 1978, a group of archaeologists and geologists finished their seventh major excavation project on the banks of Lake Nojiri, in the northern Nagano Prefecture. They concluded that the Nojiri man lived on the shores of the lake during the Stone Age, some 20,000 years ago. The large quantity of crafted bone artifacts that were found, along with many stone tool fragments, offered graphic evidence that these people had a far more diverse and complex life than was previously thought. The Nojiri man may be an important clue to unveiling the still shrouded roots of the earliest Japanese.

It is also possible that some of the early inhabitants came from the south and others from the north. The former might have been people with some attainments of an agricultural nature, and the latter—those coming from Korea—might have had some notions of pastoral culture, which once prevailed in the northeast of China, as among the Mongolians. About the third century B.C., these agricultural and pastoral tribes seem to have united into the so-called Yabadai State in the southern part of Kyushu island.

The oldest body of distinctively Japanese material is the pottery called Jomon ware, considered to be some 9,000 years old and produced continuously until the beginning of the Christian Era. The Jomon, or "rope-pattern," ware—so-called because during its manufacture ropes were pressed against the fresh clay surface as a means of decoration—has been found practically everywhere in Japan, but never in Korea or anywhere else in Asia.

A new theory, developed after World War II and expounded mainly by Namio Egami, proposes that the Japanese people derive from the Noshem horse-riding tribes of the northern Eurasian area. These tribes went south looking for the rich rice fields, where they then settled. In due time, they conquered Kyushu and the central part of mainland Japan. The imperial family and the Shinto religion, according to the same theory, derived from these Noshem people. This theory is not generally accepted but is regarded as attractive for explaining Japan's origins. Nevertheless, this and other theories agree that the state of Japan rose about the middle of the fourth century A.D.

Though Japan evolved similarly to so many other ancient societies, each of its stages, as already mentioned, showed a definite Japanese character. When the first villages were established and life became more secure, a special craftmanship replaced the more bold and spontaneous primitive ware. They started by making charming idols, called *dogū* (clay figure), resembling human beings and domestic animals, all of them deformed, which must have had some symbolic significance—perhaps ensuring fertility or exorcising evil forces. Thus, in spite of its cultural isolation, Japan was already producing aesthetic objects of memorable beauty.

After beginning their agricultural life and mastering the techniques for casting bronze and iron, there were profound changes in Japanese society: food supplies were more or less stable; the land was divided in plots; villages and more permanent communities were formed; and larger political units were established. Even a religion developed, based on the cycles of planting and harvesting. A new type of ceramic, with marked continental influence, also appeared. It is known as Yayoi ware; its name derives from a district near Tokyo where it was first found. It is simpler than the exuberant Jomon style but, once again, is distinctly Japanese and has been found nowhere else.

During this Yayoi period (from about 250 B.C. to 250 A.D.) Japan entered the first stages of advanced civilization, perhaps because in Japan, unlike other parts of the world, bronze and iron appeared virtually at the same time. Bronze weapons and aesthetic objects were common and were much appreciated. During this period, possibly due to contacts with China, skillfully wrought jewels, particularly of agate and jasper, were used as personal ornaments, indicating that the standard of living was already not one of mere subsistence. The Japanese started to form a national community, which was achieved between the sixth and seventh centuries. It was a patriarchal state, having at its head the Tenno, a system that has been retained till today, though it has been sometimes powerful and sometimes fairly weak.

Thanks to rice cultivation, agricultural villages became larger; local chieftains came into being as well as powerful landholding families, constituting the basis for something similar to small regional states. During the Kofun period (from about 250 to 522), there was a slow but marked growth of a sense of national unity and of a need for a supreme national leader, which represent the remote origins of modern Japan. The most important archaeological remains of this period are the *kofun* (ancient tombs), concentrated in the Kinki area, which corresponds to the modern Kyoto, Osaka, and Nara districts. The *kofun* contained bronze mirrors and other furnishings. Some even had small paintings. Clay figurines, the *haniwa,* were ceremonially placed around such grave mounds.

Legends, Myths, and Documents

From the two earliest extant documents of the eighth century A.D., Japanese mythology is richly embroidered with details about the divine origin of the imperial family, which have powerfully influenced Japanese culture. The second of these documents, the *Nihonshoki* (Japan's Chronicles), also known as *Nihonji*—officially compiled in 720 A.D.—was to become the "official history" of Japan. It was written in Kanji—Chinese characters—which until the end of the nineteenth century was the learned language of the Far East, as Latin was for Europe. The style of the writing follows the pattern of the chronicles of the Chinese dynasties, but there is still more legend than history.

Both documents were written at a time when national Japanese sentiments were blossoming. Both of them date the foundation of Japan impressively back to 660 B.C., when the Emperor Jimmu Tenno ascended the throne.

As the legend unfolds, Ninigi-no-Mikoto, the grandchild of Amaterasu-Omikami, the sun-goddess, comes down from heaven and lands on top of the Takachiho mountain, from where he rules the region of Hyuga, which corresponds to the present-day prefecture of Miyasaki, in southern Kyushu. Till the end of World War II, the Japanese people never questioned the historicity of Jimmu Tenno's heavenly origin. The evidence, if any was needed, was that the jewel, the sword, and the mirror that Ninigi-no-Mikoto brought with him from heaven were (and are still) the state insignia and are preserved in the Imperial Palace of Tokyo, the special Shinto sanctuary of Atsuta Jingu, and the great Shinto shrine of Ise, respectively. The Ise shrine, with its magnificent *torii* (the red gate found only before a Shinto monastery or shrine), is the most sacred of Japan, and every Japanese must pray at it at least once. Till 1945, each prime minister visited it upon taking office. This legend of the heavenly origin of the imperial family continues to constitute the essence of Shintoism.

Until the present postwar era, the orthodox Shinto view of the origins of the Japanese race was officially accepted and even enforced. However, under postwar educational reforms, this body of mythology was declared "historically improbable" and the divine origin of the emperor invalid. But it is still a strong undercurrent in Japanese life, and the "Age of the Gods" still plays an important role in Japanese culture. Nevertheless, among these decorative mythological fancies runs a thread of material facts. Archaeological and historical studies show that the Japanese state expanded from Kyushu and reached the Yamato region before 400 A.D., when the first historical capital was established.

On the other hand, the first written data about "Japan" are found in Chinese books. According to the "Chronicles of the Former Han Dynasty" of about the end of the first century A.D., there were some hundred independent but constantly warring clans in Japan. Afterward, they began to concentrate, so that by the beginning of the third century, they were all united under Queen Himiko of the state of Yamatai, an event that was considered the inception of the Japanese state. There is no doubt that southern Japan was the center of the country's early civilization, since Chinese culture arrived through Korea. Some Japanese historians believe that Himiko, who reigned about the year 200 A.D., is the real ancestor of the imperial family. Later, another emperor, Ojin Tenno, conquered Korea and may have established there the Mimana branch of the family in 369 A.D. A few centuries later, Kammu Tenno (737–806), after the battle of Hakusonko and following celestial advice, went eastward and conquered Yamato, a great and fertile valley near modern Nara and Osaka, encompassing the Asuka district. There he established a new and powerful empire, with its capital in the city of Heiankyo. In 792, as mentioned, he declared Japan a "demilitarized peace state" and created the Kondisei system, according to which the Emperor could be assisted in his multiple tasks by young bureaucrats as "case work" officers. During his reign, a number of clergymen—such as Saicho, Kukai, and others—went to China to study Buddhism.

To ensure the continuity of the imperial line, the emperor could take as many wives and concubines as he wished, but the right of succession did not go automatically to the eldest son but went to the one considered the most suitable. Among the 124 Japanese emperors, there have been good, bad, and eccentric ones and more than one downright evil one, such as Yozei Tenno, who was finally dethroned and died in 949.

The Yamato district is also the cradle of Buddhism in Japan. It not only has imperial tombs but also has the first vestiges of ancient Buddhist temples. It was well selected as the site of the capital, not just for its great fertility and beauty but mainly for its encircling mountains, which made it easy to defend. Because of the animistic concept of the impurity of death, a palace was thought to be contaminated when the emperor had died there. Thus, a new one had to be built for each new sovereign, and the capital was constantly relocating.

It is important to mention here, before turning to the historical evolution of Japan, the contemporary debate about national chronology. Japanese scholars, since Fujiwara Teikan in the eighteenth century, have realized that the *Nihonshoki* was inadequate from the historical point of view, at least insofar as the chronological information is concerned. They have suggested that Japan was founded 600 years later than stated in the *Nihonshoki*. Naka Michiyo, a historian of the late nineteenth century, argued in minute detail about the basic question of Japanese chronology. His ideas, supplemented by those of other scholars, pointed out that the reigns of the early Japanese emperors, as stated in the *Nihonshoki,* are unnaturally long; that the date of the enthronement of Jimmu Tenno has to be reconsidered; and that a chronological gap exists between the *Nihonshoki* and contemporary Chinese and Korean chronicles. For instance, in the *Nihonshoki,* the entries about the Empress Jingō and the Ojin Tenno can be identified with historical facts relating to those of Korea of the fourth and fifth centuries A.D. and must be placed some 120 years later than mentioned in the *Nihonshoki*. When the data contained in the *Nihonshoki* are compared with those of Chinese chronicles, the chronological gaps are somewhat reduced.

Historical Evolution

The Asuka Period (522–646)

From the beginning, the powerful clans surrounding the imperial throne fought each other without cease. Even Buddhism, the religion just imported from China and Korea, became entangled in these battles. When the pro-Buddhist Soga family triumphed, the religion got government support, and Soga-no-Umako's rule would last till the Taika Reformation in 645. No matter how powerful the Soga family was, the emperor was never displaced. He held at least a figurehead status for 1,500 years.

Japan under the Soga was still a barbarous land, far behind China or even Korea in political organization or technology. There was no written language, and only a few knew how to read or write Chinese. On the whole, the Japanese had very little contact with other peoples. Then, almost suddenly, during the late sixth century and the seventh century, Japan became enamorated of the great Chinese civilization and eagerly welcomed everything Chinese.

It was during this period that Prince Shotoku, working at the great Horyu-ji temple, wrote the famous Seventeen Article Constitution in 604. He was known as Shotoku Taishi, the "prince regent" (574–622), and his famous work is called *Jūsichije Kempō* in Japanese. This "constitution" seems to have been written as the basic preparation for the "moral state" that followed the Taika Reformation of 645; that is, the prince regarded his work as the first step for attaining such a "moral state." Whatever the case, it certainly represents a softening of the prevailing political regime.

The seventeen articles of the constitution, according to Professor Taro Ogawa, can be summarized as follows.

Article 1. Peace and harmony should be respected because they are very important for intergroup relations. Concord should always be honored. (This spirit of honoring concord and obeying the law is still alive in the present-day administration of justice.) Most people are egoistic, but few have a proper awareness of this.

Article 2. Great emphasis should be placed on the Buddhist belief of respecting Buddha, the laws, and the clergymen. There are very few evil men; if we teach them, they may become obedient.

Article 3. Subjects should obey the Tenno, because he is Heaven and they are ground. Everything will then go very smoothly.

Article 4. There should be orders and grades among the variety of subjects, and if the people respect these, they will certainly become obedient. (In this regard, Prince Shotoku follows the Chinese pattern. He believed in "free people on public land"—that is, that there should be no slavery. According to Japanese historians, only 10 percent of the population were then slaves, a surprising figure compared with the prevailing situation in a number of Western countries of those days.)

Article 5. Equality, speediness, and integrity should be maintained in court procedures.

Article 6. Encourage good deeds and chastise bad ones.

Article 7. Officers should be sage and benevolent to the people. Without these two virtues, they cannot give a good example.

Article 8. Officers should be at their offices early in the morning and retire late in the evening.

Article 9. Officers should believe in their work.

Article 10. Each individual should be tolerant toward others, within our common moral bounds.

Article 11. Officers should clearly understand the elements of merit and demerit and use them with moderation when deciding praise or blame.

Article 12. Officers should not receive gifts directly from the people.

Article 13. Officers should not lose time during their working hours communicating with other officials, family, or friends about illness or other matters.

Article 14. Officers should not be jealous of their colleagues but sage and benevolent gentlemen. If not, they may threaten the peace of the whole country.

Article 15. The basic philosophy in all matters should be "against privacy" and "toward public benefit."

Article 16. Officers should use people's services according to the seasons. From spring to autumn, the farmers are working, and they should not be disturbed. Winter is a good season, however, to obtain their assistance.

Article 17. Important matters should not be decided without consulting with other officers in group talks.

As can be seen, these seventeen maxims were, basically, instructions to officials, rather than a constitution in the true sense of the term.

The Early Nara (Hakuo) Period (646–710)

After a particularly bloody civil warfare, the Soga clan was driven from power, and in 645, Emperor Kotoku ascended the throne under the tutelage of another clan, the Fujiwara, who would remain predominant for the next 500 years.

In those days, people were attracted to Buddhism not so much for its basic tenets as for the sheer splendor of the temples and the decoration within them. In the center of the great Horyu-ji temple compound (also known as Ikura-dera), near the Asuka river and still standing at the village of Ikaruga, was the five-story pagoda (symbolizing earth, water, fire, wind, and sky), containing not only a number of relics and masterpieces of religious art but also the *kodo* (lecture hall) where monks talked to laymen followers. Besides its religious center, the temple was also a refuge from the turmoil and brutality of everyday life.

Together with Buddhism from China and Korea, a lesser infusion of Confucianism came from China. Having a great respect for their ancestors, the Japanese appreciated the elegant treatment afforded them in Confucianism. Meanwhile, the native religion, Shinto, receded for a while, particularly, when some emperors adopted Buddhism. Soon, ingenious theologians were able to reconcile Shintoism with Buddhism, which was vital for Japan, since the imperial family derived from the Shinto sun-goddess. Slowly, elements of Shintoisms, Buddhism, and Confucianism intermingled. Since then, religious conflicts have been rare in Japan, and a Buddhist temple and a Shinto shrine are often found in the same compound.

In 645, Emperor Kotoku, backed by the Fujiwara family, decided to establish a central government in Japan, similar to the rigid Chinese system. The resulting Taika Reformation led to an absolute monarchy, with the emperor rather than the clans in ascendancy. The large agricultural properties were transformed from the clans to the national government, which would distribute them, in small plots, to the peasants. In return, the peasants paid taxes to the state with part of their crops. This early version of state socialism was gradually enforced, and by the end of the seventh century, the government was almost totally centralized. Nevertheless, the artistocratic landowners basically retained their ranks, power, and wealth due to appointments to high offices, despite the Taika reforms. The Chinese system of appointments after rigorous written examinations never succeeded in Japan. Instead, aspirants' genealogies were carefully examined, but such a bureaucracy was anything but efficient.

The Nara (Tempyo) Period (710–94)

There was now a large sedentary bureaucracy, and the need for a fixed capital was strongly felt. In 710, a site was finally selected in the center of the Yamato plain, fifteen miles southeast of the Asuka district. Thus, Nara became the first permanent seat of government and the first real Japanese city. Soon it became not only a center for fashion and pleasure-seeking noblemen but also for culture and religion, because of its important monasteries and temples and, within them, libraries.

Power struggles continued. Priest and monks were so numerous in the city that one of them dared to aspire to the imperial throne when Empress Koken abdicated in favor of a young prince. Dokyo, the unscrupulous monk (not unlike Rasputin), got the ex-empress completely in his power and pretended to succeed her to the throne; but after she died in 770, he was banished from the city. In 784, Kammu Tenno decided that what was needed was a "priest-proof" city and ordered the transfer of the capital to nearby Nagaoka, which was abandoned ten years later because it was considered ill-omened.

The Early Heian-kyo or Kyoto Period (794–898)

Yet another city was established twenty-five miles northwest of Nagaoka, thought far enough to reduce the influence of Nara's Buddhists. It was first called—not too appropriately—Heian-kyo (Capital of Peace and Tranquility), the same name as Kammu Tenno's capital, but it came to be called Kyoto (Capital). It remained the imperial capital of Japan for over a thousand years. Within it, a distinctively Japanese culture began to develop. If during the Nara period Japanese artist were under strong Chinese influence, during the Heian period a truly Japanese pictorial style began to emerge. Kyoto soon became a flourishing cultural center. It was planned around a vast enclosed area called the Daidairi (the Great Interior), which became the ceremonial and administrative center. Emperor Kammu ruled without interference till 806, but afterward monks returned to the capital, and the Fujiwara gradually became, *de facto* or *de jure,* the real rulers of Japan. Kampaku (chancellor) was the title of the highest dignitary of the Imperial Court. Kammu was succeeded by Saga Tenno, who abolished the death penalty in the year 810, an abolition that, as we have seen, lasted till 1157.

Japan was still backward, with most of its estimated 5 million people living as peasants. Conflicts in the provinces were frequent. The non-Mongoloid Ainu tribes (thought possibly to have migrated by way of Siberia) of the north were often restive. Yet Kyoto flourished, in part, perhaps, due to Buddhism, but certainly because of the political skill of the Fujiwara, who knew how to retain support of and yet keep under control the emperor and his family.

With the T'ang dynasty breaking up on China, the relationship with the Chinese culture declined in this period. By the late ninth century, it was reduced to a trickle of scholars and traders.

The Late Heian (Fujiwara) Period (898–1185)

With Kyoto having its own rich and delightful culture, most of the noble families came to live there. This pleasant existence would continue till a new class of warrior-aristocrats arose in the provinces during the twelfth century. For the time being, the city's upper class—no more than some 3,000 out of its population of about 100,000—enjoyed a world of sophisticated life based on festivals, arts, and literature, with the emperor always at the center of the main events. Education was then largely a matter of learning to write in Chinese. Calligraphy was considered a great art by the aristocrats. There was no science or other intellectual life nor interest in other cultures.

This charming world of Kyoto began to wane by the start of the eleventh century, owing to the slow deterioration of its political and economic structure. The central government, meaning the Fujiwara family, had to cope with the violence deriving from the frequent attempts to achieve provincial independence but, at the same time, was reliant on alliances with some of the same warlike provincial families, especially with one known as the Minamoto, also known as the Genji, and another known as the Taira, or Heike. This military class (*bushi, buke,* or *samurai*) would become very prominent. In 1086, Emperor Shirakawa abdicated the throne, starting the era of the "cloistered emperors," or Insei, who, though usually members of a monastic order, would have greater freedom of movement in the power struggles of the twelfth century than the actual regnant emperor, who was often a child or a puppet of one of the contending forces.

During the eleventh century, with provincial turmoil as well as a plague of banditry, piracy, and even armed monks who threatened the Fujiwara government, much of Kyoto was burned and was never rebuilt. The curious Insei system brought power struggles between different "cloistered emperors," and the Taira and other clans were able to battle each other with increasing ferocity. By the middle of the twelfth century, Kyoto had lost its luster, and the Heian golden age gave way to a dark era of violence. Feats of arms took precedence over poetry contests. The warriors became supreme, and Japan fell under a military rule that would basically persist for about the next 700 years. With the growth of this "feudal" system, based on personal and clan loyalty, the *samurai,* the "gentlemen warriors," became a major figure. They were bound by a code of absolute loyalty to their immediate superiors in their chain of command, beyond the loyalty to wife and children and certainly beyond the fear of death. If the samurai seem to resemble the knights of medieval Europe, unlike them they were motivated not by chivalry or religious fervor but only by the need to strike terror in their enemies and serve their superiors. The warrior caste acquired considerable mystique. No one else could carry the weapons of the samurai.

An agreement between the Taira and the Minamoto families could have brought peace to the entire country, but this was against the belligerent spirit of the time. In 1156, a full-scale battle erupted between these two rival families in Kyoto itself, and the capital became the stage of great cruelty and destruction. Palaces were burned, and the prisoners were slaughtered, often beheaded. The chief of the Minamotos was captured and sentenced to death by the Tairas, and from these orgies of blood and arson the latter emerged the victors.

Once the Tairas had defeated the Minamotos in 1160, the bold and impetuous Taira leader, Taira-no-Kiyomori, seized control of the imperial family and became the real political authority. He was a clever politician who established his family with great pomp, even marrying one of his daughters into the imperial family. Emperor Antoku, who came to the throne in 1180 at the age of two, was his grandson. He developed the province of Aki, where he built the important shrine of Itsukushima, and also reopened trade on a large scale with South China, ruled then by the remnants of the Sung dynasty, building the port of Hiroshima and others for such a purpose.

But the Minamotos struck back in August 1180, under the leadership of Minamoto-no-Yoritomo, who became one of Japan's greatest statesmen. The civil wars raged across the country in an orgy of slaughter and devastation. Kiyomori died in 1181, but the war went on. By 1183, the Minamotos forced the Tairas to flee Kyoto, taking with them the child-emperor Antoku, but the "cloistered" ex-emperor Go Shirakawa stayed in the capital and supported the Minamotos. The Tairas were finally crushed in the great naval battle of the Inland Sea in 1185. Emperor Antoku, then a child of seven or eight years, was drowned, along with most of his entourage. Thus the Heian period ended.

The Kamakura Period (1185–1333)

Out of these wars grew the strongest government Japan had yet known. Yorimoto, the head of the Minamoto clan, imposed a military dictatorship based on the *samurai* code of loyalty. However, he had to put down much opposition, including the Fujiwara branch of the northern provinces. In 1189, at the end of the so-called Three-Year War, Yorimoto's army besieged the northern Fujiwara stronghold of Hiraizumi and put it to the torch. Thus, Yoritomo's power grew, but with the experience of the Tairas behind him, he did not make the mistake of moving to Kyoto. Instead, he established his headquarters in Kamakura, a fishing village at the end of a small peninsula near the mouth of Tokyo Bay in the Kanto region. Kamakura was easy to defend, thanks to the surrounding mountains and sea. Here he established the Bakufu (Central Government), with the assistance of a small but efficient bureaucracy, headed by himself. He used the title Sei-i-Taishogun (Military Commander against the barbarians), known by the abbreviation Taishogun (generalissimo). *Shogun* was a military rank, equivalent to general, that was given for a lifetime and on a hereditary basis to Yorimoto. Till the end of the sixteenth century, the Taishogun was in fact the supreme secular authority in the land, subordinated only in theory to the semidivine emperor. Samurai families settled in the area, and Kamakura became a major political and religious center, the rival of Kyoto. From then on, the emperor became only a symbol of national unity, without real power.

The stern realism of the samurai triumphed over the idealism and refinements of the aristocrats. This situation created a spiritual vacuum, and new religious movements began to develop. Zen Buddhism, recently arrived from the China of the Sung dynasty (from where Yorimoto "imported" much art and the architectural knowledge to enrich and build his new city), was encouraged by the Bakufu of Kamakura, since Yorimoto wanted to dissociate the new government from the old religious order. And Zen, with its emphasis on personal discipline and austerity, suited the samurai well.

Directly under Yorimoto there were an administrative council, a system of courts, and an all-important office called the Samurai-dokoro, which dealt with all the affairs of the samurai and was, along with the Bakufu, a major locus of power.

Yorimoto died in 1199 at fifty-two, and his government might have disappeared if not for Masakao, his strong-minded widow, who was able to arrange that members of her father's family, the Hojos, emerged as *shikken,* or regents, in control of the Bakufu and the Shogunate. For almost two centuries, the Hojo family exercised a complex rule over Japan. Its official head was the emperor at Kyoto, but his powers were administered by a "cloistered emperor," usually his father, who in turn delegated the imperial powers to the Shogun at Kamakura, who was dominated by a Hojo regent. This long chain of delegated powers functioned surprisingly well, and occasional rebellions were always crushed by the Hojo regents. The country prospered, the population increased, towns began to grow, trade with China was extensive, and there was somewhat a return to the national Shinto gods, though Zen Buddhism was on the way to becoming the national religion. Still, during this feudal period, most of the population remained peasants.

In November 1274, a great Mongol armada, under Kublai Khan, Genghis Khan's grandson, sailed into the Korean straits and took the small islands of Tsushima and Iki, landing afterward at Hakozaki Bay in northern Kyushu. The battle was inconclusive, but that night a storm sank many of the Mongols' ships and blew the others back toward Korea.

The Japanese began to prepare for another Mongol attack in Hakozaki Bay, building a wall around it. Early in the summer of 1281, a larger Mongol fleet sailed from Korea toward Kyushi. The first troops landed on the island's north coast on June 23. The Japanese, with their characteristic contempt for death, attacked immediately, and the struggle lasted more than fifty days. Then, in late August, a great typhoon roared over Kyushi, the Mongol fleet was wrecked, most of the crews drowned, and the soldiers still on the island were duly slaughtered. Thus typhoon was called *kamikaze,* the "divine wind." The Japanese suicide pilots of World War II were also named *kamikaze.*

The war, however, had drained Japan economically, especially depleting the Bakufu, which moved to the Imperial Court in Kyoto to try to regain power. In 1318, an unusually vigorous emperor, Go Daigo, ascended the throne. He was a grown-up man resolved to restore the authority of the imperial family. In 1333, the Hojo regent sent a powerful army against him, but its commanding officer, Ashikaga Takauji, changed sides and entered the capital in Go Daigo's name. Meanwhile, samurai families wanted to come back to Heian, attracted by the cultural life of the ancient capital. For a while it looked as if Go Daigo would succeed, but the ambitious Takauji managed to replace him with a puppet emperor and took over the Kyoto government as Shogun, while Go Daigo set up a rival court in the mountains south of Kyoto. The Kamakura Bakufu was burned in the resulting civil war and was finally transferred back to Kyoto.

The Muromachi or Ashikaga Period (1337–1573)

The Shoguns of the line established by Ashikaga Takauji, who assumed the rank of Taishogun in 1338, were never as strong as those of Yorimoto or his

Hojo successors. Within a century, their power had almost disappeared and, for almost three centuries after Takauji's coup d'état, Japan had practically no real central government. The southern court established by Go Daigo returned to Kyoto in 1392, but both emperors and Shoguns remained shadowy figures, while the *daimyo* (great name), the noblemen of the provinces, came to rule their more than sixty principalities like independent little nations. A new kind of feudalism had begun.

Notwithstanding all this, the country prospered. In fact, it was during the fifteenth and sixteenth centuries that Japan reached its highest point in culture and the arts. Some of the samurai married into ancient families, and during the time of the most important of the Ashikaga, Yoshimitsu (Shogun from 1367 to 1394, then ruling from retirement until his death in 1408), many powerful families moved to Kyoto and competed with Yoshimitsu and his family in the luxury and refinement of their lives. Zen Buddhism was now stronger than ever, not only setting up an elaborate school system to teach young people to read and write, but organizing and controlling Japan's foreign trade, which was particularly strong with China. The Bakufu in Kyoto imported many aesthetic objects from Ming China to replenish its treasury. China sent raw silk, elegant clothes, paintings, porcelains, and copper coins, while Japan reciprocated with sulfur (a raw material of their volcanoes), their already famous swords and armor, lacquerware, pottery, and even horses. The spiritual values of monastic Buddhism coexisted with commercial interests. In fact, some of the Zen temples served as storehouses.

As the later Ashikaga Shoguns grew progressively feebler, local wars of conquest between daimyos became common. In some provinces, vassals defied their overlords, and even the peasants revolted, assaulting tax collectors and plundering granaries. In the early fifteenth century, the disturbances mounted, and in 1441, the peasants invaded the capital itself, defying the now powerless Shogunate.

While Yoshimasa, Yoshimitsu's grandson and aesthete Shogun, was devoting most of his time to the arts, the violence came to a climax with the 1467 breakout of the Onin War, the prelude to a bloody era of civil strife known as Sengokujidai (the Age of the Country at War), which would last till 1573, the end of the Muromachi period. Much of Kyoto was reduced to ashes, and the control of the Shogun over provincial samurai virtually ended. In fact, the Ashikagas were rendered so poor that in 1500, the body of the emperor Go Tsuchimikado remained unburied for six weeks for lack of money for the funeral.

The old social order disintegrated. During the Sengokujidai, many ancient families were reduced to poverty or exterminated. Those who replaced them were families of simple soldiers seeking only to increase their wealth and prestige, a pursuit from which daughters were almost excluded, so that the subordination of Japanese women began in earnest. Each daimyo made his own laws. And small landowners banded together and took control of the local government, so that the Sengokujidai was not without some benefit for the lower classes.

Daimyos sought to swallow each other's territory, and the successful ones gained the support of young adventurers. When there was no war on land, these young warriors engaged in piracy. During the second half of the fifteenth century, Japanese pirate vessels, sometimes with Korean cohorts, attacked the entire coast of China. The Chinese called them *wako* (from the Chinese for "dwarfs") and succeeded in forcing them farther south, so the wako raided the Philippines, Thailand, Java, and the Malacca Straits. In the early sixteenth century, they began to establish permanent settlements. Their activities were extremely profitable, and part of their wealth flowed back to their protectors, the daimyos of southern Japan.

In 1542 or 1543, the first Europeans, a Portuguese party, landed in Japan, carrying with them harquebuses, the latest product of Europe's rapidly growing firearms industry. The Japanese realized at once the importance of this new weapon, and the era of firearms began in Japan soon afterward.

Jorge Alvarez, a Portuguese merchant and sea captain, arrived in 1547 and reported in detail on what he saw. Soon after came the Spanish Jesuit Francis Xavier, followed over the next century by other Jesuits (always, no matter their nationality, with the backing of the Portuguese crown), who sought to convert the Japanese and sometimes succeeded with some of them. Some powerful *bonzes* (Buddhist monks) even instigated popular revolts to expel the missionaries. About 1569, the Jesuit Gaspar Vilela converted a daimyo of a small fishing village, who was renamed Don Bartholemew and who, in return, presented the village to the Jesuits as a safe harbor for Portuguese trade. The village was to grow into the important seaport of Nagasaki, a Christian town with churches and Jesuit schools, which served as a fortress for the Portuguese merchants and was in fact governed by Jesuits.

By about 1570, the "Country at War" was approaching a turning point. A few powerful daimyos controlled most of the country, and some began to think about unifying it and restoring peace. The fear of the Europeans, the "southwest barbarians," may have inspired this urge for unification. By the end of the sixteenth century, open hostility was directed against the European missionaries and merchants. Japan decided once more to shut itself in.

The Muromachi period, despite the strife, was by no means an era of unrelieved darkness. It gave birth to a number of art forms, which were to mature during the succeeding periods, the last great expressions of traditional Japan before the process of Westernization began.

The Momoyama (Azuchi) Period (1573–1603)

The chaos of the "Age of the Country at War" was brought to an end by two remarkable men, Nobunaga Oda and Hideyoshi Toyotomi, who were able to unify Japan. The former was a fierce, heartless, and single-minded autocrat whose family were retainers of a very minor feudal lord in the province of Owari, near the present city of Nagoya. In 1560, when a powerful and ambitious daimyo, Imagawa, decided to conquer Kyoto and began his march with an army of 25,000 men, he did not anticipate much opposition from Oda, who was then the leader of a small army of about 3,000 men. Yet Oda attacked and won. It was a turning point in Japanese history, and the young Oda suddenly became a national figure. Many chieftains came over to his side, among them Tokugawa Ieyasu, who would eventually become the ruler of all Japan.

Oda adopted the new muskets for his army and won many battles against neighboring lords. By 1567, he was so famous that the emperor sent him a secret message requesting his help in regaining his lost estates, and Ashikaga Yoshiaki, one of the claimants to the Shogunate, also asked for his support. On the basis of these two requests, he considered himself authorized to take control of the country. In 1568, he marched into Kyoto with Ashikaga, whom he installed as Shogun. But Oda was able to dominate only central Japan. The rest of the country refused to obey him, particularly some warlike Buddhist sects near Kyoto. Oda hated the Buddhists and was very friendly toward the Christian missionaries, particularly the Jesuit Luis Frois, who was introduced to him in 1569, when Oda declared full war against the Buddhist sects. He also decreed that the Jesuits could live in Kyoto and freely preach Christianity. After some savage victories over the Buddhists, he defeated the daimyos in the battle of Nagashino in 1575, a landmark in the history of Japanese warfare in which a rather small army of musketeers moved down four waves of samurai cavalry.

When Ashikaga began to act on his own, Oda sent him into exile, so marking the end of the Ashikaga Shogunate. Then, one morning in 1582, Oda was suddenly surrounded by the soldiers of Akechi Mutsuhide, a supposedly loyal general. After some resistance, Oda either killed himself or was killed.

Oda's successor, Toyotomi, was a commoner below samurai rank. Many Japanese consider him the greatest man their nation has produced. He was Oda's leading general, and upon his leader's murder or suicide, he rushed back to Kyoto and soon after killed the assumed assassin. He conciliated a rival general, Tokugawa Ieyasu, putting him in charge of the eastern provinces, while he bacame the master of central Japan. He also made bloodless peace with some daimyos who were still holding out. However, to prevent the rise of other ambitious commoners like himself, he enacted many repressive measures against that social class.

In spite of the ceaseless fighting, Japan was progressing and prosperous. Hideyoshi, a more pleasant and hedonistic person than Oda, wanted to be considered a patron of the arts and gathered around him the best painters, poets, and actors. Thus, his rule, sometimes known as the Japanese rococo period, saw considerable artistic activity. The paintings of this period are detailed, exuberant, and full of bright colors. The simplicity of Ashikaga's times and the discipline and restraint of Zen Buddhism were gone. Hideyoshi was as opposed to the Buddhist monks as Oda had been, in 1586, he ordered all the Jesuits to leave Japan. His decree was never enforced, and the Jesuits continued to proselytize, but more discreetly. More disturbing was the arrival of the Spaniards in the Far East. Hideyoshi feared that they would try to overthrow him, but he still had to finish first with some internal enemies, which he did in a most successful campaign. He then decided to slam the doors of Japan to the outside world, because he feared European religions, technology, and ideas as a threat to the established Japanese order. This voluntary seclusion, known as "the national policy of isolation" or "the closed country," would last more than two centuries; it kept Japan on a separate course of development from that of Europe.

So confident was Hideyoshi that he decided to attempt something unprecedented in Japanese history: large-scale foreign conquest. First, he targeted China. In May 1592, his forces landed in Korea, then a Chinese tributary state, and quickly subdued it; but when the Japanese threatened to cross the Yalu River, in a drive toward Peking, the Chinese reacted and forced them back down the Korean peninsula. In 1597, Japan invaded again but eventually withdrew.

Meanwhile, at home, there was a new development: Spanish Franciscan friars came to Japan from the Philippines, despite Jesuit opposition. At first, their proselytizing produced no local antagonism, but in 1596, when an officer of a Spanish galleon shipwrecked in Shikoku threatened, during a dispute, that the king of Spain would conquer Japan, Hideyoshi reacted by condemning the Franciscans to crucifixion. Six Franciscans, seventeen Japanese friars-in-training, and three Japanese Jesuit lay brothers—included by mistake—were crucified at Nagasaki on 5 February 1597. Hideyoshi died a year later.

Broadly speaking, this period saw a decline in the role of religion in Japan. Today it is one of the most unecclesiastical nations in the world. Its secularization occurred in stages. First, in the eleventh century, Buddhism lost some spiritual power as its priests concentrated on ritual, aristocratic pleasures, and warfare. During the thirteenth and fourteenth centuries came the orientation toward Zen Buddhism. Finally, in the sixteenth century, Oda destroyed the Buddhists' military power, at the same time that Christianity was imparting to the Japanese its message of man's ability to control his own destiny.

The Tokugawa or Edo Period (1603–1867)

Hideyoshi's successor was his old ally, Tokugawa Ieyasu, who became Shogun in 1603, when he was sixty-one years old. The Tokugawa Shogunate ruled until 1867.

At the start of his reign, Ieyasu was eager for European knowledge and tolerant of the Christian missionaries, but the discussions he had with the pilot of a Dutch ship that docked in Japan, an Englishman named Will Adams, changed his mind. Adams convinced him that the 300,000 Christians in Japan were likely to become allies of Spain in a possible invasion by that country. Consequently, Ieyasu decreed that all missionaries must leave Japan and that all Japanese Christians must join some Buddhist sect and change their faith. This time, the anti-Christian decrees were enforced, but not in a hurry. Some hundred missionaries left in a Portuguese ship, and the Japanese Christians were not persecuted for the time being. And as Ieyasu had thought, foreign trade was not affected by all this.

Ieyasu died in 1616, at the age of seventy-four, and was buried within the magnificent Toshogu Shrine at Nikko. He was succeeded by his son, Hidetada, who was harder on the Christians. Four clandestine missionaries were beheaded in 1617, and Japanese Christians who refused to recant began to be executed in great numbers. This was only a part of a broader movement hostile to foreign influence, secular and religious. When Hidetada retired as Shogun in 1623 and was succeeded by his son, Iemitsu, a new wave of persecution began, one in which thousands of Christians were martyred. Meanwhile, in Europe, the Spanish Inquisition was burning thousands of heretics, and the Thirty-Year War was raging.

In 1633, the Shogunate started to issue the Exclusion Decrees, thus starting the "National Policy of Isolation," which would last till 1853. Japanese people were forbidden to go out of their country, or to return home if they lived abroad too long, under pain of death. In 1637, after a rebellion near Nagasaki of thousands of Christian peasants was stamped out, the Portuguese merchants were expelled, but not the Dutch or Chinese, so foreign trade was strictly controlled. The propagation of Christianity was forbidden, as was private communication with foreigners. Japan was now almost completely shut off from the outside world. This lengthy isolation not only helped to form certain aspects of the Japanese national character but also permitted the accumulation of wealth that paved the way for Japan's later industrial development.

The basic policy of the Tokugawa Shogunate was to preserve Japan's type of military feudalism and to perpetuate its own power. Japan was then ruled much like a modern police state. The Shogunate had been moved by Ieyasu from Kyoto to Edo (now Tokyo), an easily defensible site. For a while, the social structure imposed by the Tokugawas remained fairly stable. The daimyos were still rich but practically without influence in state affairs. They were subjected to humiliating regulations to keep them quiescent. The peasants lost almost all rights, and tax collectors took about half of their crops. The towns' commoners were the most fortunate: skilled artisans made a rather good living, while merchants and moneylenders grew rich.

Yet towns and cities were growing fast. Edo, no more than a village when

Ieyasu made it his capital, had a population of half a million by 1700. By the same year, Japan had a full money economy, with a great variety of coins. By the end of the seventeenth century—while the aristocracy clung to older arts, such as traditional music, the Noh plays, and the tea ceremony—the townspeople entertained themselves with the so-called Floating World of restaurants and theaters, prostitutes and bath-girls, singers and dancers, and so on. Kabuki, a form of popular drama, still flourishes in modern Japan, with its slow-moving, fabulist, and stylized characteristics. The Shogunate disapproved of the Floating World and sometimes confiscated all the wealth of a nouveau riche merchant or banker. On the other hand, some of the townsmen acquired samurai rank, most often by paying a poor samurai to adopt them into his family. Even in the villages, enterprising peasants started small businesses and freed themselves from feudal bondage.

In spite of being a "close country," Japan kept pace with the West in its own way. Education spread to all classes, so that by 1850, about 40 percent of Japanese males were literate, a proportion then higher than in some European countries. It is true that power-driven machines and industrialism were completely lacking, but Japanese artisans were as skilled as the best of the West. Japanese commerce, trading, and banking were well developed. So in 1853, when the "black ships" of the American Commodore Matthew Perry steamed into Edo Bay and forced Japan to reopen the "closed country," Japan was not an "undeveloped" nation. Once again, it adjusted to the Western ways with remarkable ease while preserving the most important aspects of its distinctive culture.

During the Tokugawa period, the gaps between central and provincial calendars disappeared after the establishment of the Jekyo calendar, the first Japanese one, which replaced the Chinese one that was in use till then. Under Emperor Meiji, Japan adopted Occidental systems, including the Gregorian calendar, as of 1 January 1873. On the same date the "Japanese era" was established, with Jimmu Tenno as its founder. Emperor Meiji also launched an expansionist program, defeating China and Russia, and Japan became a great world power. The Meiji period lasted from 1868 till 1912, when the contemporary period, known as that of Taisho and Showa, began.

The Japanese People and the Law

Before analyzing Japan's legal systems, some peculiar characteristics of its society must be understood. The Japanese people are not accustomed to the detailed processes of legal reasoning. Instead, they may react emotionally to the *ho* or *horitsu* (body of written legislation). They could say that they hate (or like) this or that *"toda nantonaku,"* which might be translated as "for no reason in particular."

New concepts are not necessarily integrated with older ones but simply coexist, creating a sort of "fashion" of ideas and concepts. Thus, their modern legal system has been based successively on French, Anglo-Saxon, and German models, not so much because one was seen to have been superseded by another but simply because it had gone out of fashion.

If the Japanese way of thinking does not favor the functioning of law as a system of rights and duties, it does not mean that Japanese society has lacked standards of conduct. Before the modern system of law was established, a nonlegal system of *giri,* or "customs," prevailed, and giri continues to operate today, side by side with the legal system.

It is difficult to explain what giri is or even to define the word, even in Japanese, because it includes many disparate items. Therefore, it might be better to try to describe it by noting some of its basic characteristics:

1. Giri regulates interpersonal relations. There is a giri of a child to his parents, of a student to his teacher, of a beneficiary to his benefactor, of one friend to another, and so on.

2. Giri relations entail an obligation (*okaeshi*) to reciprocate. Whoever does not satisfy his giri is seriously dishonored, but so is the benefactor who applies pressure to be reciprocated for his benevolent act.

3. Giri relations are perpetual, even between a merchant and his customer. If the latter buys something from another merchant, he has violated his giri.

4. Giri relationships are supposed to be based on *ninjo* (feelings of affection), not on selfish considerations. Thus, private arrangements for purposes of profit or lovemaking were frowned upon. Marital relations should be based only on ninjo, not on material considerations.

5. Giri relationships are based on the feudal hierarchical order. During the Edo period, the number of *bungen* (societal ranks) was 360. Thus, even today, in every large department store, someone is stationed to greet customers entering each floor, since customers have a higher rank than merchants. On the other hand, a head of a department knows that his giri-ninjo means giving appropriate and equitable instructions to his subordinates. This is one of the "secrets" to explain the great loyalty and harmony that exist in modern Japanese enterprises.

6. The rules of giri are sanctioned by a feeling of honor. Their great sensitivity about honor prevents many Japanese from acting immorally or against giri. The disapproval of others is a feared consequence. On the other hand— as in many other cultures—a wrongful act that no one will witness might be committed. The psychological role of honor largely accounts for why giri is so scrupulously observed even today.

In sum, giri is a system of perpetual, voluntary, emotional, and hierarchical norms, based on a customary code of honor and creating the expectation of reciprocation. The rules of giri are often opaque to outsiders.

Japanese hierarchical norms clash with the Western concept of equality before the law, so that even today, social conflicts are settled mostly outside the legal system. Even the courts, to some extent, operate less as instruments of judgment than as organs of conciliation. In rural areas, the resistance to modern law is stronger than in cities, and the relationships between landlords and peasants are still based on giri. All these considerations are, of course, subject to change. Japanese elders complain that young people do not behave according to giri-ninjo and are too materialistic and calculating. Therefore, the Japanese attitude to law may also change under the impact of time.

A second difficulty in understanding Japanese law is the Japanese language. Japanese is written in Chinese ideographic characters, which work well enough in Chinese, since its words are monosyllables that do not vary in form. But for Japanese, a language of wholly different structure, the Chinese system is considered exceedingly clumsy. Therefore, it had to be modified, but the means used were also clumsy, particularly the transformation of Chinese characters into more phonetic symbols. A positive outcome was that the Japanese vocabulary was enriched, but it also became more complex. In addition, during the feudal times, expressions for the same thing varied greatly according to the social class of the person using them. The language thus became a very complicated one, more suited to express emotions than logical arguments. And without a good understanding of its strange nuances, a good understanding of Japanese law is not easy to attain.

On the whole, the rapid imposition of capitalism on traditional feudalism has led to a society with a "double structure." Many Japanese people now believe that the sudden democratization and modernization has dislocated their society and that a return to the old morality is very much needed. For the same reason, there is a pervasive tension and duality in modern Japanese law.

The Evolution of the Japanese Legal System

If the western world's myth of the primordial crime is that of Cain and Abel, Japan's is that of *kamuyorai* (divine banishment) or Prince Susa-no-o, the younger brother of the sun-goddess. He was expelled from Heaven to the earthly world for persistent misbehavior, but first he had to present expiatory gifts to the 800 deities who had jointly condemned him. He also had his head shaved and his nails pulled out. This is not a myth of retributive punishment, as in less primitive societies, but of *harae* (ritual exorcism). Crime was abhorred because it was thought to pollute the whole community and possibly provoke divine wrath. Therefore, ritual processes—such as bathing and sacrificial offerings—were common.

Japanese law has a background of some 2,000 years, first under Chinese and Indian influence and later under Western influence. Contemporary Japanese law has retained almost nothing from the past, but an analysis of the previous legal systems is important, since its influence still underlies Japanese society in numerous ways. From Himiko's unified Japan, during the third century A.D., till 1868, the Year of the Meiji Restoration, Japanese law evolved in a discernible pattern. During the nineteenth century, and more so after that, it went through rapid changes under Western influence. But these considerations diverge from the focus of this book and will not be explored here.

Early Society

There is insufficient documented knowledge about ancient penal practices in Japan. Nevertheless, there is no doubt that Japan has a long legal history. In the chapter in the *Nihonshoki* dealing with the period of the Emperor Ingyo, it is mentioned that justice had been adminstered since the fourth century A.D., when national unity was achieved by the ancestors of the present emperor. It is true that there were then no concepts of "crime" and "punishment" in the legal or sociological sense and that the country was under strong religious influence, so that religion and law were closely related. Nor was law yet distinguished from other customary rules, particularly the religious ones. People's morality seems to have been rather strong, and there were few crimes and conflicts. Women were generally "virtuous," in spite of the fact that men usually had four or five wives, and even those of the lower classes had three or four.

Himiko, an old spinster whose brother helped her to rule, was a kind of a pontiff, since the Shinto religion considered her ancestors gods. She was believed to know the will of her god-ancestors through her prayers; therefore, her expressed oracles were law, although it was her brother who carried them out. (In early Japan, the woman-king was the rule rather then the exception.) In other cases, justice was done according to the expressed opinion of a miko—one of the young girls who performed the sacred dances, such as *kagura,* in the large Shinto temples. Some among the olde mikos claimed to have communication with gods or ancestors, so that they knew the future and could render judgment based on the divine will.

In those days, derelicts were regarded as blemishes detested by the gods, but they could be cleansed by religious ceremonials and rituals. Central to Shinto society were the concepts of *tsumi*—acts of religious injury, better to be avoided—and *harae*—the solemn rituals of offerings and cleansing by which the priests were able to eliminate evil. They were based on notions of Chinese practices, which were then more developed than in Japan.

The "judicial" procedure known as *kudadachi* seems to have existed since the fourth century. It was based on ordeals similar to others that existed in the ancient societies of Asia and Europe. After the parties had sworn the correctness of their respective statements, they were asked to obtain a piece of baked clay or stone in the boiling waters contained in a cauldron. A favorable judgment was rendered in favor of the party whose hand was not scalded. The "culprit's" wives and children were then taken away from him, and if the "offense" was a serious one, family and relatives could be destroyed with him.

A Shinto statement—*Oharai-no-Norito*—refers to the kinds of misbehaviors to be purged by dedication to *Kami,* one of the gods, through *harae* and *misogi* (offering of properties). It mentions especially two kinds of offenses: *amatsu-tsumi* (heavenly ones) and *kunitsu-tsumi* (earthly ones). The first are mainly related to agricultural crimes, including injury to animals, and the others to bodily injuries and sexual family offenses. These types of *tsumi* may have been applied to two different kinds of people, one with an agricultural background and the other with a pastoral one, particularly during the transitory period from the third to the fourth centuries. Regarding punishments, it seems that death, transportation, banishment, tattooing, and corporal punishments were already in use, but there was also a primitive system of compensation.

The Period of the Ritsu-Ryō

Just as Japan's political structure evolved into a more centralized and secularized mold, resembling the Chinese one, in the field of law during the eighth century, a number of codes were created following the general pattern of the Chinese T'ang codes. These legal documents were known as the *Ritsu-Ryō*. The *Ritsu* corresponds to penal rules, like a modern criminal code, and the *Ryō* contains all other regulations involving provisions for national organization, as well as for administrative, procedural, and civil organization. The Ritsu-Ryō system was introduced in response to the needs of the times, when the great Taika Reform and the movement for the centralization of powers were being instituted. They are also intended to instill the basic Confucian concepts among the people. As usual in ancient "codes," the Ritsu-Ryō gives more prominence to criminal matters than to civil ones.

Whereas Western law, owing to the pervasive impact of Roman law, is basically oriented toward resolving disputes, and therefore to procedure, the aim of Far Eastern law is mainly to prevent disputes. In this regard and others, the Ritsu-Ryō were a replica of the Chinese codes, except that they mitigated the punishments and were much simplified. The Ritsu-Ryō were revised five times between 645 a.d. and the Nara period. Each revision had a different name, such as Omi-Ryō, Tammu-Ryō, and others. The Taiho Ritsu-Ryō, promulgated in 701 and enforced the following year, is the best known of all of them, but unhappily is no longer extant. Still existing is most of the Yoro Ritsu-Ryō, which was promulgated in 718 and came into force thirty-nine years later. The Ritsu of this code have twelve books and the Ryō thirty. Its final, amended, and elaborated version is known as the Ritsu-Ryō Kyaku-Shiki. With it Japan became a "legal state" to a certain extent. It contained five punishments: death, transportation, forced labor, striking, and whipping. They are not called "punishments," however, because such a term—*keibatsu*—was as yet nonexistent. Instead, they were known as "crime to be killed," "crime to be transported," "crime to be expiated with labor," and so on.

The judicial procedure under Ritsu-Ryō can be divided into two parts; one is a proceeding provided by Kōshikirei, and the other is known as Dangoku, provided by Dangokurei. In the former, a lawsuit was instituted by filing the plaintiff's complaint with the local authority having territorial jurisdiction over the defendant's permanent domicile, and the judgment was rendered on the basis of oral proceedings. In Dangoku, an action was instituted by an accusation made by an injured person or the general public to the authority exercising jurisdiction over the place where the crime was committed, and a judgment, generally based on confession, was entered by referring to an article of the Ritsu-Ryō. In both civil and criminal cases, appeals were permitted.

To increase understanding of the law, a faculty of law, known as Myo-Bo-Do, was established in the daigaku (university). Legal knowledge was much appreciated during this period, uncharacteristic in Japanese history. This was because the law was not strictly related to procedure and was, in fact, not a judicial practice but an administrative one. Even so, there was no legal profession, though important studies of the Ritsu-Ryō were published, two of which are still extant.

The Ritsu-Ryō system did not last long, first because Japan was culturally quite different from China; therefore, it was rather difficult to apply these norms. Most of its provisions soon fell into disuse. Another reason was that many administrative and judicial texts were derived from these provisions, so that the original text became obscure and forgotten. Finally, this system collapsed when the imperial authority that adopted the code lost its power. Still, the Ritsu-Ryō were never formally abrogated, and some were even applied after the 1868 Restoration.

Thanks to the Ritsu-Ryō system, which lasted till about the middle of the tenth century, the imperial government succeeded in concentrating all state powers in its hands. From then on, lands and public offices were distributed by the imperial government according to the rules of the Ritsu-Ryō. A certain extension of land was given for life to everyone six or more years of age, according to the various categories of persons determined by the law. Although this resembled an agrarian system with socialistic overtones, the real purpose was to assure the state of its taxes. Public offices were apparently open to anyone, but in practice virtually only to the nobility.

The Confucian ideology was quickly neglected. Many estates were acquired by usurpation or by making tempting offers. This practice of acquiring *sho* (private property) grew progressively. Though illegal, these sho gradually acquired official status, and the *honjo* (owner) was given certain immunities, later expanded into legislative, administrative, and jurisdictional prerogatives that he could exercise over his sho. Thanks to these developments, as already mentioned, a military class was emerging. Under the Ritsu-Ryō system, the army was composed of professional officers and recruited soldiers, but gradually, from the end of the eighth century, this system was suppressed in favor of an army of samurai. And so the *samurai family feudal era* was established; it lasted from 1192 till 1867. The Japanese Middle Ages were dominated by these samurai or *bushi,* the "warrior class," with the clan in power changing from time to time as a direct consequence of the almost permanent political feuds. In the history of the Japanese legal system, this is one of the most important periods. Compared with the previous period of the Ritsu-Ryō, when emphasis was placed upon criminal trials, remarkable progress was made in regard to the law of civil procedure.

The following period can be divided in two stages: dual and unitary feudalism.

The Period of Dual Feudalism

The breakdown of the centralized state brought a mixed regime of feudalism and sho. In other words, the world of the imperial court and the honjo was still attached to the Ritsu-Ryō, while that of the samurai was feudal in structure. All this while the former was losing influence and the latter was gaining it.

During Yorimoto's rule, a hierarchical order was established. The bond of vassalage has a marked familial character, and each group of samurai, linked by blood relationship, was controlled by its head, the Katoku. This bond was based on a broad contract between the suzerain and his vassals, which, however—much unlike Western feudalism—was rather imprecise. The vassal owed his overlord absolute fidelity but had no legal rights to demand the rewards, usually in the form of *shiki* (administratrive positions), which the overlord was expected to give him. Litigation between lord and vassal, on the other hand, was strictly prohibited.

When Yorimoto defeated the Taira clans, he confiscated all their lands, which were distributed among his own vassals. Afterward, he required that the Imperial Court appoint him as chief *jito,* meaning that he was entitled to send his vassals to any *sho* and enjoy there a shiki. In such a way, this new system facilitated the gradual dispossession of the real owner of a sho, the honjo; and by the end of this period, the sho regime had largely come to an end.

Similar to this feudal relationship, and under the Confucian ideology of filial piety, a child had to obey his parents unconditionally, without corresponding parental duties. Such an almost unlimited power lent itself to abuses and encouraged a conception of the child as a kind of property; a child could be sold by his parents or bound for life to be a prostitute or acrobat. Even today there are extreme incidents of this type, such as a parent committing suicide and killing his children as well.

Apart from the feudal dualism there was a legal pluralism, with three coexisting main systems:

1. The first one was the *Kuge-ho* (*Kuge*, "Imperial Court," and *ho*, "law" or "statute"). At the end of the Ritsu-Ryō era, and gradually declining through the Ashikaga period, the administrative and judicial practices constituted a system based on a kind of customary law, incorporated into the Ritsu-Ryō, which continued to be applied in the regions reserved to the imperial authority. During the Kamakura era, the Kuge-ho was, at least in theory, common law; but in practice it was gradually limited, and it had little importance during the Muromachi period. The laws promulgated by the Imperial Court had mostly a moral importance and were meant to inculcate a moderate way of life. Nevertheless, in conflicts arising among different authorities, the legal experts based their opinions according to the rules of the Ritsu-Ryō, thereby creating an important source of customary law.

2. The Honjo-ho was the private law for all private sho, greatly varying from one region to the other. The Honjo-ho was, in fact, not more than a variant of the Ritsu-Ryō.

3. The Buke-ho covered the legal relationships—rules and customs—peculiar to the samurai class. Also known as *bushido* (the way of the *bushi* or *samurai*), these laws resembled a chivalric code. Some laws were written, but basically it was a customary system. The most important of the Buke-ho was the Goseibai Shikimoku, or Jōei Shikimoku, promulgated in 1232, during the Kamakura period. This Shogunate ordinance, or "warriors' law," contains the basic rules of the administration of justice during the Kamakura and the Muromachi periods. It is reputed as a human law, and its basic aims were to prevent underhanded dealings. Judges had to solve disputes according to its rules. There is no doubt that, consistent with the traditional conception of Japanese law, its purpose was more to prevent social conflicts than to determine right and wrong. Nevertheless, it was basically used to serve the needs of the rulers, who applied it to the ruled as they saw fit.

Basically, the law during this entire period was based on bushi customs and, to a large extent, derived from Confucian tenets. However, the Buke-ho, because it grew out of the daily life of the bushi, is considered essentially Japanese.

The Goseibai Shikimoku had only fifty-one articles, but it greatly influenced future legislation; it is based on reasoning rather than positive legal principles. It was also known as Jōei (the Japanese calendar year of 1232), and Shikimoku was a Shogunate ordinance. It was written by two righteous and selfless moralists, a fact that determined the basic conditions of this law. One was Yasutoki Hōjō, who was chief of staff of the Shogunate and had a reputation as a sage; the other, Myoe, was a Buddhist monk. Among its provisions there are ownership rules; the jurisdiction of upper bushi over lower ones; and litigation procedures, including those for conflicts between the bushi and their employees.

This Shikimoku was read by many because it was written in simple Japanese. It was also admired by a famous poet, Bashō, in one of his *haiku* (short poems): "The full moon is now shining upon the fifty-one articles." One of its most remarkable statements is that "in a quarrel or fight, both parties are to blame."

The punishments stipulated in this Shikimoku were not so harsh as in other codes. It contained the death penalty, but very frequently it was changed to transportation. Cutting parts of the body was rarely applied. Whipping and caning, as well as shackles, fetters, and the pillory, were abolished.

Finally, from this same period there are a few other documents of particular interest. One is a Saikyojō (a decision on civil and similar cases) of the year 1313, referring to a judgment rendered in favor of the Tenmangū Anrakuji temple by Chinzei Tandai, the military representative of the central government in Kyushu, concerning a dispute about the ownership of land. The other is a Migyoshō (a mandamus issues by a superior, such as a Shogun, to subordinates) of the year 1328, ordering the enforcement of the decision rendered in the aforementioned Saikyojō, which had not been done till then.

During the Kamakura Shogunate, when a man and woman were married, the woman could not seek a divorce from her husband, even if he was a wicked man and she a battered woman. To correct such a situation, a temple law was established, permitting the temple to concern itself with every woman who wished to be divorced; in such a way, the woman was set free. This law continued to function till the closing days of the Tokugawa Shogunate.

During the era of the Sengokujidai, there was an unusual development of codified laws, thanks to the *Jinkaishū* (ordinances). In 1536, for instance, one of these ordinances was enacted and promulgated by the thirteenth head of the Date family, the feudal lords of the domain corresponding to the present Miyagi prefecture. It has 171 articles and was enforced only in his domain. It started by statting the principle that ex post facto legislation may not be applied. It provided the most advanced legal system of those days. Nevertheless, torture was often used in order to obtain confessions from Japanese spies or from those belonging to the enemy.

Nobunaga Oda would issue his ordinances in the form of *seisatsu,* roadside notice-boards, such as the one issued in 1567 that proscribed arson, violent behavior, and other similar crimes in the area corresponding to present-day Senjudō, in the city of Gefu.

Regarding the judicial proceedings of this period, as a rule, civil cases were tried by *Jitō,* the feudal lords, or *Daikan,* the chief agents of the central government, while criminal cases were handled by *Shugo,* the provincial military governors. There were three kinds of proceedings; *shomuzata,* involving disputes between *gokenin* (vassals of the shogunate) on their feudal estates; *zatsumazata,* involving purely civil cases; and *kendanzata,* involving criminal cases. However, the shomuzata cases were ordinarily tried by an independent judge, called *Hikitsukeshū,* appointed for the purpose of speeding up civil trials; only the important cases were handled by *Hyōjōshō,* the equivalent to the present Supreme Court.

Civil cases were usually conducted through documentary hearing, and serious consideration was given to copies of deeds attached by the complainant, whereas defendants presented their own documents as their answer. A judgment was delivered in the form of a saikyojō (a decision of a trial court). An appeal was permitted only when it was well founded. The lower judgment was quashed in the form of a migyōsho, a decision of the apellate court involving an instruction. In addition, an adjudication by the imperial authority's official, or *kuge,* which had existed since the Ritsu-Ryō period, coexisted together with the aforementioned ordinary tribunals within the imperial estates and *shōen* (manors), owned by the Buddhist temples and Shinto shrines.

In the field of criminal trials, although the procedure of the Ritsu-Ryō period had been generally adopted, the use of torture was generally prohibited in felony cases. Furthermore, the authority of trial examiners was expanded, and few appeals were allowed.

With the decline and fall of the Kamakura and the Muromachi Shogunates, national conquest and unity were achieved by Hideyoshi Toyotomi in 1590, and law and order seemed to reign once more. However, independent local adjudications remained as before within each domain, and Toyotomi rendered ad hoc decisions, without adhering to precedents, in the form of *shuinjō,* documents bearing his seal.

The period of Unitary Feudalism

With the decline of the sho by the late sixteenth century, independent states were emerging in their stead. By 1603, as already mentioned, Tokugawa Ieyasu succeeded in establishing a solidly based unitary feudal regime. The samurai were now the overlords. Confucian principles of supremacy and subordination in relations among the people developed into the rules of giri, somewhat similar to the Chinese regulations in these matters.

In spite of the uniform and hierarchical structure, the legal system was still not unified. Every one of the *han* (lands distributed in fiefs by the daimyo)—also known as the *shugodaimyo*—had its own laws. The direct consequence of this situation was a new and far-reaching destruction of the legal order and the judicial system. However, although the laws of the Bakufu applied, in principle, only in the areas directly governed by the Shogun, the Bakufu would exhort the han to follow the model of the shogunate law, and the han gradually acceded. If diversity of laws continued, there was nevertheless a progressive diminishment, which carried on till the 1868 Restoration.

Parallel to the customary law there was also written legislation, known as *hatto*, promulgated by the Bakufu and by each han. This became the fountain for the consolidation of the Japanese indigenous law, which could be established thanks to the special relations existing between the Edo Shogunate and the han and its subordinated local authorities. The judicial system during this Shogunate was based on these local laws, which were enforced only within each domain. As a result of the Shogunate's efforts to codify these customary local laws, the Bukeshohatto of 1615 and the Kugeshoshihatto of 1632 were enacted, and so the original pattern of the feudal legal system was gradually formed. They were the expression of the trend toward the stabilization of the conciousness of the social status of each member of the community and the diversification of judicial proceedings depending on this social status. The first of the aforementioned *hatto* established the general status of the *buke* (clergy), Buddhist or Shinto; the second dealt with the status of the *kuge*, the functionaries of the Imperial Court.

Although the differentiation between judicial officers and administrative officers did not exist during the Edo period, a definite line between civil and criminal cases was drawn. The Shogunate attached much emphasis to criminal trials, whereas with regard to civil cases, it adopted the policy of settling matters out of court, recommending, as much as possible, conciliation to both parties.

It was not until 1742 that a unitary code of criminal law was promulgated, and it constituted the basis for the criminal policy during the Edo feudal system. This was the *Kujigata Osadamegaki* (written rules of procedure), also known as *Osadamegaki Hyakkajo* (the hundred written rules), which consisted of two volumes containing 184 regulations. The first volume had 81 regulations concerning the performance of the official duties of the Hyōjōshō, the orginazation of a police system, and the various legal proceedings. The second volume contained 103 articles mainly devoted to a substantive penal code, except for two or three criminal procedural provisions. These texts could be consulted only by the three *bugyō*, the top judicial court officials of the Bakufu.

A civil action began with the plaintiff's filing of his complaint with the Bugyōsho, the judicial court office. The Bugyōsho—by serving a summons containing the appointed date and time of the trial or by sending a certified copy of the complaint—commanded the defendant to appear in court or to file an answer. The trial was conducted on either documentary hearing or oral procedure. Whenever insufficient evidence was presented, the suit was dismissed. A party who submitted forged documents could be penalized. In civil cases, the judgment was rendered orally to both parties summoned before the court. However, a decision on a dispute concerning ownership and the boundaries of land was rendered by serving both parties with a map, and the judgment was written on its back as a proof for future situations. When a reconciliation was made on the recommendation of the Bugyōsho, its protocol had to be submitted.

In a criminal case, a magistrate's office had the authority to institute an action *sua sponte,* "by its own motion." When a crime was committed, a suspect could be arrested even when an accusation had not yet been lodged. Since decisions relied solely upon the confession of the accused, torture was frequently used to make the innocent confess to guilt, so the number of misjudgments was great. This situation gradually led the magistrates away from deciding cases only upon confession; as a result, the collection of other evidence was emphasized.

Because of the lack of separation of the judicial and administrative functions within a magistrate's office, the Shogun and other feudal lords often interfered in the administration of justice in those days. However, so far as important cases were concerned, consultations among magistrates, acting as a collegiate body, were held frequently, and detailed studies were made of precedents and scholars' opinions.

The provided punishments consisted of various kinds of execution, transportation, banishment, and corporal punishments such as whipping and tattooing. Prisons in those days were used only for persons awaiting trial.

There were several official collections of the laws and jurisprudence of the Bakufu. Among them were five collections of criminal cases and their judgments, four of them still extant, such as the Hyakkajo Shirabegaki and the Oshiokikuireishu. There was also a collection of judgments of civil cases in forty-five volumes, but only two are still extant. These collected judgments are all of the Hyōjōshō, dealing with matters concerning two parties whose business was not within the competence of the different Bugyōsho. There was no appeal system, so the Hyōjōshō did not function as a jurisdictional superior to the Bugyōsho. All the courts functioned with the participation and assistance of *yokiki* or *Joshi* (public prosecutors) and a number of *yuhitsu* (court clerks).

Dr. Susumu Oda of the Department of Psychiatry, School of Medicine, Dokkyo University, studied the Hyakkajo Shirabegaki's docket of criminal cases dealt by the Hyōjōshō. He found five cases of arson, committed by four men and one woman. Two were due to avarice, two resulted from grudges, and one from amorous passion. There were also four cases of accidental homicide, three of which related to business transactions, and fifty-six cases of murder or attempted murder, with three women among these offenders. He also found several cases of homicide by the criminally insane and offenses committed under alcohol intoxication. All these cases were described in such detail that Dr. Oda was able to analyze them from the modern psychiatric viewpoint. He defined three of these cases as schizophrenic, one as a melancholic, two suffering from psychomotor epilepsy, and a few chronic alcoholics. In all cases in which it was proved that the offenders were mentally insane, the punishment was commuted and the accused—if not of an excessively violent character—was left to be cared for by one of his near relatives. In order to avoid simulation by the accused, the mental disorder had to be conclusively proved with a detailed anamnesis. A minute description of the criminal act itself had to be provided by witnesses, and the written consent of members of his direct family to receive and care for him was required. In cases of alcohol intoxication, commutation was not necessarily applied. It is indeed remarkable that such ways of dealing with insane offenders in that era—when psychiatry and penology were practically nonexistent—appear so similar to contemporary methods.

As stated earlier, the law of this period was strongly influenced by Confucianism and, in this respect, resembles the Ritsu-Ryō system. However, now the purpose was less to educate the people to behave according to the law than to constrain them to obey like silent animals, following the Tokugawa political motto: "Let the people know nothing, but make them obey." Under such conditions, there was no respect for human rights. Dissent was not tolerated, and punishments for disobedience were severe. Nor were there any procedural guarantees against the caprices of judges. Torture to extract confessions was abolished only in 1873.

On the other hand, from the middle of the Tokugawa era, some scholars were interested in the problem of crime and punishment. Their penological thoughts were not too different from those of their contemporary European colleagues. They insisted on differentiating law from religion, separating prisons for convicted offenders from those used for the detention of accused people awaiting trial, separating police from the sentencing process, and so on. They paved the way for the more modern prison system of the Meiji period. However, they were able to convince the Tokugawa Shogunate to establish a "workhouse" in 1790. It was based on relatively humanitarian principles, and a conditional release system was soon adopted, pioneering the later prison reform in present-day Japan. Among these early prison reformers were Sanai Hashimoto and Shōin Yoshida, who were much influenced by the American prison systems. At the beginning of the Meiji period, their disciples occupied influential positions and were able to institute important steps in Japanese corrections, obtaining the liberation of prisoners from the physical punishments used only for slaves. (Might it be that traditional punishments had their roots in the ancient slave system?) Compensation begun to be the usual way of resolving criminal situations among equally free people, while physical punishment was used only for lower-class people who could not pay compensation—not the most just or democratic solution.

Between old and modern Japanese criminal law there is a sharp break, since the modern law considers itself a kind of heir of Western law. After the drafting of some codes based on French models, the New Penal Code, which reflects the German penal code, came into force in October 1908. With some amendments, it is still in force, but there is now a strong movement to replace it with a new code. At any rate, in the unwritten law of everyday life, the giri, there is certainly a considerable continuity with the past.

Punishments during the Different Periods

At the beginning of the eighth century, the established penal system in Japan was no more than an imitation of the Chinese system of those days. It included five kinds of punishments: whipping, beating with a rod, confinement (separating the convicted offender from the community), banishment, and death. The beating with a whip or a rod was imposed on those who committed minor offenses. Those on whom confinement was imposed had to do hard work for one to three years. The banished criminal was compelled to work for one year at a place far from the capital city of his district, and he had to stay there with his family for life. It is not known if there were special institutions for confined or banished offenders, like a modern prison or penitentiary. There were two kinds of death penalty: hanging or cutting the neck, although there were many kinds of death penalty in China. Broadly speaking, these punishments were not so severe as those applied in China, due perhaps to the prevailing strong influence of Buddhism.

Feudal Japan had a number of extremely cruel punishments—perhaps the severest in Japan's penal history—including beheading, crucifixion, sawing the neck, burning at the stake, boiling in a cauldron, and several others. The head of the executed was often exposed. *Seppuku* or *harakiri,* ritual suicide, was imposed only on samurai, for whom it was considered an honorable punishment. The death penalty was usually imposed on those who committed serious offenses such as treason, rebellion, murder, night attack, burglary, or piracy.

When Nobunaga Oda narrowly escaped an assassination attempt, he ordered that his assailant be sawed to death. The unlucky man was buried in the middle of a highway, with his head above ground; a bamboo saw was placed beside him, so that passersby could take turns as sawing his neck. The process took seven days and nights. Even collective punishments, such as the execution of the criminal with his wife and children, was common before the Meiji era.

Cruel punishments soon proved to be useless; they did not deter but led to vicious cycles of revenge and violence. Thus, from the end of the sixteenth century, the Shogunate started to apply more moderate punishments, such as fines (deprivation of property) and degrading and stigmatizing the offender at the pillory, but still keeping the death penalty. It goes without saying that none of these punishments were aimed at the rehabilitation of criminals, their main purpose being deterrence. Note that in the Western world, where the soil was more fertile for rationalism than in the East, cruel punishments were also in use in those days.

Regarding punishments during the Edo and early Meiji periods, there are only a few bibliographical references in Western texts or in Japanese texts translated into a Western language. I visited Japan four times and was able to find a little booklet, published anonymously and secretly in Japan in 1836, whose title was *Illustrated Records of Punishments,* from which I obtained a summarized translation into English. Another publication, *The History of Japanese Punishments,* by Nobuhisa Shibuya, was published in 1982 and translated by the author for me. Additional information was found at the Museum of the Training Institute for Correctional Personnel in Fuchu. From all these sources, the following picture emerges.

In the second half of the eighteenth century, there were many vagabonds in Japan who had been sentenced to banishment or had escaped from a manor because of their poverty. These vagabonds, living around Edo, the capital city, often committed thefts and arsons. If caught and convicted, they were severely punished. If they were innocent, they were ordered to go back to their manor. In 1777, the government decided to send some innocent vagabonds to the Sado Islands but forced them to work at the local gold mine. However, these measures did not prevent vagabonds from committing other offenses around Edo. So in 1790, the government built a "workhouse" for them, with a kind of regimen or prison rules, the so-called *kangakusoku.* In 1793, the average daily population at the workhouse was about 130 inmates. In 1820, as the treatment in the workhouse had produced some good results, the government decided to confine some serious offenders, particularly those with better personality traits, in the workhouse instead of imposing banishment on them. After five years of work, they could be released. In such a way, the workhouse began to function like a modern prison, and by the middle of the nineteenth century, the average daily population amounted to some 500 inmates. The complex of the workhouse was fenced with bamboo sticks, and there were a number of buildings to accommodate the inmates. Each of these buildings was used by inmates according to their work, such as rice-cleaning, carpentry, or plastering. There were separate rooms for female, sick, and old inmates, as well as factories for manufacturing charcoal balls and clam powder and one for rice cleaning, among others. In 1841, a special factory was built for producing oil. If inmates worked hard, they were released and sent back to their respective manors. Those who had nowhere to go were provided, by the government, with a place to work. In the 1850s and 1860s, there were some workhouses within the manors of a few feudal lords. Undoubtedly these were the first step in the rehabilitation process of Japanese offenders.

But in spite of the aforementioned progressive developments, there were still various types of torture. For extracting a confession from the accused, flogging with a cane was employed, or putting a very heavy stone on the thighs of a bound, seated person, or hanging him by the hands, tied up on his back, and the legs, on his front. All this went on for a good number of hours, or even days, usually till the person died or confessed.

Prisons were used mainly to incarcerate prisoners before sentencing. In 1887, the punishment stone was used in the prisons; inmates had to carry it, again and again, from place to place in the prison courtyard, similar to the system used in the early European prisons.

During the Edo period, there were two degrees of banishment or exile—to another island or to another country. For minor offenses, such as vagrancy, there was no penalty the first time, but afterward there was detention in a prison, similar to the *prison école* of some European countries. For more serious offenses, the punishment was internment in common prisons, with or without penal servitude.

The pillory was used as punishment in some special cases, as when a *bonze* was surprised having sexual relations with a woman. In cases of attempted double suicide, both partners were exposed for three days.

When whipping was applied as a punishment for a first-time thief, a medical officer was in attendance within the prison. The number of strokes— from ten to a hundred—depended on the seriousness of the offense.

In tattooing, several kinds of marks were made—usually on the arms of the offenders—varying in accordance with the kind of offense, whether the offender was a first-timer or a recidivist, and the local jurisdiction where the offense was committed. Broadly speaking, thieves were marked to indicate where they had been put on trial or to what places they had been exiled.

For persistent recidivists, the only possible punishment was beheading. The death penalty was also applied for different kinds of homicide. For instance, for killing an employer, there were several stages: The first day was devoted to the march toward the pillory; the second day was a walk to the sawing place, another kind of pillory that became merely formal, without actual sawing taking place. The third day, the condemned man went to the execution place; the fourth day was devoted to the crucifixion proper, known as *harikuze,* somewhat different from the Western system, in that it had two transversal blocks on the wooden cross instead of one, in order to fasten both the arms and the feet. Finally, the body was exposed for three days, so the entire procedure took an entire week.

In cases of parricide, there were one or two days of march to the execution place, then the crucifixion, and then the three days of exposure. For fratricide cases, there were also one or two days of march, then the beheading within the jail, and finally the exposure of the head for three days on a kind of high table, with posters to indicate the offense committed by the executed criminal. Arson cases received one or two days of march to the execution palce and then burning at the stake.

Recidivist thieves could also be executed by hanging within a prison. For such a purpose, an iron sinker was used at the Oita prison, on Kyushu Island, from 1872 to 1882. This heavy weight was used instead of the opening platform used in Europe.

Finally, the testing of a new *nihonjo* (sword) or a samurai was usually done on the bodies of executed offenders.

Concluding Summary

Early Japanese society was dominated by customary law, with a strong moral and religious character. With the introduction of the Ritsu-Ryō, the written law became the dominant legal source. After the tenth century, with the decline of Chinese influence, new administrative and judicial practices were gradually developed, based on the Ritsu-Ryō. When these practices started to decline, custom again became the main legal source; but during the Tokugawa era, the written law was strengthened, facilitating the Meiji government's conversion to modern codification. Still, even today, customary law operates side by side with the state legal system.

There is no doubt that the classical penal system, based on a kind of metaphysical criminology, is almost completely bankrupt. Something new is urgently needed. Juvenile delinquency and recidivism have reached an unprecedented level throughout the world, about three times higher since World War II than prewar levels. The immaturity of criminology, the general public's lack of enlightenment on these matters, and the still prevailing legal and judicial conservatism, among other factors, acted to obstruct a real and much needed penal reform. Some contemporaty Japanese penologists claim that their country was or still is an exception to this sad general situation. The main reasons for their comparatively better condition, they claim, are the full supply of prison industries within the penal system, providing work for every inmate, and the patriarchal relationship that exist between guards and prisoners. Could something so beautiful be true? I have the most serious doubts on the subject.

14

Oceania: A Vast Conglomeration of Islands

Geographic Background

Broadly speaking, Oceania is the generic name for all the islands scattered throughout the Pacific Ocean, between Asia and the Americas. Nevertheless, there is a large consensus to exclude from it the Japan archipelago, Indonesia, Taiwan, and the Philippines, since the people of these islands are ethnically and culturally much closer to Asia. And since Australasia is considered an independent continent, most scholars do not include it within Oceania. But even with these restrictions, Oceania comprises more than 10,000 islands, with a total land area of approximately 325,000 square miles.

Usually, Oceania has been divided into three great geographic sectors: Polynesia, Melanesia, and Micronesia.

Polynesia—from the Greek *poli* (many) and *nēsoi* (islands)—comprises all the islands in a huge triangle of the Central and South Pacific, lying east of both Melanesia and Micronesia. Its northern vortex is in the Hawaiian (formerly Sandwich) Islands, its southeastern one in Easter Island, and its southwestern one in New Zealand. *Samoa,* the Tuvalu (formerly Ellice) islands (in the Western Pacific, north of the Fiji group, between Fiji and the Gilbert Islands), and the Tonga or Friendly Islands are located along the western edge of this triangle. The Society Islands of French Polynesia, including Tahiti, are at the center. Northeast of the Society Islands are the Marquesas Islands and, in between, the Tuamotu archipelago, stretching eastward to the Mangareva group. The Cook Islands (in the South Pacific, southwest of the Society Islands) and the Tokelau or Union Islands (in the Central Pacific, north of Samoa and belonging to New Zealand) lie to the west of the Society Islands, while the Tubuai or Austral Islands, belonging to France, are to the south of them. Also included in Polynesia are the Line Islands (in the Central Pacific, south of Hawaii) and the Phoenix Islands (another group in the Central Pacific, located between the Gilbert and Tuvalu groups).

Polynesia is such a vast triangle—its land area is over 110,000 square miles—that from Hawaii to New Zealand there are some 5,000 miles and from Tonga to Easter Island about 4,000 miles. A few of the Polynesian islands are very high, mostly of volcanic origin, such as the Mauna Kee of Hawaii, which is 13,796 feet high; but most are low coral atolls. The climate ranges from tropical to subtropical, depending on the location and the predominance of the trade winds.

Because of its importance in relation to the other two parts of Oceania, Polynesia will be the main focus of this chapter.

Melanesia—from the Greek *melas* (black) and *nēsoi* (islands)—comprises all the islands of the West Pacific, lying to the northeast of Australia, south of the equator and Micronesia, and west of Polynesia. Scattered from New Guinea and eastward to Fiji, it has a total land area of 202,886 square miles. It includes the Trobriand Islands, located about 100 miles north of the extreme eastern end of New Guinea and forming part of the territory of Papua New Guinea. We shall look later at the paralegal practices of the Trobriands, since they provide an excellent sample of aspects of primitive law. Like Polynesia, Melanesia includes high islands of volcanic origin as well as low atolls. The climate is rather tropical.

Micronesia—from the Greek *mikros* (small) and *nēsoi*—comprises all the islands of the Western Pacific, north of Melanesia, west of Polynesia, and east of the Philippines. It includes the U.S. Trust Territory of the Pacific Islands—comprising the Caroline, Gilbert, Mariana, and Marshal groups—as well as the isolated island of Nauru (independent since 1968), all of them north of the equator. Except for a few high islands of volcanic origin (such as Guam, the largest Micronesian island and a U.S. possession since 1899), Micronesia is made up mostly of low coral atolls and has a total land area of 1,055 square miles (2,732 square kilometers).

Ethnic Origins and Characteristics

From the paleontological point of view, Oceania goes back some 100 million years, when the west coast of the Pacific may have stretched from Japan to New Zealand, via the Caroline and Fiji islands. As recently as 20,000 years ago, no human being lived in the region. Although they disagree on details, most scientists support the theory of a Southeast Asian origin of the people of these islands.

It seems that Oceania's first inhabitants were the Pygmoids. At the end of the last ice age some 14,000 years ago, Oceania's low-lying lands were flooded and its mountaintops became islands. To these islands, the Pygmoids—a short, dark-skinned, kinky-haired people—fled from Southeast Asia over thousands of years. Later, the Ainoids swept down from Malaya to New Guinea and farther south to Australia. These people had lighter skins, straight hair, and hairy bodies; they were similar to the Ainus of Hokkaido, in Japan. After the Ainoids came the Veddids, hunters and food gatherers of the preagricultural period, who resembled the Veddas, the aborigines of southern India. These three ethnic groups and other, later ones, each with its own distinct culture, intermingled and then subdivided into a great variety of customs, dialects, and social structures. In fact, whereas Polynesia shows greater ethnic and cultural uniformity, the far more ancient Melanesians count hundreds of different civilizations that have defied all scientific attempts at classification.

It seems that the Pacific Ocean is much older than the other oceans of our planet. Yet the people of the Mediterranean, Indian, and Atlantic oceans made history, at least from the beginning of writing, whereas the people of the Pacific were much quieter. And yet these same people were great seafarers, who—centuries before the Vikings or Columbus—conquered an enormous maritime area. Their huge canoes were manned by crews of up to three hundred and were used for warfare or for voyages lasting months and even years.

Quite a number of scholars believe today that the ancient Polynesians probably came from Indochina via Indonesia. This theory is based on the many cultural similarities between Polynesia and Indonesia: both kept dogs, pigs, and chickens and produced fire by rotating a vertical stick in a hollowed piece of wood placed on the ground; and they have many words with similar sounds and meanings. These theories have recently been challenged by Thor Heyerdahl, the Norwegian explorer, who stresses the parallels between the civilization of Easter Island and those of the pre-Columbian populations of South America, particularly those of Peru and Ecuador. His argument, having been underlined by the wonderful voyage of the raft *Kon Tiki* in 1947, seems highly persuasive.

A brown race with Negroid and Caucasian admixtures, the Polynesians loved to explore the Pacific; it seems, for instance, that a Tonga chieftain named Hui-te-Rangiora reached as far as the Antarctic about 650 a.d. The Polynesians discovered and colonized island after island; and they are credited with having reached America long before the Vikings or Columbus. In addition to being great seafarers who understand winds and weather, storms and tides, and could estimate the depth of the sea and the nearness of their destination by observing the flight of birds, they were excellent astronomers.

It is true that the Polynesians' insular communities maintained an unjust system of castes and practiced cannibalism in certain situations, despite the fact that basic material needs were assured for everyone. But it is also true that they cultivated their leisure time and knew how to mix work and pleasure; even their wars were in many respects a kind of sport. Moreover, they were healthy people, who, before the coming of the Europeans, knew of only two autochthonous diseases, leprosy and elephantiasis.

Polynesia contains the two most highly developed islands in Oceania: Hawaii and New Zealand (the latter is included because of the Polynesian origins of its native Maoris). The Polynesian cultural systems have now come under heavy Western influence; during the nineteenth century, virtually all of Oceania passed to the control of the European powers and the United States. By 1980, about 8 million islanders lived in Oceania.

The earliest human settlements in Melanesia, particularly in New Guinea, date from some 15,000 to 18,000 years ago. A later wave of horticulturalists settled the islands of this region from the second millenium B.C. and into the Christian Era. These later arrivals settled along the coast and drove the earlier, Negroid aborigines into the forests and mountains of the interior. Today there are clear distinctions between the coastal dwellers and the bush natives. The Melanesians are on the whole more Negroid than the Polynesians.

The culturally diverse Melanesian islands are today a living museum for the study of the most primitive forms of civilization. Many features are common to all of them: chipped stone tools; the bow and arrow as well as spears; pig raising; domesticated dogs; chickens; fishing; food gathering and primitive agriculture; animism; secret male societies with initiation rites; masks; and exogamy. In fact, one of the most striking characteristics of these people is their division into two or more clans, with no marriage ever taking place within the same clan, and membership in a given clan transmitted to the children by their mothers. To the Melanesian man, all the women of his generation either are taboo, like sisters, or are potential brides. To the Melanesian women, all men are taboo, like brothers, or are potential suitors. Another practice common to all Melanesians is totemism, a complex phenomenon also found in some of the Americas and in the early civilizations of Australia. Totemism is a person's belief in his blood relationship to some animal, plant, star, or the like, with the totem as the common link between a related group of people. Melanesian totemism has produced artistic creations, tribal rites, taboos (sacred prohibitions), and important festivals at which the totemic union is renewed.

In contrast to the leisure-loving Polynesians, the Melanesians were a gloomy people, obsessed with magic and witchcraft. Until lately, head-hunting and cannibalism were practiced in some of their islands, as well as euthanasia of the aged and infirm. In all their diverse linguistic world—some twenty different languages and dialects in New Caledonia alone—they had no written grammar; and yet the people seldom made grammatical mistakes in their speech, because they believed that words have a dangerous, magical power.

The racial characteristics of the people of Micronesia are medium to heavy skin pigmentation, wavy to kinky hair, and short stature. Although analysis of their blood types shows that they are distinct from their Asian,

Australian, and Polynesian neighbors, their language is closely related to that of the Melanesian and Polynesian peoples.

The Material Life of the Polynesians

As a whole, the peoples of Oceania until the arrival of the Europeans might be equated, in terms of their cultures and economies, with those of the Neolithic Age. The majority of these peoples were food gatherers and hunters, having no cattle or flocks nor knowledge of metals.

Fishing was one of the main activities of the Polynesians. In fact, their diet is one aspect of their ancient culture that has not been hopelessly corrupted since the arrival of the Europeans. The men did their fishing from canoes with nets or harpoons, and the women and children gathered shellfish from among the rocks of the shore without entering the canoes, since that was taboo for them. The Polynesians also used hatcheries, crates, and even some plants to numb the fish. Magic rituals were a vital part of the entire procedure, in order to court favor with the gods and to avoid supernatural dangers.

Since there were no savage animals, hunting was limited to the chase of birds, which was done with nets, glue, or other kinds of trickery. Eggs were eaten in great amounts. The Polynesians also domesticated the dog, which was found everwhere except Easter Island. Chickens were known in all Polynesian islands except New Zealand, and pigs were absent only from New Zealand and Easter Island.

The vegetarian diet included a few elements from natural plants such as the pandanus, ferns, and rush, with whose pollen they prepared a kind of pie. Among the cultivated vegetables, the coconut tree was a basic element, not only for food but for rubbing oils, basketry, and carpeting, and for making house pots, parts of canoes, and some types of arms. Breadfruit and bananas, though nonexistent in New Zealand and Easter Island and rare in Hawaii, were also important. With the exception of the pumpkin, all the other annual plants, such as the taro and the *yam,* were cultivated for their roots. The digging stick, three or four feet long, was their only agricultural instrument, and primitive irrigation systems were used, particularly when there was some type of rotation of crops.

Men usually did the heavy work, such as breaking the ground and burning the undergrowth, while women did the actual cultivation. In early times, there was little differentiation between the sexes regarding work, but most food gathering was done by women, with the assistance of their digging sticks, while hunting was done by men, mainly with bows and arrows. Some fish and shellfish were usually eaten raw, while others were cooked in earthen ovens (*umu*). Food was eaten with the fingers, with some exceptions, as in Fiji, where the chiefs had large forks, like tridents, for eating human meat.

There were also people in the vast Pacific Ocean who, instead of being food gatherers, found their main means of subsistence in horticulture. Still, they lacked cattle and flocks and had no metals. The majority of them lived in Melanesia, but they were also found in Polynesia—in the Solomons, Tonga, Hawaii, Samoa, and other places.

In due time, with the increase of domesticated animals and other kinds of goods, there appeared, at least in the more developed communities, a surplus beyond the immediate needs of subsistence; and some kinds of trade began. Barter between individuals or social groups was the most popular. But partly because much of this wealth, especially the animals, could easily be taken away in raids, there was now a greater trend toward warfare, a pursuit hardly known before.

Although clothes were not really necessary in the mild climate, nakedness was unthinkable. Men used a loin cloth (*maro*) and very frequently a kind of kilt (*pareu*), which was also the indispensable garment for women. Children went naked till puberty. The Polynesians had no textile industry; for making clothing, they used only the *tapa,* a kind of thick paper prepared from pounding the bark of some trees. Each one of the islands had its own sort of design for decorating the tapas. Only in the Marquesas were tapas white, without any decor. Feathers were an important decoration for clothes; and pendants from nacre or whalebone, shell necklaces, and flower garlands were common in festivals, particularly for men. Tattooing was also a very important decoration.

As for dwellings, houses built all around Polynesia used the same principle: A number of stones were assembled on a piece of land, and a light wooden structure was put up on top of them. The walls were made of bamboo, rush, or just leaves, and the roof was covered with straw. In their camps and settlements, other houses were built with branches, logs, and earth and covered with skins or hides. There were also *tipis,* conical tents usually consisting of animal skins. Where horticulture was the main activity, the people lived in relatively elaborate houses of timber. In some places, there were also long houses accomodating more than one family. And in New Zealand, each village had its own "council building"; great aesthetic care was taken in its construction.

Furniture was almost nonexistent. There were a few floor carpets and covers of tapa, used as beds for the night. In Tonga, Samoa, and the Society Islands people used wooden pillows. Pieces of basketry were part of the furniture, and a kind of envelope was made with pandanus for keeping all manner of items.

Tools were made from stone, bone, shells, or wood; there were no metals till the coming of the white men. In New Zealand, there was a kind of saw made from a brown jadeite; carpenters and sculptors used adzes of shell or granite. The Polynesians also had axes and scissors and various instruments for wood carving—in which they excelled, particularly in New Zealand. With such primitive tools, they did some good basketry, built excellent canoes, worked some crude pottery, and wove various materials.

In the area of transportation, the Polynesians were, of course, extraordinary seamen. For fishing in rivers and lagoons, they used simple dugouts; but to make these more stable for the high seas, they invented the outrigger, a piece of wood attached parallel to the canoe to serve as a counterweight. An elaboration of this was the double canoe, in which each canoe served as a counterweight to the other. The wooden logs that united the canoes, covered with wooden planks, formed a kind of bridge that facilitated long voyages. In this bridge, there was usually a small cabin for women and children and for storing the reserves of food and water. Sails were made of tapa. These canoes had no rudders; direction was assured by a larger and longer oar, usually in the hands of the vessel's captain or the chiefs or priests of the higher classes, who knew how to navigate by observing the stars and the direction of the winds and sea currents.

The war canoes, which never sailed very far, were sometimes thirty-five meters long, with a mast about twenty meters high. Usually, the bow and the stern had sculptured gods on them. Captain James Cook, during his second voyage, saw and described a fleet of war north of Tahiti that comprised about a hundred vessels.

Land travel was of no importance, since practically all transportation was done by water, on sea or rivers.

The Social, Political, Cultural, and Economic Life of the Polynesians

In the course of time, there were far-reaching changes in the social organization of the Polynesian communities.

The biological or extended family was the main socioeconomic unit. Polygyny existed almost everywhere, particularly among the chiefs; consequently, there were practically no unmarried women, though there were a few bachelors. Still, the vast majority of the men had only one wife. Polyandry existed only in the Marquesas, where it was considered normal. Wife-lending was common or even required in some places as an expression of good manners, but marriage by capture was rare, except in Tikopia, where it was the prevailing system. Marriage between near relatives was generally forbidden, but in Hawaii the families of highest rank had marriages between brothers and sisters in order to preserve "blood purity." In general, men got married when they reached twenty years of age. The virginity of women was not requested, except among the aristocracy on certain islands, because the youngsters of both sexes enjoyed great sexual liberty.

With the emergence of surplus wealth appeared the custom of the exchange of gifts on the occasion of marriage, mainly taking the form of bridewealth, brideprice, or dowry. On the whole, women's status was diminished, because such a practice had the character of a sale. Marriages were easily terminated by mutual consent or the desertion of one spouse. Infanticide was practiced almost everywhere, perhaps as a preventive measure against overpopulation, particularly on islands where food was limited. Therefore, population density remained extremely low. The size of local populations varied from less than 100 to 1,500 or more.

Besides some cases of cruelty, most families lived in peace and gave special care to children. Adoption of children was widespread, with no difference in status between the legitimate and adopted children.

Less important than the family were the age groups: groups involving persons of the same age and position in life (bachelors, warriors, elders, etc.). Some of these groups had rites of initiation and passage from one degree to the next; a few of them even functioned as secret societies. In some places, there were also groupings according to sex for socioeconomic or religious purposes.

The tribe was the second most important social unit after the family. Here a more general point is in order. The term *tribe* has acquired a pejorative connotation, evoking primitiveness and used to describe ethnic groups of Africa but not Europe. For example, in Belgium, the 6 million Flemish and 4 million Walloons are called "nations," whereas the 3 million Shona and 4 million Ndebele of Zimbabwe—despite having cultural homogeneity, a unifying social structure, and a common language and religion—are known as tribes. Such a distinction is demeaning. If the African ethnic dances look odd to Western Europeans, they are certainly no odder than those seen in discos. It is time to put an end to this misuse of a scientific expression.

In Polynesia, the tribe remained a shadowy and unstable entity, defined by a common language or dialect. With time, moieties (one of two complementary subdivisions), totemic groups (for which an animal, plant, or other object—or its carved representation—served as the emblem of the clan), and other divisions began to be formed. The tribe became less significant when camps and settlements started to grow. Tribes were sometimes matrilineal, sometimes patrilineal, sometimes a combination of the two. Moreover, in some places they were an exogamous unit (marriage between members forbidden) and in others endogamous (marriage within the group required).

Broadly speaking, three main characteristics became common to all Polynesians. One was their preoccupation with wealth and social status, due in part to the expansion of trade and to individuals' pride in their skills as fishermen, hunters, or horticulturists. Aside from warlike exploits, prestige depended mostly on wealth.

Second, great attention was paid to rank, which, in some places, comprised the familiar medieval distinctions of kings, nobles, commoners, and slaves. Slavery was actually infrequent, but where it existed, the slaves' lot was hardly human. However, many female slaves were taken into marriage, and their children were considered equal members of the community. Nobility ranks were bought more often than inherited, though where they were inherited there were real caste systems. In fact, during tribal assemblies (see below) a Polynesian had to be able to recite by heart his own genealogy—sometimes up to eighty names, some of them more mythological than historical.

Third, there was a widespread, gradual increase of the power of the chiefs. At first, chiefs and priests had both been considered of divine origin, and had enjoyed equal rank. But gradually, sacredness came to be attributed only to chiefs. The chiefs' power grew to the point that, as noted, feudal kingships appeared—in the small atoll of Ontong Java (southeast of the Solomons), on the island of Tikopia (also on the fringes of the Solomons), in Easter Island, and especially in Tahiti and Hawaii. Under the influence of the Europeans, some chiefs tried to expand their powers to previously unknown, despotic levels, including wars of conquest such as in the Society Islands, when the reigning Pomarés tried to include other islands in their rule.

Polynesia had many forms of government. The central government usually had greater authority in agricultural communities and less in the smaller, dispersed coastal and fishing communities. In fact, in some of the less organized communities, there was no government at all, nor even any chiefs; but everywhere there was usually at least a special, prominent individual, sometimes an elder or head of family, who had authority. In the more developed social entities, chiefs usually held sway, though in widely differing fashions.

As social organization became more elaborate, there appeared a kind of informal council, constituted by chiefs and heads of families. The council's authority was minimal, however, and its functions were very limited, usually no more than suggesting the activities of the people for each day: who would hunt, who would work the fields, who would gather food, and so on.

Territorially, a division into districts emerged, with each district comprising at least one village. Larger assemblies, with the participation of the chiefs of all the villages of a district, decided on matters involving the entire tribe, such as war and peace or the appointment of chiefs. In these assemblies, opinions were freely expressed, but people dared to do so only if they knew they had the backing of an important sector of the council or assembly.

War, in the form of sudden raids at dawn by parties with the approval of their communities, was rather frequent. Success in war was an important basis for status and prestige. In Melanesia, most war captives were eaten. The problem of cannibalism has been the subject of much discussion, but very few experts deny the former existence of this practice, which was once an established one among some of the New Guinea people. The frequency of cannibalism changed over time in response to situational factors, including environmental ones. For instance, whereas in some cases the Melanesians participated in a given raid specifically to get "meat," in others cannibalism occurred in the context of mortuary rituals. Cases of cannibalism have been also described, on few occasions, in the Western world. It should be enough to remember the famous trial of Alfred Packer, in Colorado in the last century—the only man ever convicted of cannibalism in the United States.

If wars took place in Tonga and Samoa mainly because of dynastic controversies, with long intervals of peace, wars were an endemic condition in the rest of Polynesia. In New Zealand, the Marquesas, and Easter Island, war was usually an intertribal affair; in Hawaii, the Society Islands, and the Austral islands, one island would fight another. When war was between nonrelated tribes, it could be finished with the extermination (rather than enslavement) of the defeated and, sometimes, cannibalism. Nevertheless, a brave warrior could be treated with magnanimity.

Religion played an important role during wars. In certain places in Polynesia, there were human sacrifices to the gods before starting a war; and images of gods were generally taken to the battlefield. The victorious side often kept the skulls of their dead enemies in their sanctuaries.

The wars were not without refinements. For instance, the Maori had trenches with pits, palisades, and even towers with several stories. Such elements, together with Maori bravery and cruelty, gave the British much trouble when they tried to conquer New Zealand.

Broadly speaking, chiefs were not also generals. In times of war, there was often a special chief of war. Soldiers were usually chosen for their abilities and military records; in some places, there was a kind of military caste for such purposes.

As we have seen, each sex had its own kind of work. A man would never prepare a *tapa,* nor would a woman participate in building a canoe. But there were some areas in which both sexes participated, such as agriculture—in which men still handled the heavier tasks—or basketry, in which women did the more delicate work.

There was always some kind of activity in a Polynesian village, and idleness was regarded as a disease. Yet work was done freely and creatively, never under pressure; great pride was taken in, and great appreciation accorded the finished product, whether a canoe or a work of art. Larger tasks were often done communally.

The concept of land ownership was greatly developed in Polynesia, with much variation from one island to another but some common general features. For instance, in some places, members of the matrilineal group might own the houses on a piece of land, while members of the patrilineal group owned the land. In others, husband and wife might have separate houses near their respective places of work. Land could be obtained by discovery, occupation, gift, or distribution by the chiefs. Land could be leased but was almost never sold, but in some places, such as Hawaii, the occupiers had to pay the chief a kind of location tax.

According to the existing political system in a community, there was often an overriding interest of the tribes, clans, joint or extended families, villages, or towns to take hold of the land communally. This land could then be subdivided into smaller tracts belonging to smaller kinship groups.

With the increase in the authority of the chiefs, land came to be considered as belonging to the head of the clan or tribe, to the sacred king (as in Tonga), or to the king (as in Hawaii), who was entitled to distribute it among lesser chiefs or people of the middle class. Even so, the owner was never the absolute proprietor of the land in the sense of contemporary law and could rarely be permanently assigned to the land.

As for movable goods—and the lightly built Polynesian house was one of them—they, too, were considered property objects. Women owned those things made by them or belonging to their sex, such as baskets, bark skirts, and so on; when they got married, they kept their rights to those objects. And all that a man acquired by his labor or used belonged to him. But crops grown by the wife in her garden were often hers, as were household furnishings and sometimes the house itself.

Rules of succession were undeveloped and similar to those prevailing among food gatherers. Usually, the goods of the deceased were destroyed or buried with him. Succession to land became progressively important in these agricultural communities, generally involving inheritance by relatives according to patrilineal or matrilineal patterns. Wills, however, were very rare.

With the exceptions of the rich New Zealand and the poor Easter Island, the rest of Polynesia showed a marked cultural similarity, though not, of course, without local variations. But under the various cultural manifestations there were a number of beliefs, some of them linked to religious practices, known everywhere in Polynesia and Melanesia as *mana* and *tapu*.

Mana was a concept embracing a continuum from simple prestige to magic power. There were some chiefs who had no *mana,* even though it was inconceivable that a man without *mana* could become chief. *Mana* could be present in objects such as the arms of a hero or the tools of a great artist. The *mana* has been compared to an electric current, that could be transmitted by contract, such as through recitations and chants.

Tapu (taboo) could be considered an extension of *mana,* in the sense that a great chief was *tapu* because of his divine origin. But whereas *mana* was a basically constructive or positive force, *tapu* is basically negative, from which derives the sense of interdiction that it has acquired. People could die for transgressing *tapu* prohibitions. In later times, chiefs started to impose this *tapu* on whomever they wanted, so that *tapu* became a form of primitive legislation.

Mana and *tapu* were essential elements in Polynesian life. Civil and religious organizations, the vast majority of creative activity, and individual life were regarded as under the sway of these forces.

The Polynesians were natural artists. Primitive looms have been found in some places. Although pottery was still incipient, there was much weaving of mats, textiles, and baskets from a great variety of materials. Their tatoos, their engraved woods and stones, and their tapas were often richly and beautifully designed. The royal cloaks and the crests of royal helmets, some of which are kept at the British Museum and the Bernice P. Bishop Museum in Honolulu, are quite striking.

Polynesian statuary was generally done in the so-called primitive fashion and was made of wood or stone. The statuary of Easter Island is widely admired for its effectively tragic and gloomy qualities.

Dancing was perhaps the best expression of the Polynesian soul. It was a mixture of poetry and music, pantomime and choreography. Psalmodic poems were accompanied by drums and flutes; gourds, used as percussion instruments, and whistles were also common in their orchestras. Perhaps the Hawaiian hula was the most expressive of the Polynesian dances, rich in descriptions of the local landscapes. Each public event produced songs and dances, and it is still so today. When I visited Tahiti in January 1935 on the Belgian sailing ship *Mercator*, its arrival was greeted with songs and dances in honor of the "blond men from Peretita" (Belgium).

The Polynesians were also great orators. The magic power of the chiefs was generally expressed through persuasive speeches. Dr. Peter Buck, Maori through his mother, was one of the greatest orators while he was a member of the parliament of New Zealand.

The Polynesians were polytheistic and animistic. Esoteric religious knowledge was reserved for the high priests and the chiefs. This was knowledge of the secret, primary god who had created and delegated powers to all secondary gods. After the gods came the heroes, founders of the most important families, who were more or less historical people who had been divinized.

As elsewhere, divinities were represented by statues; offerings were made to them—fruits or flowers, meat of animals, and in more recent times, human flesh. The British Captain Cook, who explored Polynesia in the late eighteenth century, was invited to attend one such ceremony while in Tahiti; and at the beginning of the last century, a number of white explorers visited sanctuaries where they found the wide-open mouths of the statues full of human remains in different stages of putrefaction. Not many statues of Polynesian gods have survived; most were destroyed by people or weather.

Magic also flourished. Many illnesses or deaths were attributed to witchcraft, and it was one of the main causes for local unrest, raids, and murder. As in other primitive societies, magic became a kind of pseudoscience in Polynesia—a supernatural way of producing desired results. In a few places, the widows of chiefs were strangled so as to accompany their husbands in the hereafter, somewhat similar to the *suttee* ceremony in India. Shamans and sorcerers were engaged to further socioeconomic purposes, whereas witchcraft was mainly used for antisocial purposes.

Aside from astronomy and navigation, the Polynesians had no real scientific knowledge. Yet it can be said that they were real experts in applied sciences. For instance, they had elementary systems of recording, based on mnemonic devices such as notches in sticks; and they used numbers and had calculations with a highly developed decimal system.

How much of the original Polynesian culture is still existent after the two world wars is difficult to say, but it is probably very little. If we cannot justify their cannibalism and infanticide, they undoubtedly deserve our respect and admiration in many other areas—religion, arts, family life, and so on.

Penal Customs and Practices in Polynesia

Two cautions are in order. First, as the vast majority of the people of Oceania were illiterate, without a written language, it would be inaccurate to refer to nonexistent "laws" and "codes." Therefore, instead of "penal norms" it is better to refer to "penal customs and practices," which existed practically everywhere.

Second, it is well known that when a foreigner observes the life of primitive people, the mere fact of his presence is a disturbing and distorting element. The best example of this regarding Polynesia is, perhaps, all that has been written and the punitive actions taken by Europeans in retaliation for what they understood as a natural Polynesian propensity for stealing. Admiral Jacob Roggeveen, the Dutch discoverer of Easter Island, and some of his followers, who spent only a few days ashore, had time enough to order the massacre of some natives who offended them with their petty thefts. Roggeveen was unable to give any other interpretation to their behavior.

With only a few exceptions, law was not very important in these cultures. Law can be said to exist only where (1) there are accepted canons of behavior; (2) the community can enforce them by imposing various sanctions; and (3) there is some regularity in the imposition and character of these sanctions. Thus, among these people, there was no criminal law in the field of private offenses, because even if the first condition was fulfilled, the second and third were not. As for public offenses, in certain places the first two conditions were satisfied, and sometimes even the third one—but not in any way that could be characterized as the beginnings of law, since there was no regular compliance with the punishments imposed.

Instead, for the most part, social control was based on mutual dependence for food and survival, habits and traditions, public approval, kinship ties, conformity with existing standards, fears of ridicule or charges of witchcraft for nonconformity, and the supernatural sanctions of magic and religion.

Almost everywhere a distinction was made between public (affecting the entire community) and private (affecting an individual or smaller group) offenses against the good order. Death caused by witchcraft was considered the most serious public offense. Other public offenses were incest (marriage or sexual intercourse with a person whom one cannot properly marry); adultery by a wife (especially elopement or kidnapping of a man's wife); and a few others that varied somewhat from one community to another, such as improper behavior during hunting, military raids, and tribal gatherings. Homicide, wounding, theft, and in some places adultery were considered private (civil) offenses. The most frequent disorders arose out of charges of witchcraft and disputes about or among women.

The distinction between public and private offenses, however, was far from being easily understood. Public offenses such as incest were often avenged by the same group that would avenge a private wrong—namely, the nearest relatives, the clan, or any other kinsgroup to which the victim or offended person belonged. There were few or no fixed sanctions for either type of offense. Moreover, some punishments of public offenses actually took the form of war rather than retribution for a crime. For example, killing by witchcraft was usually alleged against members of a foreign group, and the "punishment" was war.

Adding to the confusion was the general lack of fixed sanctions for either type of offense. Sometimes, in fact, there was no sanction at all, or a sufficiently powerful person could evade punishment. Homicide was a capital offense in most places, and a culprit could be killed by a relative of a victim after obtaining approval of others or of the community as a whole; or a murder could simply result in a protracted blood feud. Adulteresses were variously punished by death, mutilation, mass rape (by the husband and his friends), or expulsion from the group—or they could be accorded forgiveness.

Nevertheless, in some cases, the distinction between public and private offenses functioned more clearly. If an allegation of killing (except by witchcraft) or wounding was settled by acceptance of goods, the chief and his council would not object; but when they did claim authority to decide guilt and impose punishment, it was usually for a public offense.

As already mentioned, the notion of property rights was widespread, but it was not universally understood or accepted. Particularly vague was the concept of land as a separate thing capable of ownership, so there were few disputes on this score and, in many places, no authority to hear them if they arose; rules of succession were also primitive and undeveloped. Nevertheless, the individual's right to articles made or exclusively used by him was widely acknowledged, so theft of these was a recognized private offense.

Primitive ways existed for ascertaining the identity of an offender. Not only was there a kind of simple ordeal by oath (swearing innocence), but with the development of magic there was also a wide use of divination; for instance, the deceased could be held on the shoulders of two or more men, and a movement of the corpse in a given direction or at the mention of a name was considered enough for identifying the culprit. Magic and religion also played some role in such procedures (to determine, for instance, the identity of a witch or the committer of a sacral wrong). Eventually, as we shall now see, more advanced procedures developed.

It is important to recall that among the least developed agricultural communities as well as among the food gatherers, there were no well-established chiefs, only some heads of families or local clans. These men could give the word to begin actions after they had been discussed communally and agreed upon, but they usually could not issue orders.

With the growing authority of chiefs, however, came the emergence of jurisdiction to hear and determine disputes. The chief of a subclan, for instance, could informally adjudicate in disputes among its members. If the dissenting parties belonged to different subclans within the same parish (the largest local group having some permanent political unity), their respective chiefs presided jointly at a meeting of the local people.

There was no central authority, however, to maintain law and order within each parish. Decisions were taken in the light of group interests and local standards regarding what constituted right conduct (*hab'g*), such as being a good worker, controlling one's wives without creating public scandals, and so on. It was considered wrong (*kets*) to quarrel with kinsmen, with members of smaller groups, or with one's brothers. Men of renown, however, were at an advantage whether or not their conduct was right. The chief would rarely attempt to impose a judgment that was not in accordance with public opinion, as expressed by the parties to the dispute and their respective supporters.

The proceedings were lengthy, and the public—that is, members of the disputing groups, who were not directly affected—took part in the discussions. Precedents could be brought forth based on general standards; often there were exchanges of recrimination regarding previous misbehavior of the parties. At the close of such proceedings, shells were usually exchanged in compensation for false exchanges, harsh words, or blows.

To take an illustration from Melanesia, in a Kapauku village of western New Guinea, the headman (usually a wealthy man, as well as the political and military leader) settled most of the local disputes. He did so in accordance with the generally recognized rights of the parties, but sometimes he made decisions at variance with these ostensible rights, and once in a while, he was clearly unjust, particularly by furthering his own interests. His decisions were usually obeyed, and a kind of elementary law of crimes and torts started to develop among these people.

The jurisdiction of the chiefs grew with their authority and the aura of reverence that surrounded them. Among the people of Trobriand, off the northeast coast of New Guinea, the highest ranking chief of Kiriwana was entitled to punish misbehaviors against himself (adultery with one of his wives, theft of any of his private possessions, etc.), even by having the offender speared by one of his armed attendants. But in southern New Hebrides, the power of the chiefs was almost absolute; they could judge and punish serious offenses by death. If the parties belonged to different villages, the respective chiefs met in council and, after deliberation, could punish the offender. In the small Polynesian atoll of Ontong Java, before a permanent chief or king arose some 250 years ago, the chief priest appointed the *polepole* (a kind of police) to punish the only known crime: the theft of coconuts or taro from the common land.

In the kingdoms of Tonga and Hawaii, where there existed a kind of feudalism resembling that of Western Europe, the noble class was that of the *matapule*, the principal attendants and hereditary advisers of the kings. The father had the right to punish his children, the head of the extended family every one of its members, and the chief his subjects. The commoner could appeal a decision of a minor chief to a higher chief and even ultimately to the king.

In Samoa and other more developed places, authority was less centralized, but legality was more advanced. The local *matai* (the elected head of kindred groups) formed the *fono* (council or assembly) of each village or district and exercised the main authority. There was no chiefly class; the *matai* did not inherit his position but was elected on merit and validated by a large distribution of goods. In criminal matters—offenses against the *matai*—the *matai* and the *fono* could put the offenders on trial and had powers of life or death over them. Sentences were executed by the *aumanga*, people of the same guild and age group. Criminal offenses included disrespect for a *matai*, failure to conform to a village edict, insulting the local god, habitual theft, and incest. Adultery was on the boundary between criminal and civil wrongs. Sodomy was rarely found; among some people of Oceania, it is said to have been unknown, whereas among others, such as the Trans-Fly and Malekula, sodomy and male concubinage were an institution—that is concubinage was considered necessary for a boy's normal growth, similar to the situation in classical Greece. Fornication before marriage was ignored in some places but not in others, depending on the type of community. Theft was almost unknown before the arrival of the Europeans, since it was considered a disgrace, implying a person's weak-mindedness and inability to earn a living. Later, it became a capital offense in some places. The chief punishments for crime in Polynesia were death, beating, flogging in public, and banishment.

In the most advanced Polynesian communities, the progress of religion brought with it the institution of the sanctuary. In Samoa, there were cities of refuge, where a man was free from the dangers of a feud and was allowed instead to pay a heavy fine (in the form of food), though his house and land could be destroyed in his absence. He might also be forbidden to return to his original village. There were also some forms of oath ordeals in the name of a divinity, specifically in Tonga and Hawaii. In Ontong Java, where religion was well developed and the headmen of a few joint families were priests, the people believed in the *kipua*—the immortal spirit of a person. Four kinds of behavior could offend this *kipua*: (1) failure to fulfill duties toward members of the joint families and neglect of other relatives (especially poor ones); (2) murder or adultery between members of the same joint families, or the displacement of a true heir as headman of a joint family; (3) incest; and (4) neglect of ceremonies and the breaking of taboos. In such cases, no action was taken by the community; the execution of justice was confidently left to the *kipua* of the ancestors. In general, however, religion and magic became less important as practices of a more legal nature became more widespread.

Preliterate law may be flexible and highly effective or unpredictable and even destructive in the absence of formalized controls. In the vast area of Oceania, although there were parallel developments among all the people in relation to the emergence of law, there were also great variations. The most backward of these people, those of Trans-Fly, were behind regarding legal matters, while the Polynesian kingdoms were more developed in matters of government and law. Nor did economic growth necessarily correlate with legal growth. The people of Kapauku, who were poor in goods, were precocious in law. And among the Polynesians, the Samoans, though behind Tonga and Hawaii in centralization of government, were more advanced in the administration of justice. Some of these apparent disparities, of course, may reflect the difficulty of reconstructing the past. On the whole, however, we can say that peoples without cattle or metals have nevertheless been capable of achieving significant progress toward civilization.

Broadly speaking, food gatherers, no matter where—because of their extremely primitive economy—were unable to create anything that can be called law. A great leap forward in material culture occurred with the domestication of animals (cattle being more important than sheep and goats, though in Oceania this role was played by the pig) and the ability to use metals. In other words, where there was a combination of agriculture, domestic animals, and use of metals, there appeared the early stages of legal development, despite the fact that there was no writing, no central government, a most crude and insignificant technology, and an extremely weak authority of the chief. In many though not all places in Oceania, however, there were individuals who had some kind of ill-defined jurisdiction, with very small powers. There was no actual legislation. Homicide was treated as a civil wrong, and sanctions for it were mainly of a compensatory nature. Ordeals were found everywhere when evidence was insufficient. The main criminal offenses were witchcraft (particularly if thought to have caused someone's death), incest, and persistent theft. With the coming of the European navigators, of course, things began to change.

Penal Customs and Practices in Melanesia: The Trobriand Islands

Until the last few decades, the subject of primitive law had received the scantiest and least satisfactory treatment. The very nature of primitive law makes it difficult to study. If in every society we look for institutions similar to those in the more advanced Western societies—police, codes, courts, and penal systems—we are likely to conclude, from their absence, that primitive man simply has an inner propensity to conform to the customs of his own group. But the fact is that whenever the native can evade his obligations without risking any cost (such as the loss of prestige involved in being caught), he will behave according to his personal wishes, exactly as a civilized business-man would do.

In the Trobriands, social relations were based on a number of protolegal principles, the most important of which was mother's right, according to which a child was bodily and morally related to his maternal kinship. This matrilocal principle determined succession to rank, power, inheritance, and membership in the totemic clan. Most aspects of private and public behavior were grounded in the same strange but basic principle, influenced by certain magical and religious beliefs.

The exogamous prohibition was one of the most serious in the Trobriand islands. All females of the clan were called "sisters" and were forbidden for males of the same clan. Nothing was supposed to arouse greater horror than the breach of this prohibition; in addition to outrage, people believed that supernatural punishments such as sores, diseases, and even death might result. That is, this was the case in theory; yet in real life, the breach of exogamy was not a rare occurrence, and public opinion was lenient and decidedly hypocritical. If the affair was conducted with a certain amount of decorum and discretion, there would be gossip but no demand for harsh punishment. If, however, it was publicly revealed, a scandal broke out, everyone turned against the guilty pair, and by ostracism and insults, one or the other could even be driven to suicide.

There were also believed to be supernatural means, such as magic spells and rites, to bring about illicit unions, such as by estranging a woman's affection for her husband and inducing her to commit adultery. Thus, it was believed that the supposed supernatural sanctions against exogamous activity could be neutralized by countermagic procedures.

The seriousness of breaches of exogamy depended on the degree of relationship of the guilty pair. Incest with a sister was an almost unthinkable crime—which did not mean that it was never committed. But when it happened between a pair that merely belonged to the same clan, the breach was considered a venial offense that could be easily overlooked. In fact, the breach of exogamy was considered a spicy form of erotic experience, and many would boast about such exploits. Marriage, on the other hand, was a much more serious affair, and there were only a few cases of marriage within the same clan.

Sorcery was practiced in the Trobriands by a limited number of specialists, usually men of outstanding intelligence and strong personality who had learned a number of intricate spells. They exercised their power on their own behalf or for a fee. Since sickness and death were attributed to black magic, the sorcerer was held in great awe—leading to inevitable abuse and blackmail. Some have even claimed that sorcery was the main criminal agency in Oceania, though in fact sorcerers knew they had much to lose by flagrant abuses and were strongly deterred from them.

When a real injustice had to be punished, the sorcerer was always ready to do so and receive his full fee. Often an offender made amends and came to equitable arrangements when he knew that a sorcerer was at work against him. Therefore, black magic acted, in many cases, as a genuine legal force, preventing the use of violence and implementing the rules of tribal law.

When there was only a suspicion, or doubt, as to whether a given person had committed an offense, then the chief, as penal agent, could not use direct bodily violence against that person. Instead, he had to resort to sorcery and pay the sorcerer from his private purse. Thus, black magic was also the chief's principal instrument for enforcing his authority. This was also the main explanation for actual oppression and crass injustice. Therefore, in addition to its role in maintaining law and order, sorcery in these societies also served as a support for vested interests.

Suicide, though not a purely juridical institution, nevertheless had a distinct legal aspect, in that it was often used to escape intolerable situations in which a person had been caught breaking a taboo or had been insulted in public. It was practiced by two horrific methods—jumping from the top of a palm tree or taking the poison from the gall bladder of a globe fish; a milder method involved eating the vegetable poison used for stunning fish. In the last case, a generous dose of emetic was able to restore life; thus, both the method and its remedy were sometimes used in more amorous or domestic cases.

Suicide was certainly not a means of administering justice, but it afforded the accused—whether guilty or innocent—a way of escape and a kind of rehabilitation. It loomed large in primitive psychology as a corrective for deviations from custom and tradition. Therefore, suicide, like sorcery, was a means of ensuring adherence to the law as well as a conservative force.

Theft and murder played no substantial part in the life of the Trobriand natives. Theft was categorized into lawful appropriation of objects of personal use, on the one hand, and food items such as crops or livestock (i.e., pigs), on the other. The first type was regarded as a greater nuisance but the second as more despicable, because such an act represented the admission that the thief was in a state of need and therefore entailed the greatest humiliation conceivable. The penalties in either case consisted of shame and ridicule for the culprit. The vast majority of thefts were committed by social outcasts, feeble-minded people, or minors.

Murder was an extremely rare occurrence. It might take the form of a spearing at night of a sorcerer in defense of a sick man who was his victim. There were also some cases of killing as punishment for adultery, when caught *in flagrante* or for insults to high-ranking people, or in brawls or skirmishes. In such cases, if the killer was a member of another subclan, there was a theoretical obligation of talio (*lugwa*). In practice, however, the talio was regarded as obligatory only when the victim was an adult male of an important rank; and even then it was considered superfluous if the victim had been killed for something for which he was clearly to blame. In almost all cases, the talio could also be evaded by the substitution of blood money (*lula*)—a regular institution in peacemaking after war, when a compensation was given the other side for everyone killed or wounded.

To sum up, in the Trobriands as in other primitive societies, the principles according to which crime was punished were rather vague, and the methods of carrying out retribution were irregular, based more on chance and personal passion than on an established system. These methods were a by-product of nonlegal institutions, such as customs, sorcery, the power of the chiefs, supernatural sanctions, and personal acts such as revenge or suicide. Such institutions fell well short of administration of justice per se, but they were the only means of ensuring social equilibrium and satisfying personal feelings of injustice.

The Coming of the Europeans

The first contacts of the Europeans with the indigenous populations of Oceania—which began in the late sixteenth and early seventeenth centuries, when various explorers such as the Spanish Alvaro de Mendaña Neira (1541–95), the Portugese Pedro Fernandez de Quiros (1565–1615), and the Dutch Abel Janszoon Tasman (1601–59) began to land on various islands of the region—were often difficult and violent. A number of early explorers—particularly the

Dutch, the English, and some of the French—brutalized the natives and treated them like animals. Later, the French treated them somewhat better on the whole, but there were always misunderstandings from which the natives suffered. Captain Cook was the first to win the genuine respect and esteem of the islanders; and the French explorer Jean-François de la Pérouse (1741–88) gave these people some idea of the possible greatness of the white man.

But later came the whaling men, sandal hunters, and slave traders—cruel men who spent long months on the high seas and found on these islands healthy men to turn into slaves and lovely women to satisfy their sexual needs. These white men inspired a hatred in the natives that might have become permanent had not the missionaries begun to arrive and to achieve, from their perspective, remarkable results.

Missionaries and colonial officials did their best to "liberate" the Polynesians from their "outmoded" ancient civilization, to accustom them to clothes, soap, religion, schools, and whatnot. Yet whatever white men did led to the annihilation of the traditional culture. If the traffickers were dangerous to their lives and liberty, the missionaries destroyed their religious beliefs. The natives also fell prey to European maladies they had never known before; alcoholism was one, and there were also foreign microbes and viruses. The *kokongo* (the disease of the ships) was a real epidemic, one that still appears today in some of these islands after the arrival of a foreign ship.

Thus, the equilibrium acquired over centuries of slow evolution was shattered in a short time. With the changing of the original religion came the collapse of the entire sociopolitical organization. The festivals and tribal assemblies disappeared, and the people's lives became progressively emptier; some of their previous conviviality could be revived only in clandestine gatherings. The depopulation was horrendous. The people of the Marquesas, who numbered about 100,000 in Cook's time, were only some 3,000 by the middle of this century. The same thing happened in Easter Island after the raids of the Peruvian slave traffickers. Pure Polynesian people are becoming scarcer every day, and the day will come when they will disappear altogether what with the ethnic mixing with the whites and now, too, the Chinese and Japanese. This seems sad when we think of those bold navigators who, without compass or chart, were sailing the vast spaces of the Pacific long before Columbus ventured across the Atlantic.

Primitive people—without a written language, with religious ideas and means of social control radically different from our own—have unconsciously been working out experiments on the potentialities of human nature. They have invented new tools, new forms of government, new interpretations of good and evil, new views of man's place in the universe. Sometimes they have tested the social effects of rank and simple types of democracy. All these are their unique contributions to the history of human development, and now that so many of these fragile primitive cultures have been destroyed, we should be all the more grateful for their achievements.

Historical and Criminological Facts about Easter Island and Pitcairn Island

It seems that Easter Island—a speck of undulating volcanic rock, mostly shorn of trees but green with scraggly vegetation—was the first island discovered in Polynesia. It is, nevertheless, the loneliest inhabited island in the world. Lying 2,350 miles west of the mainland, the Chilean port of Valparaiso, this eastern-most basalt, triangular island, with its massive stone statues—some of them forty-six feet high, standing or sprawling on the island beaches, hillsides, and volcanic slopes—still represents the greatest enigma of Oceania. Its culture is so markedly different from all the other prevailing Polynesian cultures that some scholars believe that it should not be lumped together with the rest of Polynesia, even though the natives were indeed Polynesians when the island was discovered.

Today there is a consensus that this island, known to be natives by a number of names (among them *Te Pito te Henua,* the "navel of the world"), was discovered by the Dutch navigator Admiral Jacob Roggeveen (1669–1733), on 5 April 1722, when he was in a voyage around the world with a small fleet of three warships: the *Den Arend,* the *Thienhoven,* and the *Afrikaansche Galie.* He arrived at the island on Easter Sunday, from whence its name of Easter Island, which he called in his own language *Paasch Eyland.*

When some of the natives came swimming and went on board, they snatched everything they could find at hand—here hats and bonnets, there a handkerchief or a table cloth. The puritan Dutchmen considered this theft and larceny, forgetting that for the poor natives, all these little things meant a great deal, since they had nothing and had no understanding of the notion of private property and, therefore, no idea of committing a crime. Roggeveen decided to send a punishing expedition of 134 armed men. As soon as they arrived at the shore, they were surrounded by a great number of natives who, for reasons of natural curiosity, tried to touch the arms of the sailors or take the blouse of one of them. The Dutchmen started to shoot, and the natives ran away, but not before ten or twelve of them were dead on the spot. The Dutchmen left on 11 April, having created the concept that these islanders were natural thieves. This "tradition" would accompany the natives of Easter Island for a couple of centuries. And from the very beginning, blood would mark the first contact of the natives of Polynesia with the people representing Western civilization.

On Friday, 11 March 1774, Captain James Cook, during his second voyage through the Pacific Ocean, on board the *Resolution* and accompanied by the *Discovery,* saw the island, disembarking the following Sunday. Once again, the natives took all kinds of objects from the seamen who accompanied him. There was some shooting, and a few natives were killed or hurt. He wrote: "They are expert thieves and they do not only steal from foreigners, but one from the other."

Jean François Galaup, Count de la Pérouse, in charge of the vessels *Boussole* and *Astrolabe,* arrived at the island on 8 April 1786. Immediately, a great number of natives came swimming and were allowed to come on board—where, once again, they showed how expert they were in the art of small theft. La Pérouse and his men did not react. They considered such behavior a kind of play of the natives, and firearms were not used. As a sensible man, La Pérouse wrote in his diary: "The theft of the hat of a seaman could not be a sufficient reason to kill a native."

Later, the crimes of Westerners against the natives became more serious. The tragic events started with the visit of the American schooner *Nancy* in 1805; it was engaged in the hunting of seals. Needing cheap workers who were also good swimmers, they looked for them in the many Pacific islands, whose people were already known not only as excellent swimmers but also as fine hunters and fishermen. As soon as they arrived, the captain and a number of sailors disembarked. Many natives came to greet them, as was their custom. The sailors tried to catch a number of them by force, but the islanders resisted. There was a fight, the foreigners used their firearms, and a number of natives were killed or wounded. They eventually took twenty-two native prisoners (twelve men and ten women), put them in the hold of the *Nancy,* and left immediately. After three days of navigation, the prisoners were brought up to the deck and delivered from their chains. The moment they felt they were free, they jumped into the sea and started to swim back home; most probably, they all drowned in their dramatic flight for freedom.

It was therefore not at all surprising that from then on, hostility against all kinds of foreigners became the natural reaction of the natives, as against enemies. The next five visiting ships were not allowed to disembark their crews.

Another tragic event occurred during the stopover of the American whaler *Pindos* in 1811. A couple of boats were sent ashore to get fresh water, vegetables, and women. They brought back as many young women as there were seamen on board. The next morning, the women were taken back to the island, but before reaching the coast, they were ordered to swim the rest of the way. And while they were swimming, Waden, the second in command, exercising his sadism and mastery in shooting, started to shoot, killing a few of them as a matter of sport. This is what might be called the process of "civilization through crime."

On 28 March 1816, the Russian vessel *Rurick* arrived, with its commander, Otto von Kotsebue. Because of the number of scientists and artists on board, this could have been a visit of considerable importance, but it failed because of the hostility of the natives. First, they attracted the sailors by offering them some of their fruits, but then they stole everything they could get their hands on. Shots were fired, and again a number of natives were killed or wounded.

Similarly, *HMS Blossom,* with Captain F.W. Beechey, arrived on 16 November 1825. The next day, a boat was sent full of presents for the natives, but they received it with a rain of stones, slightly hurting practically all the sailors. Again there was some shooting and a few natives were killed.

There is nothing particular to mention about the history of the island till about 1859, besides the internal wars among the different clans of natives, which perhaps arose from thefts by one or the other group, thefts that were not so kindly tolerated as those committed on foreign visitors. That brought, as a direct consequence, the downfall of all the statues on the island. From 1859 to 1862, all the visitors had only a commercial interest, whether they were American whalers or Peruvian slave traders.

The first Peruvian ships that tried this new slave trade made good profits, which tempted a number of entrepreneurs to send their ships in order to bring more workers. They never "bought" these natives but enticed them on board with small gifts, then got them intoxicated with alcoholic drinks; while they were sleeping, the ship left the island. More than 2,000 natives were kidnapped in this way for American whalers or were taken to the Guano Islands of Peru. The most devastating raid was the one that took place on 19 December 1862, when the Peruvian ship *Cora,* with its commander Antonio Aguirre, together with seven other ships, carried away some 900 natives. Among them were the last king, Maurata, and his family, as well as many noblemen and native "scholars"—those who were still able to read the "talking tablets." With them, most of the island's tradition were definitely lost. This real catastrophe created an irreparable gap between the past and the present of Easter Island. Even worse, when the government of Peru decided to stop such activities and to send the remaining natives—some 700 in total—back home, they were so ill and tired that only 15 of them came back. And since some of them were carriers of the dreadful smallpox virus, the local natives died in the hundreds because they had no natural or vaccinal immunity. As a result, by the end of the last century, there were only 111 natives left. (Today the population is a bit more than 2,000, including the majority of the Pascuences—native Polynesians—and the Conties, as the minority of the Chilean mainlanders are known.)

Very soon after this tragedy, there was a remarkable change in the relationship between the frequent visitors to the island and the natives. Those who came now had a real interest in studying the natives and their island, their archaeology and anthropology, their history and their customs. But the natives were living in an incredibly miserable state, lacking almost every elementary thing to satisfy their basic needs. This situation started to change for the better from 6 November 1866, when the schooner *Tampico,* under the French commander Jean Baptiste Onesime Dutrou Bornier, brought to the island—besides two missionaries—a cow, two calves, a number of rabbits, some pigeons, and even a horse and a wheelbarrow. In 1867, Dutrou Bornier came back to the island with the purpose of engaging some natives to work on the plantations in Tahiti, but he had no success, because the islanders were aware of what had happened when the Peruvian raiders came with a similar purpose. A year later, he returned once more with the intention to start a small sheep ranch. In May 1868, his schooner was destroyed when a sudden gust of wind threw it on the rocks of the shore. "Condemned" to remain on the island, he decided to become a land proprietor, so he initiated the "commercial exploitation" of the island. He became the first European settler and colonist and the one and only resident to have firearms at his disposal. He was keenly aware of the opportunities available on the rather depopulated island, which lacked an effective European jursidiction. Together with his business associates, the well-known Brander family of Tahiti, he stuck to his main goal of converting most of the island into a sheep ranch. He started by purchasing tracts of land, which was then easy and cheap. He kept at such activities till the early 1870s. In the beginning, his relationships with the two missionaries were correct and positive, but then they started to object to the harsh way in which he bought the land and treated the natives. An open conflict developed among them, which finished when the missionaries left the island in 1871. Free from their presence, he and his associates started to build a fortune, mainly as plantation owners in Tahiti. Some 200 natives were brought to work there, and a further 150 were distributed among their properties on the Gambier Islands. Only about 175 remained on Easter Island under the autocratic rule of Dutrou Bornier.

In October 1871 one of the Branders and Dutrou Bornier formed a legal partnership for the exploitation of the island. Dutrou Bornier was to administer the island, and John Brander was to provide the shipping communication with Tahiti and Valparaiso. From then on, Dutrou Bornier ruled the island without interference. The population had been reduced to little more than 100, who served as slaves under his brutal rule. He proclaimed himself the representative of France and displayed the French flag above his dwellings in Mataveri, which he renamed Saint Marie de Rapa-nui. His ranch now had some 40,000 sheep, and each year he exported about sixty to seventy tons of wool.

After a few years of his brutal rule, his luck changed. On 6 August 1876, Dutrou Bornier—some claimed—had an "accident": he fell from his horse and died. This explanation is very difficult to accept, given that he was an expert rider. It is more probable that he was murdered by the natives, and there are a few versions about how that happened. According to one, he was killed by an unnamed native who was upset by the continuous ill treatment he received from Dutrou Bornier. Another version is that he was killed by a group of natives who beat him with their clubs. And a third version says that he was killed by a single native, Huki, who, tiring of the everyday "jokes" of Dutrou Bornier—who used to prick him with the bayonet he always had at the end of his rifle—killed him with the same bayonet.

With his death, the Brander–Bornier partnership came to an end, and Brander replaced Dutrou Bornier with Alexander P. Salmon, a relative of Queen Pomaré IV of Tahiti. Salmon visited the island in 1878, a year after John Brander's death. With his death, the entire business was involved in a series of legal proceedings lasting till 1893. By then the island was beyond French jurisdiction, having been annexed by Chile in 1888.

Nothing notable happened till 1892, when a French businessman from Valparaiso, Enrique Merlet, became interested in obtaining the transfer of the Brander–Bornier–Salmon business to his company, E. Merlet and Company, which was finally agreed in September 1895. In 1897, when Merlet became the sole owner of practically the entire island, he visited it for the first time. For the next few years, the Merlet operation seemed to be successful, but early in this century, his company was in dire straits and he had to get into a financial relationship with the powerful Scottish firm of S. Williamson and Company, established in Liverpool in 1851, with the main purpose of transporting goods to the west coast of South America. This company had its overseas headquarters at Valparaiso. In 1863, its Chilean branch, being extremely successful, became the new Williamson, Balfour and Company, which was a real economic empire at the turn of the century. As Merlet was unable to repay to this company the loans he had received from it, they agreed to form the so-called Compañia Explotadora de la Isla de Pascua, registered on 30 July 1903. In 1908 this new company, which I shall call attention to later, became, in fact, a branch of Williamson, Balfour and Company, which then had its own local manager on the island who was the island's real administrator and only authority. This situation remained unchanged till November 1953, when the company's lease was finally and definitely revoked.

The islands of Tahiti and Pitcairn are linked not only by the fact that they were discovered the same year but also because they were the stage of a dramatic event—namely, the mutiny that took place aboard *HMS Bounty*. Few minor incidents in world history have received more attention than this mutiny. The criminal acts associated with the mutiny had two singular consequences: an exceptional feat of navigation and the establishment of a British settlement still flourishing today.

The tragic history of the *Bounty,* a tiny ship only ninety-one feet long, began when Lieutenant William Bligh (1753–1817) arrived at Tahiti. He was sent, in charge of the *Bounty,* to take samples of the breadfruit tree for the West Indies, where they could serve as a most valuable food supplement for the slaves of the local plantations. He was received with great hospitality and got the breadfruit plants he required. For some unknown reasons, he remained on the island for more than five months. As idleness seems to be the enemy of discipline, Bligh lost control of his men, and a number of incidents occurred on board. Finally, on 4 April 1789, the *Bounty* left Tahiti with 1,015 breadfruit plants and, on April 21, arrived at the Friendly Islands, the Tonga group. On 28 April Fletcher Christian, aged twenty-six—one of the two master's mates and second in command—decided, after a number of most serious clashes with Bligh, to organize a mutiny with a number of seamen who followed him. In fact, it was a simple and almost spontaneous takeover. The *Bounty* was then not far from Tofua, one of the islands of the Tonga group. The mutineers decided to put Bligh and his eighteen followers into the twenty-three-foot launch of the ship, which was provided with the most indispensable food and water supply, only enough for one week, as well as with a compass and a quadrant. Cast adrift in the middle of the great Pacific, the tiny boat was dangerously overloaded, and only a hand's length separated the water's surface from the gunwale. Incredibly, on 12 June, after a long trip of forty-seven days and innumerable mishaps, the boat reached Dutch Timor, the only white settlement in the South Seas, located some 3,600 nautical miles to the west, constituting one of the most extraordinary known naval adventures. On 14 March 1790, Bligh and the other ten survivors returned to England. All credit goes to Bligh, for without his genius and his prim leadership, they would never have reached their destination. It was the longest open-boat voyage in the history of the British Navy.

Meanwhile the *Bounty,* with twenty-five people on board and Christian as its new captain—after a short stay at Tubuai (of the Austral group), where the natives were most unfriendly to them—returned to Tahiti to get some livestock and other supplies. Christian fell into a deep depression, not only at the thought of the immensity of his crime but also because sixteen men of his crew decided to stay in Tahiti in spite of the dangers of remaining there, since British vessels used to visit the island rather frequently. The other eight men decided to stay on board with Christian. A fair division of the ship's arms and stores was accepted by both groups, and on 21 September 1789, Christian left Tahiti for a place unknown to those left behind. They had on board six native men and twelve women, tricked aboard the *Bounty.* Christian had a copy of the narrative of Captain Carteret's voyage around the world on board the *Swallow* between 1766 and 1769, which had resulted in the discovery of Pitcairn Island, a tiny island with an extension of only five square miles, located southeast of the Tuamotu archipelago—that is, far from the usual course of ships. The island had vegetation and water, was uninhabited, and had no good harbors that might tempt ships to come in. After sailing about the Pacific for about three months, he put the helm over at Pitcairn Island. It is not known on what exact date the *Bounty* reached the island, but once there, they decided to stay. The ship was stripped of every bit of valuable material and was then burned and sunk on 23 January 1790 to avoid betraying their presence to a passing ship, but also to prevent anyone from leaving the island.

Not all of the crew who stayed with Christian were mutineers. Some, like the sixteen-year-old midshipman Peter Heywood, simply could not be accommodated aboard the overloaded launch of Bligh and his men and were forced to remain on the *Bounty*, but they were not spared their share of the ordeal. In the beginning, everything went well. They divided the island into nine plots, built themselves houses, and began to cultivate the land. But then the natives conspired to kill the white men. Betrayed by one of their own women, two of the natives were killed instead. From then on, the history of Pitcairn Island is one of jealousy, hatred, and murder. The Englishmen started to treat the natives as slaves. Three years later, in 1793, the natives rebelled again and killed five of the mutineers, including Christian himself. In fact, while he was patiently digging at his yams, one of the Tahitians shot him from behind at point-blank range and afterward axed him until his face was unrecognizable. The four remaining male natives became the masters of the island, but very soon they quarreled over the possession of the women who had lived with the murdered white men, and within a few days, none of these four remained alive. The surviving four Englishmen had to apportion among them the eleven native women (one was killed in an accident). But then one of them produced an intoxicating liquor from a local plant, and after a lot of drinking, fell or flung himself over a cliff. Another was killed when he attacked the two remaining white men. Young died of asthma in 1800, leaving Alexander Smith, better known as John Adams, the sole survivor of the mutineers who had arrived ten years before. The first child to be born was Christian's son, named Thursday October. Slowly, Adams turned religious and brought up the growing community in strict Christian principles. The present inhabitants of the island, which since 1839 has belonged to Great Britain, are all the descendants of these men and women.

The settlement of Pitcairn remained a secret till 1808, when the American ship *Topaz*, with its captain Mayhew Folger, unraveled the mystery that had puzzled the Admiralty and the English people for so long. Folger informed the British authorities about the discovery, but British ships next reached the island only in 1814. These were *HMS Briton*, with its captain Sir Thomas Staines, and the *Tagus*, with its captain Pipon. So impressed where these visitors by the exemplary conduct and fatherly attention with which Adams cared for the small community that instead of arresting him and bringing him to England, they allowed him to remain there as the shepherd of his small flock. Adams died in 1829.

Although none of the mutineers who went to Pitcairn Island were ever tried for their crime, those who remained in Tahiti were not so fortunate. In fact, on the morning of 23 March 1791, *HMS Pandora* with its captain

Edward Edwards, entered Matavai Bay in search of the mutineers of the *Bounty*. Very soon, all of the remaining mutineers were apprehended, put in irons, and kept in the "Pandora's box," an ill-ventilated, round iron cell built at the afterpart of the quarterdeck, by order of Captain Edwards. The unfortunate "pirates," as they were called, remained there, amid filth and privation, for about five months. On 8 May 1791, the *Pandora* left Tahiti; and for the next three months, they looked, without success, for the other mutineers. On the night of 28 August the *Pandora* struck a submerged reef off the northern coast of Queensland and sank early the next morning. Thirty-one shipmen were drowned, as well as four of the fourteen prisoners, who cried for help but were freed only at the last moment. The survivors continued their voyage on the *Pandora's* four boats and reached Timor after sixteen days. Finally, on 19 June 1792, all of them reached Spithead, where the prisoners were transferred in custody of *HMS Hector*. On 12 September the trial of the ten surviving mutineers began on board *HMS Duke* in Portsmouth harbor. They were charged for "mutinously running away with the *Bounty* and deserting from His Majesty's service." Four men were acquitted; three others were sentenced to death but subsequently pardoned; and the remaining three were convicted and publicly executed on 29 October 1792. As for William Bligh, he died as rear-admiral of the British Navy, at the ripe old age of sixty.

This tragic story of the mutiny of the *Bounty* seems to end on a note of cynicism—for the natives of the West Indies found the breadfruit too insipid for their taste!

The Situation in the Other Polynesian Islands

From Samoa, there is nothing special to be mentioned except the work done there by Margaret Mead (1902–78) in 1925 and the opposition to her conclusions by Derek Freeman in 1983.

New Zealand, so rich in many aspects of its cultural anthropology, has a few items deserving a special note from the criminological point of view. Besides the already mentioned early stealing from foreign visitors, noteworthy was the *whakapohane,* considered by the Maori the highest form of insult. It consists in dancing a protest jig, which includes parting the grass skirt and baring the buttocks. This old custom is still kept today, as seen during the recent visit of Queen Elizabeth II of England to New Zealand in February 1986, when a "heavily built" Maori sprang from the roadside, danced a protest jig, parted his grass skirt, and bared his buttocks, where he had inscribed offensive slogans with a ballpoint pen.

Regarding Tonga and the Friendly islands, it should be recalled that Tasman (in 1643), and particularly Cook (in 1773), and afterward La Pérouse, D'Entrecasteaux, and others had already observed that mischief was stirring among these natives. One of the early missionaries stated that they were without law and not withheld from wrongdoing either by divine command or by human restraint. They had no dread of eternal punishment to deter them from sin and no hope of eternal reward to urge them to virtue. Their only drive was to satisfy every desire of their earthly great chiefs, because punishment followed refusal. And to appease the wrath of their gods, they self-inflicted such punishment by wounding or piercing their bodies. It was common practice, for instance, to cut off the little finger in order to avoid supernatural calamities. Like all the other Polynesian natives, they were afraid of darkness and dared not venture out after nightfall.

On the other hand, starting with the earliest visitors, the ships' crews indulged in all sorts of excesses, leaving the natives far worse than they found them. They robbed women and amused themselves with them; encouraged the natives to drink alcohol; and made their weapons more deadly, such as by barbing their spears with iron or fastening burning brands to the points of their arrows and showing them how to project them into an attacked enemy village. They also taught them to use guns, muskets, and swords.

When Cook and his party returned to these islands in 1777, a couple of startling incidents occurred. One of the natives seemed to have offended the rest of the local population, who rushed after him, struck him down with clubs, broke his thigh, and would have certainly killed him if the Englishmen had not interfered and saved his life. Shortly after, one of Captain Cook's people, walking alone, was surrounded by a number of natives, who threw him down and stripped him of everything he had with him. Later, observing the respect with which the natives approached and entered a certain building in which the great chiefs were buried, Cook understood that it was a place of worship, and he laid down on the floor an offering of blue pebbles, nails, medals, and so on, which were immediately pocketed by one of the natives, who ran away. Cook, who twice visited these islands, came to the conclusion that the natives were expert and unceasing thiefs. They took everything, from shoes to jackets and books and even guns, in spite of the many guards who were on board and on the shore and the fact that they sometimes fired on and wounded some of the natives. They were also cruel—the chiefs mercilessly beating natives who had been disobedient; Cook saw one of them being killed in such a way. In their great ceremonies, human victims would be slain to deter an angry god from destroying their king.

During the last quarter of the eighteenth century, Spanish, English, and French ships visited the islands, and their accounts were similar; the natives were fearless thieves, and their women were immodest. Quarrels with the natives were frequent, and some sailors were wounded, while a few natives were killed. The result was distrust on both sides. From then on, they were "Friendly" islands no more. Fighting among the natives themselves was rather frequent, often becoming real wars in which the prisoners were cut up alive and eaten raw. The second half of the last century witnesses a more quiet period in the history of these islands, lasting practically till today.

On the other hand, children were always much desired and greatly prized; therefore, infanticide, so common in the Society Islands, was unknown in Tonga. Moreover, the Tui-Tonga, the king of Tonga, issued a written code of laws in March 1839, with the assistance of the missionaries. He appointed four of his chiefs as magistrates. Each of them had to sit once a month to hear and decide all cases of complaint that might arise. This first code, though far from perfect, served to establish principles of order and justice. After a preamble praising the will of God, it refers to open acts of crime, the worship of God, the way the chiefs should rule their people, the industry and cultivation of the land, the conduct of foreigners visiting the island, and so on. The last code of 1850 has forty-three sections. The following are examples: It is unlawful to leave hogs outside a fenced place; the owner should shut up the pig and shall make amends for the possible damages done. If he does not pay attention and his pig misbehaves a second time, it may be killed, and the offended party may claim it. A person retailing ardent spirits shall pay a fine of twenty-five dollars to the king, and the spirits shall be taken from him. If a man leaves his wife, she shall claim whatever property he has. If a woman forsakes her husband, she cannot marry any other man while her husband lives. Any man not willing to work shall not be fed or assisted in any way. The woman who does not work shall not be fed or assisted. Supporting her is evil. In spite of all this, lying or stealing was not considered a disgrace unless detection followed, and even then these acts were rarely punished.

Human sacrifices occurred even in 1842, when a boy eleven years of age was chosen in order to save the life of the ailing king. He was anointed with oil and decorated in the most splendid manner. A cord was placed around his neck and drawn tightly by two persons, one of them the boy's father. The dead body was carried to the spirit house, but the king did not recover and died a few days later.

As for the Sandwich or Hawaiian Islands, before the arrival of the Europeans, there were independent kingdoms on the four largest islands: Hawaii, Maui, Oahu, and Kauai. The smaller ones (Molokai, Lanai, and Niihau) were sometimes independent and at other times held by one of the larger kingdoms as tributary communities. King Kamehameha I of Oahu later established the united kingdom of the entire archipelago. The will of the king was the supreme law, with the exception of some customs related to religious observance and fishing rights.

The most distinctive and impressive feature of Hawaiian life was the taboo (*kapu* in Hawaiian), meaning "forbidden" or "sacred." A commoner could not stand in the presence of a chief. Women could not eat pork, bananas, and some kinds of fish; they had to cook their food separately and eat it apart from their male masters. The penalty for violating a *kapu* could be severe, and the death sentence was not unusual.

The natives were superb vocalists and liked to sing for the pure joy of making music, mainly based on drum beats. Their hula was a combination of song and dance, a blending of erotic invitation, religious and physical exercise, and a form of entertainment. The early missionaries condemned many native practices, particularly polygamy, infanticide, and human sacrifices, and what they considered their many unhygienic habits, as well as the frequent application of the death penalty for trifling offenses and the harsh way in which the majority of the chiefs treated their people.

Captain Cook was the first European who saw these islands, in January 1778. He left after spending a few days on Maui, when gifts were exchanged. He returned by the end of the same year, but this time friction broke out between the natives and the British. On 13 February 1779, a native stole a pair of blacksmith's tongs and, when caught, received a severe flogging. The same night, the natives stole a large boat from one of the British ships. The next day, Cook went ashore with the intention of kidnapping the king and holding him until the boat was returned, a stratagem that had been successful elsewhere in Polynesia. The natives became violent, and during the scuffle Cook himself was hit with a club and stabbed. His violent death was another omen that harmony would not result from this first contact.

In 1819, at the end of the reign of Kamehameha I, there were about 200 foreigners as permanent residents, many of them drifters and some of them ex-convicts of the British penal colony in Australia who had been able to escape. The presence of these foreigners and the sporadic visits of foreign ships created serious problems and a generally debauched atmosphere in which everyone was ready to cut his neighbor's throat. Treachery was the order of the day, and the truth was never spoken. Moreover, besides the venereal diseases, many other diseases were common, such as measles, whooping cough, and smallpox, as well as cholera and bubonic plague, which killed thousands of natives because they had no natural immunity against them. The natives were also helpless against the liquors introduced by the foreigners. Famous novelists such as Herman Melville and Robert Louis Stevenson had given appalling accounts of native drunkenness everywhere in Polynesia. Traders and sailors were mainly interested in profit or vice, not in checking the progressive deterioration of the native population. The climax of this process of demoralization came in November 1819, when the new young ruler, Kamehameha II, abolished the *kapu* system and ordered the destruction of the ancient idols. In the confusion so created, the entire native population, originally estimated at 300,000, declined to about 135,000 in 1820; to some 85,000 in 1850; and to only 40,000 in 1890. When the first Calvinist missionaries arrived in 1820, the natives were well along in their decline. Their reports mention dreadful abominations, drunkenness and adultery, gambling and theft, deceit, treachery and killings, as well as prostitution, incest, and sodomy.

Kaahumanu, the favorite of Kamehameha I, who acted as regent and premier till her death in 1832, issued a code of laws against murder (particularly against the old custom of infanticide), theft, fighting, drunkenness, breaking the Sabbath, gambling, and sexual immorality and made it mandatory to learn to read and write (*palapala*). In 1839, a new code of laws was established, and in 1840, a liberal constitution. The king and the regent (*kuhinanui*), together with the other chiefs, formed the Council or Upper House, but there was a Representative Assembly elected by the common people. A Supreme Court was also created. Hawaii retained its independence and did not become part of the United States till 1898. In 1959 it became the fiftieth state of the United States of America.

Some Criminological Conclusions

Two important criminological issues are related to the population of Easter Island—namely, the supposed natural inclination toward theft (not only of the natives of Easter Island, but also of all the other Polynesians), described by all the early navigators and explorers, and the killing of Dutrou Bornier. My almost five-month stay on Easter Island in 1934 led me to views on these matters that are at variance with the accepted ones.

Besides the stealing from occasional foreign visitors, E.N. Ferdon (mentioned also by Heyerdahl in his volume *The Art of Easter Island*) refers to "steal trading" on the island. He believes that it had a decisive influence on the island's culture, inasmuch as the considerable number of underground caves of volcanic origin, with artificially concealed entrances (first discovered during Heyerdahl's expedition of 1966), are known to present-day natives, but their whereabouts are kept rigidly secret, even from near relatives. That is, the islanders spend considerable time searching for caves belonging to others, because if occasionally they may contain remains from burials, they were usually storage places for material possessions, protected by the family's spirits (known as *aku-aku*)—dangerous spirits that could disable or kill any trespasser. According to Ferdon, these caves were required to store the stolen goods and represented the one secure place in which the natives could keep their private and secret possessions. The fact that these caves were not previously known is obviously attributable to their sacred nature, in contrast to the giant stone statues (*moais*) and burial structures (*ahus*) that dominated the open landscape. These secret storage caves were a functional necessity for the personal preservation of family belongings, facilitating the "steal trading" that was an integral part of the local communal life. Because these caves were discovered after I left Easter Island, I will not refer to them further.

Many authors were convinced that the natives never regarded stealing as something immoral and claim that they even had a god of thieves (I never heard about such a god). Moreover, they point out that even though a thief captured *in flagrante* while stealing from a foreigner was punished by the administration of blows, he never lost his social status. A thief who was not caught was even considered a kind of hero, particularly if the victim was a foreigner. I personally never heard about such practices while I was on the island, perhaps because there were no other foreigners besides the members of our mission.

Stealing among the natives themselves was a different matter. The theft had to be confirmed beyond any doubt, and the victim had the right to indemnify himself with goods belonging to the thief. Alternatively, he was entitled to destroy the thief's property up to the value of the stolen goods. Every native was entitled to this type of revenge, including the weak and incompetent against the powerful and strong. If the thief resisted, the victim could count on the support of the entire community. Therefore, there was a clear disctinction between stealing from another native or doing the same thing to a foreigner.

Dealing only with the second type of stealing (from foreigners), I was convinced—based on my personal experience during the time I spent on the island—that the notion that the natives were natural thiefs was mainly based on a different interpretation of the facts. The early European explorers already knew the legal concept of theft, and they applied it to the natives' behavior without realizing that the natives had no such notion. For instance, when a native was walking from one place to another on the island and the weather was hot, he would take a pineapple from the first grove he saw and eat it to quench his thirst. If he was hungry, he would eat a few bananas wherever he found them, again with no idea of committing a "theft." And when the natives needed some meat to enrich their diet, they simply took a sheep from the Compañia Explotadora de la Isla de Pascua. The administrators of the Compañia complained to the governor of the island, who promised to take care of the matter but never did. As a matter of fact, when I was on Easter Island, there was no jail or anything even resembling such an institution.

My interpretation is based on the fact that the natives lived an incredibly deprived sort of life, lacking the most elementary items that already existed in Europe, in the Americas, and even in other Polynesian islands. Therefore, when the first explorers arrived at the beginning of the eighteenth century, the natives had an urge to get their hands on anything they could—even a sailor's hat or a handkerchief. For them, such items were of the greatest value, and they seized them without thinking of committing what the Europeans called a theft. Whatever the case, while I was on Easter Island, besides the stealing of a sheep once in a while—which could be seen as a case of *furtus familicus*—no violent criminal behavior occurred. The natives were kind and peaceful; they all had work to do, and all of them tried to help us as much as they could.

Regarding the killing of Dutrou Bornier, according to what I heard from the most important natives on the island, he was the victim of a plot. The natives, tired of his abuses and excesses, decided to kill him. Pieces of straw, one of which was short, were offered to all participants in the plot. The one who drew the short piece of straw was to be the executioner. However, I was never told who he was.

When I visited Pitcairn Island, there were only ninety inhabitants, all of them of mixed ethnic origin (English and Tahitians) and direct descendants of the mutineers of the *Bounty*. During the two days we spent there, the natives received us with great kindness. When we inquired about certain types of behavior, such as stealing or homicide, the people were very surprised; they could not recall any incidents of such a nature, despite being the descendants of the *Bounty*'s mutineers. I found only one young man of an unbalanced character; he was the only one on the island that was not working. He would wander from place to place, trying to catch birds with a catapult, but he was not of a violent character. He did not disturb the other islanders, and they did not disturb him. In short, it was a perfect arrangement.

Bibliography

Adamson Hoebel, E. *The Law of Primitive Man*. Atheneum, New York, 1972.

Adler, Morris. *El Mundo del Talmud*. Editorial Paidos, Buenos Aires, 1964.

Aldred, Cyril. *The Egyptians*. Thames and Hudson, London, 1961.

Alexiou, Stylianos. *La Civilization Minoènne*. Spiros Alexiou Fils, Heraklion, Crete, no date.

Anales de la Universidad de Chile, 161–162, November 1980, Santiago, Chile (totally devoted to the publication of papers on Easter Island by William Mulloy, Gonzalo Figueroa G.H., Claudio Cristino, and others).

Atkins, Harry. *A History of Ethiopia*. Central Press, Addis Ababa, no date.

Ayarragaray, Carlos A. *La Justicia en la Biblia y el Talmud*. Librería Jurídica Abeledo, Buenos Aires, 1948.

Babini, Rosa de. *Los Siglos de la Historia*. Fondo de Cultura Economica, Mexico, 1960.

Bamberger, B.J. *La Biblia: Un Enfoque Judío Moderno*. Editorial Paidos, Buenos Aires, 1963.

Barandarian, Jose Miguel de. "Ciertos Delitos en el Pais Vasco." In *Estudios Vascos de Criminología* (pp. 35–42) Mensajero, Bilbao, Spain.

Baron, Salo Wittmayer. *A Social and Religious History of the Jews*, Vol. II (2nd ed.). Jewish Publication Society of America, Philadelphia, 1958.

Barrera Carrasco, Carlos de la. "Informe del Estado Actual del Programa para el Control de la Lepra en la Isla de Pascua" (a typed document). Santiago, Chile, 1978.

Beaglehole, John Cawte. "The Development of New Zealand Nationality." *Journal of World History* (UNESCO), Vol. II, # 1, Librairie des Meridiens, Paris, 1954.

Bengtson, Hermann (ed.). *The Greeks and the Persians*. (translated from the German by J. Conway). Weidenfeld and Nicolson, London, 1969.

Beristain, Antonio (ed.). *Estudios Vascos de Criminología*. Mensajero, Bilbao, 1982.

———. "Las Violencias y las No-Violencias en Euskadi." In *Estudios Vascos de Criminología* (pp. 43–55). Mensajero, Bilbao, 1982.

———. "El Fuero de San Sebastian y su Continuación en el Derecho Penal Vasco." In *Estudios Vascos de Criminología* (pp. 103–58). Mensajero, Bilbao, 1982.

———. "La Violencia como Desafío en España y en el Pais Vasco: 1936–1978." In *Estudios Vascos de Criminología* (pp. 201–67). Mensajero, Bilbao, 1982.

————. "La No-Violencia y el Perdon Revolucionario." In *Estudios Vascos de Criminología* (pp. 269–74). Mensajero, Bilbao, 1982.

Beristain, Antonio; Larrea, Maria Angeles; and Mieza, Rafael Maria. "Fuentes del Derecho Penal Vasco (Siglos XI–XVI)." *Gran Enciclopedia Vasca.* Mensajero, Bilbao, 1980.

Berman, Harold. *The Interaction of Law and Religion.* Abingdon Press, Nashville, 1974.

Berrondo, Pedro. "Algunos Modos Pasionales del Vasco." In *Estudios Vascos de Criminología* (pp. 63–64). Mensajero, Bilbao, 1982.

Bevan, E.R. *History of Egypt under the Ptolemaic Dynasty.* Methuen, London, 1927.

Bible, The, Revised Standard Version. Fontana Books, London, 1952.

Bickerman, Elias Joseph. *Chronology of the Ancient World.* Cornell University Press, New York, 1968.

Biscardi, Arnaldo. *Diritto Greco Antico.* Giuffrè, Varesse, 1982.

Boas, Franz. *El Arte Primitivo.* Fondo de Cultura Economica, Mexico, 1947.

Bobula, Ida. *Herencia de Sumeria* (translated from the original by Leonardo Castañeda). Museo de las Culturas, Mexico, 1967.

Bock, Albert de. *Met de "Mercator" naar de Stille Zuidsee. Reisdagboek van een Kadet.* Tweede uitgave, De Sikkel, Antwerpen, 1944.

————. *Croisière du "Mercator" au Pacific* (translated from the Dutch by Richard Lavaque). Imp. L. Vaumelle, Gent, Belgique, 1985.

Bodde, Derk, and Morris, Clarence. *Law in Imperial China* (Taiwan ed.) 1971.

Bonner, Robert, and Smith, Gertrude. *The Administration of Justice from Homer to Aristitle* (2 vol.). AMS Press, New York, 1970.

Bose, Sukumar, and Varma, Paripurnanand. "Philosophical significance of Ancient Indian Penology." *Journal of Indian Philosophy,* Vol. 10, # 1, March 1982 (pp. 61–100).

Bouzon, E. *O Codigo de Hammurabi.* Imp. "Vozes," Petropolis, Brasil, 1976.

Bowra, C.M. *Classical Greece.* Time-Life International, Nederland, N.V., 1966.

Braidwood, Robert J. *The Near East and the Foundation of Civilization.* Eugene, Oregon, 1962.

Brasiello, V. "Diritto Penale Romano." *Novissimo Digesto Italiano,* Vol. V, Torino, 1960 (pp. 960–66).

Breasted, James Henry. *A History of Egypt* (2nd ed.) Scribner, New York, 1923.

Bregeault, J. "Proces contre les Cadavres dans l'Ancient Droit." *Revue Historique du Droit Français et Etranger,* Vol. 1 (pp. 619–22).

Bright, John. *A History of Israel.* SCM Press, London, 1962.

Bronowski, J. *The Ascent of Man.* Little, Brown, Boston, 1973.

Brown, Jose David. "India." In *Biblioteca Universal de Life en Espanol,* Offset Multicolor, S.A. Mexico, D.F. 1961.

Buck, Sir Peter (Te Rangi Hiroa). *The Vikings of the Sunrise.* Fred A. Stokes, New York, 1938.

————. *The Coming of the Maori* (2nd ed.). Maori Purposes Fund Board, Whitecomb and Tombs, Wellington, 1966.

Burn, A.R. *Persia and the Greeks.* Edward Arnold, London, 1962.

Burton, John. *The Collection of the Qur'an.* Cambridge University Press, Cambridge, 1977.